eTourism

Information technology for
strategic tourism management

We work with leading authors to develop the
strongest educational materials in tourism, bringing
cutting-edge thinking and best learning practice
to a global market.

Under a range of well-known imprints, including
Financial Times Prentice Hall, we craft high-quality
print and electronic publications which help readers
to understand and apply their content, whether
studying or at work.

To find out more about the complete range of our
publishing, please visit us on the World Wide Web at:
www.pearsoned.co.uk

eTourism

Information technology for strategic tourism management

Dimitrios Buhalis
University of Surrey

 Prentice Hall
FINANCIAL TIMES

An imprint of **Pearson Education**
Harlow, England • London • New York • Boston • San Francisco • Toronto • Sydney • Singapore • Hong Kong
Tokyo • Seoul • Taipei • New Delhi • Cape Town • Madrid • Mexico City • Amsterdam • Munich • Paris • Milan

Pearson Education Limited
Edinburgh Gate
Harlow
Essex CM20 2JE
England

and Associated Companies throughout the world

Visit us on the World Wide Web at:
www.pearsoned.co.uk

_____

First published 2003

ISBN 0582 35740 3

British Library Cataloguing-in-Publication Data
A catalogue record for this book is available from the British Library

Library of Congress Cataloging-in-Publication Data
Buhalis, Dimitrios.
    eTourism : information technologies for strategic tourism management / Dimitrios Buhalis.
        p. cm.
    Includes bibliographical references (p.).
    ISBN 0-582-35740-3
        1. Tourism—Information technology.   2. Tourism—Management.   I. Title.

    G155.A1 B79 2002
    338.4′791′0285—dc21

                                                            2002033933

10 9 8 7 6 5 4 3
08 07 06 05 04

Typeset in 9.5/12.5pt Stone Serif by 35
Printed and bound by Ashford Colour Press, Gosport

The publisher's policy is to use paper manufactured from sustainable forests.

To my family Maria and Stellitsa for tolerating me . . .

To my parents Theodoros and Stella, and my sister Diamantoula, for supporting me . . .

To my teachers and colleagues for challenging me . . .

Brief contents

List of figures, tables and case studies   xv
Foreword   xix
Acknowledgements   xx
About the author   xxiii
Preface   xxiv

Part A
**The information and communication technologies revolution
and strategic management: issues – challenges – trends**   1

  1 Information and communication technologies:
      evolution and revolution   5
  2 Implications of the ICT revolution for business and strategy   29
  3 eTourism: the dynamic interaction of ICTs and tourism   75
  4 Demand-driven eTourism   109
  5 Supply-driven eTourism   137

Part B
**ICTs for strategic and operational management in the various
sectors of the tourism industry**   173

  6 Operational management and distribution in eTourism   177
  7 eAirlines   193
  8 eHospitality   219
  9 eTour operators   241
10 eTravel agencies   261
11 eDestinations   279
12 eTourism: synthesis and a vision of the future   311

Glossary   342
Bibliography   353
Index   367

Contents

List of figures, tables and case studies   xv
Foreword   xix
Acknowledgements   xx
About the author   xxiii
Preface   xxiv

Part A
The information and communication technologies revolution and strategic management: issues – challenges – trends

      1

1   **Information and communication technologies: evolution and revolution**   5
   Chapter objectives   5
   1.1   Introduction   6
   1.2   Defining ICTs, information systems, information management and their interrelationships   6
   1.3   The stages of ICT evolution   11
   1.4   ICTs and new business tools   13
   1.5   Networking and the information superhighway: the Internet, intranets and extranets   15
   1.6   Technological convergence and new ICT developments   20
   1.7   A new wave of technological evolution   22
   1.8   Conclusions   25
   Chapter questions   25
   Further reading   26
   Websites   26

2   **Implications of the ICT revolution for business and strategy**   29
   Chapter objectives   29
   2.1   Introduction   30
   2.2   Implications for business and strategy   30
   2.3   The impact of the ICT revolution and the information society   33
   2.4   Value chains and the influence of ICTs   35
   2.5   The development of the information marketplace, eCommerce and cyber-markets   38

2.6	Strategic management and competitive advantage	42
	2.6.1 Defining strategy and strategic management	43
	2.6.2 Strategic management processes and tools	44
	2.6.3 Competitive strategy, competitive advantage and competitiveness	49
2.7	ICTs, strategic management and competitiveness	51
	2.7.1 Using ICTs to achieve generic strategies and strategic competitive advantage	52
	2.7.2 Using ICTs to support strategic initiatives	54
	2.7.3 Conditions for optimal use of ICTs	56
2.8	Prerequisites for achieving competitive advantage through IT	57
2.9	ICTs in the contemporary competitive arena: business re-engineering and paradigm shift	60
2.10	The virtual corporation: concepts and definitions	63
2.11	ICTs and innovation as the nucleus of organizational processes and strategy	67
2.12	A multidimensional framework for strategic management and marketing	69
2.13	Conclusions: ICT info-structure and strategic management	71
	Chapter questions	71
	Further reading	72
	Websites	72

3 eTourism: the dynamic interaction of ICTs and tourism   **75**

	Chapter objectives	75
3.1	Introduction	76
3.2	The impact of ICTs on tourism	76
3.3	The transformation of best operational practices in tourism by ICTs	78
3.4	The tourism system and ICTs	80
3.5	The use of hardware and software in tourism organizations	83
3.6	Applications of ICT in tourism and hospitality	87
3.7	Telecommunications and networking in the tourism industry	89
3.8	The evolution of Computer Reservation Systems	93
3.9	Multi-integration of ICTs for the tourism industry and destinations	96
	3.9.1 Technological integration and convergence	96
	3.9.2 Tourism industry integration and collaboration	98
	3.9.3 Local economy and society integration and coordination	98
3.10	A multidimensional framework for ICTs in tourism	99
	3.10.1 Intra-organizational functions (using intranets)	101
	3.10.2 Inter-organizational functions through extranets (and the Internet)	101
	3.10.3 Consumer and stakeholder interaction over the Internet	102
3.11	Dynamic partnerships and constant movement	104
3.12	Conclusions: the tourism info-structure and organizational performance	105
	Chapter questions	106
	Further reading	106
	Websites	107

4 Demand-driven eTourism   **109**

	Chapter objectives	109
4.1	Introduction	110
4.2	Leisure vs business travel demand and the Internet implications	110

4.3 Quantitative growth of tourism demand and on-line population 113
    4.3.1 On-line population and on-line tourism demand 115
    4.3.2 Demand for tourism on-line and eCommerce 121
4.4 Barriers and catalysts for on-line consumers and travellers 125
4.5 Qualitative growth of tourism demand 127
4.6 The ICT revolution and tourist satisfaction 132
4.7 Conclusions: the rapid growth of on-line population and travel demand 134
Chapter questions 135
Further reading 135
Websites 135

5 Supply-driven eTourism **137**
Chapter objectives 137
5.1 Introduction 138
5.2 eTourism and the requirements of the tourism industry 138
5.3 ICTs and SMTEs vs larger tourism organizations 140
5.4 Strategic aims and objectives for tourism suppliers 144
    5.4.1 Private and for-profit tourism organizations 144
    5.4.2 Public and not-for-profit tourism organizations and destinations 146
5.5 ICT-empowered strategic management in the tourism industry 147
    5.5.1 Monitoring the environment and dynamic response:
        proactive management and neural organizations 149
    5.5.2 Building and maintaining competitive advantage using ICTs 151
    5.5.3 Using ICTs for sustainable competitive advantage 160
    5.5.4 Using ICTs to avoid competitive disadvantage 161
5.6 ICT-empowered strategic decisions and directions 163
    5.6.1 ICT-empowered strategic alliances and partnerships 163
    5.6.2 ICT-empowered scope of operations: expansion and
        portfolio management 165
    5.6.3 ICT-empowered distribution strategies 165
    5.6.4 ICT-empowered building and protecting of brands on-line 167
    5.6.5 ICT-empowered customer relationship management and
        dynamic marketing (loyalty boosters) 169
5.7 Conclusions: eTourism empowers tourism management 171
Chapter questions 171
Further reading 172
Websites 172

Part B
ICTs for strategic and operational management in the various
sectors of the tourism industry
173

6 Operational management and distribution in eTourism **177**
Chapter objectives 177
6.1 Introduction 178
6.2 Tourism distribution mechanisms and practice 178

6.3	ICT tools for managing the digital tourism organization	182
	6.3.1 Internet-supported eTourism management	183
	6.3.2 Internal systems and intranet-supported eTourism management	183
	6.3.3 Partner systems and extranet-supported eTourism management	186
6.4	Conclusions: managing eTourism sectors through ICTs	189
	Chapter questions	190
	Further reading	190
	Websites	190

7 eAirlines — **193**

	Chapter objectives	193
7.1	Introduction	194
7.2	From Computer Reservations Systems to Global Distribution Systems	194
7.3	Airline types and ICT utilization	198
7.4	Strategic and tactical roles of ICTs for airlines	198
	7.4.1 Internal systems and intranets	199
	7.4.2 Interconnecting partner systems and extranets	203
	7.4.3 Connecting with all stakeholders through the Internet	206
7.5	ICT-empowered strategic alliances for airlines	209
7.6	Critical issues for the future success of airlines	211
7.7	Conclusions	213
	Chapter questions	213
	Further reading	214
	Websites	215

8 eHospitality — **219**

	Chapter objectives	219
8.1	Introduction	220
8.2	Accommodation establishment types and ICT utilization	220
8.3	Strategic and tactical role of ICTs for hotels	221
	8.3.1 Internal systems and intranets	222
	8.3.2 Interconnecting partner systems and extranets	225
	8.3.3 Connecting with all stakeholders through the Internet	227
8.4	Larger vs smaller accommodation properties	231
8.5	Lessons and issues for the future of eHospitality	234
8.6	Conclusions	237
	Chapter questions	237
	Further reading	238
	Websites	239

9 eTour operators — **241**

	Chapter objectives	241
9.1	Introduction	242
9.2	Tour operator functions, types and structures	242
9.3	The use of videotext as an early leisure travel network	243
9.4	Strategic and tactical roles of ICTs for tour operators	244
	9.4.1 Internal systems and intranets	244
	9.4.2 Interconnecting partners and extranets	246
	9.4.3 Connecting with all stakeholders through the Internet	250

9.5 Disintermediation vs re-intermediation for tour operators 254
9.6 Lessons and issues for the future of tour operators 256
9.7 Conclusions 257
Chapter questions 258
Further reading 258
Websites 259

10 eTravel agencies **261**

Chapter objectives 261
10.1 Introduction 262
10.2 Travel agency functions, types and structures 262
10.3 Videotext for leisure travel agencies and GDSs for business agencies 263
10.4 Strategic and tactical roles of ICTs for travel agencies 265
10.4.1 Internal systems and intranets 265
10.4.2 Interconnecting partner systems and extranets 267
10.4.3 Connecting with all stakeholders through the Internet 267
10.5 Disintermediation vs re-intermediation for travel agencies 270
10.6 Lessons and issues for the future of travel agencies 272
10.7 Conclusions 276
Chapter questions 276
Further reading 276
Websites 277

11 eDestinations **279**

Chapter objectives 279
11.1 Introduction 280
11.2 eDestination types, SMTEs and ICT utilization 280
11.3 Strategic and tactical role of ICTs for destinations 281
11.4 Developing a destination management system (DMS) 285
11.5 DMS challenges and developments to date 287
11.6 From operational DMSs to strategic DICIRMSs 288
11.7 DICIRMSs using intranet–extranet–Internet tools 293
11.7.1 Internal systems and intranets 294
11.7.2 Interconnecting partner systems and extranets 295
11.7.3 Connecting with all stakeholders through the Internet 296
11.8 Challenges and critical issues for destinations 297
11.9 The optimization of the impacts of tourism 301
11.10 Lessons and issues for the future of DMSs 302
11.11 Conclusions 306
Chapter questions 306
Further reading 307
Websites 308

12 eTourism: synthesis and a vision of the future **311**

Chapter objectives 311
12.1 Introduction 312
12.2 ICTs as tools for the industry and inelastic expenditure 312
12.3 Developing interactivity between consumers and suppliers through ICTs 313

12.4   Multi-channel strategies for tourism distribution   315
        12.4.1   eTourism intermediaries: the revolution of intermediation   316
        12.4.2   eTourism intermediaries: using multi-channel strategies   318
        12.4.3   eTourism convergence and platforms   324
12.5   Strategic implications of eTourism for tourism management and
        marketing   325
        12.5.1   Strategic implications of eTourism for the consumer of the
                 future   326
        12.5.2   Implications of eTourism for principals and SMTEs   328
        12.5.3   Implications of eTourism for travel intermediaries   329
        12.5.4   Implications of eTourism for destinations and the public sector   333
12.6   The virtualization of the tourism industry   334
12.7   Conclusions: change is the only constant   337
Chapter questions   340
Further reading   341
Websites   341

Glossary   342
Bibliography   353
Index   367

List of figures, tables and case studies

List of figures

1.1	Information and communication technologies	7
1.2	Information and communication technologies convergence	8
1.3	Information systems characteristics	9
1.4	Relationship between business strategy, information system strategy and information technology strategy	11
1.5	Internet capabilities and functions	16
1.6	Electronic networking for organizations	18
1.7	The electronic nucleus of organizations	18
1.8	Lines of technological evolution	23
2.1	Value-chain analysis	36
2.2	Value chains within the entire industry value system	37
2.3	Strategic management processes and tools	45
2.4	Portfolio analysis and generic strategies	46
2.5	Opportunities and threats matrix and strategic implications	47
2.6	Market growth share matrix	47
2.7	Determining a product/market strategy	47
2.8	Porter's three generic strategies	50
2.9	Strategic ICT systems classified into four main categories	51
2.10	Using ICTs to develop competitive advantage	53
2.11	4Rs framework for ICT training	59
2.12	Organizational change and ICTs	60
2.13	Paradigm shifts influencing business	62
2.14	Information technology as the nucleus of organizational processes and strategy	68
2.15	Organizational info-space for strategic management	69
3.1	The eTourism concept	77
3.2	The tourism industry and tourism system	82
3.3	Examples of information technology applications used in tourism	88
3.4	Critical tourism and hospitality functions supported by ICTs	88
3.5	Need for and mission of CRS services	94
3.6	Integrated IT for an integrated tourism industry and local economy management	97
3.7	Tourism industry communication patterns and functions facilitated by ICTs	100
3.8	Dynamic tourism partnerships in the info-space	104
4.1	The top European travel and tourism groups, September 2000	112
4.2	On-line population per country, in millions	117
4.3	On-line population per country, in percentage	117
4.4	The rapid rise of on-line adoption	118

4.5	On-line pleasure trip planning activities in the USA	123
4.6	Types of website used for planning and booking leisure trips in the USA	124
4.7	Travel products booked on-line	125
4.8	Reasons that discourage people from purchasing tourism on-line	127
4.9	Tourism demand transformation	129
4.10	Customer satisfaction for travellers as a result of ICT tools	133
5.1	Key strategic and operational functions empowered by ICTs	139
5.2	Push and pull factors determining the introduction of ICTs in SMTEs	143
5.3	Strategic management and marketing objectives for destinations	147
5.4	Cost-and-benefit analysis for incorporating ICTs and developing on-line presence	152
5.5	Potential golf-related activities and products offered by a specialized provider	157
B1	The tourism system	175
6.1	Functions and benefits emerging through the tourism distribution channel	180
6.2	Tourism distribution mechanism	180
6.3	Tourism distribution channel members' needs and wants	181
6.4	ICT-enabled tactical planning and operational management	182
7.1	eAirlines' ICT functions	200
7.2	Planned ICT investment as percentage of airline's revenue in 2001	201
8.1	Variables characterizing accommodation establishments	221
8.2	Planned ICT investment as percentage of hotels' revenue in 2001	222
8.3	Use of the Internet for reservations by accommodation establishments	227
9.1	Arguments for and against the disintermediation of tour operators	255
10.1	Developments and trends in the marketplace affecting travel agencies	270
10.2	Arguments for and against the disintermediation of travel agencies	271
10.3	The future of travel agencies	275
11.1	Types of destination – main target markets and activities undertaken	281
11.2	Tourism distribution mechanisms and the role of DMOs and DMSs	283
11.3	Services and features for DMS advanced systems	283
11.4	A guide to designing a destination website	286
11.5	Barriers to the successful development of DMSs	288
11.6	The 6A framework for the analysis of tourism destinations	290
11.7	Contents of a destination integrated computer information reservation management system	291
11.8	Multi-entry search variables for destination management systems	298
11.9	Distribution of a destination integrated computer information management system	300
11.10	Success criteria for DMS stakeholders	303
11.11	Characteristics of successful destination systems of the future	304
12.1	Old eTourism intermediaries	316
12.2	New eTourism intermediation and intermediaries	318
12.3	Traditional eTourism intermediaries vs new eTourism intermediaries	319
12.4	eTourism: stakeholder ICT requirements for the future	327
12.5	The 'I' framework – increasing the virtuality of eTourism	337

List of tables

2.1	Benefits from enterprise-wide Internet and eCommerce strategy	40
2.2	Interaction in the electronic marketplace, with examples from tourism	42

2.3 Characteristics of virtual corporations 66
3.1 Software classification scheme 86
3.2 Computer reservation systems and global distribution systems as drivers
for the globalization of tourism and hospitality 96
4.1 Forecast of international tourist arrivals by region (in millions) 114
4.2 Forecasted growth of worldwide travel 1995–2010 114
4.3 Ranked top nations in Internet use in 2001 (by size of population) 116
4.4 Ranked top nations in Internet use in 2001 (by percentage of population) 116
4.5 Motivation factors for Europeans to purchase more products on-line 120
4.6 Mobile phone usage in European countries 121
8.1 Typologies and examples of hotel computer reservation systems 223
8.2 Hotel Internet reservations in 1997 and 2000 228
8.3 Internet opportunities for innovative SMTEs 232

List of case studies

1.1 Fidelio's OPERA hotel Property Management System 19
2.1 The Corisande Hotel in Cornwall and the www.cornwall-calling.co.uk website 31
3.1 Lonely Planet's Thorntree 103
4.1 Size of the German travel market in turnover and travel agencies 113
4.2 Internet population – catching a moving target 119
5.1 Hotel Segas 142
5.2 The Airtours business and strategic business units 166
6.1 The Biz2Biz Hospitality Marketplace 189
7.1 Amadeus, global travel distribution 196
7.2 The British Airways in-flight catering system extranet 205
7.3 WorldTracer – the mishandled baggage system 206
7.4 easyJet on-line 207
7.5 Southwest Airlines on the Internet 208
7.6 The Opodo travel portal 210
8.1 Active Hotels 224
8.2 Revenue management system at the MGM Grand Hotel, Las Vegas 226
8.3 Accor hotels on-line 229
8.4 worldres.com, the hotel reservation network 233
8.5 Six Continents Hotels use wireless devices 236
9.1 Anite's PowerRes system 245
9.2 The European Commission Harmonise project 248
9.3 Tapestry Holidays offers a virtual tour on its website 251
9.4 Thomson and World of TUI on-line in the UK 253
9.5 On-line and eCommerce for tour operators in Scandinavia 254
10.1 Via Voyager travel agency solution 266
10.2 Thomas Cook on-line 269
10.3 lastminute.com 273
11.1 The Australian portal australia.com 284
11.2 The Finnish Tourism Board info-structure 294
11.3 Cyber-squatting – the barcelona.com legal battle 299
11.4 Tiscover: development and growth 305

Foreword

Travel and tourism is one of the world's largest and most rapidly expanding industries, contributing over ten per cent to global GDP and generating employment for 200 million people, according to annual research by the World Travel & Tourism Council (WTTC). Travel and tourism can be part of the solution to world problems, such as bridging the gap between the 'haves' and 'have-nots'. In many areas, it is one of the few possibilities for economic activity. It can create jobs and opportunities for entrepreneurs. It offers training in management skills, education and technology to local people as well as increasing incomes in rural and remote economies. It can help contribute to the alleviation of poverty in developing countries.

Technology plays a vital enabling role in travel and tourism and is crucial to the expansion of the industry. It was to accelerate this enabling role that the WTTC established the WTTC IT/eCommerce Task Force. The task force recommended a transformation programme comprising seven major initiatives that suppliers and intermediaries must jointly and independently execute:

- Intermediary infrastructure transformation
- Supplier integration and service transformation
- On-line systems transformation
- Off-line systems transformation
- Experience delivery transformation
- Revenue management transformation
- Distribution management transformation.

This book provides an insight into the tourism industry and the transformation taking place in information and communication technologies. Dr Dimitrios Buhalis, who contributed to the work of the WTTC IT/eCommerce Task Force, captures these trends and offers a vision of how travel and tourism can expand through technology-enabled and customer-focused distribution systems.

Jean-Claude Baumgarten
President
World Travel & Tourism Council

London, June 2002

Acknowledgements

Author's acknowledgements

This book brings together almost fifteen years of active interest and research activity in the issue of information technology and tourism. Throughout my academic and professional life I have been lucky to be associated with a lot of people who have contributed enormously to the ideas discussed here. Several colleagues and friends have shaped my interest and provided the tools for exploring and navigating through this area and I feel obliged to acknowledge them here. The first opportunity came at the University of the Aegean in Greece where Nikolas Litinas gave me the opportunity to research the impacts of ICTs on Greek tourism through the European Community STAR programme. Gerassimos Zacharatos, Odisseas Sakellaridis and Roi Panagiotopoulou trained me in tourism, ICT and research methodology respectively. My classmate and good friend George Paraskevadis provided tireless technical support at the time. Once in the UK, I was fortunate to meet Chris Cooper, John Fletcher and John Westlake, all then at the University of Surrey. Chris directed my doctorate research and John Fletcher financed the project through a Surrey Research Group scholarship.

Working with Peter O'Connor, a self-confessed 'hi-tech hotelier', kept me up to date with recent developments and advanced thinking. Hannes Werthner always made difficult technological issues sound fun and encouraged my involvement with the International Federation of Information Technology and Tourism and the ENTER conferences. I also had the opportunity to work closely with Hilary Main, Karsten Kärcher, Inkeri Starry, Josef Margreiter, Roger Carter, Peter Dennis, John Rafferty, Walter Schertler, Daniel Fesenmair, Andy Frew, Anna Pollock, Pauline Sheldon, Alex Paraskevas, Valeria Minghetti and Olivier Dombey. Karsten Kärcher also contributed Case Study 11.4. Working closely with the World Tourism Organization, the World Travel and Tourism Council and the European Commission has also developed several ideas explored in the book. Finally, prolific authors Chris Cooper, Dick Butler, Mike Hall and John Swarbrooke, who lead by example, have been instrumental in encouraging this book. Colleagues at the University of Surrey, David Airey, Andrew Lockwood, Panos Louvieris, Jan Powell-Perry and Gareth White, contributed to this book by accommodating my research interests and by debating some of the ideas presented. Also many of my ex-students at the University of Surrey, at IMHI (Cornell University-ESSEC) in Paris and the University of Westminster, London contributed to the development of the material and concepts. In particular, Antonella Spada, Cristina Licata, Adria Lacorte and Steve Keeling undertook research on eTourism and some of their findings are reflected in the book.

Feedback from several anonymous reviewers as well as from Tony Jolley of Bournemouth University has also contributed to this book. Finally, a word of appreciation to Maria Sega-Buhalis and Dimitra Darabara who provided invaluable support with this text, and to Andrea West for secretarial support.

Thank you all and I hope the result justifies your efforts to train, encourage, motivate and support me.

Dimitrios Buhalis
Guildford, May 2002

Publisher's acknowledgements

We are grateful to the following for permission to reproduce copyright material:

Figure 1.8 after *Information Technology and Tourism – A challenging Relationship*, Werthner, H. and Klein, S., 1999, © Springer-Verlag, reprinted with permission of Springer-Verlag, Hannes Werthner and Stefan Klein (Werthner, H. and Klein, S. 1999); Table 3.2 adapted and reprinted from *Tourism Management*, Vol. 13(1), Go, F., 'The role of computerized reservation systems in the hospitality industry,' pp. 22–26, © 1992, Figure 3.7 adapted and reprinted from *Tourism Management*, Vol. 19(3), Buhalis, D., 'Strategic use of information technologies in the tourism industry,' pp. 409–423, © 1998, Figures 11.7, 11.8 and 11.9 adapted and reprinted from *Tourism Management*, Vol. 14(5), Buhalis, D., 'Regional integrated computer information reservation management systems as a strategic tool for the small and medium tourism enterprises,' p. 376, © 1993, Figures 12.1 and 12.2 reprinted from *Tourism Management*, Vol. 23(3), Buhalis, D. and Licata, C., 'The eTourism intermediaries,' pp. 207–220, © 2002, with permission from Excerpta Medica Inc. (Go. F. 1992; Buhalis, D. 1998a; Buhalis, D. and Licata, C. 2002); Figure 3.6 from and Figure 11.9 adapted from 'Information and telecommunications technologies as a strategic tool for small and medium tourism enterprises in the contemporary business environment,' pp. 252–275, in Seaton, A. *et al.* (eds), *Tourism the State of the Art: The Strathclyde Symposium*, © 1994 John Wiley, reproduced by permission of John Wiley & Sons Limited (Buhalis, D. 1994); Table 4.1 after *World Tourism Organization's Tourism 2020 Vision* (WTO 2000), Figure 10.3 after *Marketing Tourism Destinations Online* (WTO 1999), and Figure 11.4 after *Marketing Tourism Destinations Online* and after *EBusiness for Tourism: Practical Guidelines for Destinations and Businesses*, World Tourism Organization (WTO 1999; WTO 2001); Tables 4.3 and 4.4 adapted from 'How many on-line?' www.nua.ie/surveys/how many on line/, 1 June 2001, © Nua Internet Surveys; Table 4.5 after and Figure 4.4 from 'European online commerce and travel: serving the directed shopper,' in Jupiter Communication presentation at the conference 'Changing Distribution Channels in the Travel Industry,' 8–9 December, London, © 2002 Jupiter Research, a division of Jupitermedia Corporation (Jones, N. 1999); Figures 4.5, 4.6 and 4.7 from 'Travel planners: how they use the web today,' presentation at ENTER2001 Conference, Montreal, © Travel Industry Association of America (Cook, S. 2001); Case Study 4.1 after http://www.fvw.com, reprinted with permission of FVW International; Figure 7.2 from 'IT trends survey 2001,' *Airline Business*, August, Airline Business (O'Toole, K. 2001); Figure 8.3

from 'Hotels technology survey,' *Hotels*, February, © HOTELS magazine, a Reed Business Information publication (Hensdill, C. 1998); Figure 11.10 from 'Destination management systems: criteria for success,' in *Information Technology and Tourism*, Vol. 3, No. 1, pp. 41–58, Cognizant Communication, Corporation (Buhalis, D. and Spada, A. 2000).

In some instances we have been unable to trace the owners of copyright material, and we would appreciate any information that would enable us to do so.

About the author

Dr Dimitrios Buhalis is Course Leader of the MSc in eTourism and Director of the Centre for eTourism Research (CeTR) in the School of Management, University of Surrey. Dimitrios is also Adjunct Professor for the MBA in Hospitality Management at the Institut de Management Hotelier International (Cornell University-Ecole Superieure des Sciences Economiques et Commerciales, ESSEC) in Paris and he contributes regularly to post-graduate courses around the world. Other activities include: Vice Chairman of the International Federation of Information Technology and Tourism (IFITT); Chair of the Meetings and Events committee and Member of the Executive Council of the Tourism Society. He is also the immediate past Chairman of the Association of Tourism Teachers and Trainers (ATTT). He was Chair of the Scientific Board of the ENTER '98, '99 and 2000 conferences on tourism and information technology and he chaired the ENTER 2002, Destinations and ENTER 2003 conferences. His industrial experience includes managerial roles in the Aegean tourism and hospitality industries, as well as more than ten years of international tourism and hospitality research and consultancy. Dimitrios regularly works as adviser for the World Tourism Organisation, the World Tourism and Travel Council and the European Commission. He has written or co-edited eight books and a plethora of scientific articles in academic journals.

Preface

Information and communication technologies (ICTs) and tourism are two of the most dynamic motivators of the emerging global economy. Not only do they offer employment to millions of people around the world, but they also provide growth opportunities to otherwise peripheral, underdeveloped and neglected regions of the planet. Tourism (in the widest possible sense, including hospitality, catering, attractions, travel, public and private organizations) is frequently able to develop economies through the infusion of international and national demand and expenditure into local resources, services and products. Increasingly, people have access to incredible resources and knowledge through the Internet. Several communities around the world are following India's example in gradually using technology to improve their participation in world affairs and to attract financial resources. **Tourism and ICTs are therefore the two key catalysts** for enabling dynamic, innovative and knowledgeable communities and organizations to communicate and interact with the outside world in order to import expenditure and benefits. In this sense, both tourism and ICTs increasingly provide strategic opportunities and powerful tools for economic growth, redistribution of wealth and development of equity around the globe.

However, they also instigate new challenges and threats for players that are unable to cope with the developments and are left behind technologically. Increasingly, these players will fail to participate in the wealth-creation process and will be excluded from the emerging prosperity provided by the new tools. ICTs offer both strategic opportunities and threats not only for commercial organizations but also for governments, economies, sectors and nations at large. ICTs enjoy a particular relationship with tourism. On the one hand, ICTs propel the globalization and expansion of tourism, and on the other, tourism's geographical and operational expansion generates further demands that need to be resolved by advanced technology (in other words, a chicken-and-egg situation).

This book defines eTourism as the digitization of all the processes and value chains in the tourism, travel, hospitality and catering industries that enable organizations to maximize their efficiency and effectiveness. eTourism revolutionizes all business processes, the entire value chain as well as the strategic relationships of tourism organizations with all their stakeholders. It takes advantage of intranets for reorganizing internal processes, extranets for developing transactions with trusted partners and the Internet for interacting with all its stakeholders. eTourism increasingly determines the competitiveness of the organization and therefore it is critical for the competitiveness of the industry in the longer term.

This book aims to provide a strategic overview of the use of ICTs in the tourism industry and to explain the impact of the emerging ICTs on a wide range of players. It concentrates on the strategic management and marketing perspective for tourism enterprises and destinations. It examines a wide range of ICT techniques and developments that relate to the tourism and hospitality industries and provides guidance for organizations to enhance their competitiveness in their dynamic environment. Two major assumptions are made. First, in the long term, which is estimated to be less than three years in the ICT industry, the available technology will be adequate to facilitate all organizational functions required by the rapidly emerging business models. Therefore the book advocates that managers need to understand and believe in technology and to create a vision that will enable them to achieve long-term competitive advantage in an increasingly dynamic and fluid marketplace. Second, ICTs will be affordable, understandable and implementable by most organizations within a reasonable time-frame. This implies that committed managers can actually achieve their vision if it is properly designed. It also means that other players, empowered by technological tools, will be able to enhance their competitiveness. Thus, it will become incredibly difficult for organizations to maintain competitive advantage unless they adopt dynamic, innovative and constantly evolving structures and processes.

The book takes a positive stand towards technology in general. This is not because the limitations and costs of ICTs are not being recognized and considered, but because it is only a matter of time before technological progress provides trouble-free solutions at a justifiable cost that makes them cost effective. This has been demonstrated by a whole range of technologies that have surpassed their initial expectations to become commonplace, enabling people to rely on them. Inevitably in the process several organizations have not managed to achieve their objectives and some have even faced catastrophic failure. In the long term, however, technological innovations have been adopted by and contributed to the management of organizations. The book also suggests that organizations that fail to follow dynamic developments and undertake suitable action to strengthen their competitiveness will be endangered, just as other organizations have failed before – only this time developments will take place at a much faster pace, and therefore organizations will succeed or fail in a fraction of the time required before. Time and speed are therefore key factors for the business environment of the future.

The need for sound business models and a clear understanding of market needs, size and growth remain unchanged, however. Only organizations that create real value for their customers and partners will survive in the long term. This can be demonstrated by examples in both the on-line and off-line world. In retail, C&N decided to close its UK operation and Marks and Spencer decided to close its overseas outlets in the struggle to maintain their profitability; at the time their offerings were considered out of fashion and lacked customer appeal. Similarly, many dot.com companies failed in recent years mainly because they could not develop their market share and income fast enough, or because they could not raise capital to pay for technological investments or, as often happened, because they had miscalculated their business proposition. The speed with which ICT-related organizations often achieve their media profile makes these examples more visible than the off-line operations that fail on a daily basis. Developments during the last few decades support the validity of these assumptions and the positive attitude towards technology.

This book is written mainly for final-year undergraduate and postgraduate students in business, tourism and hospitality programmes who need to explore how they can use ICTs in a strategic context. International examples and case studies are aimed at making the book relevant on a global scale. It is also anticipated that researchers and practitioners will find it useful and stimulating. The book assumes that readers have a fairly good understanding of tourism/hospitality management, marketing, and planning issues. Should readers need to develop their understanding on tourism, they are advised to read specialized books in order to appreciate the different aspects of the field (Cooper et al., 1998; Mill and Morrison, 1998; Goeldner et al., 2000; Hall, 2000; Horner and Swarbrooke, 1996). This book does not pretend to be information technology focused and its technical coverage is rather limited. Instead it aims to interpret the new technological developments and assess their implications for the tourism industry as well as to illustrate the emerging opportunities and challenges. Rather than focusing on the 'hands-on' approach, this book concentrates on the strategic implications of ICT developments and illustrates how tourism organizations should take advantage of the emerging tools to achieve sustainable competitive advantage. Readers may find it beneficial, therefore, to complement their reading with technology texts and manuals (e.g. Laudon and Laudon, 2002; Oz, 2000; Turban and Aronson 2001; Gupta, 2000). These texts will enable them to study technological solutions in greater detail and to explore technical implementation suggestions further.

During the last few years several books have been published dealing with information technology in tourism. Most of these books offer a new angle on the study of the topic. Therefore, they do not compete with but rather complement this volume. For example, Poon (1993) offers a theoretical framework on innovation and ICTs in tourism; Sheldon (1997) offers an overview and examines how each industry sector uses ICTs; O'Connor (1999a) and Peacock (1995) illustrate the use of ICTs in hospitality operations; Inkpen (1998) explains the use of ICTs in the travel trade; Kärcher (1997) proposes strategic frameworks for the development of ICT for tour operators; O'Connor (1999b) and Marcussen (1999a) demonstrate the impacts of the Internet on the distribution of European tourism organizations; the WTO (1999, 2001) provides an overview of ICT in tourism and particularly for destinations; and Werthner and Klein (1999) explore a wide range of ICT, management and tourism techniques and their interrelationships. In addition, the ENTER proceedings of the past nine conferences (Schertler et al., 1994; Schertler, Schmid et al., 1995; Klein et al., 1996; Tjoa, 1997; Buhalis et al., 1998; Buhalis and Schertler, 1999; Fesenmaier et al., 2000; Sheldon et al., 2001; Wöber et al., 2002) offer a plethora of conceptual frameworks, case studies and techniques from around the globe. Academic papers published in journals, and in particular in *Information Technology and Tourism*, discuss several key issues both from a theoretical and a practical stand. This book aims to distil knowledge from all these resources and to encourage readers to explore these texts for their contribution.

The book follows a straightforward structure. Part A aims to establish a basic level of understanding of the new technologies driving change, the main strategic management choices and the generic impacts of ICTs on strategic management. These should illustrate that the changes discussed in the book are not unique to tourism and that a great transformation is evident throughout the business world and all organizational processes. Then it explores the relationships between tourism and ICTs from a strategic management perspective. In Part B, the book concentrates on the key sectors of the tourism and hospitality industry. It provides a comprehensive overview of the use of ICTs in their strategic and tactical management. Finally, the book concludes by discussing the future under the theme of multi-integration, arguing that increasingly we shall face more integrated technologies, which will drive a great integration of the tourism industry, and as a result, a collaboration between all partners will be required. Enjoy . . .

This book is accompanied by a website (**www.booksites.net/buhalis**) that provides **annotated weblinks**. For lecturers and facilitators who have adopted the textbook, there are also **PowerPoint slides** to aid in preparation.

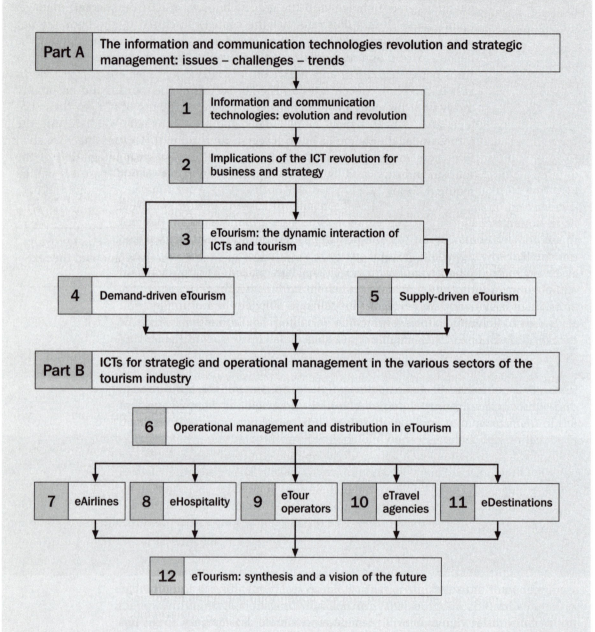

Part A

The information and communication
technologies revolution and
strategic management:
issues – challenges – trends

Introduction to Part A

Tourism and technology go hand in hand together. Indeed, technological progress during the last century has revolutionized work patterns and enabled the industrialization of most production functions. As a result, the way we live and work in most societies around the globe has been significantly altered. Automated industrial production has enabled a greater total output as well as better planning and quality control. This has led to the production of sufficient products to cover increasing demand, as well as the production of new standardized and consistent commodities that can be traded at a global level.

During the Industrial Revolution, organizations were forced to re-engineer their processes in order to take advantage of the changes in organizational capabilities and emerging tools, and thus improve their competitiveness. Productivity was increased dramatically and gradually workers were able to concentrate on 'lighter' but more intelligent work, leaving the hard labour to machinery. The Industrial Revolution and the developments in production during the first decades of the twentieth century allowed a great proportion of the workforce to leave agriculture and migrate to urban centres in order to find work, and then to demand and achieve paid leisure time as part of their working contracts. The availability of time and disposable income propelled the industrialization of tourism as a new phenomenon, allowing working-class people to include travel and holidays in their annual activities and budget.

Over the last few decades, the progress in information technology has revolutionized both the global economy and enterprises. The development and application of computerized systems has accelerated rapidly and enabled their use in a wider range of functions and activities. More importantly, the development of powerful personal computers (PCs) in the 1980s provided individuals with reliable and affordable computing without having to invest in mainframes or mini-computers, which were expensive to acquire and maintain. In addition, the emergence of the Internet towards the end of the twentieth century enabled the networking of computers globally and the access to multimedia information and knowledge sources free of charge. Thus, a huge number of people can effectively access unprecedented levels of information and knowledge.

At the same time, people can contribute to a web of interactive communication, by publishing material on the Internet, participating in discussion forums and exchanging electronic mail. Although only three per cent of the global population is currently estimated to have access to the Internet, predominantly in the developed world, it is increasingly evident that people from developing countries are gradually gaining access to the Internet and often use technology to improve their living conditions. Perhaps India is a leading example of that. Many young scientists specialize in information and communication technologies (ICTs) and pursue international careers from India or by emigrating to developed countries. ICTs are now a key determinant of organizational competitiveness as a result of several major developments, including:

- massive enhancements in processing capabilities;
- increase of computing speed;
- decrease of equipment size;
- reduction of hardware and software costs;
- improvement of reliability, compatibility and interconnectivity of terminals and applications;
- evolution of business models to collaborative models; and
- globalization of demand and supply, particularly in tourism.

These developments have a great effect on the operation, structure and strategy of innovative and technological advanced organizations. Not only do they reduce both communication and operational costs of most enterprises internationally, but they can also restructure their **management** practices and processes to take advantage of emergent opportunities. As a result of the technological development around the world, production systems, methods of organizing work and consumption patterns are currently undergoing changes, which, in turn, will have long-term effects comparable with those of the first Industrial Revolution. At a personal level, these developments enable individuals to enhance their personal productivity and to be able to use computers for entertainment, education and leisure, as well as for planning their leisure time. ICTs, therefore, on the one hand allow people to increase, via higher productivity, their disposable income and leisure time and thus enjoy their recreational activities. On the other hand, they provide the info-structure for the development and operation of tourism suppliers who can attract and serve consumers from all over the world. Hence, ICTs increasingly empower and enable both tourism consumers and suppliers to communicate, enhance awareness of needs and offers, inform, negotiate and, more importantly, develop bridges to reduce distance, cultural and communication gaps.

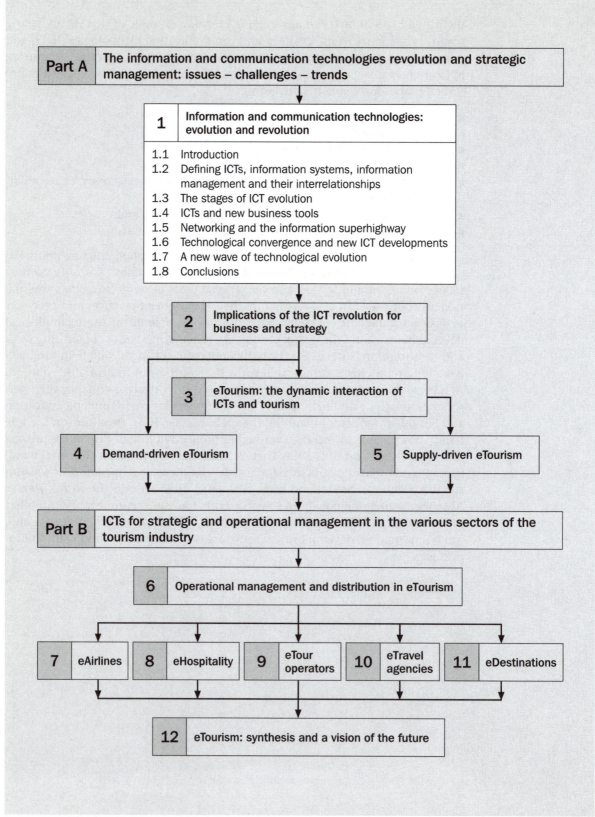

Part A | The information and communication technologies revolution and strategic management: issues – challenges – trends

1 | Information and communication technologies: evolution and revolution

1.1 Introduction
1.2 Defining ICTs, information systems, information management and their interrelationships
1.3 The stages of ICT evolution
1.4 ICTs and new business tools
1.5 Networking and the information superhighway
1.6 Technological convergence and new ICT developments
1.7 A new wave of technological evolution
1.8 Conclusions

2 | Implications of the ICT revolution for business and strategy

3 | eTourism: the dynamic interaction of ICTs and tourism

4 | Demand-driven eTourism

5 | Supply-driven eTourism

Part B | ICTs for strategic and operational management in the various sectors of the tourism industry

6 | Operational management and distribution in eTourism

7 | eAirlines

8 | eHospitality

9 | eTour operators

10 | eTravel agencies

11 | eDestinations

12 | eTourism: synthesis and a vision of the future

1

Information and communication technologies: evolution and revolution

Chapter objectives

The purpose of this chapter is to introduce technological concepts and to establish a level of understanding of ICTs, enabling readers to appreciate the key elements of the technological revolution. A number of implications for business and for society in general are also highlighted. This chapter provides the foundation for discussion of the impacts of ICT upon business and the tourism industry dealt with later in the book. Thus the chapter objectives may be defined as to:

■ Increase awareness of technological developments and some major trends

■ Establish a level of understanding of terminology and critical issues

■ Demonstrate that ICT developments have a profound impact on organizations

■ Explore the relationship between the Internet, extranets and intranets

■ Discuss the growth of the on-line population and the issues related to it

■ Identify the need for integrated managerial solutions within the business strategy context

1.1 Introduction

Information and communication technologies (ICTs) enhance the ability of organizations to manage their resources, increase their productivity, communicate their policies and market their offerings, and develop partnerships with all their stakeholders, namely consumers, suppliers, public sector organizations, interest groups, etc. ICTs also enable organizations to expand geographically and coordinate their activities regionally, nationally and globally. Operational expansion is also assisted as ICTs enable the management of more resources and thus facilitate expansion, mergers, acquisitions and growth in general. Technological tools offer unprecedented tools for managerial control and coordination. As a result, they not only facilitate expansion, they often instigate it. Hotel chains, for example, can expand because of their ability to control and coordinate their functions at remote locations and in larger properties.

Perhaps more importantly, ICTs support the development and maintenance of organizational competitiveness and competitive advantage. Constant innovation in applications of hardware, software and **network computing** means that only dynamic organizations that can assess the requirements of their stakeholders and respond efficiently and effectively will be able to outperform their competition and maintain their long-term prosperity. Rapid technological development paradoxically means that the more powerful and complex ICTs become, the more affordable and user-friendly they become, enabling more people and organizations to take advantage. Moreover, advanced education for younger people means that they are often more competent in using new technologies than their parents are. It is, therefore, anticipated that by the year 2010 an integrated system of technologies will be at least as widely available and easy to use as the telephone was in the 1980s, providing enormous capabilities for consumers as well as opportunities and challenges for suppliers in all industries.

1.2 Defining ICTs, information systems, information management and their interrelationships

It is quite difficult to define **information and communication technologies (ICTs)** in an accurate and succinct manner. ICTs include not only the **hardware** and **software** required but also the groupware and netware as well as the intellectual capacity (humanware) to develop, program and maintain the equipment (Figure 1.1). Several authors have attempted to define ICTs:

- Thomas (1988) philosophically suggests that technology consists of 'society's poll of knowledge concerning the industrial, mechanical and practical areas'.
- Peppard (1993) defines information technology (IT) as the enabling mechanism that facilitates the processing and flow of information in an organization and between organizations, encompassing the information the business creates, uses and stores, as well as the technologies used in physical processing to produce a product or provide a service.

Figure 1.1 Information and communication technologies

Terminology box	Examples from the hospitality industry
Hardware: physical equipment such as mechanical, magnetic, electrical, electronic or optical devices (as opposed to **computer programs** or method of use)	Computers, printers and restaurant terminals
Software: prewritten detailed instructions that control the operation of a **computer system** or of an electronic device. Software coordinates the work of hardware components in an information system. Software may incorporate standard software such as **operating systems** or applications, software processes, artificial intelligence and intelligent agents, and user interfaces	Micros-Fidelio – the property management system that enables hotels to control their assets and to debit and credit departments and guests' bills
Telecommunications: the transmission of signals over long distances, including not only data communications but also the transmission of images and voices using radio, television, telephony and other communication technologies	Telephone centre, fax systems
Netware: equipment and software required to develop and support a network or an interconnected system of computers, terminals and communication channels and devices	Networking of hardware and software between all departments in a hotel
Groupware: communication tools, such as e-mail, voice mail, fax and videoconferencing, that foster electronic communication and collaboration among groups	Applications that allow employees to share files, customer profiles and operational information such as prices
'Humanware': the intellect required for the development, **programming**, maintenance and operation of technological development. Humanware incorporates the knowledge and expertise pool of society	The IT/IS team in the hotel as well as their liaisons with departments and functions

Adapted from: Gupta (1996); O'Brien (1996); Laudon and Laudon (2002); Werthner and Klein (1999); Halsall (1996)

- Runge and Earl (1988) include telecommunications in ITs and propose that '*telecommunication* networks provide the information highways over which new products and services can be offered, thereby redefining concepts of customer service, opening up new arenas of innovation and altering the economics of distribution'.
- Poon (1993) defines ICT as 'the collective term given to the most recent developments in the mode (electronic) and the mechanisms (computers and communications technologies) used for the acquisition, processing, analysis, storage, retrieval, dissemination, and application of information'.

For the purposes of this book we consider ICTs as the entire range of electronic tools that facilitate the operational and strategic management of organizations by enabling them to manage their information, functions and processes as well as to communicate interactively with their stakeholders, enabling them to achieve their mission and objectives. This range, which represents a convergence of hardware, software, telecommunications, netware, groupware and humanware, is illustrated in Figure 1.2 (Gupta, 2000; Beekman, 2001; Oz, 2000).

This convergence effectively blurs the boundaries between equipment and software (Werthner and Klein, 1999, p. 72). For example, mobile phones increasingly have access to the Internet and in the near future will be used as mini-computers

Figure 1.2 Information and communication technologies convergence

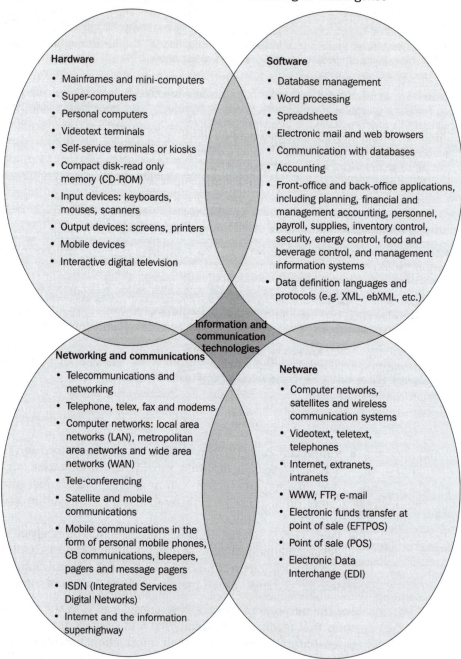

Hardware

- Mainframes and mini-computers
- Super-computers
- Personal computers
- Videotext terminals
- Self-service terminals or kiosks
- Compact disk-read only memory (CD-ROM)
- Input devices: keyboards, mouses, scanners
- Output devices: screens, printers
- Mobile devices
- Interactive digital television

Software

- Database management
- Word processing
- Spreadsheets
- Electronic mail and web browsers
- Communication with databases
- Accounting
- Front-office and back-office applications, including planning, financial and management accounting, personnel, payroll, supplies, inventory control, security, energy control, food and beverage control, and management information systems
- Data definition languages and protocols (e.g. XML, ebXML, etc.)

Information and communication technologies

Networking and communications

- Telecommunications and networking
- Telephone, telex, fax and modems
- Computer networks: local area networks (LAN), metropolitan area networks and wide area networks (WAN)
- Tele-conferencing
- Satellite and mobile communications
- Mobile communications in the form of personal mobile phones, CB communications, bleepers, pagers and message pagers
- ISDN (Integrated Services Digital Networks)
- Internet and the information superhighway

Netware

- Computer networks, satellites and wireless communication systems
- Videotext, teletext, telephones
- Internet, extranets, intranets
- WWW, FTP, e-mail
- Electronic funds transfer at point of sale (EFTPOS)
- Point of sale (POS)
- Electronic Data Interchange (EDI)

or to interconnect computers. As it becomes more difficult to distinguish between each element of the technology, ICTs should be regarded as the entire range of electronics, computing and telecommunication technologies and all hardware, software and netware required for the development and operation of the 'info-structure' of an organization. Thus, ICTs are an integrated system of networked equipment and software that enables effective data processing and communication for organizational benefit.

Synergies emerging from the use of these systems effectively mean that information will be widely available and accessible through a variety of media and locations. Users will be able to use mobile devices such as portable **computers** and mobile phones as well as digital television and self-serviced **terminals**/kiosks to interact and perform several functions. Negroponte (1995, p. 82) asserts that 'personal computers have moved computer science away from the purely technical imperative. Computing is no longer the exclusive realm of military, government and big business. It is being channelled directly into the hands of very creative individuals at all levels of society, becoming the means for creating expression in both its use and development. The means and message of multimedia will become a blend of technical and artistic achievement.'

Information systems (IS) are defined as the 'interrelated components working together to collect, process, store and disseminate information to support decision making, coordination, control, analysis and visualization in an organization' (Laudon and Laudon, 2002; Turban et al., 2002). Martin et al. (1999) explain that information systems represent the collection of computer hardware and software, as well as procedures, documents, forms and people responsible for the capture, movement, management and distribution of data and information. Each of the elements of the system needs to be coordinated and work efficiently together. Information systems can be defined as having seven characteristics (Figure 1.3).

Figure 1.3 Information systems characteristics

Terminology box	*Examples from the airline industry*
Boundary: clear distinction between internal and external elements. Internal elements are controllable by organizations	Distinction between internal and external systems of an airline
Environment: external elements to the system including assumptions, constraints and inputs to the system	External computerized and non-computerized systems that influence the airline, such as immigration systems and regulations or weather-forecasting systems
Inputs: all resources imported to the system including data, material, supplies and energy	Reservations by consumers, data on procurement, aircraft planning rota, weather forecasts
Outputs: products and resources of the systems in various formats including reports, documents, displays, announcements provided to the environment of the system	Flight manifests, crew requirement reports, in-flight catering orders
Components: activities or processes within a system that transform inputs to outputs	Software programs that order catering, generate crew requirements based on reservations, weather forecasts and other inputs
Interfaces: point of contact between system and its environment	Point of interaction between a customer or a travel agency computer and the computer of an airline
Storage: holding areas used for the temporary and permanent storage of information	Memory for storing reservations as well as management reports and information

Source: Based on Martin et al. (1999); Turban et al. (2002)

Information systems contain therefore the entire range of ICTs as well as raw data representing events, entries and information (i.e. process data into meaningful and useful representations). They take into consideration input and use interfaces to interact with the external environment to collect more data. Through a number of procedures and processes, they produce output that supports organizational functions and business purposes.

Information management is responsible for providing information and communication services and resources for the products and services, operations, management and control activities and cooperative work of an organization. It is, therefore, charged with planning, developing, implementing, operating and maintaining the information technology infrastructure (**info-structure**) and portfolio of applications for an organization. Information management overlooks information technology and information systems and ensures that they are co-ordinated with the goal of achieving the business **strategy**. This includes a range of functions and processes that produce strategic information planning, system building and maintenance, change of management, systems operation and information advisory services. This is an ongoing process, which requires feedback and adjustment at each stage. As a result, the implementation of a business strategy, as well as the development and adoption of an information system strategy, is often fed back and formulates the business strategy. This is increasingly the case, as innovative tools may enable organizations to expand their business strategy through partnerships and development of additional business applications. In contrast, innovative technologies may not be adopted early enough or may prove to be unsuitable for particular users, in which case again organizations may need to change their business strategy and models. Information management enables organizations to develop systems and processes in order to transform raw data and input from the external and internal environment through software to meaningful and useful information, which can support business processes and managerial decisions (Turban et al., 2002; Earl, 1988).

As demonstrated in Figure 1.4, the organizational mission and business strategy generates the strategic directions and objectives for any enterprise. As a consequence, a wide range of needs for information and business processes is created. This generates the information systems strategy, which identifies the user requirements and the types of applications needed to fulfil the business strategy. As a result, an ICT strategy is determined, which enables technology experts to develop and operate suitable technological solutions for achieving the information systems strategy. At this stage, the ICT infrastructure and the technical capabilities of organizations are assessed and fed back to the information system strategy. This process may alter the business strategy in order to take advantage of the technological strengths and to avoid weaknesses and deficiencies in the systems.

Researchers often enquire whether technological developments drive business strategies or vice versa. It is becoming evident that the business strategy and mission of organizations should lead their processes and technological developments. However, it is also evident that unless managers appreciate their technological strengths and weaknesses, they will be unable to implement these strategies. A wide spectrum of results may arise if this is the case. Managers may

Figure 1.4 Relationship between business strategy, information system strategy and information technology strategy

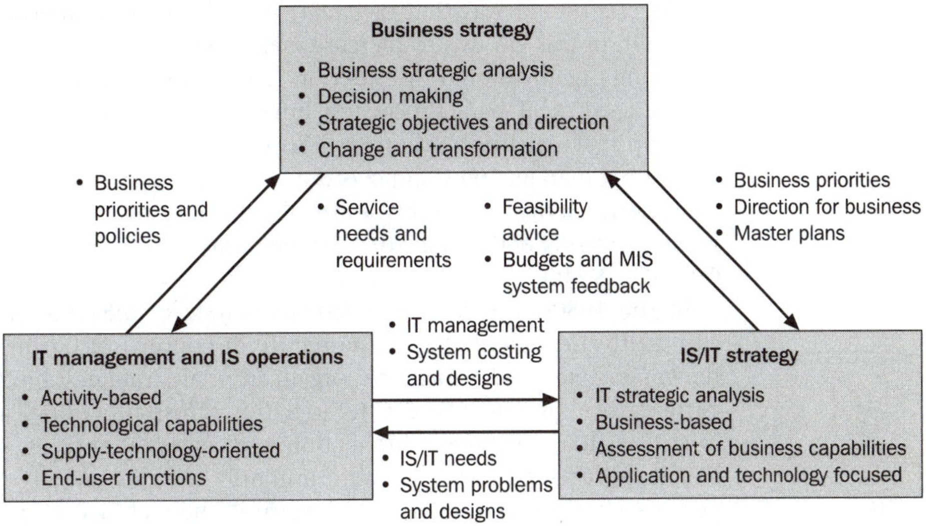

Business strategy

- Business strategic analysis
- Decision making
- Strategic objectives and direction
- Change and transformation

- Business priorities and policies

- Service needs and requirements

- Feasibility advice
- Budgets and MIS system feedback

- Business priorities
- Direction for business
- Master plans

- IT management
- System costing and designs

IT management and IS operations

- Activity-based
- Technological capabilities
- Supply-technology-oriented
- End-user functions

- IS/IT needs
- System problems and designs

IS/IT strategy

- IT strategic analysis
- Business-based
- Assessment of business capabilities
- Application and technology focused

Source: Based on Robson (1997)

fail to exploit a particular market or opportunity if they miscalculate their strengths and weaknesses, with catastrophic results. It is therefore increasingly apparent that the business strategy of an organization should go hand in hand with its ICT strategy if the organization is to succeed in its mission and strategic objectives. For example, a leisure travel agency that would like to expand its operations to attract business travellers may need to do a comprehensive audit of its ICT infrastructure. This may identify the necessity for new systems or additional software for managing the business. They may also decide that investing in these systems may not provide adequate returns and thus decide against this expansion. Therefore business strategy needs to take into account ICT resources and the development of the ICT infrastructure to ensure that the business strategy can be served effectively.

1.3 The stages of ICT evolution

It is important to appreciate the four main eras of technological evolution. In these different eras, ICTs have contributed in different ways to organizations and have required variable resources and commitment. More importantly they have concentrated on different functions, and as a consequence, have had a dissimilar importance for the strategy and operations of organizations.

In the first era, *data processing*, the main objective was to improve operational efficiency by automating information-based processes. This era took place from the 1960s onwards and mainly used **mainframe computers** and mini-computers. Computers were only used by major corporations such as airlines. Hardware and programming were very expensive and could only be justified for organizations that had a significant amount of transactions daily.

The second era was that of *management information systems* (MIS). The principle aim of this era was to increase management effectiveness and efficiency by satisfying organizational information requirements. It commenced in the 1970s and it used local data processing linked to information resources to support decision-making. Information systems were used primarily to address the needs of internal management and coordination. Emphasis was also given to administrative and clerical functions, especially accounting or inventory management, while delivering **added value** to customers was a lower priority (Strassmann, 1990; Gamble, 1994a).

In the 1980s, the *strategic information systems* (SIS) era aimed at improving competitiveness by changing the nature or conduct of business. Integrated ICT networks were used to achieve organizational strategic objectives, to enhance performance, and to coordinate activities across functional and business unit lines as well as to support interaction with external entities, in pursuit of **competitive advantage**. Thus, SISs were primarily used to support or shape the competitive strategy of the organization and their ability to gain and maintain competitive advantage. Personal computers enabled managers to manipulate data and create their own management reports, statistics and follow-up mechanisms by using standard and fairly **user-friendly** spreadsheets and statistical packages. They were also able to forecast, budget and plan, using past data and simulation models, enhancing their ability to undertake strategic decisions. This process brought power back from programmers to end-users and enhanced the personal efficiency of individuals as well as of the organization as a whole (Robson, 1997; Peppard, 1993; McGee and Thomas, 1988; Earl, 1988; Jackson, 1989; Wiseman, 1985).

Since the late 1990s, a fourth and more profound era has been emerging, *the network era*, in which intra- and inter-organizational networking has proliferated. **Local area networks** and **wide area networks** as well as the Internet, intranets and extranets have revolutionized communication and enabled multilevel integration and efficient collaboration. It also supported both **centralized and distributed computing** to maximize the performance of the available resources. This era is gradually altering the competitiveness of firms in the global marketplace and reducing the significance of location and size in the product delivery processes. ICTs are used as indispensable tools for almost all business functions from production to marketing as they facilitate:

■ quick communication;
■ reliable and timely information transfer and retrieval;
■ integration of the different divisions within organizations;
■ flexibility of product specification;
■ sharing of information; and
■ achievement of common objectives.

The development of **electronic commerce (eCommerce)** has signified the instigation of a new global economy in which everybody is interconnected and competes on a worldwide scale. Global competition is generated through transparency in offerings and prices. Therefore, ICTs have been driving the globalization and re-engineering of most business processes and practices. Operators at different locations and different sectors of the economy may experience these changes at a variable level of growth although it is becoming more evident each day that we all live in an incredibly networked society and economy that is based on partnerships and interrelations on a global scale (Laudon and Laudon, 2002; Peppard, 1993; Tapscott, 1996; Ward et al., 1990; Blois, 1987).

1.4 ICTs and new business tools

As a result of these developments, various systems gradually became available to support business management and to enable organizations to enhance their efficiency and productivity. Operation support systems and transaction processing systems automated clerical functional and repetitive transactions, such as payroll, accounting, orders and stock management. The aim was to process business transactions, control industrial processes, support office communications and update corporate **databases**. In addition, they assisted production management and rationalized the supply and inventorying processes by forecasting the needs for raw material and input and ordering supplies accordingly.

Perhaps more importantly, **management information systems (MIS)** deal with processing data that already exist in operational systems, in order to improve the managerial efficiency of organizations. MISs have updated clerical and record-keeping functions to an interrelated and integrated computerized system that can support the tactical goals of organizations. They assist the monitoring, controlling, decision-making and administrative tasks of middle management. MISs include reports, displays and advance warnings pre-programmed by managers using data from operational databases. Hence, MISs provide managers with information and mechanisms to support their decision-making processes, by pre-planning, designing and specifying the types of information required on a regular basis. MISs normally address structured and predictable decisions at an operational and tactical level as well as measure, monitor and illustrate the performance of a process or function.

Decision support systems (DSS) are the natural progression from MISs and transaction processing systems. DSSs are interactive systems that use decision models as well as specialized databases and operation support systems to extract information to assist the decision-making process. They can provide managers with ad hoc information when needed, rather than through pre-designed formulas (as in the MIS case), and thus they support non-routine decision-making. DSSs enable managers to acquire information for unstructured types of decisions and problems in an interactive way and to personalize their enquiries and reports. Thus, they can develop and test scenarios for different developments in the external environment or to assess the risk of decision alternatives (O'Brien, 1996; Laudon and Laudon, 2002).

Strategic information systems (SIS) enable organizations to use all data and processes available to define their strategy and strategic objectives in order to improve their competitiveness. These systems support decisions related to organizational main competencies, the markets an organization operates in, its external environment, what it offers, as well as partnerships, mergers, acquisitions and alliances. By evaluating issues relating to the external environment, SISs support managerial decisions and enable managers to identify and evaluate risks based on historical data and projected trends. The aims of SISs are to enable organizations to achieve long-term competitive advantage, to avoid strategic disadvantage and to protect or improve their position. SISs are often instrumental in changing the nature of organizations and in restructuring all business processes.

Executive information systems (EIS) aim at offering top and middle management with immediate and easy access to selective information about key factors that are critical to accomplish the strategic objectives of an organization. EISs use aggregate data and easy-to-read graphs to demonstrate the current status of an organization and the projected trends for key factors selected by executives. EISs can also incorporate information from the external environment of the organization and predict its implications. Although EISs cannot solve specific problems, they can address unstructured decision making (O'Brien, 1996; Robson, 1997).

Expert systems lead the development of ICT applications as they attempt to develop and manage knowledge in a specific area in order to advise users accordingly. Expert systems consist of a specialized knowledge base and software to perform human-like inferences on the knowledge and thus answer specific questions; they can explain the reasoning process and conclusions. They are related to knowledge-based decision-support systems, which add a knowledge base to the database and model base of traditional decision-support systems. Expert systems often use **artificial intelligence**, which ultimately aims to imitate human functions such as thinking, seeing, hearing, tasting, smelling and feeling. The Massachusetts Institute of Technology (MIT) defines intelligent agents as 'computer systems to which one can delegate tasks', noting that they 'differ from conventional software in that they are long-lived, semi-autonomous, proactive, and adaptive'. To flesh out MIT's definition of agent technology, think about some of the tasks an agent might carry out: they can make airline reservations, order new books from an on-line store, find out about the latest song from a favourite musician, or monitor stock portfolios. They can scour the Internet to find information for us.

Some of the more sophisticated software agents can negotiate the purchase of raw materials for a factory, schedule factory production, negotiate delivery schedules with a customer's software agent, or automate the billing process. Intelligent software agents act on behalf of the user to find and filter information, negotiate for services, easily automate complex tasks, or collaborate with other software agents to solve complex problems. Ultimately artificial intelligence applications aim to develop a structured set of rules and procedures, which will enable the system to reason and solve problems. By collecting and interrelating information and user preferences the system can gradually 'learn' from experience as it acquires and processes new knowledge in order to improve future results (Werthner and Klein, 1999; Winston, 1992; Russell and Norvig, 1995).

It is becoming increasingly evident that unless all systems operating in an organization are integrated, it will be impossible to optimize their contribution. Synergies between operational and managerial systems can enhance the total output of an organization and maximize its efficiency and productivity. Developing a knowledge base by using the different levels of managerial systems described and incorporating new tools will be of vital importance for organizations that seek to develop their competitiveness. Integration is required not only between the technical equipment but also between all business processes; organizations that use their information systems wisely and develop responsive mechanisms can react to dynamic changes in their external environment and maximize their benefit.

1.5 Networking and the information superhighway: the Internet, intranets and extranets

The **Internet** as an idea emerged in the 1960s as a military tool by the US army (Defense Advanced Research Projects Agency). The aim was to link together mainframes and enable them to communicate with each other and share data through a flexible system that could remain operational if a few systems were destroyed or out of order. The system was known as ARPANET and used a **Transmission Control Protocol/Internet Protocol (TCP/IP)** for linking all computers together. Over time its use spread from the military to other government departments to non-government organizations such as universities and research laboratories, and ultimately to the business community and the general public (Dertouzos, 1997). The Internet supports a wide variety of different tools and functions that enable communication and sharing of data such as electronic mail, Usenet, Listserv, Gopher, Telnet and File Transfer Protocol (FTP), as illustrated in Figure 1.5. These **Internet tools** were, in the main, only accessible to technologically competent users, primarily scientists and academics. However, it was Tim Berners-Lee at CERN who in 1994 developed a user-friendly graphical interface supported by the **HyperText Mark-up Language (HTML)**, which provided the opportunity for the convergence of information processing, multimedia and communications through the **World Wide Web (WWW)**.

The WWW is effectively a global protocol of communication, which uses web pages that contain text, graphs, animations, sounds and videos for storing, retrieving, formatting and displaying multimedia information in a networked environment. The WWW uses a client/server architecture and the Internet for its distribution. Information and processes are hosted/saved on a server, which enables 'clients' (i.e. users' remote computers) to access and process the information and perform pre-programmed functions. For example, if a user logs into their 'Hotmail' account from a remote terminal, the server on the **host computer** identifies the name and password, enables them to read their eMail and to perform several activities such as reply or delete a message.

Users navigate through a plethora of networked multimedia web pages by using web browsers to access **Uniform Resource Locators** (URLs) and retrieve HTML documents. Browsers, such as Netscape Navigator and the Microsoft's Internet Explorer, use hypertext's point-and-click ability to enable users to navigate or surf

Figure 1.5 Internet capabilities and functions

Electronic mail	Person-to-person messaging and document-sending mechanism
Usenet newsgroups	Discussion groups on electronic bulletin boards
LISTSERVs	Discussion groups using eMail mailing list servers
Chatting	Interactive conversation between special-interest groups
Telnet	Remote login to one computer from another
FTP	File transfer protocol for transferring files between computers
Gophers	Locating information using a hierarchy of text-based menus
Archie	Search database of documents, software and data files available for downloading
Veronica	Very Easy Robent-Oriented Netwide Index to Computer Archives enabling speed search of gopher sites by using keywords
WAIS	Wide Area Information Servers locate files on Internet databases using keywords
World Wide Web	Retrieve, format and display multimedia information including text, audio, graphics and video using hypertext links
WAP	Wireless Application Protocol for using the Internet from mobile phones and other devices

Source: Adapted from Laudon and Laudon (2002)

from one site to another on-line. Each time they request data from a web page they count a 'hit'. Several web directories such as Yahoo.com, or **search engines** such as Altavista.com, Lycos.com and Infoseek.com, emerged to assist the organization of information in manageable categories and also the identification of relevant information through the searching of all available web pages (O'Connor, 1999b; Laudon and Laudon, 2002).

The Internet, often described as 'the network of all networks', uses a collection of over 100 000 private and public networks. It enables the instant distribution of media-rich documents worldwide and revolutionizes the interactivity between computer users and servers. The Internet provides a window to the external world and facilitates the interactivity of organizations globally. This development instituted an innovative platform for efficient, live and timely exchange of ideas and **products**. It also provided unprecedented and unforeseen opportunities for interactive management and marketing to all service providers. The development of the Internet introduced a whole range of new tools as well as benefits and challenges for organizations. It supported several business functions and organizations were forced to transform their processes in order to take advantage of the new business realities. As a result organizations were able to:

- accelerate knowledge and information distribution;
- reduce their transportation, postage and communication costs;
- increase their efficiency and productivity;
- enhance their communication and coordination efficiency;
- improve and shorten the decision-making process; and
- support their interactivity with all **stakeholders**.

Once these benefits were apparent for the macro-environment, organizations were quite keen to establish internal and secure systems of communication and knowledge share exclusively for their employees and partners. However, the Internet has been limited by the relatively slow development of on-line speeds. Most computers operate 56K (kilobits per second) **modems**, delaying the delivery of bite-hungry multimedia information, slowing down the system and increasing phone bills. As a result, good Internet designers maintain low graphics and inter-active interfaces in order to support fast and trouble-free downloading. Although **integrated service digital network (ISDN)** lines provide better speeds, they are still expensive and thus not widely used. The proliferation of the asymmetric digital subscriber line (ADSL) will make possible the sending of high volumes of data at high speeds across the existing copper cables of the telephone line. This will speed up and support communications as it will provide Internet access at speeds 20 times faster than a modem over a normal phone line. In addition, ADSL will be permanently connected for an estimated fee of £300 annually, and therefore there will be no extra charges per call.

Internal systems or **intranets** have also been developed as 'closed', 'secured', 'controlled' or 'firewalled' networks within organizations or individual depart-ments. Using Internet standard protocols and thus offering user-friendly **multi-media** interfaces, intranets allow authorized personnel to access information, knowledge and mechanisms across the enterprise in order to perform their tasks efficiently. Intranets use similar software and hardware to the Internet. However, they are protected from unauthorized users by **firewalls**, which use hardware and software to identify users and prevent outsiders from invading classified networks and data. Intranets enable organizations to improve their internal management at all levels by sharing media-rich data and processes, using Internet interfaces.

Increasingly, enterprises realized the need to formulate close partnerships with their partners and other members of the **value chain** for the production of goods and services. As a result, they developed **extranets**, which use the same principles, computer equipment and networks as intranets to allow access to pre-selected sections of an organization's data, knowledge base and mechanisms. User-friendly and multimedia interfaces mean that users require limited training for using the systems. As a result, extranets can enhance the interactivity and transparency between organizations and their trusted partners, by linking and sharing data and processes to format a low-cost and user-friendly electronic commerce arrangement, similar to **electronic data interchange (EDI)**, which was attempted in earlier stages of ICT development. Extranets therefore empower the **cooperation** between partners by enabling a certain degree of transparency and interactivity. Both partners can enjoy mutual benefits and enhance their efficiency, productivity and effectiveness without compromising on security and confidentiality (Laudon and Laudon, 2002). Figures 1.6 and 1.7 illustrate the entire networking of organizations that incorporate the Internet as well as intranets and extranets and explore their interrelationships.

Figure 1.6 Electronic networking for organizations

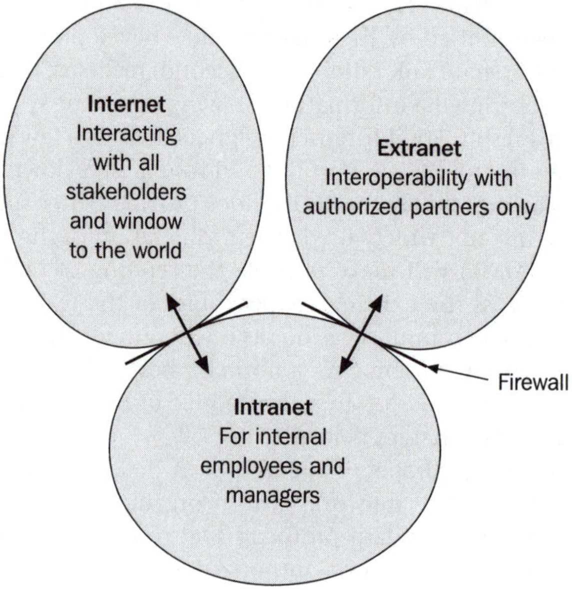

Internet
Interacting
with all
stakeholders
and window
to the world

Extranet
Interoperability with
authorized partners only

Firewall

Intranet
For internal
employees and
managers

Figure 1.7 The electronic nucleus of organizations

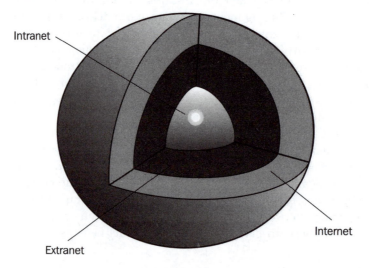

Intranet

Internet

Extranet

Case Study 1.1

Fidelio's OPERA hotel Property Management System

Fidelio was founded in 1987 in Munich and emerged as one of the leading and most innovative international systems integrator for the hospitality industries, changing the way hotels computerize and operate. Its software is adaptable to changing business requirements and integrates both the ongoing technological developments of industry-standard computer and software systems and the organizational change experienced. Fidelio allows hotels and chains of any size and type, restaurants, cruise ships and catering and conference operations to computerize their operations and to integrate major industry software products through analysing individual requirements and appreciating their uniqueness.

The latest Fidelio product is the OPERA Enterprise Solution. The OPERA Enterprise Solution is a fully integrated suite of products consisting of modules that can be easily added or expanded allowing effective and easy deployment from smaller operations to global, multi-branded hotel chain environments. OPERA can be deployed in any size environment, from a single property with just Front Office to a large, full-service hotel with Sales & Marketing, Catering, Revenue Management, Quality Management, Back Office, and Materials Management. In addition, the OPERA Enterprise Solution offers products for a hotel chain's corporate office that includes a central reservations system (CRS) for both centralized guestroom and function-space sales, and an enterprise information system, the customer relationship management (CRM) package specifically designed for the hotel industry.

The OPERA Property Management System (PMS) is designed to scale according to the requirements of any size hotel or hotel chain. The OPERA Back Office is a powerful financial software suite that provides hotels with a fully integrated, flexible financial and eBusiness solution. The OPERA Reservation System (ORS) manages the hotel inventory efficiently as it is integrated with the OPERA Property Management System and OPERA Sales and Catering System. The system emulates traditional CRS functionality, while at the same time integrating the bold new technologies shared in the OPERA Enterprise Solution, including system access via web client or any Java-enabled browser. With the power of the Internet, ORS is easily deployable and globally accessible. The OPERA Revenue Management provides both property-based and centralized yield management and is interfaced with the OPERA Sales and Catering System to analyse the value of particular group business and maximize revenue. The Customer Information System collects and manages guest, travel agent, source, group and company profile information from designated hotel properties in a centralized database. Guest stays with detailed revenue information are also collected. The system includes a whole range of interrelated modules, including:

- OPERA Property Management System
- OPERA Sales & Catering
- OPERA Back Office
- OPERA Revenue Management System
- OPERA Central Reservations System
- Central Reservations System (plus web engine)
- OPERA Quality Management System
- OPERA Materials Management System
- OPERA Palm
- Customer Information System
- Enterprise Information Systems

All of these systems are interrelated and interconnected, enabling hotels to use the system internally (intranet), externally with partners (extranet) and as a window on the world (Internet).

For more information see **www.fidelio.com**

Case Study 1.1 *continued*

Questions

- Examine the Fidelio website and identify how a Property Management System can take advantage of the Internet.
- Discuss the critical factors that will enable Property Management Systems to be delivered through an Application Service Provider (ASP) mode.
- Visit the web pages of Microsoft, Nokia, Ericsson and Motorola and
  - identify the latest technological developments that will influence tourism;
  - explore which business functions will benefit most from the new tools;
  - identify the unique contribution of each technology in the tourism industry.

1.6 Technological convergence and new ICT developments

At the dawn of the new century and the new millennium it is evident that the technological revolution has just begun, and nothing will escape its impact. Rapid technological developments and also the gradual reduction of prices illustrate that ICTs will be reaching a mass market within a few years rather than remaining accessible to only competent computer users. This is also propelled by schoolchildren who are being trained to use computers in their educational environment and are consequently demanding that their parents purchase personal computers for them at home. Although their first motivation may be to play electronic games, they often use electronic mail, **chat groups** and rooms and Internet resources for their homework. In this way it is predicted that the majority of households in the developed world will own personal computers at the same level as televisions and refrigerators.

Both satellite and cable televisions provide a wide range of opportunities for piping information to households and for facilitating interaction (Dertouzos, 1997). The introduction of digital and interactive television will bring the Internet to the living room and will allow technologically challenged people to access the **information superhighway**. Television is often associated with prestige or crisis events, and is considered to be a medium that can bring live multimedia information that is accurate and trusted. Negroponte (1995) suggests that television becomes a tollbooth that will integrate all systems into a general-purpose and less proprietary computer design. The development of global players, such as CNN and other networks, will enable users not only to watch the channels that they require from a global selection but also to subscribe to a wide range of new services worldwide. Already digital television sets supporting Internet functions have become available in hotels, where business travellers can use their screen to surf the WWW, check their eMail and connect to their company computers for entertainment and information retrieval purposes. The introduction of digital and interactive television at home will enable families not only to access a wide range of entertainment avenues but also to retrieve information for school homework or shop on-line 24 hours a day through interactive shopping malls.

Cellular phones will also change from being voice communicators to being mobile data providers, enabling consumers to have constant access to relevant data through the Internet. **Global System for Mobile Communications (GSM)** has been established as an open, non-proprietary system for global mobile telecommunications. One of its great strengths is the international roaming capability and its ability to evolve continuously. This gives consumers seamless and standardized, same-number contactability in more than 159 countries. GSM satellite roaming has extended service access to areas where terrestrial coverage is not available. Further ability to download information from the Internet is also becoming possible through the development of the technology. High-bandwidth services have become available through the evolution of second- (and second-and-a-half-) generation technologies. The development path to third and future generations of mobile networks and devices is clearly mapped out and brings with it the possibilities of sophisticated data and multimedia applications. The GSM standard will continue to evolve, with wireless, satellite and cordless systems offering greatly expanded services. These will include high-speed, multimedia data services, inbuilt support for parallel use of such services, seamless integration with the Internet and wireline networks.

The **Wireless Application Protocol (WAP)** was introduced by the mobile manufacturers as the de facto world and industry-wide standard for Internet services on mobile phones and other wireless devices and aimed to enhance interactivity between data providers and mobile phones. WAP was born in 1997 through a joint initiative called the WAP forum set up by Ericsson, Motorola, Nokia and phone.com. Using Wireless Markup Language, which is a development of XML, WAP enables standard Internet pages to be modified so that they can be accessible from mobile phones. That can include not only browsing through information but also using eMail and connecting to specific providers for content such as news, weather, traffic, banking, personal calendars and on-line transactions. 'Alerts' and user-specified information will enable consumers to follow news and events as they happen, and 'intelligent' electronic assistants will provide services that users require without having them initiating the process. For example, when the football team you support scores, a message is forwarded to your mobile phone. Similarly, if your mobile is at a range that will not be possible for you to catch your flight, an alternative seat can be booked on the next flight available (**www.wap.com/forum**; Curtis, 1999).

Despite the promising start and the overhyped marketing campaign, the WAP has failed to inspire consumers partly because of the long periods required for people to log in, making it both inconvenient and expensive. The text interface is also not very attractive for Internet users, while the entire system is not user-friendly. In addition the small number of useful applications currently available as well as the small screen make it impractical and difficult to maintain.

In Japan, however, the NTT DoCoMo's I-mode had a much better rate of success, as it is estimated that in March 2001 about 20 million people were using mobile Internet services. This can be attributed to a lower level of Internet usage in Japan (about 30 per cent in comparison to 60 per cent in the USA). Other reasons included:

- the I-mode had significantly more developed content than WAP providers;
- the I-mode offered variety in content to suit all users;
- Japan has a low level of personal computer ownership;
- the Japanese are early adopters of technology in comparison to Europeans;
- there is a lack of real privacy in Japanese houses;
- services are affordable as most of the telecom expense is covered through advertising.

Third-generation (3G) mobile technology services include the *Universal Mobile Telecommunications System (UMTS)*. There are two new technologies to bridge the gap between current capabilities and those arriving with UMTS: High-Speed Circuit Switched Data (HSCSD) and General Packet Radio Services (GPRS). While **third generation (3G)** technology is still being defined by the standards bodies, HSCSD and GPRS have been established with defined characteristics and projected availability. Third-generation mobile technologies are expected to be commercial some time in 2003. The world is moving gradually towards universal connectivity between digital devices. Eventually, of course, people will be able to watch a football match or to track flights on-line from their mobile devices. They will also be able to use their mobile phones for **electronic cash** transactions and micro-payments. Hence, mobile phones will become interactive mini-portable computers, personal assistants and entertainment devices to assist users constantly. **Bluetooth** provides a new kind of freedom and convenient connection without direct line-of-sight requirements. It allows usage of Bluetooth-empowered phones as a GSM modem connecting to a laptop within the range of 10 metres in order to download eMails, browse the Internet and send faxes. It also facilitates the synchronization of calendar and contact data between compatible PC office applications and the mobile devices. The introduction of video-mobile phones, pioneered by Kyocera in Japan, offers the ability to transmit both pictures and voice over mobile phones. This enables mobile videoconferencing and will support a much more dynamic interaction between people as well as between consumers and suppliers. Operated in parallel with the Internet presence of organizations, video-phones will allow remote face-to-face contact and will empower the human touch.

1.7 A new wave of technological evolution

Werthner and Klein (1999) have identified the most significant technological developments forcing a new wave of technological evolution, as demonstrated in Figure 1.8. The underlying trend of all developments is the integration of hardware, software and intelligent applications through networking and advanced user interfaces. Technological convergence will therefore lead ICT developments. Interestingly, most of the technological tools required already exist. The classification represented has no clear boundaries but only blurring boundaries to illustrate dependencies and relationships. However, all technologies need improvements in order to enhance their speed, **interoperability**, reliability and adaptation to the industry and consumer needs.

Figure 1.8 Lines of technological evolution

Network(ing)	Information management	Intelligent applications	User interface

ISO/OSI
SGML
Internet
World Wide Web
HyperText Markup Language
XML
Cryptography
GSM
WAP
ATM ◄►IPv6
System architectures
Client–server
Distributed and mobile computing
	Databases, relational,
	    object-oriented
	Multimedia
	Data modelling
	Data mining and warehousing
	Unified Modeling Language (UML)
	Programming languages
	Java
	CSCW (Computer Supported
	Cooperative Work)
	Authoring tools
	Participatory design
		Artificial intelligence
		Logics
		Optimization
		Simulation
		Statistics
		Knowledge discovery
		    and data mining
		Learning systems
		Agents
		Artificial life
			What You See Is
			    What You Get
			    (WYSIWYG)
			Multimedia
			Windowing
			User modelling
			Natural language
			    processing
			Metaphors
			Visualization
			Adaptive interfaces

Distributed architectures *Object orientation* *Agents – ontologies* *Adaptive interfaces*

Integration
Metadata
Mediated architectures
Facilitators
Wrappers – legacy systems
Added services – ePayment and eCommerce

Source: After Werthner and Klein (1999)

Fast and reliable **networks** are emerging to support media-rich applications and on-line video presentations required by both consumers and suppliers. Distributed and mobile communications as well as network architectures and protocols effectively support mobile computing and facilitate access to information from a wide range of **media** and geographical coverage. This will increasingly enable mobile phone users to access databases of information, purchase products and interact regardless of location. Development of client–server interfaces empowers end-users and reduces new users' training required and reluctance. Advanced **cryptography** improves on-line security through **encryption, authentication** and **digital signatures** and provides trusted and robust financial systems for electronic commerce. The development of electronic commerce, especially through the introduction of digital television and the mobile media, forces a re-engineering of all business models and propels new practices and distribution channels, such as specialized shopping malls for individual needs, **electronic** auctions and consumer-predetermined acceptable prices (as in priceline.com), etc. More importantly, eCommerce enhances the opportunity for interaction with consumers and, thus, the specialization of products and services. Eventually, networking will take advantage of the convergence of a wide range of equipment such as portable computers and palmtops, digital television as well as the Internet, intranets and extranets, on-line kiosks and entertainment systems, in order to network all users and suppliers globally.

The above developments both support and require more effective *information management*, as they enable both organizations and consumers to take advantage of the information they gain. The development of object-oriented, relational databases enables inter-linking between all information kept by organizations in order to generate synergies. Data modelling and knowledge management increasingly enhance the usage of operational data in decision-making processes and will enable better informed operational and strategic choices. Automation of procedures reduces manual working procedures by using **smart cards** and expert systems. Computer Supported Cooperative Work (CSCW) facilitates the development of organizational knowledge management and enables employees to share experiences and solutions to established problems. Hence, intelligent applications can incorporate knowledge from all sections of an organization into decision-making at the level required. Finally, authoring tools can also be used to facilitate information management end-user programming, to support the customization of software to user requirements.

Recent software evolution has been driven by the development of *intelligent applications* using artificial intelligence and complex algorithms to provide customized information and services. Office automation and full integration of all business processes enhance efficiency and effectiveness. In addition, the use of simulation and the processing of statistics improve the quality of information used for decision-making and enable organizations to adopt more proactive approaches to management and marketing problems. Optimization and simulation applications also enable organizations to develop alternative scenarios and to predict situations and potential outcomes based on previous experience. Knowledge discovery and **data mining** support management and marketing functions by sharing experiences throughout organizations and enabling proactive and relationship marketing. Personalized records and **cookies** can provide opportunities for interaction with consumers and identification of trends. Learning systems and agents increasingly accumulate and use knowledge productively to support employees and organizations.

Perhaps the most significant development during the last decade has been the development of user-friendly *interfaces*, which have enabled non-specialists to use computers without extensive training on each particular program or interface. The development of multimedia presentations and particular interfaces based on the 'What You See Is What You Get' (WYSIWYG) and Windows protocols have enabled most systems and applications to become accessible to the majority of people in organizations and consumers, saving time and enhancing efficiency. Adaptive interfaces and the visualization of computing functions simplify processes and allow users to take advantage of systems and applications. In addition, user-friendly interfaces enable partner organizations to share resources, empowering interaction and maximizing the outcome of value chains. Intelligent **geographical information systems** will increasingly relate information and functions to the regional and geographical situation of end-users; users on the road will be targeted according to the location of their mobile phone, while suppliers will be able to display local information on mobile phones to satisfy consumer needs. Obtaining information on the exact location of users will also be useful for tourists needing directions in an unfamiliar environment.

The most challenging task for the technological revolution experienced is the **integration** of all applications and systems to enable interoperability on different platforms and through different media. Werthner and Klein (1999) define interoperability as 'the provision of a well defined and end-to-end service, in a consistent and predictable way. This covers not only technical features, but also, for example in the case of electronic market environments, contractual features as well as a set of institutional rules'. Integration will enable end-users to access a broad knowledge base; suppliers will be able to appreciate the information requirements as well as product and service needs of their consumers and partners; information and services will be delivered by the most convenient method. The right information can be delivered at the right time to the right user at the right cost.

1.8 Conclusions

Technological developments have introduced a wide range of new tools for the strategic and operational management of organizations. Increasingly technological convergence integrates software, hardware and netware and supports interoperability and interconnectivity. In addition, the integration of the Internet, extranets and intranets enables organizations to interact dynamically with different actors and stakeholders. Mobile devices and interactive digital television also provide new electronic platforms, supporting access to data and processes on-line through different channels. These innovations require management to keep abreast of developments and be ready to adopt suitable technological solutions in order to maximize organizational competitiveness.

Chapter questions

1 What are the different elements of ICTs that are used in tourism?

2 Why is it difficult to define ICTs?

3 Explore the relationships between the Internet and extranet and intranets for an organization of your choice.

4 Which is more important for the tourism industry: software, hardware or netware?

5 Explain the relationships between information management and information systems with regard to a tourism organization of your choice.

6 Does technological development drive business strategies or vice versa?

7 What is technological convergence and why it is significant in the tourism industry context?

8 What do innovative organizations need to do with regard to technological developments?

Further reading

Beekman, G. (2001) *Computer Confluence: Exploring Tomorrow's Technology*, 4th edn, Prentice Hall, New Jersey.

Gupta, U. (2000) *Information Systems: Success in the 21st Century*, Prentice Hall, New Jersey.

Laudon, K. and Laudon, J. (2002) *Management Information Systems: Managing the Digital Firm*, 7th edn, Prentice Hall, New Jersey.

O'Brien, J. (1996) *Management Information Systems: Managing Information Technology in the Networked Enterprise*, Irwin, Chicago.

Robson, W. (1997) *Strategic Management and Information Systems: An Integrated Approach*, 2nd edn, Pitman, London.

Turban, E. and Aronson, J. (1998) *Decision Support Systems and Intelligent Systems*, 5th edn, Prentice Hall, New Jersey.

Turban, E., Lee, J., King, D. and Chung, H. (2002) *Electronic Commerce: A Managerial Perspective*, Prentice Hall, New Jersey.

Werthner, H. and Klein, S. (1999) *Information Technology and Tourism – A Challenging Relationship*, Springer, New York.

Websites

Technology manufacturers and suppliers

www.sun.com

www.ibm.com

www.nokia.com

www.ericsson.com

www.motorola.com

www.labs.bt.com

www.cisco.com

Technology news and developments

www.w3.org

www.xml.org

www.ebxml.org

www.news.zdnet.co.uk

www.mformobile.com

www.informit.com

Management and ICT issues

Electronic markets: **www.electronicmarkets.org**

Government initiatives: **www.ukonlineforbusiness.gov.uk**

Accenture on management: **www.accenture.com**

IBM: **www-3.ibm.com/e-business**

Ernest and Young International: **www.ey.com**

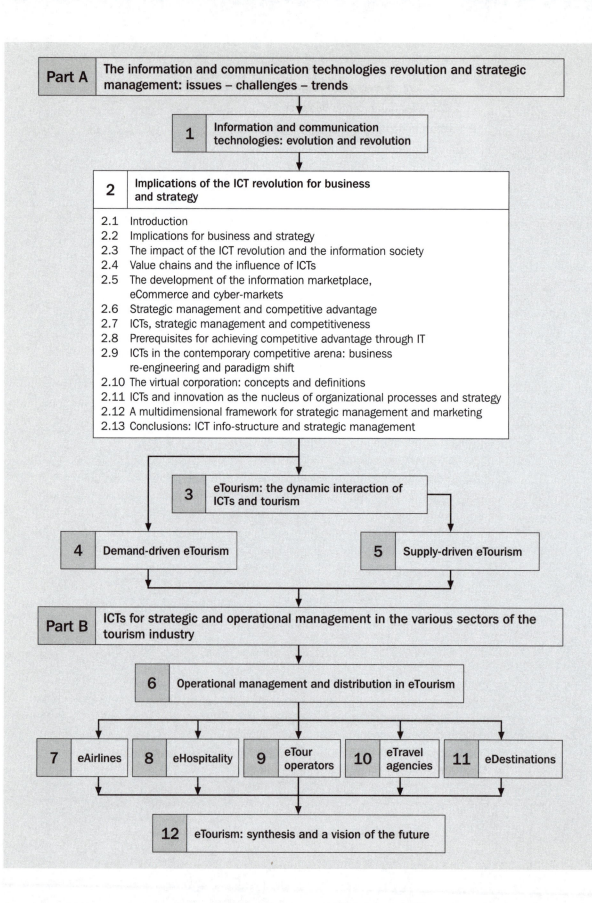

Part A — The information and communication technologies revolution and strategic management: issues – challenges – trends

1 Information and communication technologies: evolution and revolution

2 Implications of the ICT revolution for business and strategy

2.1 Introduction
2.2 Implications for business and strategy
2.3 The impact of the ICT revolution and the information society
2.4 Value chains and the influence of ICTs
2.5 The development of the information marketplace, eCommerce and cyber-markets
2.6 Strategic management and competitive advantage
2.7 ICTs, strategic management and competitiveness
2.8 Prerequisites for achieving competitive advantage through IT
2.9 ICTs in the contemporary competitive arena: business re-engineering and paradigm shift
2.10 The virtual corporation: concepts and definitions
2.11 ICTs and innovation as the nucleus of organizational processes and strategy
2.12 A multidimensional framework for strategic management and marketing
2.13 Conclusions: ICT info-structure and strategic management

3 eTourism: the dynamic interaction of ICTs and tourism

4 Demand-driven eTourism

5 Supply-driven eTourism

Part B — ICTs for strategic and operational management in the various sectors of the tourism industry

6 Operational management and distribution in eTourism

7 eAirlines

8 eHospitality

9 eTour operators

10 eTravel agencies

11 eDestinations

12 eTourism: synthesis and a vision of the future

2

Implications of the ICT revolution for business and strategy

Chapter objectives

The purpose of this chapter is to introduce how ICTs have revolutionized modern society and how they affect business strategy. The chapter also outlines the strategic management process and demonstrates how ICTs can contribute to the competitiveness of organizations. The chapter objectives can be summarized as:

- Demonstrate how ICTs revolutionize societies and businesses
- Understand the basic structure and tools for strategic analysis for organizations
- Introduce the issue of eCommerce and how it grows
- Demonstrate how organizations can achieve competitive advantage and strengthen their competitiveness
- Explore how ICTs can support organizations to enhance their strategic position

2.1 Introduction

The rapid progress of ICTs since the 1970s has illustrated that organizations have ever more powerful tools for enhancing their efficiency. More importantly, the proliferation of the Internet in the 1990s networked the global economy and changed the way organizations operate and compete locally and internationally. Hence, ICT developments have revolutionized not only the global economy but also enterprises around the world, regardless of their size, product and geographical coverage. Although the potential is there for all to explore, it is generally the wealthy countries and the larger organizations that have the expertise and resources to enable them to invest in and increase the benefits offered by the Internet. However, a number of innovative small organizations led by determined entrepreneurs have already demonstrated that with a minimal investment they can also compete on an equal footing with larger organizations. Less wealthy regions and nations are gradually using the Internet for educating their youth and for having access to learning resources available only in wealthy regions and for economically privileged societies; India Malaysia and are typical examples, with young scientists and ICT professionals working for a large number of global operators and therefore importing significant income to their home countries.

2.2 Implications for business and strategy

Even before the era of the World Wide Web, Tapscott and Caston (1993) illustrated that information technology propels a 'paradigm shift', which generates fundamental changes in the nature and application of technology in business and has far-reaching implications for organizations and societies. The proliferation of the World Wide Web introduced the 'age of networked intelligence', which brings both promise and peril. This new situation gives birth to a new economy, new politics and a new society, reinventing businesses, governments and individuals. The new economy is also a knowledge economy, based on human know-how and intellect, which adds value to all products and services. Intellect is critical for this, hence human resources emerge as one of the most critical assets for organizations. Competition intensifies and as information becomes digital and networked, enterprises need to protect their market share globally from both traditional and new competitors (Tapscott, 1996; Tapscott et al., 2000).

At the macroeconomic level, ICTs are increasingly regarded as instrumental in regional development and long-term prosperity. All enterprises become global, as they can be present in the international marketplace at an affordable cost. Frontier controls and limitations are gradually eased through international trade agreements enabling easier global trade. As a result the location of buyers and sellers becomes less important for transactions. The European Commission illustrates that as a result of the ICT development 'throughout the world, production systems, methods of organising work and consumption patterns are undergoing changes which will have long-term effects comparable with the first industrial revolution'. The report suggests that 'a new information society is emerging, in which management, quality and speed of information are key factors for competitiveness: as an input to the industries, as a whole and as a service provided to ultimate consumers, information and communication technologies influence the economy at all stages'. Thus, 'the competitiveness of the European economy will to a great extent depend both on the conditions of utilisation and on the development and application of these technologies' (EC, 1993). The new information society and the knowledge-based economy therefore transform regional politics, economics and societies, illustrating the need to enhance the global competitiveness of both enterprises and regions.

Similarly, at the microeconomic level, recent ICT developments have enormous implications for the operation, structure and **corporate strategy** of organizations. Porter (1989) illustrates that ultimately technology can totally transform the way an entire business operates, as ICTs help to improve the efficiency, productivity and competitiveness of both inter-organizational and intra-organizational systems. The real benefit of information technology lies in the linking and reconfiguring of businesses and organizational functions, reducing both the communication and operational costs of most enterprises while enabling them to interconnect with all their stakeholders (e.g. suppliers, distributors, customers, facilitators) and operate internationally. ICTs play a profound role in the competitiveness of organizations in the global economy, as 'globalization and technology are mutually reinforcing drivers of change' (Bradley et al., 1993). Information provides power where it is controlled, manipulated or where it provides the ability to absorb critical uncertainties. Metakides (1994) also asserts that the global information revolution obliges enterprises to 'act local and think global', while dramatically transforming both production and consumption patterns. ICTs also drive a shift from product-oriented organizations to a flexible and responsive marketplace, where success depends on sensing and responding to rapidly changing customer needs. Hence, ICTs increasingly become one of the most important strategic considerations at the corporate level, as successful ICT strategies based on innovative and dynamic management can provide organizations with competitive advantage (Piercy, 1983; Haeckel and Nolan, 1993). Even small organizations are increasingly able to capitalize on ICT opportunities, as demonstrated in Case Study 2.1.

Case Study 2.1

The Corisande Hotel in Cornwall and the www.cornwall-calling.co.uk website

The Corisande Manor Hotel in Cornwall is an example of best practice in ICT usage. Not only does it receive 90 per cent of its bookings through the Internet, but it has also developed a new part of the business in which it assists other companies to develop their Internet presence for a fee. David and Chris Grant bought the Corisande Manor Hotel in 1996. They were trying to reach their customers but felt that advertising in the national

▶

Case Study 2.1 *continued*

newspapers was both expensive and unproductive. David taught himself how to use the Internet and gradually learned how to develop a web page promoting his property. Instead of David creating the usual page about his own hotel, he registered the domain name **www.cornwall-calling.co.uk** and provided information on Cornwall and its attractions. On each page was an invitation to stay in his property by means of a link to his hotel (**www.corisande.co.uk**). He managed to gain a respectable return on his investment, which cost the equivalent of one regular advertisement in a Sunday newspaper.

Following this success David Grant developed the Soft-Options Internet company (**www.soft-options.co.uk**), which registered Internet domains for all the UK regions (such as **www.greatbritain.co.uk, www.capital-calling.co.uk, www.wales-calling.co.uk**). He offers a package solution for small properties whereby the design and management of their web presence is charged at £950 for the first year and less during subsequent years. He suggests that a minimum of 100–200 hits per day is needed to make the Internet a valuable generator of bookings. Based on his experience Grant suggests that around 1 per cent of browsers normally eMail hotels for information and 50 per cent of those book a room depending on the speed in replying to eMails and the quality of the site and the hotel. The cost for the development was always kept to a minimum with a PC that cost about £1200 and Front Page, which costs about £100. David also co-authored the book *Guide to the Internet: Get Your Business Online*, published by Butterworth-Heinemann.

For more information see **www.corisande.com**

Questions

- What are the unique characteristics of the Corisande Hotel's web page?

- How can small and medium tourism enterprises take advantage of the Internet?

- Explore the cost of putting a small hotel on-line and identify the key issues associated with this.

- Examine several commercial but non-tourism websites (such as amazon.com, www.multimap.com, tesco.com, virgin.com) and identify:
  - the main features and unique added-value services offered on each page;
  - whether they are succesful, and why;
  - how they implement customer relationship management;
  - the transferrable lessons that can be learned for tourism.

- Explore the UK government services on-line (**www.ukonline.gov.uk**) and the eEurope initiatives (http://europa.eu.int) and:
  - discuss how the government initiatives at the national and European levels are moving more people and enterprises on-line;
  - discuss what the impact will be on their competitiveness;
  - explore which business functions can be influenced as a result.

- Identify several tourism organizations and explore how their on-line strategies are helping them improve their positions in the growth–share matrix.

2.3 The impact of the ICT revolution and the information society

The Internet established an innovative and user-friendly **platform** for efficient, live and timely exchange of ideas and products. The pace of development demonstrates that the Internet restructures the lives of people and social interactions worldwide. Dertouzos (1997) suggests that ICTs alter how we work and play and will revise deeper aspects of human life and humanity, such as how we receive healthcare, how children learn, how the elderly remain connected to society, how governments conduct their affairs, how ethnic groups preserve their heritage, whose voices are heard, even how nations are formed. On the one hand, technology enables the personalization of information, products and services to individual needs and desires. People will have the tools to design the information they require and ask service providers and **intelligent agents** to filter all external messages according to their needs, circumstances and even moods (Negroponte, 1995). On the other hand, ICTs also enable people to socialize and interact not only with their local community but also with a virtual community, which may be scattered around the earth.

On-line communities emerge to assist people to meet, network and establish communication channels. This often happens at a geographical level or at a special-interest level. People meet, talk to, work with and, in the extreme, even fall in love with and marry individuals that they have never met in person. At the local level, websites such as UpMyStreet (**www.upmystreet.com**) provide local information. In some areas they also aim to introduce neighbours and establish social relationships and activities, such as organizing street parties and car boot sales. This can enable people in urban centres who do not have the opportunity to meet their neighbours to develop virtual communities and reverse the paradox of human isolation in overcrowded areas (O'Brien, 2000).

Virtual communities may also be established between people with common interests. Thousands of bulletin boards, discussion groups and chat pages assist people to communicate all over the world. For example, TRINET, a discussion group formed by Professors Jafari and Sheldon, was established in 1995 and has connected more than 800 tourism academics and researchers around the globe, leading to research cooperation, publications and discussion of critical issues. Others use websites, such as lonelyplanet.com, to exchange information, to upgrade and update the contents of the page, and to enhance the global knowledge base by sharing advice based on personal experience and discoveries.

Digital living increasingly places less and less emphasis upon people being in a specific place at a specific time, and people increasingly operate from a distance. The Internet therefore introduces new practices, such as home shopping, tele-entertainment, tele-working, tele-learning, tele-medical support and tele-banking. This will be particularly critical for remote, insular and peripheral communities, which hitherto have been deprived of important services in their vicinity. Parents with young kids who were pressurized to move to central places to take advantage of education and medical facilities may be able to use tele-services and **distance learning** in order to stay in their societies. Increasingly tele-medicine enables specialized consultants to direct local doctors in their diagnosis and treatment while surgical procedures can take advantage of ICT tools: doctors located in metropolitan regions can use robots to undertake operations that require precision and accuracy. The results are already dramatic with better and faster recovery rates. The implications of ICT advancements in medicine will be the ability of specialized personnel to carry out medical procedures from a distance, taking expertise to patients and regions that have never had the opportunity to be treated by experts in their field (Dertouzos, 1997).

Equally the Internet offers opportunities for tele-working and several communities in some countries emerge to provide services from a distance. For example, computer programmers and data importers in India can provide competitive services for international companies and at the same time transform their region by exploring significant services and participating in the global wealth creation. Eventually people in developing countries and continents will be able to share knowledge and educate their workforce through the Internet, in the process possibly reducing the world's wealth gap. The electronic/interactive/intelligent/virtual home and enterprise gradually emerge, to facilitate the entire range of communications with the external world and to support all functions of everyday personal and professional life through interactive computer networks.

Paradoxically, ICT-supported media get bigger and smaller at the same time. International broadcasters and content providers such as CNN, BBC, Yahoo and AOL reach larger audiences globally. At the same time, however, they can be tailormade to individual needs and demands and include localized content. This is often called 'glocalization' in the ICT jargon. In addition, economies of scope allow organizations to provide specialized information and services to niche markets worldwide, catering for specific market segments. Eventually, products will be designed for individuals, reflecting their personal taste and ability to pay (Negroponte, 1995). The Internet also influences global political life, as it introduces a democratic, transparent, uncontrollable and difficult-to-dominate way of communication, where everyone is more or less able to broadcast their views, regardless of hierarchical rankings and political power. International events and protests are broadcast live on the Internet, providing the opportunity for people to share their political views with the entire world.

Abuse of resources or humans by political regimes, powerful multinational corporations or even local authorities is easily exposed by using the network and forces the international community to take immediate action. Countless examples can be offered. Shell has been accused for its environmental policies and practices in Africa, Macdonald's for the quality of its food and employment conditions, and Nike for exploiting young children in its manufacturing bases in Asia. Recent political conflicts and incidents have provided the opportunity for both sides in the argument to air their views without having to go through the control and political agenda of traditional media. Examples include the protests against capitalism and imperialism during the World Trade Organization Conference in Seattle in December 1999; the arrest of the Kurdish leader Abdullan Ocalan by Turkish security forces; the East Timor vote process and the troubles in Indonesia; the Russian attacks on Chechnya, and so on (Evans, 2000).

This has led several people to predict that the Internet 'has the capacity to change everything – the way we work, the way we learn and play and even maybe the way we sleep or have sex' (Symonds, 1999).

The late Director of the MIT Laboratory for Computer Science, Michael Dertouzos, drew the comparison between the Internet and an Athens flea market. He explained that stretching the Internet to a global market and society can be similar to traditional markets, which sell everything to everyone and at the same time are frequented by people who are friendly and talkative and can tackle every conceivable topic between deals. The market provides the opportunity for forming a community that can debate all issues and market all commodities. This is similar to the ancient *agora* where Athenians would meet, discuss, trade and philosophize. The difference of course is that location becomes less important and the emerging marketplace is global. Therefore, the information marketplace offers a much broader geographical scope in the 21st century (Dertouzos, 1997).

However, the Internet can also introduce a wide range of *social, economic and political threats* as it enables organizations and individuals with antisocial, racist, unethical and fraudulent motives to share views and to organize their actions. Terrorism, narcotics, racism, paedophilia, political propaganda and fraud are all facilitated by the Internet, as people feel to a certain degree free to broadcast their views and to recruit other members to fulfil their agenda. Instructions on how to construct bombs and other lethal weapons, as well as other illegal and unethical behaviour, are increasingly found on the Internet and spread on a global scale. In return, international policing and security forces are obliged to develop skills and expertise to battle globalized crime. On balance, though, through transparency and interactivity the Internet enables the world to become better informed. Even in countries and regions where human rights are not respected, people can access and, more importantly, generate and share information with the entire world. As a result, democracy spreads gradually, empowering individuals to decide for themselves.

2.4 Value chains and the influence of ICTs

Every organization benefits from a number of resources and inputs; these undergo processing and are transformed into customer offerings. One of the most commonly used tools for examining the available resources of organizations is the value-chain analysis. A value chain represents an organization as a chain of activities that add value to its products and services. This is within a broader **supply chain** that includes all suppliers and distributors and requires **supply chain management**. As a consequence the organization generates a margin of value (profit margin) as a benefit. Figure 2.1 represents the value-chain concept diagrammatically. Although the value-chain model is mainly associated with manufacturing products, service and in particular tourism and hospitality organizations can draw useful conclusions provided that they appreciate the differences in their processes. Operations and production in a restaurant, for example, may start only once the customer has arrived and, therefore, the chain needs to be adjusted within the tourism and hospitality context.

Figure 2.1 Value-chain analysis

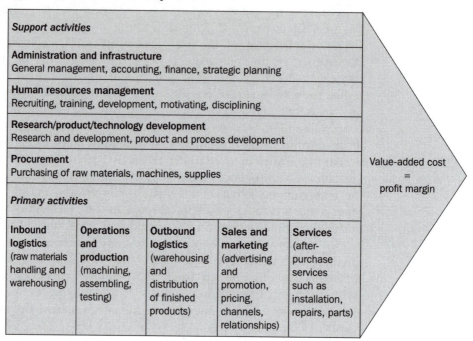

Source: Adapted from Porter (1985a); Robson (1997); Turban et al. (2002)

The resources are divided into support and primary activities. In tourism, most of the primary activities are called 'front of house' as they are visible to the consumer, while most of the support activities are called 'back of house' as consumers do not meet or interact with their employees. Primary activities examine the process of transformation of raw material or information to products and offerings and then their delivery to customers and partners through the sales and marketing as well as the service functions (Porter, 1985b; Robson, 1997; Turban et al., 2002).

For a hotel, for example, a room is the product and goes through this circle each time it is rented. Raw materials include clean linen and toiletries as well as all other articles arriving from suppliers. The production process may include cleaning and preparing a room as well as welcoming guests, all services offered to the customer upon arrival, and facilitating their stay. Outbound logistics will involve housekeeping, announcing to the front office that a room is ready to be rented, as well as all preparations for the room to be put on the market. Sales and marketing will include all the efforts undertaken to sell the room and services. The difference between tourism services and other products is that the consumer actually goes to consume the product at the place of production and, therefore, all logistics and distribution mechanisms are reversed.

Support activities facilitate the smooth functioning of primary activities and have an indirect relationship with the process of adding value to the product. They include all the administration and infrastructure required to run any business, such as accounting and finance. The human resources management is in charge of making available the right human resources for the operation of the organization. Product development aims at improving the existing products and redesigning them in a way that maintains their attractiveness and appeal to new target markets; and procurement deals with ensuring that all materials required for the organization are purchased at appropriate prices. Naturally the higher the difference between the value added to the product and the cost to the organization, the higher the profit margin and the benefit for the organization.

The value chain of each organization is incorporated within a greater value system. This includes the value chains of its suppliers, distributors and retailers. Ultimately, the value chain of all actors involved in the chain should be coordinated for the system to work efficiently and to deliver seamless products. If any of the partners fails to deliver appropriate value and products, the entire chain can break and the system can even collapse. If the water supplier of a hotel fails to deliver water, for example, or if the **tour operator** goes into liquidation, the entire system will probably collapse. Therefore, it is critical that value chains are carefully constructed, balanced, managed and robust.

Figure 2.2 illustrates that each organization, an airline in this example, operates its value system in parallel with those of its competitors. Every other organization in the system will also have a value chain that it supports. They may share some

Figure 2.2 Value chains within the entire industry value system

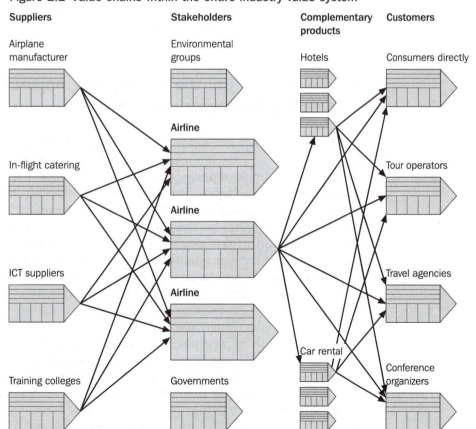

common suppliers or distributors and they may decide to outsource some of the functions together or separately.

Similarly, the broader value system for one industry also includes the value chains of competitors. Often their value chains run in parallel, but it is not unusual for tourism organizations to share some of the value-chain partners. For example, competing hotels may purchase materials from the same supplier and may also use the same tour operators or travel agencies to distribute their products. This is quite common in services, where the lack of physical products encourages flexibility in collaborations. It will be increasingly common as consumers gradually use many access platforms and channels to research and purchase products. Destination portals, for example, distribute most of the local tourism products, while eProcurement sites supply a large number of hotels operating in the same area.

In an even broader sense, each organization operates within an economic system, which can be represented as a series of value chains running in parallel and supporting each economic sector. Understanding the value chains of other sectors may be beneficial for organizations. They can appreciate factors and processes that operate better in other industries, as well as being able to identify opportunities for cross-promotion and selling opportunities. Tourism activities are supported by almost the entire range of industries at the destination level, from energy to agriculture and manufacturing. Thus, the ability of the hotel in our example to develop and deliver its products will depend to a great extent on other sectors of the economy and their value chains.

2.5 The development of the information marketplace, eCommerce and cyber-markets

The impact of the ICT revolution is more evident in the commercial world. The rapid development of the Internet has intensified on-line trading and globalized the market for all types of products and services, gradually transforming the marketplace into a 'virtual' or 'electronic' marketspace – a 'cyber-market' or **electronic market** (Bakos, 1991; Adamson and Toole, 1995). Dertouzos (1997) defines the information marketplace as 'the collection of people, computers, communications, software and services that will be engaged in the intra-organizational and inter-personal informational transaction of the future. These transactions will involve the processing and communication of information under the same economic motives that drive today's traditional marketplace for material goods and services'. The electronic-business revolution gathers momentum every day and transforms communication, collaboration and commerce. eBusiness replaces some of the off-line business transactions, but more importantly it enhances the total transaction volume as both organizations and consumers take advantage of the new tools to purchase products and services that many were unable to purchase before. Although the Internet is more suitable for trading services, which do not require the transportation of products, it is increasingly evident that no organization can escape its impacts. For example, new and used cars are one of the fastest expanding commodities trading on-line today, especially since the launch of a promotional website by Vauxhall (**www.vauxhall.co.uk**), offering special Internet discounts, and the advertising campaign that backed this initiative. In the UK, the price of cars has dropped significantly following the development of the Consumer Association car trading site, which enabled the public to compare prices with those in continental Europe and to import their vehicles.

As a result of the developing information marketplace and electronic commerce, new opportunities and challenges emerge. Although it is not clear who will be the final winners and losers of this process, it is quite apparent that the Internet bridges the gap between consumers and suppliers and provides opportunities for **disintermediation** and **re-intermediation**. To the degree that producers develop their presence in the global marketplace and offer their products in favourable terms in comparison with intermediaries, they will be able to attract consumers and sell directly, saving commissions and distribution costs. On the other hand, traditional retailers and intermediaries (e.g. Tesco supermarkets) as well as electronically empowered newcomers (e.g. Amazon.com) fight back to increase their global market share. They develop their presence on the electronic marketplace by adding value to the needs of the customer, providing a trusted one-stop shop, attracting better deals from producers due to the volume of their business and by using information collected for marketing research and **promotion**. Only organizations that have a clear and valuable business proposition and offer value on top of an easy and accessible service using all possible platforms will be able to survive and grow in the future. Expedia.com, marriott.com and easyJet.com are some of the more shining examples of using the Internet strategically to increase their market share and to interact profitably with their clients. These companies clearly offer value to the customer, have efficient web pages and achieve eFulfilment, i.e. deliver what they set to do in a consistent and hassle-free manner.

Electronic commerce (eCommerce) can be defined as the secure trading of information, products and services via computer networks and the exchange of value on-line, as well as the support for any kind of business transactions over a digital infrastructure (Kalakota and Whinston, 1996; Turban et al., 2002). eCommerce refers to electronic trading, both from **business-to-consumers (B2C)** and, perhaps more importantly, **business-to-business (B2B)**. Interactions with government organizations (**business-to-government – B2G**) can also be included. Dertouzos (1997) distinguishes 'indirect eCommerce', which is the support information exchanged in supporting transactions (e.g. advertising, contracting, settling), and 'direct eCommerce', where people purchase information products (such as software, books and music) on-line. In addition, eCommerce can be divided into two main categories. B2C transactions incorporate the trading and delivery of commodities and services to consumers as well as the entire support information and mechanisms required for these transactions. This category also includes personal services, such as home banking, stock trading and investment advice. Although these transactions have a higher profit margin, they tend to be time consuming, require a great amount of support and may generate a relatively low level of turnover. In contrast, B2B transactions include trading between producers and intermediaries and also transactions between producers towards the final manufacturing of a product. In this case, the Internet is used to add value and to support the functions at each stage of the value chain before the final product or service reaches the consumer. Although eCommerce transactions have a lower profit margin, it is normally the volume of trading and the relatively low level of information and support required that make them profitable and desirable for organizations. The latter type of transaction is in fact the fastest growing section of the Internet and generates a considerable amount of trade (Turban et al., 2002).

The Internet provides the network backbone or info-structure over which businesses can create secure trading consortia, allowing flexibility within the **supply chain** and significant cost reductions (Sun, 1998). Business-to-business transactions across the Internet increased tenfold between 1996 and 1997 and grow faster across Europe than do consumer sales. The sheer growth of eCommerce and consumer acceptance of it means that companies that do not embrace this new way of doing things will be left out in the cold. Consumers who cannot find their favourite company on the Internet will simply go somewhere else (Barsoum, 1999).

Table 2.1 illustrates the benefits available to organizations by adopting an enterprise-wide Internet and eCommerce strategy. These benefits can be classified as growth, protection, differentiation, management of change and developing trust. It is critical to integrate on-line tools and strategies with the off-line world, however, and particularly to re-engineer all processes and practices in order to maximize benefits.

The most suitable approach for each organization will vary in accordance with products, industries and business strategies. However, technological innovations need to be guided by long-term business strategies and marketing plans that integ-

Table 2.1 Benefits from enterprise-wide Internet and eCommerce strategy

Grow	■ Customer base and market share ■ Share of customer's disposable income ■ Global presence all day every day ■ Efficiency in business processes ■ Profit by increasing turnover and reducing cost
Protect	■ Customer base and market share ■ Brand name and property ■ Markets, investments and ultimately business
Differentiate	■ Specialize and 1-2-1 marketing ■ Improve customer service/information/knowledge ■ Time to market ■ Price/value proposition
Manage and create change	■ Enhance your environment ■ Organizational structure and culture ■ Business process to incorporate customers and partners ■ Enhance competitiveness
Trust	■ Leverage the trust and values of your brand ■ Implement a secure and reliable system ■ Develop trust in all your eCommerce applications

Source: Based on Sun (1998)

rate both off- and on-line strategies. eCommerce is becoming more widespread with the Internet proliferation and the **convergence** of media, as new distribution mechanisms are created that enable consumers to purchase products electronically via a wider range of devices. Major advantages such as lower transaction costs, convenience, ubiquity and premium pricing emerge rapidly and transform the nature of all businesses. Businesses therefore have to rethink their new products, their entire internal procedures and structures and their relationships with consumers. Often organizations evolve gradually to take into consideration the influences of the external environment (Whiteley, 2000; Perry and Schneider, 2001); however, a large number of tourism and hospitality businesses may need to undertake a more fundamental review of what they do and how. **Business process re-engineering (BPR)** may be needed to redesign the entire range of processes, thereby possibly transforming the nature of a business. For example, a resort hotel in the Mediterranean may have depended entirely on a few tour operators to distribute its products. As a result of the concentration of the tour-operating business in Europe, they would normally offer contracts that maintain prices at a very low level in exchange for a high occupancy level during the shoulder months. Perhaps developing and promoting a web page as well as creating local events and attractions may assist a property to achieve a better yield and to attract a more loyal clientèle. Identifying the elements of value offered to customers by distributors can support the hotel in improving its offerings and attracting direct customers, increasing its turnover and customer loyalty and at the same time reducing its dependency.

It is evident that there are profound implications for the distribution of products and services as a result of revolutionary methods of interaction between producers and consumers. Information, speed and interactivity become crucial for all enterprises worldwide and their competitiveness will be assessed according to their ability to outperform both traditional competitors and newcomers. Because the Internet enables business to deliver real-time information to the point of customer contact without any regard for geographical boundaries, this frequently reduces the buying cycle and improves the time to market of new products and services. As these developments are extremely dynamic, strategic planners wanting to benefit from new opportunities need to follow constantly the major trends in the new environment (Turban et al., 2002; Porter, 1985b; Rayport and Sviokla, 1994).

However, employing the *right technology at the right time* is a particularly difficult task. Technology and its applications and capabilities move much faster than the planning systems of corporations. Thus, making rational investment decisions and selecting systems that will enable organizations to achieve their objectives, rather than spending money on technologies that will become obsolete in a short period of time, becomes really difficult. On the one hand, organizations can invest heavily in technologies and accept the associated risk; on the other they can wait until the marketplace and technologies are settled, by which time they may have lost their positioning and market share in the new marketplace. This book suggests that only innovators and organizations that are in the forefront of technological solutions will be able to gain competitive advantage in the future. However, this does not mean that organizations should invest heavily in all new technological developments that appear; it means that they need to develop a close understanding and association with their target markets and use appropriate and affordable technological solutions to serve their requirements.

Increasingly eCommerce and the marketplace will be dominated by the interaction of business, consumers and governments. A number of tourism examples are offered in Table 2.2. Not only will B2B and B2C transactions take place but the entire range of combinations between these three players, maximizing their interactivity, efficiency and effectiveness. The interaction between governments and business will lead to a better understanding of each other's needs while enhancing their operations. Perhaps consumers are the main winners in the process, as not only will they be able to receive promotional messages of an individualized nature but they will also be empowered to interact with organizations, offer feedback and make complaints more powerfully than ever before. The introduction of complaint websites (e.g. untied.com for dissatisfied United Airlines passengers) will provide customers with a powerful voice and will force both businesses and governments to pay more attention to customer complaints and issues.

Table 2.2 Interaction in the electronic marketplace, with examples from tourism

eBusiness	Business	Consumer	Government
Business	**B2B** Extranets between hoteliers and tour operators	**B2C** eCommerce applications where consumers purchase air tickets	**B2G** Business interacting with government departments, e.g. hotel developer requires planning permission
Consumer	**C2B** Consumers registering their preferences on airline or hotel loyalty/ executive clubs	**C2C** Consumers informing other consumers over good or bad practice (e.g. **www.untied.com**)	**C2G** Consumers applying for visas, requesting maps and local destination information
Government	**G2B** Government informing hotels about food safety legislation or taxation	**G2C** Government informing consumers on regulations, visa or vaccination requirements	**G2G** Governments interacting in tourism policy matters or asking technical assistance through organizations such as the World Tourism Organization

2.6 Strategic management and competitive advantage

The fusion of information technology and telecommunications creates new industries, restructuring existing industries and radically changing the way organizations compete (Bradley et al., 1993). Increasingly, unless organizations appear on the Internet and provide a comprehensive mechanism for interacting, they will not exist on the decision set of consumers and buyers. This will intensify by the year 2010, when a much greater proportion of the world population will use the Internet regularly and today's schoolkids who have been trained on ICTs and the Internet as part of their basic skills will be entering their working life. To them, using computers and the entire range of new technologies will be as natural as using the telephone is for most of the current working population. Not only will the customer base increase but also the business model for several industries will be redesigned as global competition and the rapid development of Internet-based brands, such as priceline.com, lastminute.com and amazon.com, reinvent and reshape the value chain, developing their market share rapidly and dominating several markets.

Porter suggests that ICTs reshape not only products but, more importantly, the nature of the competition. Entire industries are affected if ICTs have a significant role in determining relative cost position or differentiation. To gain competitive advantage over its rivals, an organization must either perform the activities involved in adding value to a product or service at a lower cost or perform them in a way that leads to **differentiation** and premium pricing (more value). To the degree that a company operates within a system of competition and dynamic developments, gaining and sustaining competitive advantage depends on understanding not only a firm's value chain but also how the firm fits in the overall value system (Porter, 1985b, 1989, 2001; Porter and Millar, 1985). As ICTs change the entire economic system dramatically, organizations need to constantly update their business models and enhance their competitiveness through new technological tools.

2.6.1 Defining strategy and strategic management

Defining **strategy** accurately is challenging. Different authors provide alternative explanations and use the term differently. Unfortunately this book cannot explore in detail all issues involved in strategic management. Readers are therefore urged to explore several strategic management books (Porter, 1980, 1985a; Johnson and Scholes, 1999; Kotler, 1998; Day, 1986; Mintzberg, Quinn and Ghoshal, 1998).

Strategy is often defined as the 'top management's plans to attain outcomes consistent with the organization's mission and goals' (Porter, 1980). Mintzberg, Ahlstrand and Lamplel (1998) explain that strategy can be a 'plan, a pattern, a position, a perspective or even a ploy!' Mintzberg, Quinn and Ghoshal (1998) define strategy as a 'pattern or plan that integrates an organization's major goals, policies and action sequences into a cohesive whole. A well-formulated strategy helps to marshal and allocate an organization's resources into a unique and viable posture, based on its relative internal competencies and shortcomings, anticipated changes in the environment and contingent moves by intelligent opponents'. Emphasizing the long-term perspective, Johnson and Scholes (1999) propose that strategy is 'the direction and scope of an organization over the long term which achieves advantage for the organization through its configuration of resources within a changing environment, to meet the needs of markets and to fulfil stakeholder expectations'. They also define corporate strategy as the overall 'purpose and scope of organization to meet the expectations of owners or major stakeholders and add value to the different parts of the enterprise'. Lynch (1997) describes corporate strategy as an organization's 'sense of purpose'.

Strategic planning and management involves the entire range of strategic issues of an organization. Undertaken by top management, it is about 'seeking and understanding the strategic position of the organizations, strategic choice, which is to do with the formulation of possible courses of action, their evaluation and the choice between them and strategy implementation, which is concerned with both planning how the choice of strategy can be put into effect and managing the changes required' (Johnson and Scholes, 1999). In an attempt to synthesize these issues, Hax and Majluf (1991) explain that 'strategy can be seen as a multi-dimensional concept that embraces all of the critical activities of the firm, providing it with a sense of unity, direction and purpose as well as facilitating the necessary changes induced by its environment'. They propose that there are six critical dimensions in the strategy concept, and thus, a strategy can be regarded as:

- a coherent, unifying and integrative pattern of decisions;
- a means of establishing the organizational purpose in terms of its long-term objectives, action programmes and resource allocation priorities;
- a definition of the competitive domain of the firm;
- a response to external opportunities and threats and internal strengths and weaknesses in order to achieve competitive advantage;
- a channel to differentiate managerial tasks at the corporate, business and functional levels;
- a definition of the economic and non-economic contribution the firm intends to make to its stakeholders.

For the purpose of this book, we can therefore synthesize all these definitions and address strategy as the dynamic decision-making process, at the highest level of an organization, that takes into consideration available resources and mechanisms, desired outcomes, all elements of the external environment and competition, and stakeholders' needs, wants and interests, before designing plans and mechanisms for outperforming their competitors and optimizing their benefits in the long term. The time horizon for 'long term' is variable according to the industry, location and cultural setting of each enterprise. In the technology industries, for example, the long term is less than three years and as a result of the ICT revolution, the time-frame of all other industries has gradually been reduced.

2.6.2 Strategic management processes and tools

Identifying the stages of strategic management is critical for appreciating how ICTs can contribute to the competitiveness of organizations. Only a brief summary can be offered in this book, but several books deal with strategic management (Hax and Majluf, 1991; Finlay, 2000; Lynch, 1997; Johnson and Scholes, 1999; Mintzberg, Quinn and Ghoshal, 1998; David, 1997) and should be revised. Figure 2.3 illustrates the main steps in the strategic process and the following paragraphs briefly outline the process.

Where are we now?

A **competitive analysis** for organizations often commences with the diagnostic question 'Where are we now?'. This implies that the organization is keen to evaluate the existing situation before developing plans for improving its performance and prospects. This process includes the collection of **competitive intelligence**. At the corporate level, organizations need to examine the whole range of areas in

Figure 2.3 Strategic management processes and tools

Stage	Technique	Activities
Where are we now?	Situation analysis	Strategic business units, performance and trends, returns on equity
	Strategic business units analysis	Assessing products, markets, geographical scope, unique competence
	Future analysis: forecasting and scenarios	Future trends and estimates Potential opportunities and challenges
	Demand and supply	Demand-and-supply analysis for all products and services traded by company
	External (PEST)	External factors affecting the position of the organization and the attractiveness of the organization
	Internal analysis	Resources, processes, mechanisms auditing
	Competition analysis and industry	Existing and potential competitors Suppliers and buyers Porter's industry competitors analysis
	Stakeholders mapping	Stakeholders, interests, needs and wants
	Competitive SWOT analysis	Internal performance and potential against external opportunities and threats
Where do we want to go?	Mission statement	Unique competencies and business scope/vision
	Strategic options	Alternative strategic opportunities Definition of strategic business units
	Strategic choice	Specific action programmes to maximize long-term benefits
	Portfolio management and SBUs review	Allocation of resources to maximize outcome Manage portfolio of markets and products to ensure long-term growth
How do we get there?	Strategic direction	Provide the road map for organization
	Portfolio analysis and adjustment	Strategic action for each portfolio Assess competitive strength versus market attractiveness
	Implementation	Departmentalization, human resources management, procurement management Marketing mix
	Strategic alliances	Networks, opportunistic alliances, subcontracting, licences and franchises; consortia, joint ventures, acquisitions and mergers
	Tactical planning	Measurable strategic objectives and accountable departments
	Budgeting	Draw detailed budgets for each plan, function and outcome
How do we know we got there?	Control and feedback	Definition of performance indicators and measurements Assessment against tasks and providing feedback to the strategic process
	Setting of indicators, warnings	Identification of indicators' follow-up mechanisms
	Incorporate feedback and reaction mechanisms	Tactics to follow developments and to assess developments on the external environment, assessment of competitor moves and reaction

Source: Based on Hax and Majluf (1991); Finlay (2000); Lynch (1997); Johnson and Scholes (1999)

which they operate through autonomous **strategic business units (SBUs)**. An SBU analysis offers the opportunity to revise these areas; market trends and developments in the external environment will indicate whether the organization needs to restructure its SBUs or whether it should liquidate or develop new ones. The SBU analysis can focus on particular industries and activities and quantify organizational performance against competitors.

The positioning of an enterprise can be assessed via a **PEST (political/legal/ economic/social/technological) analysis**. This process includes a thorough business audit as well as an **industry and competitive analysis**. It assesses the position of the enterprise against elements of its external and internal environment, as well as its **market share** and product and market portfolio. A wide range of management tools are available for this purpose including **portfolio matrix analysis**, **strategic business-planning grid** and identification of company positioning; Figures 2.4 to 2.7 illustrate these tools and suggest strategic actions based on the evaluation outcome (Hax and Majluf, 1991).

Figure 2.4 Portfolio analysis and generic strategies

		Market and industry attractiveness		
		High	*Medium*	*Low*
Business strength and competitive position	*High*	**Protect position** Concentrate effort Grow Seek dominance Maximize investment	**Build selectively** Identify growth segments Invest in most attractive segments Invest strongly Maintain position elsewhere	**Protect and refocus** Maintain overall position Specialize and defend strengths Concentrate on attractive segments Seek cash flow Invest at maintenance level
	Medium	**Invest to build** Evaluate potential for leadership Challenge the leadership Identify weaknesses Reinforce vulnerable areas Build strengths	**Selectivity/manage for earnings** Protect existing position Intensify growth segments Specialize Invest selectively in profitable but low-risk segments	**Limited expansion or harvest** Prune lines Protect profitable position Specialize segments Position to divest
	Low	**Build selectively** Specialize around limited strengths Seek ways to overcome weaknesses Seek niches Consider acquisitions	**Limited expansion or harvest** Expand but minimize investments and risk Specialize Seek niches Minimize investment and consider exit	**Divest** Cut fixed costs and avoid investments Seek competitors' cash generators Sell at time to maximize cash value

Source: After Hax and Majluf (1991); Kotler (1998); Day (1986)

Figure 2.5 Opportunities and threats matrix and strategic implications

		Strategic implications		
		Positive	*Average*	*Negative*
Probability of occurrence of external environment trends	*High*	Potential opportunity Invest	Prepare for change	Major threat Diversify portfolio
	Medium	Opportunity Investigate and invest selectively	Prepare for change	Potential threat Examine the possibility and take action
	Low	Observe trends	Low risk Take action to improve competitive position	Low risk

Source: After from Kotler (1998)

Figure 2.6 Market growth share matrix

		Relative market share	
		High	*Low*
Market growth	*High*	**Star – GROWTH** Maintain leadership Reduce high business risk	**Question mark – LAUNCH** Invest to increase market share
	Low	**Cash cow – MATURITY** Invest in question marks and future research and development for new markets	**Dog – DECLINE** Divest Sell at highest price Avoid financial risk

Source: Based on Johnson and Scholes (1999)

Figure 2.7 Determining a product/market strategy

Existing products: *market penetration*
New products: *product development*

Existing products: *market development*
New products: *diversification*

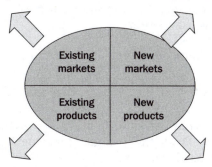

Existing markets: *market penetration*
New markets: *market development*

Existing markets: *product development*
New markets: *diversification*

Source: Based on Ansoff, 1965

Trends and indications are assessed against the potential opportunity or threat they may raise for an enterprise. In addition, its products, markets, geographical scope and unique competence can also be revised against future trends, estimates, forecasts and scenarios. To the degree that ICTs influence these factors in a very dynamic manner, the strategic process time-frame can be reduced gradually. A demand-and-supply analysis for all products and services traded by an organization will illustrate market trends and the reaction of competitors. A **SWOT (strengths–weaknesses–opportunities–threats) analysis** can illustrate the internal performance, resources, processes and mechanisms as well as potential against external opportunities and threats. A competition analysis includes both existing and potential competitors while identifying relationships with suppliers and buyers (Porter, 1985a). In addition, stakeholders' interests, requirements and wants also need to be identified and taken into consideration. The situation analysis should provide a clear indication of the major issues on which organizations need to concentrate in order to strengthen their competitiveness and performance.

Where do we want to go?

Once the situation has been analysed and understood, organizations need to define their strategy and their strategic objectives, or ask 'Where do we want to go?'. This process normally starts with the **mission statement**, which illustrates the organization's broader direction, vision, main activities and values as well as its unique competencies and business scope. British Airways, for example, identified its mission as 'to fly, to serve'. At this stage, organizations need to examine all their strategic options and decide which ones will be compatible with their long-term development. A number of options are available including **market development**, **market penetration** and **market positioning**. For example, a hospitality organization may have a choice between purchasing a hotel chain, developing a new restaurant concept or merging with an airline. As resources are limited, the best alternatives should be adopted. Alternative strategic opportunities are therefore assessed and a choice is made, based on a long-term assessment of the situation in the markets and product-portfolio management. The organization's SBUs may be redefined at this stage, to allow resources to be handled in a more efficient way. Resources are allocated accordingly and the long-term outcome should be examined. A variety of measurable strategic objectives will provide targets for executives and will allow the organization to benchmark its performance against competitors.

How do we get there?

A set of programmes, tasks and objectives are normally set to ensure the implementation of the strategy. They normally answer the question 'how do we get there?'. At this stage managers will allocate available resources, draw timetables and recruit personnel to undertake specific action programmes. Implementation plans provide the road map for achieving the strategic objectives. Organizations may be divided into manageable and accountable departments and tactical planning of functions, such as human resources management, procurement management and marketing. To the degree that ICTs change business processes, organizations need to be able to adopt flexible and changeable structures that will enable them to maximize their performance and effectiveness.

In addition organizations may undertake a market and product-portfolio analysis and assess competitive strength versus market attractiveness, as demonstrated in Figure 2.4. Strategic actions can be taken for each product portfolio and strategic alliances may be formulated in various structures such as networks, opportunistic alliances, subcontracting, licences and franchises, consortia, joint ventures, and acquisitions and mergers in order to allow the product portfolio to capitalize on its positioning and strengthen its competitive position. All necessary adjustments need to be undertaken at this stage in order to set realistic and achievable goals. Detailed budgets and plans are drawn for each activity and accountable personnel are appointed.

How do we know we got there?

Finally at the feedback and control stage, the question is asked: 'How do we know we got there?'. This process aims at addressing changes in the external environment of the organization as well as at improving the implementation process should unpredictable difficulties arise. This process includes control and feedback mechanisms through the definition of performance indicators and measurements at each stage of the strategy implementation. Assessing against tasks as well as benchmarking against industry standards and performance indicators and providing feedback to the strategic process can trigger changes in the procedure, focusing on a strategy or even demanding the re-evaluation of the entire strategy. Setting of indicators, warnings and other measurements is therefore critical at each stage, in order to enable organizations to assess developments in the external environment, assess competitor moves and react effectively.

2.6.3 Competitive strategy, competitive advantage and competitiveness

Competitive strategy 'is the search for a favourable competitive position in an industry, the fundamental arena in which competition occurs' and 'aims to establish a profitable and sustainable position against the forces that determine industry competition' (Porter, 1985a). **Competitive strategies** can be achieved by developing and sustaining competitive advantages. Porter (1985a) explains that 'competitive advantage grows fundamentally out of value a firm is able to create for its buyers, that exceeds the firm's cost of creating it. It represents the ability of an organization to sustain an above the average performance and to outperform competitors'. He suggests that there are two basic types of competitive advantage – cost leadership and differentiation which, combined with the organization's scope of activities, lead to three generic strategies, namely 'cost leadership', 'differentiation' and 'focus', aimed at achieving above-average performance. Organizations need to evaluate their situation and choose the best strategy for their needs. **Generic strategies** should be reflected not only in the final outcome of the value-adding process, but rather throughout all activities, functions and phases of the value chain. Figure 2.8 illustrates Porter's three generic strategies that aim to 'outperform other firms in an industry' as well as includes 'time' as the fourth dimension emerging in the marketplace:

- *Cost leadership*, in which organizations are required to minimize their costs, is based on mass production and strict cost control of the main business functions. Cost leadership may emerge, for example, from standardization, economies of

Figure 2.8 Porter's three generic strategies

		Strategic advantage		
		Perceived product uniqueness	Cost advantage	Time
Target market	Industry-wide and broad target	• Differentiation	• Cost leadership	• Efficient and effective communications and transactions
	Particular segments only and narrow target	• Differentiation focus	• Cost focus	• Proactive approach and time saving for particular market segments

Source: Adapted from Porter (1980, 1985a)

scale, or better deals with suppliers. An example from the tourism industry may be no-frill airlines, such as easyJet or Go, which offer limited service and charge for all catering offered on board in order to reduce their price. Destinations can perhaps include mass tourism resorts, such as Benidorm or Magaluf.

■ *Differentiation* can be achieved by creating products through a **unique selling proposition** or services that are appreciated industry-wide as being unique and valuable. Products should be perceived as above average, represent good value for money, and encourage consumers to pay premium prices. For example, Mauritius as a destination, and the Orient Express or Swiss Airlines as transport, emphasize the uniqueness of their products and their superior attributes and charge premium prices.

■ *Focus* refers to the strategy in which a narrow competitive scope within an industry, such as a particular buyer group, segment of the product line or geographical market, is targeted and a cost leadership or differentiation strategy is tailored exclusively for their needs. For example, business class on airlines normally focuses on business passengers and aims to provide full and unique service through a wide range of value-added elements. Thus, it aims at differentiation for that particular segment, while economy class may target leisure and price-conscious travellers and aims to achieve cost advantage.

■ *Time* In this book we also introduce 'time' as a source of competitive advantage. In a society where time and responsiveness are increasingly rare commodities, organizations that offer efficient and effective communications and transactions for the entire marketplace, as well as those who develop systems and mechanisms to save time for particular market segments will be able to gain competitive advantage. This is a result of the emerging ICTs as well as the globalization of the marketplace.

Competitiveness can therefore be defined as the effort towards and achievement of long-term profitability above the average of the particular industry an organization operates in, as well as profitability above alternative investment opportunities in other industries (opportunity cost). Competitiveness is a function of the structure, abilities and performance of an organization, as well as the industry situation and the external environment, which an organization often cannot control. It represents both the attractiveness of the industry and the relative competitive position of the organization within that particular industry, as well as alternative activities that an organization can undertake by using its resources. In simpler terms, competitiveness is the ability of organizations to outperform their competitors and use their resources in such a way that they gain greater benefits from their activities. This definition includes therefore the concept of opportunity cost and illustrates that successful organizations should compete not only within their particular industry but also against alternative investment opportunities. For example, the competitiveness of an airline will depend on the routes it flies, the external environment it operates in and its ability to perform better (i.e. to maximize profitability, reduce costs and attract more passengers) than its competitors. In addition, in a broader sense, the competitiveness of an airline should also be measured against the profitability of other routes, markets, products or even activities that may have improved its financial performance in the long term. Similar principles also apply to non-profit organizations by measuring their performance against their strategic objectives.

2.7 ICTs, strategic management and competitiveness

ICTs are increasingly recognized as a critical part of the strategic management of organizations, as they have the power to change the competitive game for almost all companies of all sizes. ICTs assist strategic management by supporting the research process through strategic and executive information systems as well as by influencing all stages of the evaluation of organizations against their environment and competitors. For example, the ICT capabilities of an organization are critical for its ability to expand into new markets and products or to decide on alliances and mergers. Hence, ICTs empower organizations to undertake and implement their strategic management process and also clearly determine their capabilities and potential. ICTs can also empower employees within an organization. More members of staff can have access to vital information and knowledge bases, enabling them to make decisions more efficiently (Wijnhoven and Wassenaar, 1990). Technological developments therefore alter both the attractiveness of industries and the competition between organizations, affecting both their strategies and competitiveness. There are several strategic ICT systems, which can be classified in a number of ways, as demonstrated in Figure 2.9. Coordinating the entire range of systems is critical for an organization's ability to achieve its strategic objectives.

Ultimately, firms rely on ICTs to gain a competitive advantage by lowering the cost of doing business or by improving customers' perception about the qualities of their products and services, i.e. differentiating their approach. To the degree that ICTs affect the cost leadership or differentiation strategies of organizations, by reducing the cost of production and distribution or by enhancing the features of a product or service, technology is in the heart of organizational competitiveness as well as strategic management and marketing. ICTs emerge as one of the most critical strategic resources and tools for determining the competitiveness

Figure 2.9 Strategic ICT systems classified into four main categories

- Systems that link the organization via technology-based systems to its customers/consumers and/or suppliers

- Systems that produce more effective integration of the use of information in the organization's value-adding process

- Systems that enable the organization to develop, produce, market and deliver new or enhanced products or services based on information

- Systems that provide executive management with information to support the development and implementation of strategy

Source: Based on Ward et al. (1990)

of organizations. ICT-enabled eCommerce is instrumental in accessing global markets and in developing the ability of organizations to enhance their market share. Moreover, globalization, empowered by ICTs, enhances the dynamics of all industries to a global electronic marketplace and alters the ability of organization to survive in the future. The dynamic developments of ICTs therefore provide both opportunities and challenges for the competitiveness of organizations and, consequently, demand the attention of all enterprises at the strategic level. ICTs need to be treated as a strategic resource and tool, as well as an opportunity and, threat at the highest level of decision making (McFarlan, 1984; Feeny, 1988; Clemons and McFarlan, 1986; Parsons, 1983; King et al.,1988).

Peppard (1993) and Earl (1988) suggest that ICTs can offer new management and business opportunities, which can be applied strategically in at least four different ways, namely:

- to gain a competitive advantage;
- to improve productivity and performance;
- to facilitate new ways of managing and organizing; and
- to develop new businesses.

2.7.1 Using ICTs to achieve generic strategies and strategic competitive advantage

ICTs can support organizations in achieving Porter's (1985a) generic strategies and strategic competitive advantages in a number of ways, as demonstrated in Figure 2.10. *Cost leadership* can be achieved by reducing the price of a product and thus making it more attractive than its competition. By using ICTs, organizations can reduce the cost of customers or suppliers through re-engineering all business processes and enhancing cost efficiency. Techniques such as 'just in time', for example, rationalize the procurement policy of enterprises as well as ensuring that products are produced when and where required, reducing storage and distribution costs. Using ICTs enables organizations not only to reduce the production and distribution cost per unit but also to follow up the pricing tactics of competitors; organizations can ensure that they remain competitive by maximizing the utilization of their resources, especially for fixed costs.

Figure 2.10 Using ICTs to develop competitive advantage

STRATEGIES	
Cost leadership	Use ICTs to reduce the cost of customers or suppliers Reduce cost of business processes Increase cost efficiency Ensure competitive pricing Decrease supply costs and ease supply Maximize resources utilization especially for fixed costs
Product differentiation	Use ICT to develop unique products and add value Differentiate products/services of a company Reduce differentiation advantage of competitors Use information as a product itself
Focus	ICT-enhanced segmentation and targeting Develop relationship marketing Aim to develop mini-market segments Enhance the ability to create niche markets
Time	Provide timely solutions to consumer and trade problems Maximize interaction and reduce response times Enable just-in-time initiatives, reducing stock and distribution costs
STRATEGIC INITIATIVES	
Speedy reaction	Proaction and reaction are important Business at the speed of thought
Marketing research	Use ICTs to interact with consumers Continuous marketing research Scenario building and testing
External environment	Interact with external environment and appreciate influence Set indicators and sensors React first
Innovate	Identify and develop new niche markets and products Create new products and add value to existing products Re-engineer business processes Use ICTs for communicating with consumers and partners
Promote growth	Geographical expansion Operational expansion to gain from economies of scale Develop networks and partnerships to gain economies of scope Promote horizontal, vertical and diagonal integration
Alliances	Develop virtual organizations and concentrate on core business Integrate value chain Develop flexible network of partners based on ICTs
Outsourcing	Outsource non-core business to partners
Efficiency	Redesign processes to maximize output with minimum resources Reduce time required for development and delivery of product
Quality	Standardization and quality-control systems Offer before–during–after service
ICT platform	Integrate all internal and external processes Develop info-structure and info-space

▶

Figure 2.10 continued

Loyalty	Provide incentives to create loyalty Add value through personalized interactions with consumers Develop relationship and 1-2-1 marketing
Fight competition	Use ICT to avoid substitution and barriers to entry Establish entry barriers Effect switching costs and mechanisms Build closer relationships with suppliers and customers Limit access to distribution channels

Source: Based on O'Brien (1996); Robson (1997); Peppard (1993)

In addition organizations can use ICTs strategically to enhance their **product differentiation** by developing unique products and adding value to existing offerings. Information becomes a product in its own right as well as an added value for consumers. For example, information about the latest restaurant news or theatre performances may be sold individually as well as being incorporated in a tourism package. Organizations can therefore differentiate and specialize their products/services to meet the specific requests of consumers as well as enhance the unique attributes and, thus, increase the perceived value of a product. Similarly organizations can reduce the differentiation advantage of competitors by using ICTs to identify what they offer and what is appreciated and undertake a detailed cost-and-benefit analysis before developing counter-offerings.

Focus offers differentiation advantage or cost leadership for specific market segments. Perhaps this becomes the most critical contribution of ICTs, as it makes the identification, development and servicing of mini-market segments feasible. Armed with responses from on-line questionnaires and promotional campaigns, organizations can cross-reference information with consumer behaviour from actual data. This enables them to develop **data warehouses** and to bring together and manage their knowledge in a way that allows organizations to define their market segments with greater precision than before. Customized production and promotional campaigns are therefore empowered by ICTs and eventually the market segment 'of one' will be targeted with uniquely specialized products. Relationship marketing can develop a mutually beneficial exchange between organizations and consumers.

Bill Gates (1999) suggests that increasingly business is conducted at the speed of thought. Thus *time* is also becoming a source of competitive advantage. Consumers are often cash-rich but time-poor, and therefore organizations that can offer practical solutions to consumer requirements at a fraction of the time required by others can enjoy strategic advantages. Thus, consumers may actually purchase a product that is more expensive or less differentiated or even technically inferior, just because it might be available at the right time or because it was offered through a convenient distribution mechanism. This element requires organizations to maximize their reactiveness to consumer requirements and to ensure that they streamline all processes, maximize internal efficiency and enhance interactivity with all stakeholders. As a result, organizations become neural networks that can use all information in order to satisfy needs, add value and achieve their objectives.

2.7.2 Using ICTs to support strategic initiatives

Apart from the generic strategies, several *strategic initiatives* can assist organizations to enhance their competitiveness. As a consequence, organizations need to be both *proactive and reactive* in constantly assessing the external environment and the interests of all stakeholders. This will enable them to formulate virtual corporations with partners and to design flexible products for consumers. The development of a set of indicators and sensors may alert organizations and provide a competitive edge for those that can envisage the opportunities and threats and react accordingly before their competitors do. Innovative, dynamic and ongoing **marketing research** is thus becoming the driving force of organizations. Loyalty clubs provide a huge opportunity for organizations to explore the shopping patterns of their customers, to analyse their consumer behaviour, to bundle them into specific market segments and to design suitable tourism products. As consumers undertake more of their functions on-line, organizations can ask marketing research questions during the registration process in order to establish a profile as well as collect information during each transaction. Not only is the information collected on-line richer and more accurate, but it also costs a fraction of traditional marketing research. In addition, organizations are also able to understand the shopping patterns and the decision-making process of online customers better than before, as they can examine the information required, the critical factors in purchasing products and the association between variables. Constant interaction with consumers also provides unforeseen levels of marketing-research insights mainly of a qualitative nature, which is much more difficult to acquire.

Constant **innovation** enables organizations to identify and develop new niche markets and products as well as to create and add value to existing offerings (Tidd et al., 1997). ICTs facilitate the innovation process by providing new tools for organizations and at the same time by driving new consumer needs and demands. Using ICTs for communicating efficiently with consumers and partner organizations can support a very flexible and constantly evolving product. Consumers may have special requests, which may formulate, enhance and even develop the product further. This is particularly the case for service organizations that have great flexibility and are required to accommodate more intangible and personalized needs.

ICTs also support the *growth* of organizations in several dimensions. Geographical expansion is supported as technology allows easier, more reliable and more advanced communications. Using standardized systems and packages, organizations can control the operations and performance of their branches on a global scale. Operational expansion is also empowered and allows organizations to gain from economies of scale. Developing networks and partnerships by using computerized systems also allows organizations to gain economies of scope and to enhance and evolve their product continuously. The globalization of all major industries is propelled by this horizontal, vertical and diagonal integration. The development of virtual corporations allows organizations to develop *alliances* with partnerships; by outsourcing to partners, organization can concentrate on their core business while enhancing their value-added offerings. Flexible networks of partners offer the best of everything by using ICTs as the info-structure and by bringing together their core competencies.

ICTs can enhance *efficiency* by redesigning and re-engineering all business processes to maximize output with minimum resources and also by reducing the time required for development and delivery of products. Both these qualities are increasingly critical for the competitiveness of organizations. However, in a world of global competition, *quality* is equally critical. Standardization and quality-control systems allow organizations to ensure the delivery of products that at least match the expectations of consumers. In addition, benchmarking against competitors' products also enables organizations to aim constantly at enhancing their quality and outperforming competition. Offering service before, during and after the consumption of goods and services will also be increasingly critical for the ability of organizations to retain their clientèle and to provide a proper service.

Consumer *loyalty* is one of the most important assets for organizations, as retaining customers is much more cost efficient than attracting new ones. Adding value through personalized interactions with consumers and providing incentives can create loyalty. Although small businesses have traditionally capitalized on personal relationships, larger organizations can only develop and maintain loyalty by using ICTs in order to encourage all their staff to share their knowledge and understanding of their consumers. Relationships with consumers are supported by loyalty schemes such as frequent-flyer clubs, privilege clubs and guest histories that register the profile of users and track all their transactions, actual purchases and preferences. Collecting all this information in a dynamic data warehouse enables organizations to constantly update their consumer research and to reposition themselves against mini-segments, enhancing the loyalty of their clientèle. As a result, they can narrow their targeting to the market segment 'of one' and introduce one-to-one (1-2-1) marketing initiatives, regardless of their size and industry.

Organizations not only need to enhance their competitiveness; they should also *fight their competition*. ICTs can be used to avoid substitution by developing barriers to entry and by applying switching costs and mechanisms. Once organizations invest in equipment and training for their employees, they are most likely to remain with particular suppliers even if their interests are not fully met because of the costs and mechanisms involved in switching. In addition, ICT can institute barriers to entry if the cost of their systems is prohibitive or if organizations cannot penetrate the market segments of the partners they require in order to become competitive. In addition, limiting access to distribution channels may also reduce competition. In order to develop and deliver a competitive advantage, organizations increasingly have to establish an ICT *platform* and integrate all internal and external processes through constant collaboration and interaction with all stakeholders. The critical element here is that organizations need to adapt constantly to the changes of their external environment and to aim to capture new market opportunities on a dynamic basis.

2.7.3 Conditions for optimal use of ICTs

ICTs can provide competitive advantages only 'if they are critical to operations on a daily basis; planned applications are critical to future competitiveness; and information content/intensity of products and functional area is high' (Robson, 1997). Since these lines were written less than a decade ago, it is difficult to think of any industry that has not been altered significantly by the technological developments of the last years. Every innovative and competent organization, from car manufacturers to bakers and butchers, turns to the Internet to take advantage of the global market-space and to promote their products on a world-wide scale. ICTs often act as a 'competitive weapon' that assists organizations to compete in the marketplace.

Figure 2.10 illustrates how ICTs can support organizations to achieve competitive advantages and also how they can enhance strategic tasks to improve competitiveness. There are several ways of using ICTs to strengthen the competitiveness of organizations, aimed at influencing the main sources of competitive advantage. However, ICTs are pervasive and thus initiatives often influence the entire range of activities and processes in an organization, generating synergies and enlarging the scope of a single initiative.

Decision-making can become more accurate, decentralized and flexible to the needs of all people involved. By using knowledge-management methodologies, employees can benefit from the knowledge base built within the organization and thus take advantage of previous experience and expertise, improving their ability to make the right choice. Having to go through less repetitive and bureaucratic procedures, employees can offer better attention to customer service and use technology to personalize the product, contributing to product differentiation. Releasing employees from monotonous, repetitive jobs and giving them the opportunity to concentrate on more sophisticated or interesting jobs can also improve personnel morale and enhance the human resources of organizations.

As information is a source of power in negotiations with trading partners, the adoption of ICTs often alters the power balance in **distribution channels** (Burt and Dawson, 1991). Thus, perhaps, the most relevant competitive advantage from the use of ICTs would be the shift in buyers' bargaining power and the relationships between an industry and its buyers (Parsons, 1983; Jackson, 1989; Porter, 1985b). Porter and Millar (1985) suggest that ICTs 'have had a particularly strong impact on bargaining relationships between suppliers and buyers since they affect the linkages between companies and their suppliers, channels and buyers'. This enables organizations to enhance their position within distribution channels and can assist them in increasing their profit margin.

2.8 Prerequisites for achieving competitive advantage through ICTs

ICTs are not a panacea for organizational problems and in fact they can create new problems if enterprises fail to introduce adequate, appropriate, rational and innovative ICT resources. Although there is evidence that ICTs can be a source of competitive advantage, several authors have questioned whether this advantage is genuine. There is often no significant correlation between information systems spending and profitability. ICTs frequently fail to add value in an organization's operation and the costs associated (capital, training, staff) often exceed the benefits generated (Gamble, 1990; Beaumont and Sparks, 1990). Technology does not guarantee profitability and it may even worsen the competitive position of firms and the attractiveness of an industry (Porter, 1985b). This is evident in tourism, as on several occasions new organizations have failed to generate sufficient funds, ultimately going bankrupt (e.g. Dreamticket.com). Others have invested heavily in systems that may be unsuitable for their needs and similarly have suffered financial problems. The increasing number of dot.com companies that fail to generate adequate sales and investments and consequently go into receivership with spectacular losses has also alarmed the stock exchange markets around the world. Indeed, Robson (1997) emphasizes that organizations should 'realize that ICTs contribute to both sides of the general business equation, since they recognizably add to both the revenue and the cost streams'. Perhaps the most significant lesson learned from failures is that ICTs are merely tools for supporting sound business models. If the business proposition is not strong enough and if the technology used is not suitable for the objectives of the organization, ICTs simply speed up the failure process and make the problems evident sooner. A competitive **cost and benefit analysis** is therefore required for all ICT investments and projects.

Whether ICTs can assist organizations to achieve **sustainable competitive advantage** is also debatable. To the degree that each investment in technology by one company can be matched by another, it would appear that the application of the technology is necessary merely to sustain what might be called competitive parity (Gamble, 1994b). Gaining sustainable competitive advantage through ICTs seems, therefore, unlikely, mainly due to imitation from competitors and substitution by consumers. 'To survive in the future, firms must meet or beat the competition in delivering value to the customer. With industries being fundamentally restructured by the integration of information technology and telecommunications, it is often absolutely essential that these investments be made to avoid genuine strategic vulnerability' (Bradley et al., 1993; Hickey, 1993). ICTs can assist organizations to avoid competitive disadvantage, as doing nothing is no longer an option, with competitors and newcomers in the industry enhancing their competitive position at the expense of others. This is particularly evident in the travel business where Expedia and Travelocity managed to attract a large proportion of the market share from traditional organizations such as American Express or Rosenbluth Travel.

It is gradually recognized that ICTs can no longer be treated as stand-alone initiatives but rather should be addressed at the strategic level through an integrated approach to all business functions. The use of ICTs has therefore to be coupled with a redesign of organizational structures and management control systems (Freedman, 1991). ICTs can enable organizations to achieve and sustain competitive advantage only if certain prerequisites are satisfied. These include:

- long-term planning and strategy;
- innovative processes introduction;
- top management commitment; and
- training throughout the hierarchy.

Legacy thinking and failure to address these issues can jeopardize competitiveness, prosperity and even an organization's existence.

Research demonstrates that the attitude of managers and training, as well as the degree of ICTs' capitalization, play a critical role in the successful contribution to organizations. Thus, Freedman (1991) suggests that 'rather than trying to build a flashy application that will sew up a market – something that these systems never did – organizations need to construct a broad, flexible ICT platform, hone managers' skills at applying information to decision making and continually search for more effective ways of doing business with support from ICT'.

Integrating all functions of an organization through **enterprise resource planning (ERP)**, which can help to integrate all facets of the business, including planning, manufacturing, sales and finance, is critical for the sharing of information and processes across the organization (Laudon and Laudon, 2002). Enterprise resource planning also supports organizations in taking advantage of internal and external synergies.

Perhaps the greater challenge is to identify and train managers to be effective users of ICTs and to lead technology-based decision-making in order to achieve quantifiable gains and competitive advantage for their organizations. Intellect, therefore, becomes one of the major assets of organizations, while continuous education and training are the only methods of developing and maintaining this asset. Provided that rational and innovative planning and management are exercised constantly and consistently, ICTs can support the success of organizations. Training at all levels of an organization is critical for enabling employees and managers to appreciate the strategic dimension of ICTs as well as the emerging opportunities and challenges. Figure 2.11 proposes a '4R' framework for training programmes.

Refocusing in tourism is gradually achieved through younger generations of professionals and a few pioneers who have appreciated ICT developments. This has gradually led to *retooling*, although in reality retooling is supply-driven, where software companies such as Micros-Fidelio develop applications and then promote them to organizations. A gradual *reskilling* is evident mainly because ICT professionals are increasingly employed in tourism and hospitality organizations. Proprietors of smaller hospitality properties are frequently trained in programmes sponsored by local tourism boards or they learn about computers through their children at school. Gradually computers become yet another household appli-

Figure 2.11 4Rs framework for ICT training

- **Refocusing:** raising executive management awareness and understanding how important ICTs are for business

- **Retooling:** developing management or application skills and knowledge to follow up any new initiatives identified in refocusing

- **Reskilling:** educating and training the information systems community in technology, management and business skills for the new ICT era

- **Reinforcing:** building top management understanding, confidence and commitment to support the effects of the other programmes

Source: Based on Earl (1988)

ance and more people find them easy to use. *Reinforcing* is perhaps the most difficult challenge in the tourism industry as the vast majority of top managers have not yet appreciated the magnitude of change experienced in the industry and consistently fail to move forward. Only a small number of travel dot.com companies are driving their organizations by appreciating that their business model can only be delivered by innovative ICTs and vice versa.

2.9 ICTs in the contemporary competitive arena: business re-engineering and paradigm shift

In order to maximize the benefits of ICTs, organizations need to re-examine their entire operation and to redesign their processes according to the new opportunities and challenges. Figure 2.12 illustrates that during the four different eras of ICT development, the organizational use of ICTs as well as risk returns

Figure 2.12 Organizational change and ICTs

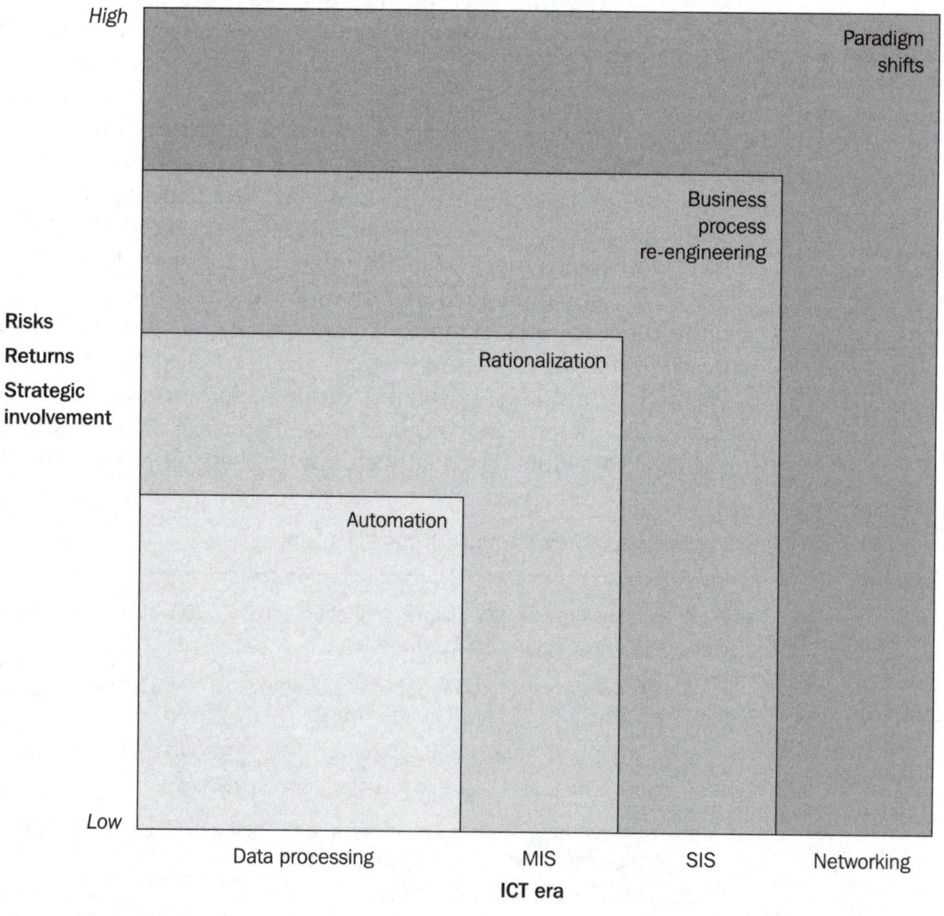

Source: After Laudon and Laudon (2002)

and strategic involvement have changed accordingly. In the data-processing era, automation was used to enhance the speed and quality of existing tasks and procedures. In the management information systems era, organizations could rationalize by identifying procedures and processes that could be improved.

It was not until the strategic information era, however, that organizations had to rethink and redesign their operations from scratch in order to address the radical changes, challenges and opportunities. Business process re-engineering (BPR) provided 'the fundamental analysis and redesign of everything associated with a business area to achieve dramatic performance improvement and the management of associated business changes' (Reynolds, 1992). Re-engineering argues that yesterday's practices, traditional hierarchical and organizational structures, revered and habitual procedures are almost irrelevant, as new systems can eliminate repetitive and paper-intensive tasks to improve cost, quality and service and to maximize the benefits of ICTs. Business process re-engineering urges corporations to respond to current and future challenges by redesigning the entire range of their processes, jobs, structures and systems, starting from scratch (Hammer, 1990; Robson, 1997). By capitalizing on the potential of ICTs, corporations need to convert their entire operations from business functions to business processes, as well as re-conceive their corporate values and culture. This is a major prerequisite for organizations that would like to address the future with contemporary tools and mechanisms, rather than being locked in traditions and obsolete tools (a situation often described as driving forwards looking at the rear mirror). There is also a clear need for a long-term strategic vision and a commitment to incorporate ICTs at the heart of strategic management. ICTs should take a central role as a key enabler of the entire range of new cross-functional business processes (Obeng and Crainer, 1994; Hammer and Champy, 1993).

However, BPR has several limitations. Firstly, in the 1990s BPR was widely perceived as a rationalization measure that could save costs, often by reducing the amount of employees. Secondly, BPR focuses on processes and therefore is inevitably occupied by structured problem solving. The new Internet economy requires ad hoc intelligent networking between individuals and organizations, hence processes become less structured and much more flexible. Thirdly, BPR often ignores the human imperative. As a cost-cutting exercise, BPR is often blamed for cutting jobs, while a top-down approach has often been adopted that alienates, demoralizes and demotivates employees. Finally, several organizations have tried to implement BPR without upgrading and networking their organization through ICTs, and have therefore failed to introduce the appropriate tools for the new networked enterprise. Research often criticizes BPR as having been used as a way to implement evolution rather than revolution in organizations, and as a result it has rarely delivered the promised benefits.

The networking era and the proliferation of the Internet are a challenge to most organizations as they threaten traditional business models. Instead they support new inter-networked organizations that concentrate on their core competencies while teaming up with others for added value. Tapscott (1996) suggests that a radical change of all business forms is required. This change should not only re-engineer companies but also transform the entire system in order to maximize its benefits. A *paradigm shift* is therefore experienced in the marketplace, forcing all organizations to identify new ways of looking at their own operations and radically re-conceptualize the nature of their business. This generates fundamental changes in the nature and application of technology in business and has far-reaching implications for organizations and societies.

A paradigm shift refers to the 'fundamental new ways of looking at something. It is necessitated by new developments in science, technology, art or other areas of endeavour. Such shifts are necessary because important changes in reality demand a shift in conceptualization' (Tapscott and Caston, 1993). The new paradigm offers 'a radical transformation of the prevailing engineering and managerial common sense for best productivity and most profitable practice, which is applicable in almost any industry' (Freeman and Perez, 1988). This paradigm has profound implications for the world geopolitical situation and the international business environment, while at the micro level it stimulates the rise of the new open, networked enterprise, which constitutes a new organizational paradigm. Haeckel and Nolan (1993) propose a new innovative management method, which takes advantage of the new paradigm: 'managing by wire' is defined as 'the capability to run a business by managing its information representation'. Figure 2.13 illustrates that four main paradigm shifts drive changes in organizations and society (Tapscott and Caston, 1993), namely:

■ new technology,
■ new geopolitical order,

Figure 2.13 Paradigm shifts influencing business

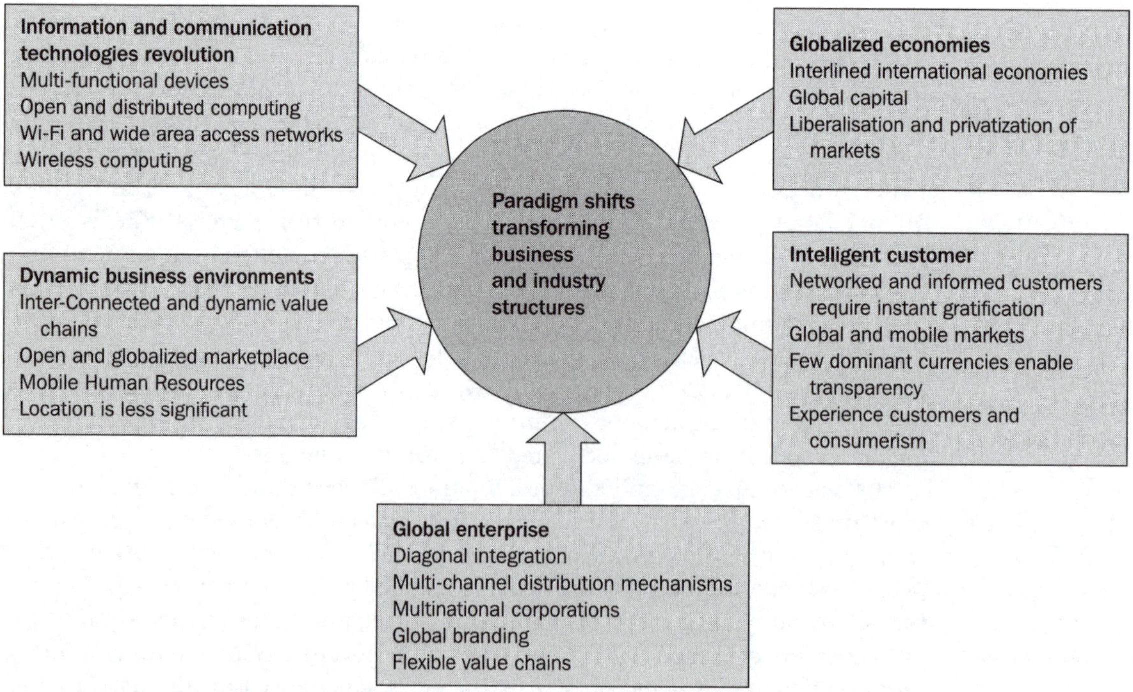

Information and communication technologies revolution
Multi-functional devices
Open and distributed computing
Wi-Fi and wide area access networks
Wireless computing

Globalized economies
Interlined international economies
Global capital
Liberalisation and privatization of markets

Paradigm shifts transforming business and industry structures

Dynamic business environments
Inter-Connected and dynamic value chains
Open and globalized marketplace
Mobile Human Resources
Location is less significant

Intelligent customer
Networked and informed customers require instant gratification
Global and mobile markets
Few dominant currencies enable transparency
Experience customers and consumerism

Global enterprise
Diagonal integration
Multi-channel distribution mechanisms
Multinational corporations
Global branding
Flexible value chains

Source: Based on Tapscott and Caston (1993)

- new enterprise, and
- new business environment.

Technology helps improve the performance of teams, to integrate organizations and to develop relationships with external partners, establishing the networked or extended enterprise. A new geopolitical order, enabled by global media, provides a more open, volatile and multi-polar world, which challenges old conformities and propels global democratization and international accountability. This generates a new and more open, competitive and dynamic international marketplace with intensified competition. As a result, organizations and enterprises need to transform the way they operate, network their activities, enhance the role of information in their processes and compete in the emerging global marketplace. ICT developments propel the four main paradigm shifts and vice versa. Due to global competition, new technological developments are required to support the expansion of global business and organizations and to facilitate the opening of markets and activities.

It is therefore apparent that ICTs increasingly play a vital role in the achievement of the strategic objectives of organizations. Despite their inability to solve all business problems, ICTs provide opportunities to increase competitiveness and efficiency. However, it is essential to re-engineer the entire range of management and marketing processes, as well as to redefine best practices in order to gain maximum benefits. The dynamic nature of ICTs suggests that only consistently innovative organizations will manage to gain sustainable competitive advantage (Davenport, 1993; Tapscott and Caston, 1993).

2.10 The virtual corporation: concepts and definitions

The latest paradigm shift established the networking era and propelled the concept of virtual corporations. In their book *The Virtual Corporation*, Davidow and Malone (1992) attempt to introduce a wide range of concepts that will characterize the competent corporation of the 21st century. They claim that a new kind of product or service is required by consumers, which delivers instant customer gratification in a cost-effective way. Virtual products and services are produced instantaneously and are customized in response to customer demand. Flexible production lines and computerized systems enable managers to accumulate expertise and develop procedures that can transform organizations into virtual corporations. In order to achieve the production of virtual products, firms will need to revise themselves, control ever more sophisticated types of information and master new organizational and production skills. Hale and Whitlam (1997) define the **virtual organization** as an 'organization which is continually evolving, redefining and reinventing itself for practical business purposes'. Virtual organizations have numerous characteristics. They institutionalize organizational change and demonstrate focused strategic direction and purpose. Hence they enable individuals to optimize their potential to contribute, by developing dynamic communication and creating cultures that support continual organizational adaptation.

Byrne et al. (1993) emphasize that virtual corporations are 'temporary networks of companies that come together quickly to exploit fast-changing opportunities by sharing costs, skills, and access to global markets, with each partner contributing what it is best at'. Organizations emerge out of this dynamic process as virtual corporations and aim to produce cost-effective, instantaneous, mass-customized goods and services. Virtual corporations develop dynamic interfaces with their suppliers and consumers, while a constant reform of traditional offices, departments and operating divisions is undertaken according to need. Consumers increasingly play a more dominant role in the design and production of virtual products as they can feed their needs and desires back to the organization through interactive mechanisms.

A virtual company is not an isolated facility of production, but rather a node in the complex network of suppliers, customers, engineering and other service functions. By developing and maintaining integrated and ever-changing data files on customers, products, production, plans and design methodologies, virtual corporations are able to deliver products which adapt in real time to consumer changing needs. 'Building virtual products requires taking a sophisticated information network that gathers data on markets and consumer needs, combining it with the newest design methods and computer integrated production process, then operating this system with an integrated network that includes not only highly skilled employees of the company but also suppliers, distributors, retailers and even consumers' (Davidow and Malone, 1992). Unlike traditional organizations, the virtual corporation appears less a discrete enterprise and more an ever-varying cluster of common activities in the midst of a vast fabric of relationships. In order to enhance their competitiveness, virtual corporations need to excel not only at producing superb products, but also in managing their relationships with all other members of the value-added chain, such as consumers, suppliers, stakeholders and employees.

Virtual organizations can operate on a global scale and can act more dynamically towards markets with high demand. Developing partnerships with local people, virtual organizations can customize global practices to local cultures and adapt products accordingly. Hollister (1995) emphasizes that 'increasingly there is much less justification for geography to play a role in the structure of the company. The advent and continual enhancement of globe-spanning telecommunications and data communication networks in parallel with other factors such as more accessible air travel is challenging the traditional site-based emphasis of business. Employees, in theory at least, should be as much in contact whether they are in the same room or on a different floor or in a different office, a different country, or in a car or plane'. The virtual organization concept 'overcomes geographical constraints and alleviates the traditional dichotomy between centralised and decentralised organizational structures and processes' and thus creates a much more customer/service-oriented company (Loebbecke and Jelassi, 1997). Dynamic networks and constantly emerging structures take advantage of flexible specialization, in order to improve their efficiencies and delivery of suitable products (Barnatt, 1995).

Virtual corporations undertake an extensive outsourcing policy. Only the core, strategic business functions are performed inside the company while the remaining support activities are outsourced to a network of external companies that specialize in each function. Functional and strategic alliances are formed between these firms to manufacture products or provide services for consumers (Davis and Darling, 1996). The goal is to extract the maximum added value from these partnerships, while making the minimum investment in permanent staff, fixed assets and working capital. Hence, lean production ensures that 'virtual corporations use less of everything compared with mass production – half the human effort in the factory, half the manufacturing space, half the investment in tools and machinery, half the engineering hours to develop a new product in half the time' (Davidow and Malone, 1992). In this way, not only does it not have to invest heavily in fixed costs but, more importantly, being lean the organization can adapt and alter its operations easily according to market trends and opportunities. The virtual corporation positions itself at the centre, drawing the cooperating companies together and organizing the work flow. Developing alliances with the right organizations can support the development of the 'best of everything' organization, able to react to external challenges instantly. Companies that wait to develop what they need for themselves will simply be left behind, but fast-moving flexible organizations, which appreciate that opportunities are brief in the global marketplace and have discovered that they can access world-class competencies, can strike new deals, make new partnerships and take immediate advantage of those opportunities (Prochak, 1997).

The key reason for the virtual enterprise is therefore speed and efficiency. The result of this 'shift from physical to virtual does not simply reduce costs, speed up communications, or provide players with more timely information, although that's all true. Rather, when information exchange becomes electronic, a world of subtle and not so subtle changes in the nature of human and organizational communication occurs – changes that support new kinds of relationships between organizations and people. The value chain becomes a value network, as new relationships become possible. And rather than value-added the technology enables the organization to create new institutional structures that can be value-generative' (Tapscott, 1996). During the shift organizations have to support multi-channel strategies and use a wider range of media to reach their customers, resulting in expensive and difficult-to-maintain processes. This is already evident in tourism where consumer still research, shop and purchase products from a number of alternatives: from high-street shops, to direct telephone calls and virtual travel agencies on-line. This results in companies building a range of interfaces to suit every potential revenue-generating avenue.

Technology facilitates informational networks to help far-flung companies and entrepreneurs link up and work together from start to finish. The partnership is normally based on electronic interchanges, contracts and processes to speed linkups. Because each partner brings its 'core competence to the effort it may be possible to create a best-of-everything organization. Every function and process could be world class-something that no single company could achieve. Partnerships however will be less permanent, less formal and more opportunistic. Companies will band together to meet a specific market opportunity and more often than not, fall apart once the need evaporates' (Davidow and Malone, 1992). This new corporate model redefines the traditional boundaries of the company and enables firms to constantly innovate and evolve. More cooperation among competitors makes it harder to determine where one company ends and another begins, whilst these relationships make companies far more reliant on each other and require far more trust than ever before. They share a sense of co-destiny, meaning that each partner is dependent on the other (Davidow and Malone, 1992). Trust between employees, partners and consumers is central in the development and operation of virtual corporations, as often these individuals have no face-to-face interaction (Handy, 1995).

Despite the variety of definitions and the ambiguity of the terminology, they share some characteristics that address most of the emerging issues. The essence of virtual corporations is evidently flexibility and responsiveness; empowered by skilled and continuous learning personnel; developed through strategic partnerships with consumers and suppliers (co-destiny); and facilitated by using innovative information technologies. The ability of virtual organizations to collect and integrate a massive flow of information throughout their organizational components, and intelligently act upon that information, becomes critical. Using advanced technology not only reduces the manufacturing time required for the design and production of goods and services but also enables the delivery of products just in time. In addition, a culture of continuous learning throughout the ranks of the organization is required in order to ensure the familiarization of employees with new technologies, as well as the understanding of the needs and wants of consumers and strategic partners. Table 2.3 attempts a synthesis of the characteristics attributed to virtual organizations.

Interestingly, small and medium enterprises (SMEs) seem to have always been closer to this new model of organizations. Their small size has always meant that they have a much more flexible production function than larger counterparts,

Table 2.3 Characteristics of virtual corporations

- Virtuality: process and direction, journey not a destination
- Focus on consumer gratification
- Responsiveness and promptness: just in time
- Cost-effectiveness
- Trust partners/consumers/suppliers/employees
- Continuous organizational adaptation to market needs
- Continuous learning and training towards innovation
- Networking and partnerships
- Synergies in communication and technologies utilized
- Lean production through outsourcing
- Dynamic involvement of suppliers/consumers/employees
- Co-destiny throughout the value chain
- Teamwork and empowerment
- Innovative use of information technology
- Flexible and intelligent location
- Proximity to the needs of the marketplace

Source: Based on Tapscott (1996); Davidow and Malone (1992); Handy (1995); Hollister (1995); Loebbecke and Jelassi (1997)

while their proximity to the marketplace enables them to formulate close relationships with their **markets**, as well as **suppliers** and other stakeholders. Tailor-made and customized products therefore comprise the bread and butter of their existence. Personal relationships frequently result in personalized services as well as strong partnerships and 'co-destiny' with other members in the value chain. Ad hoc partnerships are continuously formulated in order to satisfy consumer demand and thus achieve flexible specialization, illustrating the ability of SMEs to adapt and innovate (Poon, 1988, 1989, 1990). As a result, SMEs frequently achieve a differentiation advantage that enables them to compete with mass-oriented large organizations that can supply their products at a fraction of the cost. However, small firms have traditionally been reluctant to invest in ICT and to develop their human resources through training and life-long learning. This has resulted in a major inability in understanding consumers' demand and also in developing similar quality products and competitive prices compared with mass producers. However, increasingly, small enterprises realize that networking and developing partnerships at the local level can provide 'virtual size' and, thus, compensate for their strategic weaknesses (Cooper and Buhalis, 1992).

2.11 ICTs and innovation as the nucleus of organizational processes and strategy

Within this framework of change, **innovation** and ICTs become the nucleus of organizational processes and strategy, as illustrated in Figure 2.14. Innovation in interacting with all stakeholders, identifying business opportunities and delivering competitive products and services are the main qualities required by organizations for their future survival. ICTs are instrumental in researching consumer needs, investigating competition, assessing the external environment, and for reshaping business functions and processes accordingly. Constant communications with all stakeholders enables the identification and analysis of their needs. Moreover, a constant interaction with the external environment provides insights and assists organizations to predict events as well as their impact on the markets and to react accordingly.

ICTs should only be regarded as the tool for undertaking innovative strategic management and marketing that can enhance the competitiveness of organizations. Unless organizations have the tool they will be unable to perform the job; however, having the tool does not necessarily guarantee that they will be able to outperform others. The competitiveness of firms depends on the ability of their strategic management and marketing to take advantage of the new tools and to design products, procedures and mechanisms that will enable organizations to achieve their objectives. Constant innovation is therefore essential in order to outperform competition and implement strategic actions to support managers in identifying niche markets. Innovation is increasingly based on ICTs, as technology provides the info-structure for constant interaction with consumers and the external and internal environment of enterprises. Innovation

Figure 2.14 Information technology as the nucleus of organizational processes and strategy

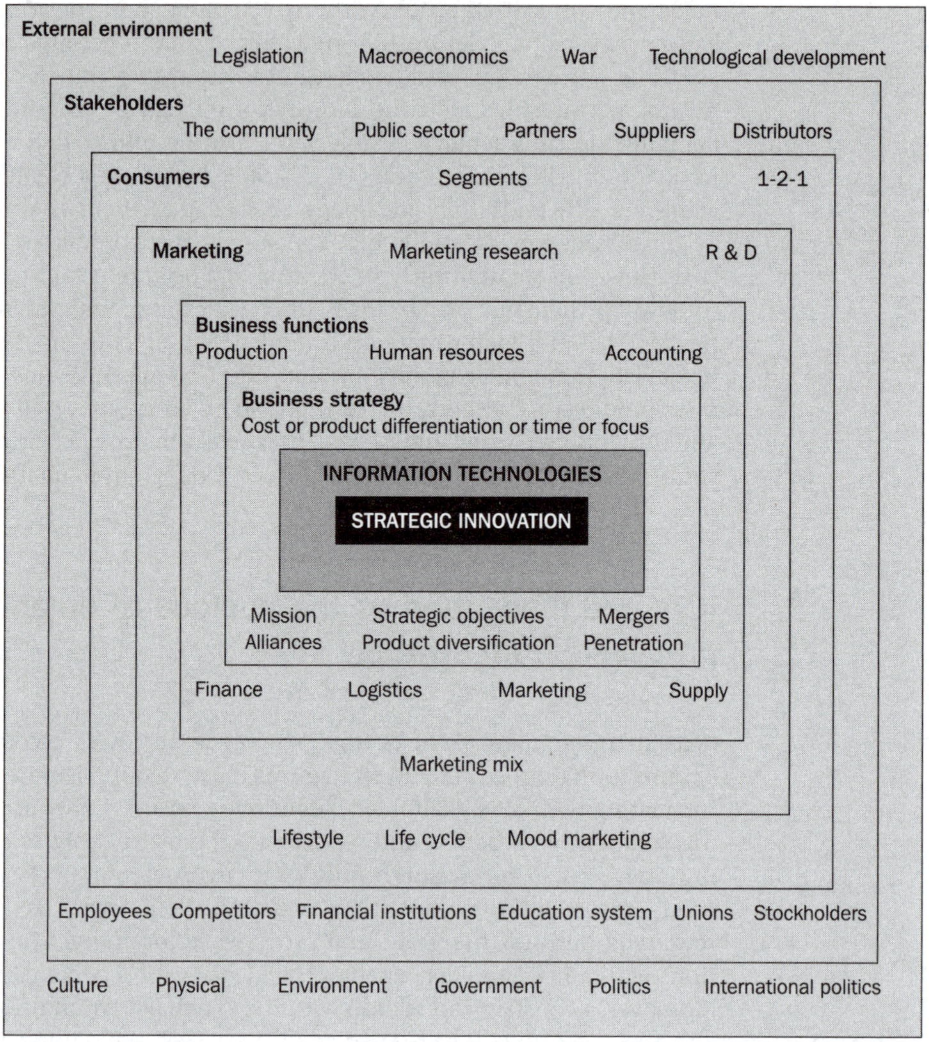

External environment				
Legislation	Macroeconomics	War		Technological development

Stakeholders
The community   Public sector   Partners   Suppliers   Distributors

Consumers   Segments   1-2-1

Marketing   Marketing research   R & D

Business functions
Production   Human resources   Accounting

Business strategy
Cost or product differentiation or time or focus

INFORMATION TECHNOLOGIES

STRATEGIC INNOVATION

Mission   Strategic objectives   Mergers
Alliances   Product diversification   Penetration

Finance   Logistics   Marketing   Supply

Marketing mix

Lifestyle   Life cycle   Mood marketing

Employees   Competitors   Financial institutions   Education system   Unions   Stockholders

Culture   Physical   Environment   Government   Politics   International politics

should be driven by a long-term mission and business strategy, which appreciates the dynamic nature of global competition and the aims for enhancing the long-term competitiveness of organizations. Strategic decision-making should take into consideration the opportunities and challenges emerging as a result of both technological developments and their implications in the marketplace. Business functions need to be reshaped accordingly, to maximize efficiency and effectiveness. Within this process, **marketing** offers a mechanism for interaction with all external and internal stakeholders, identifying their needs and wants and designing appropriate offerings. Primarily **marketing research** identifies consumer needs and develops potential products for their satisfaction. ICTs can enhance the interactivity with consumers and support the segmentation process by dividing the market into well-defined **target markets** and establishing **one-to-one marketing** and **relationship marketing**. ICTs also support organizations' interaction with the external environment and empower rapid reaction to opportunities and threats; the time element becomes much more critical in the electronic marketplace where global markets react at the speed of thought (Gates, 1999).

2.12 A multidimensional framework for strategic management and marketing

A conceptual synthesis of ICT usage in business strategy yields a strategic multidimensional framework or an 'info-space'. This attempts to systematize our understanding of the use of ICTs in business and to illustrate all strategic implications for organizations. Figure 2.15 demonstrates the multidimensional character of the framework, as well as the technologies it uses in order to perform its business functions. The framework develops a space of interaction, which can be represented as the internal part of a cube. The cube is formed by three principal dimensions and technological enablers, namely:

Figure 2.15 Organizational info-space for strategic management

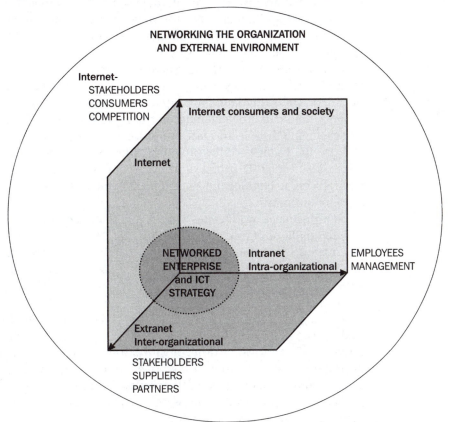

- intranets for employees and managers of the organization internally;
- extranets for external but privileged-access stakeholders such as partners, suppliers, loyal and authenticated customers; and
- the Internet, which offers a window to the world and enables everybody to interact with the organization.

The ICT strategy is at the heart of the networked enterprise, as illustrated in Figure 2.15. Effective organizations will need to use the Internet, extranets and intranets to communicate with their main stakeholders and to manage all their affairs. The Internet supports global interaction and customized websites can be offered to each of the main stakeholders, with access to appropriate information and interactivity channels. For example, an organization may have one **web page** for their customers but alternative pages for their local community, recruitment or press and media. However, due to its nature most of the information distributed by the Internet would be public. Password protection may require users to register, offering their identity or profile or both before they can use the website. This is particularly the case on websites with an electronic commerce element, where a degree of authentication is essential for security reasons. An extranet can be used for sharing information with trusted partners and for enhancing the interactivity on particular functions. The content is protected and only authorized partners can use designated areas of the data and processes of the organization. Intranets are restricted to internal users only and therefore can only be used by employees and managers of the organization. Different employees can have access to different levels of information in the organization according to their job specification, rank and responsibilities.

ICTs provide an info-structure across the industry and marketplace for effective and efficient management as well as for internal and external communications. Endless combinations of interaction can occur within this info-structure. Organizations can take advantage of this framework by undertaking research and by developing flexible and reactive processes to monitor external developments and use the framework for providing efficient and effective service when and where it is needed. The framework incorporates the paradigm shift and the business process re-engineering experienced, which effectively reshapes the entire range of business.

Each organization operates within a global electronic info-structure, which includes millions of other organizations. Increasingly each of these organizations can move around the info-structure to identify the markets they can serve best and potential opportunities, thus becoming able to formulate new partnerships with other organizations and establish flexible value chains that serve specific markets or purposes.

Selecting appropriate partners is fairly easy as through the Internet organizations can collect information and have a fairly good picture of the areas of activity and expertise of other organizations in the marketplace. Approaching organizations is also easier through electronic means of communication. Once a connection is made, organizations may use their extranet to maximize their efficiencies and to create seamless links. The challenge therefore lies on using the three axes strategically in order to:

- maximize the efficiency and effectiveness of each organization,
- capitalize on the market opportunities;
- position the organization effectively for taking advantage of partnership opportunities;
- formulate successful value chains;
- maximize consumer benefits.

ICTs propel changes in several directions between the three main axes. The resulting combinations illustrate how strategic marketing and management can be utilized in order to achieve mutual benefits for all stakeholders. The new ICT developments therefore lead to the integration of different stakeholders within an info-space, which forces them to interact constantly and to form ad hoc partnerships for mutual benefit.

2.13 Conclusions: ICT info-structure and strategic management

ICTs not only empower the research and development process but also determine which strategic plans are achievable. Hence organizations have to assess the ICT requirements and capabilities for each prospective product they plan to launch for each market they hope to target. In order to be competitive, organizations need to design their operations and products in a way that offers either cost or differentiation advantage and ICTs already play a critical role. In an increasingly global marketplace, ICTs provide opportunities for constant interaction, close relationships and endless reaction to external factors, trends, moods and preferences. Unless organizations therefore use a certain level of info-structure, they will be unable to expand, produce certain products or serve particular market segments, illustrating the role of ICTs as a competitive driving force. In addition, failing to use ICTs for networking with all stakeholders and to design, distribute and communicate product efficiently and effectively will jeopardize an organization's competitiveness. Organizations need to base their interactivity on their organizational info-space that operates within the framework of the market info-structure.

Chapter questions

1 Do ICTs reduce or expand the prosperity gap between the developed and the developing worlds?

2 How can developing societies take advantage of the emerging technologies?

3 Apply the value-chain concept to a tourism organization of your choice.

4 What is the difference between eCommerce and eBusiness?

5 Why is strategic management critical for ICT management?

6 How can ICT support strategy and competitive advantage?

7 What is constant innovation and why is it critical for the tourism organization of the future?

8 Why are ICTs becoming the nucleus of organizations?

9 Explain the info-space and info-structure concepts in relation to a tourism organization of your choice.

Further reading

Hax, A. and Majluf, N. (1991) *The Strategy Concept and Process: A Pragmatic Approach*, Prentice Hall, New Jersey.

Negroponte, N. (1995) *Being Digital*, Coronet Books, London.

Porter, M. (1985a) *Competitive Advantage*, Free Press, New York.

Porter, M. (1985b) Technology and competitive advantage, *Journal of Business Strategy*, Winter, 60–70.

Porter, M. (2001) Strategy and the Internet, *Harvard Business Review*, **103D**, 63–78.

Tapscott, D. (1996) *The Digital Economy: Promise and Peril in the Age of Networked Intelligence*, McGraw-Hill, New York.

Tapscott, D. and Caston, A. (1993) *Paradigm Shift: The New Promise of Information Technology*, McGraw-Hill, New York.

Tapscott, D., Ticoll, D. and Lowy, A. (2000) *Digital Capital: Harnessing the Power of Business Webs*, Harvard Business School Press, Boston.

Turban, E., Lee, J., King, D. and Change, H. (2002) *Electronic Commerce: A Managerial Perspective*, Prentice Hall, New Jersey.

Websites

Follow the Corisande Hotel in Cornwall and the www.cornwall-calling.co.uk case study

www.cornwall-calling.co.uk

www.corisande.com

www.soft-options.co.uk

www.soft-options.co.uk/disillusioned.htm

www.corisande.com/news-reports.htm

See the eEurope and Information Society pages of the European Commission

http://europa.eu.int/information_society/index_en.htm

http://europa.eu.int/information_society/eeurope/index_en.htm

http://europa.eu.int/information_society/newsroom/library/referencedoc/
   eEurope_EN.pdf

Explore some of the Internet pioneers

www.upmystreet.com

www.expedia.com

www.marriott.com

www.easyjet.com

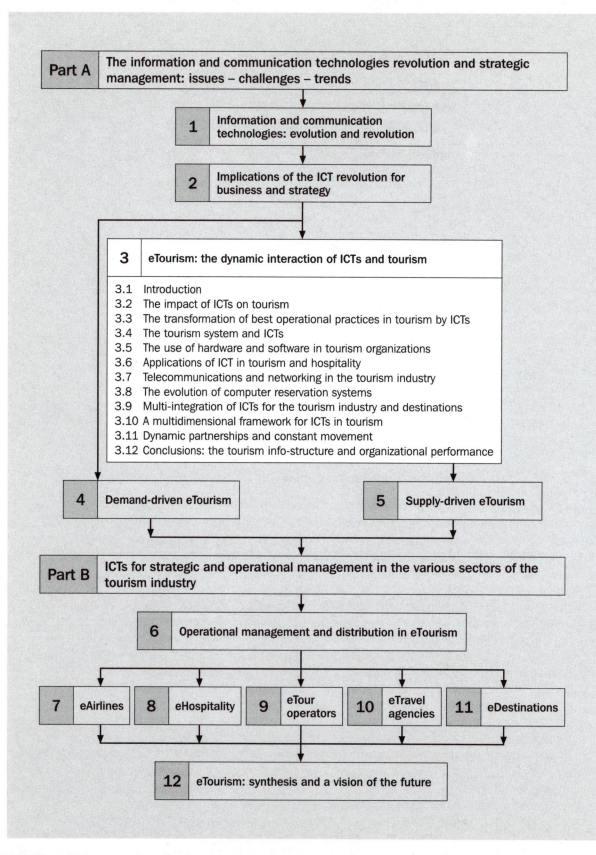

Part A	The information and communication technologies revolution and strategic management: issues – challenges – trends

1	Information and communication technologies: evolution and revolution

2	Implications of the ICT revolution for business and strategy

3	eTourism: the dynamic interaction of ICTs and tourism

3.1 Introduction
3.2 The impact of ICTs on tourism
3.3 The transformation of best operational practices in tourism by ICTs
3.4 The tourism system and ICTs
3.5 The use of hardware and software in tourism organizations
3.6 Applications of ICT in tourism and hospitality
3.7 Telecommunications and networking in the tourism industry
3.8 The evolution of computer reservation systems
3.9 Multi-integration of ICTs for the tourism industry and destinations
3.10 A multidimensional framework for ICTs in tourism
3.11 Dynamic partnerships and constant movement
3.12 Conclusions: the tourism info-structure and organizational performance

4	Demand-driven eTourism

5	Supply-driven eTourism

Part B	ICTs for strategic and operational management in the various sectors of the tourism industry

6	Operational management and distribution in eTourism

7	eAirlines	8	eHospitality	9	eTour operators	10	eTravel agencies	11	eDestinations

12	eTourism: synthesis and a vision of the future

3

eTourism: the dynamic interaction of ICTs and tourism

Chapter objectives

The purpose of this chapter is to introduce the eTourism concept and to demonstrate technological solutions and equipment used in tourism. The chapter also explores how each element of ICT is utilized in the tourism industry. Technological convergence combined with the integration of the tourism industry and the local economy can offer powerful technological solutions, supporting organizations in the industry and enhancing their competitiveness. Thus, the learning objectives may be defined as:

- Define the eTourism concept
- Introduce ICTs that are used extensively in tourism
- Understand the basic structure and components of the tourism system
- Explore some generic ICT applications and identify them as technological enablers for the tourism industry
- Engage with the concepts of computer reservation systems and global distribution channels
- Appreciate the issue of technological convergence in the tourism field
- Conceptualize a framework for dynamic use of ICTs
- Identify the tourism organization stakeholders and explore how ICTs can integrate the entire industry and economy

3.1 Introduction

The tourism system is inevitably influenced by the new business environment created by the diffusion of ICTs. Information technology is one of the external environment elements for tourism, travel and hospitality, although in recent years technological developments have supported tourism innovation and vice versa. ICTs have become an imperative partner, increasingly offering the interface between consumers and suppliers globally. 'Tourism is a very information intensive activity. In few other areas of activity are the generation, gathering, processing, application and communication of information as important for day-to-day operations as they are for the travel and tourism industry' (Poon, 1993). Unlike durable goods, **intangible** and variable tourism services cannot be physically displayed or inspected at the point of sale before purchasing, as tourism services are normally bought before the time of their use and away from the place of consumption. Tourism products are therefore almost exclusively dependent upon representations and descriptions, i.e. information in printed or audio-visual formats. Often these representations are made by friends and relatives, as well as the travel trade, rather than tourism principals or destination authorities. Communications and information transmission tools are therefore indispensable to the **global marketing** of the **tourism industry** (Sheldon, 1997). As a result, consumers undertake a significant amount of risk, not only financially but also psychologically. Holidays are one of the largest expenditures in the annual family budget and consequently they enjoy a large amount of involvement from the entire family.

3.2 The impact of ICTs on tourism

As ICT and tourism developments are closely interrelated, it is often difficult to identify whether ICTs generate or simply facilitate the changes in tourism demand and supply. Perhaps the reality is somewhere in the middle. ICTs provide the tools and enable the evolution of tourism demand and supply by facilitating existing needs and business prospects. Consequently, the tourism industry increases its requirements from ICTs, by expanding its needs and user requirements and by sponsoring technological developments which facilitate its functions. In turn, developments in ICTs offer further tools and greater potential, which are then matched by the requirements of the industry. This is a step approach where one section motivates the other and both move forward at a fast pace. The continuous development of ICTs during the last decade has had profound implications for the whole tourism industry. ICTs incorporate not only software, hardware and netware but also information, management and telecommunication systems to enable the processing and flow of tourism information within and between organizations, as well as all equipment utilized for the production of commodities and the provision of services.

eTourism reflects the **digitalization** of all processes and value chains in the tourism, travel, hospitality and catering industries. At the tactical level, it includes eCommerce and applies ICTs for maximizing the efficiency and effectiveness of the tourism organization. At the strategic level, eTourism revolutionizes all business processes, the entire value chain as well as the strategic relationships of tourism organizations with all their stakeholders. eTourism determines the competitiveness of the organization by taking advantage of intranets for reorganizing internal processes, extranets for developing transactions with trusted partners and the Internet for interacting with all its stakeholders. The eTourism concept includes all business functions (eCommerce and eMarketing, eFinance and eAccounting, eHRM, eProcurement, eR&D and eProduction) as well as eStrategy, ePlanning and eManagement for all sectors of the tourism industry, including tourism, travel, transport, leisure, hospitality, principals, intermediaries and public sector organizations. As demonstrated in Figure 3.1, eTourism bundles together three distinctive disciplines, namely:

■ business management,
■ information systems and management, and
■ tourism.

The importance of and necessity for using ICTs in the tourism industry is a relatively new subject in the literature. Following the general routes of ICT penetration into business environments, several authors have demonstrated the benefits of ICTs for the operations of tourism enterprises (O'Connor, 1999; Inkpen, 1998; Marcussen, 1999a, 1999b). Hitherto the literature is dominated by applications that belong to the 'data processing' era, and thus illustrate how technology can improve traditional operational business practices. Fewer examples elaborate on the use of ICTs for strategic and tactical management and purposes. The strategic dimension is gradually emerging in the literature, with a number of

Figure 3.1 The eTourism concept and eTourism domains

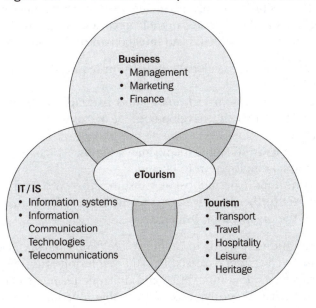

studies on strategic ICT applications and tourism business re-engineering recently appearing.

3.3 The transformation of best operational practices in tourism by ICTs

ICTs transform the best operational practices and provide opportunities for business expansion in all geographical, marketing and operational senses. However, the industry has long been regarded as a labour industry and, as a result, several practices are still carried out in a traditional manner. The dominance of small enterprises means that ICT utilization has been kept to a minimum. Similarly with other industries, ICT penetration in tourism should provide strategic tools for across-industry networking, for adding value to products and for enabling organizations to interact with all stakeholders in a profitable way. In addition, ICTs can improve the managerial processes in order to ameliorate control and decision-making procedures, and to support enterprises in reacting efficiently to environmental changes and consumer trends. Increasingly ICTs play a critical role in **customer relationship management (CRM)** as they enable organizations to interact with customers and continuously alter their product for meeting and exceeding customer expectations. Managing customer relationships on a continuous (365/24) and global basis is of paramount importance for the successful tourism organization of the future.

ICTs should also protect organizations from competitive disadvantages, as they now have to compete on a global basis and to fight against traditional and new competitors who use ICTs to access consumers and enlarge their market share (e.g. Travelocity, Expedia.com, Marriott.com). Gradually the industry attempts to identify possible ways of enhancing its competitiveness by employing the emerging tools and re-engineering all processes. Hoffman (1995) suggests that several major drivers make ICTs an integral part of the tourism industry, namely:

- economic necessity, as global competition requires maximum efficiency on a worldwide basis;
- rapid advancements in technology and particularly the proliferation of the Internet as well as the development of 3G mobile devices and interactive television;
- improvements in ICT price/performance ratios, which yield better productivity for capital employed in ICTs; and
- rising consumer expectations, as consumers become used to advanced products, expect further improvements to the service and anticipate communicating with the organization interactively.

The tourism industry needs to become *more flexible, more efficient and quicker* in responding to consumer requests. The ICT revolution offers a variety of tools and mechanisms that allow innovative and dynamic players to take advantage and strengthen their competitiveness. ICTs enable tourism organizations to have a global presence as well as to formulate partnerships with organizations around the world in an efficient and cost-effective manner. In addition, ICTs offer unique opportunities for research and development that enable the industry to provide specialized products to niche markets, and thus achieve competitive advantage through differentiation. ICTs can also assist the reduction of operation and communication costs by:

- integrating operational systems;
- maximizing internal efficiency;
- decreasing the number of people required for back-office jobs;
- reducing the amount of face-to-face or telephone communications; and
- enabling consumers to have access to all information that was previously obtainable only by direct contact with tourist organizations.

Constant interactivity with consumers and partners supports flexible and competitive pricing, which can maximize the yield of enterprises. Monitoring sales by the minute allows marketers to undertake the appropriate adjustments to the product and price or/and to initiate promotional campaigns in order to maximize sales. ICTs can alert organizations about excess capacity or demand, and thus provide more flexible management. This is particularly valuable for organizations that do not necessarily operate in one location (e.g. tour operators or airlines) as they can divert their capacity towards profitable segments or regions. As tourism products are perishable they cannot be stored for later consumption, and therefore on-line auctions and last-minute offers provide a new and interactive avenue for disposing of excess capacity. Specialist organizations such as last-minute.com and QXL.com have developed their entire business model around this proposition and allow organizations to dispose of unwanted inventory anonymously without spoiling their brand.

However, it needs to be recognized that ICT developments also contribute to the *cost* equation of tourism organizations, thus a detailed cost-and-benefit analysis should be drawn for each enterprise. The cost of purchasing hardware, software and communication packages as well as developing and maintaining their on-line presence is considerable for many organizations. The development of an info-space for each organization requires the design and construction of its Internet presence, hosting on reliable servers as well as ongoing maintenance and regular updating. Developing interfaces between internal **legacy systems** and the systems of other organizations may also require a considerable investment. Marketing the Internet service and registration of **domain name** may include advertising fees for representation in search engines and other sites. Interconnectivity with travel **intermediaries** and portals, such as TravelWeb, Travelocity and Expedia would normally cost a standard fee plus commission. Development of new procedures may also create more costs, as organizations need to be prepared to support a wider range of interaction with their stakeholders – such as eMail, telephone calls and requests for on-line help. Finally, although ICTs become increasingly user-friendly, recruitment of experts and training costs of personnel should also be calculated in the costs.

These developments have direct impacts on the *competitiveness* of enterprises, as they determine the two fundamental roots to competitive advantage, i.e.

differentiation and cost advantage. On the one hand, ICTs enable organizations to differentiate and specialize their products to each consumer. By unwrapping the tourism product and by enabling consumers to put together all the elements for their individual needs, ICTs offer the opportunity to target the market segment of one, i.e. each individual customer. This is only possible because ICTs support flexible and responsive value-added chains and allow consumers to repackage products through endless combinations. On the other hand, ICTs become instrumental for cost management in the industry and particularly for distribution and promotion costs. Organizations around the world have reduced their costs by reducing commission to intermediaries, by trading directly from their web page, or by paying lower distribution fees to electronic intermediaries, or by cutting commission levels and fees. In addition, redesigning processes and eliminating repetitive tasks reduced labour costs and increased efficiency (Buhalis, 1998).

Perhaps more importantly for tourism, ICTs support the newly important element in generating competitive advantage, i.e. *time*. The latter not only assists organizations to share information internally and with partners, and thus maximizes their efficiency, but also allows consumers to interact constantly with tourism suppliers. Consumers can undertake entire transactions from their office or home using the Internet, on a 24-hour, 365-days-a-year basis. Instant confirmation and purchasing means that consumers can also maximize their own efficiency and as a result appreciate the competitive advantage of organizations based on time. Increasingly, consumers will be able to interact through mobile devices and interactive digital television, developing their capabilities further as they will be able to be connected instantly through simpler equipment and interface without having to log on to their computer (Puhretmair et al., 2001; Zipf and Malaka, 2001).

The rapid increase of the *reliability, speed and capacity* of ICTs, in combination with the decrease of their cost, propels enterprises in the tourism industry to adapt and use these new organizational tools heavily. Innovative organizations throughout the industry, such as easyJet, Marriott Hotels and the Tyrolean Tourism Board, have strengthened their competitiveness, increased their market share and enhanced their position by using advanced ICTs and by driving their sector towards a higher level of ICT utilization. However, tourism organizations that fail to incorporate the new tools in their strategic and operational management will increasingly be left behind and will lose market share, jeopardizing their future prosperity. The paradigm shift illustrates that only dynamic and innovative organizations will be able to survive in the future.

3.4 The tourism system and ICTs

It is beyond the scope of this book to discuss the conceptual framework of tourism and to analyse the tourism industry in detail. However a short introduction to the tourism system will perhaps assist readers to appreciate the industry as an enormously complex system of independent providers who aim to serve consumers, normally for profit. A variety of stakeholders have often conflicting needs, wants and interests and the industry has to please an increasingly discerning traveller who is not easily impressed. To appreciate tourism principles, practices and mechanisms readers should read well-established textbooks on the subject (Cooper et al., 1998; Mill and Morrison, 1998; Goeldner et al., 2000).

There are countless *definitions of tourism* and the tourism industry, from a wide range of perspectives. For the purposes of this book, we use the World Tourism Organization's definition of tourism as 'the activities of a persons travelling to a place outside their usual environment for not more than one consecutive year for leisure, business and other purposes'. Leiper (1995) illustrates that the entire tourism system can be defined by five different elements, including a traveller-generating region and a destination region as well as a transit region, a travel and tourism industry and finally the external environment to the system. Figure 3.2 develops this framework further. Not only does it identify the most important service providers at each part of the system, but it also includes several support and supply industries, which are responsible for feeding the tourism industry at the destination level with the necessary **infrastructure** and supplies for its function.

ICTs prevail over the tourism system by establishing an info-space for each tourism organization and by constituting an info-structure within which the entire industry can operate. Within this info-space, industry members can identify market niches, develop partnerships with suppliers and intermediaries, and form virtual corporations for the development and production of tourism products. Hence, a wide range of potential benefits and challenges emerge for all stakeholders, as the technological revolution enables efficient cooperation and offers tools for the globalization of the industry. Effectively, ICTs empower, propel, boost and underpin the emerging globalization of tourism demand and supply experienced worldwide by providing effective tools both to consumers for identifying and purchasing suitable products and to suppliers for developing, managing and distributing their offerings on a global scale (Buhalis, 1998).

ICTs have therefore contributed to the massive *growth* of tourism and the increased volume of supply and demand. This makes ICTs one of the imperative partners of the tourism industry. This partnership is set to become much stronger in the near future, as ICTs become instrumental for the marketing, distribution and industry linkage functions of tourism enterprises whilst consumers depend on technology for fulfilling their dreams and for maximizing the value of their money and time when travelling.

Sheldon (1997) suggests that information is the life-blood of the travel industry, therefore effective use of ICTs is pivotal for its competitiveness and prosperity. Tourism is inevitably influenced by business process re-engineering and the paradigm shift experienced due to the technological revolution. 'A whole system of ICTs is being rapidly diffused throughout the tourism industry and no player will escape its impacts' (Poon, 1993). The penetration of ICTs in tourism is to a large extent *customer driven*, as consumers familiarize themselves with new ICTs and seek electronic interaction with the industry. Interestingly, most of the technological innovations are demanded by consumers or are introduced by a very

Figure 3.2 The tourism industry and tourism system

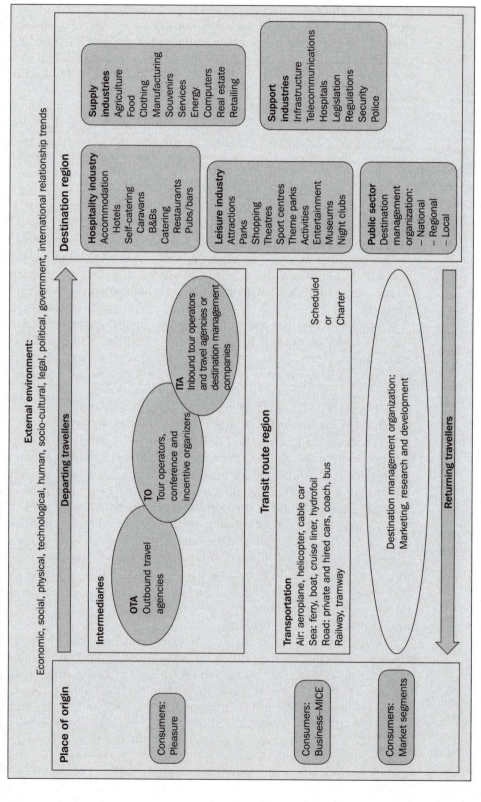

Source: Adapted from Leiper (1995); Cooper and Buhalis (1998)

small number of far-sighted tourism organizations. Increasingly it is evident that timely and accurate information relevant to consumer needs has great implications for tourist experience. It is one of the key determinants of demand satisfaction and of the ability of enterprises to offer suitable products (Buhalis, 1998; O'Connor, 1999; Vlitos-Rowe, 1995; Stipanuk, 1993).

3.5 The use of hardware and software in tourism organizations

A very wide range of ICTs is used in order to exchange information and to facilitate the operations of the tourism industry. Most of these technologies enable tourism distribution channel members to communicate with each other and with consumers in order to exchange information, contracts, reservations and payments. The technologies used in tourism and hospitality can be examined under the following headings:

- hardware,
- software and computer applications, and
- communications (including telecommunications) and networking.

Often these elements are inseparable, and hence it is almost impossible to isolate each element from the entire picture. The nature of each medium is briefly analysed below, while its contribution to the tourism industry operation is explained. This is inevitably very brief and non-technical but other resources offer much greater detail for the interested readers.

Firstly, *hardware* components of computer systems include the central processing unit (CPU), *input devices* such as keyboards, mouses and touch screens, as well as storage devices such as **hard disks**, CD-ROMs and magnetic tapes. *Output devices*, such as display terminals, printers and audio output, are critical for the operation of all tourism applications, as they not only enable operators to interact with computers but also provide displays and communication media with consumers. *Mainframes and mini-computers* have been widely used in the tourism industry in order to support the reservation and operational functions of most large organizations, in particular airlines and hotel chains. Mainframes were the only computers in the early 1970s capable of processing massive data and supporting hundreds of terminals. This made them very useful for handling and disseminating information, as well as for distributing tourism products to airline branches and airport stations through **computer reservation systems (CRS)**. Mainframes have a massive computing power and are nowadays used by global distribution systems. Some of the most information-intensive intermediaries use them to support their eCommerce applications. However, in recent years, as smaller computers have gained greater capabilities, the popularity of mainframes has declined due to their cost and complexity. Today, a **personal computer (PC)** can probably do much more than a mainframe would have been able to do in the 1970s. Contemporary mainframes have massive memory and extremely rapid processing power. They are widely used to empower most of the reservations and management departments in airlines and hotel chains. Mini-computers are smaller (perhaps the size of an office desk), cheaper and equally reliable but with less process capability than mainframes. They can also support several terminals, and therefore allow users from different departments to share files, reservations, accounts and to work in parallel. Often mini-computers are used within big hotels, theme parks or regional airline branches. The major advantages of mainframes and mini-computers in comparison with PCs include their speed, reliability, computing capability and the ability to support many users at the same time. However, they cost more, require more space and controlled climate conditions, and need skilled personnel to operate them as they use less user-friendly software and interfaces (Beekman, 2001).

It was personal computers, or microcomputers, in the 1980s that revolutionized the modern business world, introducing massive processing capabilities on the desktop while becoming remarkably affordable and user-friendly. Laptops even enabled executives to carry all this computing capability with them and to connect to their central systems for access to the entire network of files and resources. Although most PCs operate as stand-alone terminals, they are increasingly able to support parallel operations with several other terminals, as well as being used as networking terminals. PCs are widely used in most types of tourism and hospitality organizations. They are particularly useful for smaller organizations as they support most of their operations through a single computer. PCs are also used to connect with mainframe and mini-computers in order to give access to data kept there. They are used in both the front and back office of tourism enterprises, as they support the entire range of business functions including reservations, ticketing, billing, guest history, administration, marketing, personnel, accounting, control and departmental communication.

Compact Disk–Read Only Memory (CD-ROM) technology enables PCs to store and present information in text/images/photos/video forms that require massive storage capabilities. This technology empowers the rapid diffusion of multimedia technology for individual users. Tourism organizations often provide CD-ROMs as part of their promotional material and enable both individuals and the travel trade to experience multimedia presentations from a destination or a tourism product. CD-ROMs are ideal for the creation and distribution of electronic brochures by using multimedia, as organizations can provide data-heavy applications that can be viewed instantly without having to download them from the Internet, thus saving time and money. However, the development of high **bandwidth** will inevitably offer the opportunity to download files instantly, and therefore the future of CD-ROMs is questionable.

Self-service terminals or kiosks are expanding in usage in the tourism industry as points of information and sale. In most cases they sell tickets for transportation media, while being widely used as a 'night room seller' or 'night clerk' in USA hotels/inns/airports/stations. They often incorporate a computer, a credit card reader, a cash receiver, a printer and a modem and they administrate transactions and issue necessary travel documentation or keys. They can be stand-alone kiosks or they can be connected with reservation facilities to provide up-to-date availability and support reservations. Information on weather forecasts, attractions, transportation, catering and entertainment is usually found in self-service terminals. Although travel agencies such as Thomas Cook have experimented selling package holidays through kiosks in several locations, this has not proved financially viable, and thus self-service terminals are used for only fairly simple products at the place of demand. The integration of the Internet with self-service terminals makes them powerful tools for information and distribution as it enables them to access a wide range of resources on a global basis. Providing location-dependent information and interacting with mobile devices will enable users to download large applications, presentations and graphs and print maps, vouchers and programmes at the destination. Self-service terminals can have great benefits for tourism enterprises and destinations, as they increase their distribution network, labour efficiencies and ubiquity. Consumers would be able to navigate the screens successfully and acceptably quickly, and identify and purchase the products they require at convenient locations and times. Existing self-service terminals such as ATMs and telephone booths can all be integrated into a global web of interaction and service delivery. In several countries, bank ATMs are increasingly used as self-service terminals for distributing local tourism products. As telephone services are under-utilized due to the proliferation of mobile phones, British Telecom, for example, is gradually installing intelligent self-terminals in phone booths in order to provide this kind of service. Consumers can benefit enormously as they normally find these terminals informative, convenient and available when required.

Mobile devices are already used widely in tourism. Voice dominates and mobile telephony is one of the most frequently used media for communication between customers on the move and the tourism industry. This has greatly improved the efficiency of the communications between employees and their organizations as well as with consumers. Text messaging is also increasingly used through SMS and pagers. Although mobile communications and 'Internet on the go' will clearly have a major impact, there will be several problems to be resolved on the way. The recent introduction of WAP services has demonstrated that consumers find it frustrating to access information through small screens and are not prepared to wait and pay for long periods of time for the information to be downloaded. Eventually the technical issues will be resolved and by the year 2005 a range of third-generation (3G) terminals and applications will be in use. The 3G mobile devices, which will enable interactivity with the Internet and instant communication, will revolutionize the tourism industry once again as they will support the impulse buyer. Being permanently on the Internet will allow consumers to access location-dependent information, making reservations on their way, cutting travel planning requirements significantly. The industry will find it extremely challenging to cope with this type of consumer behaviour as it will need to be enormously flexible and capable of responding to consumer demand at very short notice (Puhretmair et al., 2001; Zipf and Malaka, 2001).

Software and computer applications are used to operate the above-mentioned apparatus in order to perform tasks for end-users. Software can be either purpose-built and **proprietary** for an organization or a standardized (off-the-shelf) package that performs the same functions for all users. Werthner and Klein (1999) classify software in a number of generic categories, as illustrated in Table 3.1.

Table 3.1 Software classification scheme

Type of software	Characteristics
Standard software	Operating systems such as Windows and UNIX, programming languages with graphical programming tools and databases used in tourism for generic business functions
Applications	Business applications supporting human and business functions, such as property management systems or computer reservation systems. These include expert systems and artificial intelligence
Software process	The process of designing and implement software, software engineering, such as workflow procedures, Computer Supported Cooperative Work (CSCW)
System architectures and networks	Worldwide distributed systems accessible from remote locations such as the Internet with its TPC/IP protocol. These support extranets and Internet representations
Media	Handling of text, graphics, sound and video in a comprehensive way, these enable the development of multimedia presentations
User interfaces	Development from character-oriented terminals to window-based and graphical user interfaces (GUIs). **Virtual-reality** applications enable users to be part of the digital world

Source: Based on Werthner and Klein (1999)

Most of the ICT applications used in the tourism industry are a combination of purpose-built and standardized software. Software houses tend to develop a comprehensive application for a particular client and then develop generalized solutions to make them suitable for other prospective clients of the same sector. Additional modules are often added to address particular requirements of individual clients. In addition, tourism and hospitality organizations use standardized business software such as Microsoft Office for word processing, presentations, computations, etc.

Software in tourism and hospitality is often divided into front-office applications, in other words ICTs that facilitate transactions with customers such as reservations, check-in, check-out and ordering systems, with applications that include travel agencies' terminals, airlines' check-in systems and restaurant terminals, and back-office applications, which support organizational needs and managerial requirements. These include planning, financial and management accounting, personnel, payroll, supplies, inventory control, security, energy control, food and beverage control and management information systems. Integration of these two types of applications maximizes efficiency and reduces the cost of data processing.

Multimedia combine time-based data (such as voice, animation and video) with space-based data (such as graphics, text and images) and create animated and attractive presentations (Szabo et al., 1994). In the tourism industry a number of these different **media**, such as video, computer animation, photography and music, are used in order to present tourism information for destinations or tourism products. Multimedia are used for distribution through the Internet as well as through self-service kiosks located in information centres or key points at destinations. CD-ROMs are often used to store the different multimedia components as they can be stored, copied and transferred relatively easily. The major advantage of this technique is that it can provide users with an aesthetically appealing presentation while it demonstrates images of the tourism products at a fraction of the time required to download and at no telecommunication cost. However, multimedia are still quite expensive to produce and operate while dependent on broadband capacity on the Internet, which is not always available to end-users. A wide range of audio-visual equipment as well as artistic skills for the producer are essential, and thus it can be expensive to put them together. Finally, multimedia systems should be flexible enough to adjust to their users' wishes, depending on the degree of familiarity with a product or destination.

Electronic funds transfer (EFT) facilitates the electronic transfer of money from customers' to service providers' accounts through credit and debit card transactions. Electronic funds transfer at point of sale (EFTPOS) reads and prints credit card details, thus the time and paperwork required are substantially reduced. The wide usage of EFTPOS enables purchasing through self-service terminals. International credit and debit cards offer an established clearance centre, and thus offer great benefits for the tourism industry as they facilitate money transactions globally. In addition, **Point of sale (POS) systems** enhance intra-organizational transactions and facilitate the billing process within a hotel or a catering enterprise by connecting the different **points of sale** with the central accounting system. POS systems offer many advantages, as they reduce paperwork, and therefore save time, money and labour effort, while minimizing potential mistakes through manual transmission. Better food and beverage control, stock control and supply ordering procedures are also improved.

3.6 Applications of ICT in tourism and hospitality

A wide range of hardware, software and netware is used in the tourism and hospitality industries, as illustrated in Figure 3.3. Technological solutions are normally incorporated to increase efficiency and reduce the cost and time required for undertaking particular activities and processes. Although each of these systems may be standing alone, it is their integration in to a comprehensive information management system that can maximize their operational effectiveness and enable them to contribute to the organizational strategic competitiveness. Each of these systems will be examined in greater detail within the context of industry sectors in Chapters 7 to 11.

ICTs support all business functions and so the use of ICTs in tourism and hospitality is pervasive, as information is essential for both the day-to-day operations and the strategic management of tourism. Traditionally technological solutions have been used as stand-alone entities and until recently a fairly low level of technological integration was evident. Figure 3.4 illustrates that technology supports vital everyday functions and enables organizations to communicate and cooperate with other tourism and hospitality enterprises, their consumers as well as their partners and suppliers. These functions are not only part of the core business of the organization but also inform the strategic considerations as they determine the competitiveness and the ability to grow. **Scalability**, robustness and integration are therefore critical.

Figure 3.3 Examples of information technology applications used in tourism

- Entire range of hardware, software and netware
- Stand-alone computers and network devices
- Office automation, reservation, accounting, payroll and procurement management applications
- Portable/wireless communication devices
- Internal management tools such as management support systems, decision support systems and management information systems
- Tailor-made internal management applications
- Databases and knowledge management systems
- Internet/intranets/extranets
- Networks with partners for regular transactions (EDI or extranets)
- Networking and open distribution of products through the Internet
- Computer reservation systems (CRSs)
- Global distribution systems (GDSs) (e.g. Galileo, SABRE, Amadeus, Worldspan)
- Switch applications for hospitality organizations (e.g. THISCO and WIZCOM)
- Destination management systems (DMSs)
- Internet-based travel intermediaries (e.g. Expedia.com, Travelocity.com, Preview Travel, Priceline.com etc.)
- Mobile/WAP-based reservation systems
- Traditional distribution technologies supporting automated systems (e.g. videotext)
- Calling centres
- Interactive digital television (IDTV)
- CD-ROMs
- Kiosks and touch-screen terminals

Figure 3.4 Critical tourism and hospitality functions supported by ICTs

- Front office: reservations, check-in, payments
- Back office: accounting, payroll, human resources management, marketing
- Customer entertainment and service
- Communication with consumers and partners
- Marketing research and industrial espionage
- Reaction and management of unexpected events
- Flexible and dynamic pricing through yield management
- Differentiation and personalization of products
- Monitoring performance indicators and building feedback mechanisms
- Control of business processes and personnel

3.7 Telecommunications and networking in the tourism industry

All types of telecommunications (telephone, telex and fax) have been used extensively throughout the tourism industry worldwide. Although *telephone* conversation is a personal and direct way of communication, linguistic problems, time-zone differences and its prohibitive cost limit its international usage. Mobile telephony in the 1990s revolutionized communications as it enabled people to be constantly in touch. Other *mobile communications* such as CB communications, bleepers, pagers and message pagers, widely used in the 1990s, are being integrated with mobile phones, which offer all these services through one device. Mobile telephony has been widely used by tourism firms that need to be constantly in touch with tour guides, coach drivers etc., and has contributed to their efficiency dramatically. The third- and future-generation mobile phones will allow the transfer of data as well as location-dependent information and are expected to provide the next major technological revolution in tourism. On the one hand the mobile revolution will enable travel and hospitality organizations to target consumers who are currently at their location, and on the other hand it will empower consumers to search available products that meet their search criteria and are accessible locally.

Telex was for years the most prominent communication method and has contributed greatly to communications in the tourism industry. As it transmits text reliably and inexpensively without requiring the simultaneous availability of sender and receiver, it has been extensively used especially in regions with inadequate telephone networks. However, as computer communications and faxes prevail, the telex is limited to communication with developing-world countries with unreliable telecommunications infrastructures and it is gradually being transformed into a computer-based system using a different communication network. The commercial introduction of the *telefax* in the 1980s allowed the transmission of images over phone lines and enhanced the efficiency of tourism operations significantly. Although its operational cost is the same as a phone call, information can be communicated more efficiently, as it allows transmission of readily available documents and graphics. Fax technology does not require technical skills or the simultaneous presence of sender and receiver, and therefore has penetrated the tourism marketplace very efficiently (Beekman, 2001).

Despite the above rapid developments, a large percentage of the travel industry in the UK and several European countries still use **videotext** (often referred to as Viewdata in the UK, Bildschirmtext in Germany and Minitel in France) as a main communication tool. Videotext is a widely used communication **protocol** that enables two-way communication between a user's display terminal and a host computer via telephone lines (Inkpen, 1998; Beaver, 1993; Bennett and Radburn, 1991). The system is based on a special modem, a **dumb terminal** that can be a TV monitor or a PC, and a telephone line. Users select a host computer and 'log in', in order to exchange information, request availability, make a booking, as well as offer personal and credit card details for purchasing a product. Three networks of dedicated telephone lines are used in the UK, namely AT&T (originated from Istel), Prestel and Imminus (based on the original British Midland Bank–Thomas Cook's system Fastrac) (Inkpen, 1998). Videotext used to be the standard technology in the European tourism industry, helping tour operators to communicate with travel agencies in the 1980s and most of the 1990s. Beaver (1993) suggests that 'all UK travel agencies, nearly 7000 of them have connections to viewdata networks averaging around 3 terminals an agency, enabling every type of booking to be undertaken electronically. Similarly, all French agencies have Minitel connections, while German agents are connected to BTX'. However, the life of videotext is nearly at its end. Despite the cost advantage of purchasing videotext terminals and the relatively easy operational environment, its limited capabilities, slow speed, lack of compatibility with CRSs, unsophisticated animation and low reliability drive the industry towards the adaptation of PC terminals and full adoption of the Internet as their preferred communication method. Only a few die-hard old-fashioned agencies will continue to use these systems until they are disconnected by tour operators and airlines, which is anticipated before 2005.

Teletext is an one-way communication media that utilizes the television broadcasting systems to provide the public with information. Users with appropriate TV sets can watch menu-driven pages with information and simplified graphs. The system normally provides information such as news, weather reports, airport arrivals and departures as well as last-minute package holiday offers and is being recognized as a primitive type of home travel shopping. Teletext is also widely used in the UK tourism industry as a way of communicating distressed inventory to lower socio-economic classes. Traditionally tour operators would demonstrate their distressed capacity and viewers would call to enquire about and purchase heavily discounted packages. Teletext is a time-consuming method of retrieving only limited information, such as destination, day of departure and price; viewers have to telephone for details and reservations. Nevertheless, it has proved to be one of the most efficient ways of announcing special last-minute offers to the price-conscious market and it was certainly one of the few vehicles to bridge the gap between consumers and suppliers in the pre-Internet era. It is still used by lower economic classes as a method to get access to distressed capacity while the medium is gradually being modernized through the development of an Internet site (**www.teletext.com**), which offers similar information in a much more interactive interface.

In the pre-Internet era, *Electronic Data Interchange (EDI)* used computer networks to enable computer file interchange of standard transaction documents such as invoices, bills or purchase orders between organizations. EDI transmits structured transactions with distinct fields, such as transaction data, amount, sender and recipient's name. This assists organizations in exchanging information, orders and invoices without human involvement. In tourism, for example, this can be used for travel agencies to transfer bookings to a tour operator's database and again for a tour operator to provide rooming lists for their hotel suppliers. Invoices can be directed backwards and payment receipts can be generated automatically by the system. EDI therefore enhances communication efficiency and reduces labour and transaction costs and encourages firms to continue doing business with their partners. Although EDI is still used for large amounts of transactions mainly between larger organizations, transactions and interchanges on the Internet have replaced EDI with extranets and have also enabled smaller players to take advantage of the efficiency that networking provides (Laudon and Laudon, 2002; Reynolds, 1992).

Computer networks link together computers in order to allow users to exchange information and share data and peripherals, such as memory units and printers. Not only do networks enable users to share resources but they are also more reliable, as should one system fail another may continue undertaking tasks (Werthner and Klein, 1999). The marriage of computers and telecommunications, defined as the communication of information by electronic means over some distance, has enhanced the scope and scale of ICT usage in tourism. In the 1990s, networking through the Internet enabled *inter-organizational networking* on a global scale and empowered tourism firms and destinations to communicate directly with prospective travellers, demonstrating their products and services. Even the smallest organizations now have the opportunity to promote their offerings on the Internet as well as communicate with partners around the world efficiently and effectively.

Connecting the power of the Internet with *intra-organizational networking* empowers the re-engineering of business processes and functions within an enterprise resource planning framework that allows organizations to integrate all their processes, functions and resources towards maximizing their efficiency and effectiveness. Intra-organizational networking is supported by two main types of networks, i.e. *local area networks (LANs)* and *wide area network (WANs)*. LANs are frequently used by single organizations, over a limited distance, and help users to share information and resources. LANs are widely used in hotels and travel agencies, where different departments use the same databases, such as inventory or guest history, for planning, billing, accounting and reports production. National tourism organizations often use LANs for managing and distributing information in their headquarters. Similarly, travel agencies use LANs in order to enable multiple usage of their resources and to share fewer ports to CRSs, databases and specialized ticket printers. WANs interconnect computers in a larger geographical area and allow information communication between headquarters and branches. These are used particularly by organizations that have to support a network of branches, typically airlines and hotel chains. Braham (1988) analysed the WAN utilized by Hilton, which facilitates organization, administration and reservations tasks. WANs are normally used in CRSs and GDSs, as they can offer on-line room/seat inventory management for multinational corporations. Connections may either be dedicated to a WAN, and therefore, undertake all transactions and processes at real time on-line or they can be used occasionally when it is required ad hoc and/or during prearranged times (batch process). A range of connection methods are used, such as cable connections, microwave transmission and satellites. LANs and WANs are indispensable tools in the tourism industry, as they enable staff in different locations to share information on schedules and inventory, as well as reservations and customers' history. Despite their installation and operation costs, computer networks assist employees to share information and resources, and therefore, ultimately improve efficiency and reduce costs.

The growth of international *networks* has prompted organizations to change from using centralized database applications to collaborative computing and client–server architectures, where resources are stored centrally within a world-wide distributed network enabling the sharing of information, programmes and networks (Werthner and Klein, 1999). To explore the capabilities of the Internet and interconnectivity further, networks need to increase their speed and reliability. Broadband connections offer a faster, more reliable service that can take advantage of multimedia content. *ISDN (integrated services digital network)* is an international standardized network capable of facilitating voice, images, data and video distribution at a fraction of the time required by other systems (Bubley and Bennett, 1994). The ISDN key characteristics are integration of different existing networks; continuous capability of signalling; digital transmission quality for all information including voices; sharing of one interface by several terminals; and fast transmission rates. Many telephone companies offer **digital subscriber lines** (**DSL** or IDSL or HDSL) as a newer, faster and cheaper alternative to ISDN. Their ultra-high-speed and constantly connected signals bring the advantages of a direct reliable and fast Internet connection to home and small businesses (Laudon and Laudon, 2002; Beekman, 2001). As ISDN and DSL lines facilitate high-bandwidth transmission and assist the operation of multimedia applications, they are used increasingly by the tourism industry for providing electronic and interactive brochures and video on demand, as well as for the ability to undertake simultaneous transactions over one physical line. Prospective travellers can select their holidays through multimedia experiences, book products and perhaps talk to assistants in a calling centre if they require help simultaneously through one single line. This is expected to stimulate consumer interests and desire for travelling activity, while it will provide the travel trade with an overwhelming tool for promotion and communication.

Virtual reality will be the next stage, where users will be able to experience a destination or tourism product through all their senses. By integrating multimedia and also by incorporating sense stimulants, virtual reality aims to simulate a 'real' experience. Users will be able to see and navigate within a space, hear local sounds, and smell, taste and touch local products and items, all from the comfort of their armchairs. Sceptics maintain that this will reduce the desire of prospective travellers to go to places, while others believe that the majority of virtual-reality users would then like to experience the 'real thing', increasing the travel demand.

The integration of a series of high-capacity communication channels in the *information superhighway* essentially converges media, telecommunications and information technology. This increases the interactivity between consumers and tourism suppliers and enables the provision of tailormade information and marketing material to meet the needs of individual tourists. As a result, ICTs have increased their overall contribution to the tourism industry and have become the nucleus of the entire industry by bridging demand and supply. This will gradually lead to the development of personalized electronic and multimedia brochures, designed to reflect the requirements, preferences and past experiences of individual travellers. Blended with mobile devices, ICTs will be able to provide every type of information on the go and will support travellers by identifying personalized information wherever they are. Not only will this mean a reduction in wasted paper brochures, but there will also be the opportunity to demonstrate more parts of the tourism product in a more attractive and realistic way. The provision of textual data, graphics, pictures, video and sounds easily and inexpensively and, perhaps more importantly, the personalization of the information, will gradually empower marketers to target mini-segments with specific information with regard to needs and desires.

3.8 The evolution of Computer Reservation Systems

Several major applications are based on the computing and telecommunication technologies described above to offer services in the tourism industry. Undoubtedly, *Computer Reservation Systems (CRSs)* have had the most crucial contribution of ICTs to the tourism industry in the 1980s and have dominated the industry. Essentially they are computerized systems that assist tourism enterprises with handling their inventories profitably and with facilitating the tourism products distribution. CRSs are normally operated by tourist producers such as airlines, hotels and tour operators and are distributed nationally or globally, via computerized or videotext systems. They normally use mainframes and extensive networks to support many remote terminals in travel agencies or other tourism enterprises. Since the 1980s, CRSs have experienced a great expansion, affecting almost all tourism enterprises. The instant update of the information and the ability to provide specific information and to support reservation/confirmation/ purchase of a wide range of tourism products, are the greatest advantages of a CRS. However, the installation and usage costs, lack of user-friendliness and bias in favour of their vendors are significant disadvantages.

They originally appeared in the early 1960s, aiming to offer an efficient tool for handling and managing inventory. The rapid growth of both tourism demand and supply in previous decades had demonstrated that the industry could be managed only by powerful computerized systems. Airlines were the pioneers in introducing this technology, as they replaced their manual booking systems with electronic databases. Soon, international hotel chains and tour operators realized the potential and followed suit by developing centralized information and reservation systems. CRS is often used as an umbrella term to include the entire variety of systems used. CRSs can provide important strategic tools for both enterprises and destinations, while they can also form autonomous strategic business units (SBUs) and act as a new independent tourism distribution industry. Figure 3.5 illustrates the specific needs of all parties operating a CRS as well as their mission.

Airline computer reservations systems emerged to become *global distribution systems* (GDSs), incorporating a comprehensive range of services and products and providing a global distribution info-structure for the entire industry. CRSs and GDSs were the most important facilitators of change in the tourism industry before the arrival of the Internet, as they were established as a comprehensive

Figure 3.5 Need for and mission of CRS services

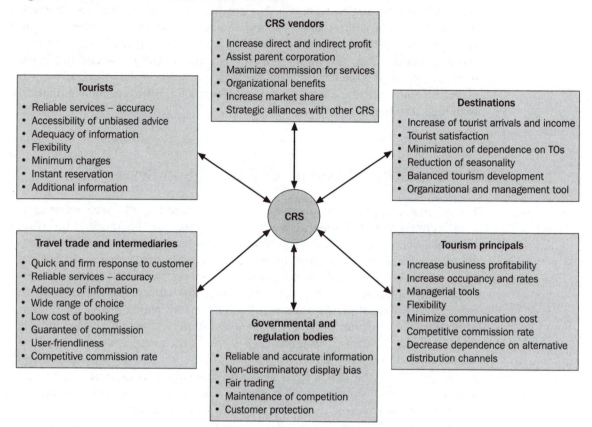

travel marketing and distribution system and were often called travel supermarkets (Go, 1992). The need for GDSs arises from both the demand and supply sides as well as from the expansion of the tourism industry in recent decades.

GDSs satisfy the need of **consumers** for easy access to transparent and easily comparable information on a wide variety of choices of travel, lodging and leisure services, and to the actual prices and availability of such services. Consumers also want immediate confirmation and speedy documentation of their reservations; they require information on attractions and travel formalities, as well as inexpensive and standardized communication with prospective suppliers. The satisfaction of tourism demand depends on the accuracy and relevance of information as well as the promptness of responding to consumers' requests.

As information is described as the life-blood or the cement that holds together the industry, ICTs are used to facilitate and manage the drastic expansion of tourism enterprises and destinations globally. **Tourism suppliers or principals** use CRSs and GDSs to manage and distribute their capacity. CRSs offer internal solutions for controlling inventory and for demand management. GDSs can be characterized as the 'circulation system' of the tourism product in the international market. CRSs and GDSs enable tourism providers to control, promote and sell their products internationally, while assisting them to increase **occupancy/**

load factor levels and to reduce **seasonality**. In addition, GDSs often cost less in comparison with other distribution options, while enabling flexible pricing and capacity alterations, in order to adjust tourism supply to demand fluctuations. CRSs and GDSs can also reduce communication costs, while they may also provide managerial information on demand patterns or competitors' position (Sheldon, 1993).

GDSs also serve the *travel trade (intermediaries)* as they support quick and firm responses to customers' enquiries by making tourism products accessible efficiently and inexpensively. The reliability, adequacy and accuracy of the information listed in the system are of course critical factors for the success of a GDS. Moreover, they reduce communication/reservation costs and facilitate commission payments within the tourism industry. GDSs also tend to generate net financial benefits for their owners/vendors in return for their investment on the system. This return includes:

- gross income from commissions generated by the system and subscription;
- participation and rental fees;
- assistance in the promotion of the parent company through preferential display, especially in airline CRSs and in GDSs (although this has been made illegal in GDSs);
- organizational and information management benefits from the efficiency improvement.

The GDS industry emerges as a market in its own right, and therefore causes fierce competition between suppliers. Often GDSs' owners attempt to increase commissions charged to participants as well as bias the system in favour of their own products. GDSs attempt to maximize their market share through strategic alliances and mergers, which essentially increase the concentration in this industry. GDSs' efficiency and reliability enable principals to distribute and manage their reservations globally, by bridging consumer needs with the tourism supply. Hence, great synergies are achieved, where globalization drivers stimulate GDS developments and vice versa. Go (1992) identifies four major sets of conditions, namely cost, market, government and competitive drivers (Table 3.2), and demonstrates why the globalization of the tourism industry is closely interrelated with its ability to use computerized systems. Ultimately CRSs and GDSs should aim to increase the satisfaction of their stakeholders (i.e. consumers, principals, travel agencies and shareholders), offer superior products and enable partners to maximize their profitability.

Governmental and regulatory bodies attempt to protect consumers and smaller enterprises in the tourism industry. Consequently, they impose non-discriminatory and anti-trust regulations, in order to ensure that reliable, accurate, and unbiased information is displayed, while a satisfactory level of competition is maintained.

Tourist destinations, increasingly, realize the potentials and build *Destination Management Systems (DMSs)* in order to provide information on locally available attractions and products, and therefore, stimulate their visitation. As discussed in Chapter 11, DMSs can assist regions to reduce their seasonality problems by providing the tools for spreading and balancing tourism demand. Furthermore,

Table 3.2 Computer Reservation Systems and Global Distribution Systems as drivers for the globalization of tourism and hospitality

Cost drivers	Market drivers	Government and regulatory drivers	Competitive drivers
■ Increase efficiency ■ Low distribution cost ■ Low communication cost ■ Low labour cost ■ Minimization of waste factor ■ Facilitator of flexible pricing	■ Satisfy sophisticated demand ■ Flexibility in time of operation ■ Support specialization and differentiation ■ Provide last-minute deals ■ Accurate information ■ Support relationship marketing strategies for frequent flyers/guests ■ Quick reaction to demand fluctuation ■ Multiple/integrated products ■ Yield management ■ Corporate intelligence ■ Marketing research	■ Deregulation ■ Liberalization ■ Government supported	■ Managing networks of enterprises ■ Value-added skill building ■ Flexibility ■ Knowledge acquisition ■ Strategic tool ■ Barrier to entry

Source: Adapted from Go (1992)

DMSs provide organizational tools for destination management and can assist in the reduction of dependencies on existing distribution channels.

3.9 Multi-integration of ICTs for the tourism industry and destinations

The computer hardware and software, telecommunications and applications analysed above highlight that the tourism industry uses a wide range of ICT tools for its operational and strategic management. However, it is larger organizations that use these technologies the most and consequently gain the most benefits. Smaller players have been reluctant to capitalize on these technologies and have only recently become engaged in new technologies. ICTs have progressively become the nucleus for a multi-integrated activity, where integrated ICTs provide a platform for efficient communication in an integrated tourism industry, which, in turn, is integrated with the local business and economy. Thus, there are three levels of **integration**, as illustrated in Figure 3.6, which effectively determine tourists' satisfaction, the prosperity of SMTEs and the economic impacts of the destination at the macro level:

- technological integration and convergence;
- tourism industry integration and value-chain partnership;
- local economy and society integration and coordination.

3.9.1 Technological integration and convergence

The diffusion of ICTs yields a whole system of integrated technologies that facilitate the operation and global distribution of the tourism industry. These include

Figure 3.6 Integrated ICTs for an integrated tourism industry and local economy management

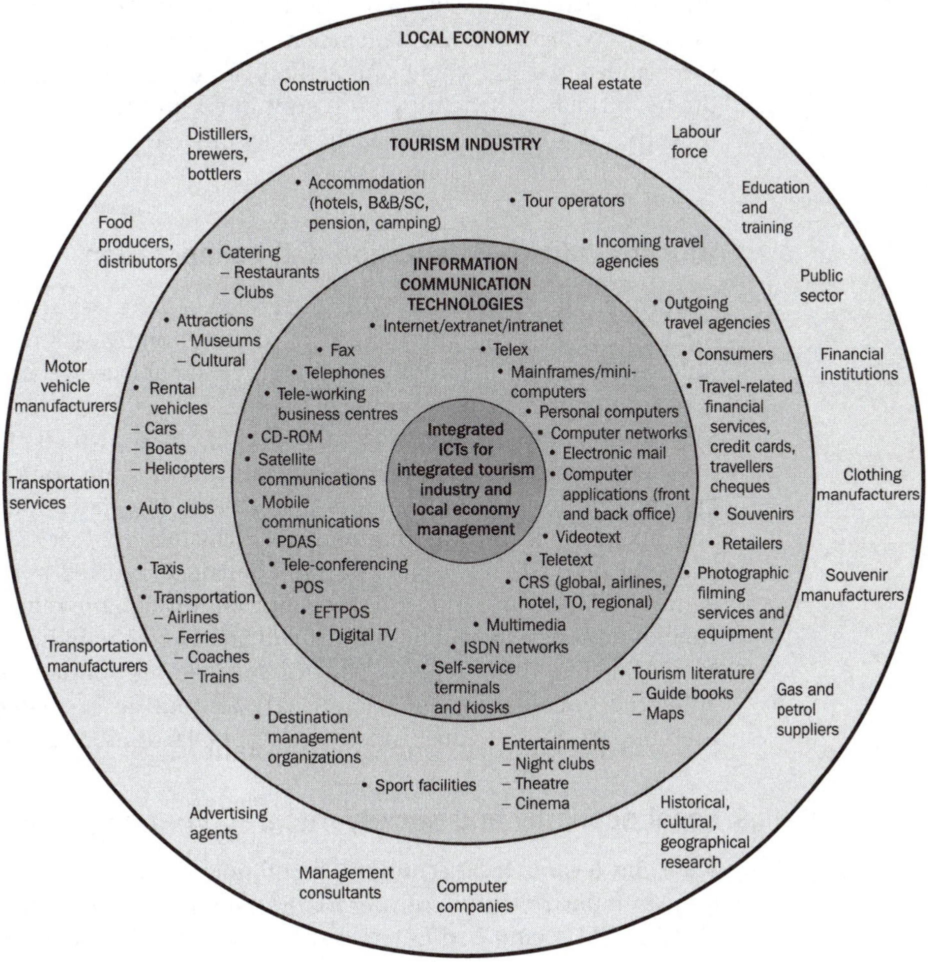

Source: Buhalis (1994, p. 258)

software, hardware and netware, which blend together to support the industry. Porter (1989) predicted that 'the world of the next decade is going to be a world where people struggle with how to connect systems, how to make them compatible, how to deal with the complexity of systems that span many activities within the firm and cross functional boundaries'. This could not be more applicable to any other industry than it is to tourism and hospitality. Interconnectivity, interoperability and integration of CRSs and other ICT systems dominate most of the industry, as information technology is particularly pervasive in the value chain with every value activity creating and using information. The gradual integration of the Internet, mobile devices and interactive digital television enables the convergence of ICT platforms for the industry, which needs to find methods to make information as well as content, processes, mechanisms and practices transparent and interoperable on all channels.

Hence, an integrated system of ICTs emerges to facilitate the operation of the tourism industry. ICTs effectively play an executive role in managing and unravelling the complexity generated by the interrelationships within the tourism industry (Williams, 1993). Benefits emerging from the integration of ICTs create value-added chains, where one activity supports the cost and effectiveness of others, ultimately benefiting both consumers and the prosperity of the tourism industry. As a result, several authors demonstrate that technology and tourism are 'ideal bedfellows' (Poon, 1993).

3.9.2 Tourism industry integration and collaboration

Tourism products are perceived as integrated experiences and they are ultimately evaluated as the total experience at the destination by each individual consumer. This assessment relies heavily on building reasonable expectations for consumers, which consequently depend on providing adequate and accurate information. Most destinations are effectively networks of SMTEs, which offer an amalgam of products and services, in order to generate an integrated outcome – the tourism experience. This approach implies the need for integrated tourism development and operation at the destination level, which requires close cooperation and networking of all local enterprises and partners involved in the tourism service delivery. ICTs can facilitate this **collaboration** through the integration of the value chain, and thus enable destinations and SMTEs to strengthen their competitiveness. Therefore the prosperity of both destinations and local enterprises can be enhanced since the total impact of ICTs on tourism is greater than the sum of their impact on individual functions or organizations (Poon, 1990).

3.9.3 Local economy and society integration and coordination

The third level is local economy integration. A closer relationship between the tourism industry with local non-tourism enterprises that provide goods and services for SMTE and consumers can be achieved. Regional development theory demonstrates that in order for destinations to maximize their economic benefits all economic sectors should participate and contribute to the products consumed by tourism. By doing so destinations can benefit by multiplier effects and the tourist expenditure can fuel many economic sectors in the society. Porter (1985b) claims that 'technology is pervasive in a firm and depends in part on both the buyers', channels', and suppliers' technology'. ICTs can facilitate inter-organizational communications at the local level and can engage all economic sectors in the production of the tourism experience. Therefore, the efficiency and benefits of all enterprises involved in the tourism industry can be improved and the macro-economic benefits can be supported. In addition, ICTs offer an opportunity to diffuse knowledge about demand for raw materials and services. Tourism producers need to be aware of the entire production scenario in their region so they can incorporate elements in their own production. Consequently, imports can be reduced and a higher usage of local products achieved, boosting local economic activities. The systematic adaptation of ICTs by all members of the tourism value chain as well as their suppliers provides the necessary platform for wealth creation on the supply side and consumer satisfaction on the demand side.

In the new strategic information system era the principle strategic development goal is to increase system-wide productivity by linking all the travel industry's computers and to make it as easy to send and receive data as it is to use a telephone. Hopper (1990) recommends that companies 'will focus less on being the first to build proprietary electronic tools than on being the best at using and improving generally available tools to change what their organizations already do well. Within their companies they will focus less on developing stand-alone applications than on building electronic platforms that can transform their organizational structures and support new ways of taking decision'. Tourism organizations therefore have to take advantage of the emerging ICTs and in particular the unprecedented opportunities that technological convergence and the Internet have introduced, redeveloping their **business processes** and models accordingly in order to maximize the benefits for the entire tourism system and value chain.

3.10 A multidimensional framework for ICTs in tourism

The contribution of ICTs in tourism is multidimensional, as they empower organizations to improve their internal efficiency, develop their effectiveness in their communication with their external world and establish partnerships with trusted collaborators and stakeholders. Figure 2.15 in Chapter 2 can be developed further to offer a conceptual synthesis of the usage of ICTs by tourism organizations.

Each cube can represent one tourism organization. ICTs enable organizations to use the opportunities provided by the three axes and to develop combinations of the available tools for facilitating communication and interaction with partners and stakeholders. They use the three key ICT axes to perform internal processes (intranet), to communicate with external established partners (extranets) and to interact with consumers and the society at large (Internet). The info-space between the axes provides endless combinations for the development and delivery of products as well as for adapting procedures and business processes. Given the dynamic nature of the industry as well as the rapid development of the technological tools, organizations will need to keep updating their offering, processes and partnerships to continually improve their competitiveness and to keep abreast of developments. Although the Internet and internal networks are currently the main technological tools for achieving these tasks, increasingly a wide range of devices and channels will be employed to allow further flexibility and interactivity. The ability of principals and destinations to use this framework effectively will determine their future competitiveness. The framework incorporates the paradigm shift and the business process re-engineering experienced, which effectively reshape the tourism industry. ICTs propel changes in several directions between the three main axes and enable organizations to use a wide range of communication methodologies for establishing partnerships with stakeholders and achieve mutual benefits.

Based on this multidimensional framework for strategic management and marketing, Figure 3.7 illustrates several applications of the framework in the tourism industry and the functions undertaken by tourism organizations. This framework attempts to systematize our understanding of the role of ICTs in tourism.

Figure 3.7 Tourism industry communication patterns and functions facilitated by ICTs

Intra-organizational communications and functions INTRANET	Inter-organizational communications and functions EXTRANET (AND INTRANET)
Information exchange within a tourism organization	*Information exchange between tourist product suppliers and intermediaries*
Management	*Before travelling*
• Strategic planning	• General information
• Competition analysis	• Availability/price inquiries
• Financial planning and control	• Negotiations and bargaining
• Accounting	• Reservations and confirmations
• Marketing research	• Ancillary services
• Marketing strategy and implementation	• Travel-related documentation
• Pricing decision and tactics	– lists of groups/visitors
• Middle-term planning and feedback	– receipts/documents
• Management statistics/reports	– voucher and ticket production
• Operational control	
• Management functions	*During travelling*
	• Follow up progress
Communication between departments	• Keep partners informed about plans
• Business functions	• Amend plans should unexpected developments arise
• Networking and information exchange	• Follow up developments
• Human resources management	
• Staff coordination	*After-travelling*
• Operational planning	• Payment and commissions clearance
• Accounting/billing	• Feedback and suggestions
• Payroll	• Complaint handling
• Supplies management	• Building loyalty through data mining
Communication and function with branches	
• Coordination of operations	
• Reports and budgeting	
• Availability/prices/information	
• Orders from headquarters/administration	
• Share of common resource databases for customer and operational information	
Consumer communication with tourism industry INTERNET	**Tourism enterprise communication with non-tourism enterprises INTERNET (AND EXTRANET)**
• Electronic commerce	• Other suppliers and ancillary services
• Travel advice	– vaccinations
• Request availability/prices/information	– travel formalities and visas
• Reservation and confirmation	• Insurance companies
• Amendments for a reservation	• Weather forecasting
• Deposits and full settlements	• Entertainment and communications
• Specific requests/enquiries	• Banking/financial services
• Feedback/complaints	• Credit cards
	• Other business services

Source: Adapted from Buhalis (1998)

It also demonstrates how the networked tourism enterprise can take advantage of ICTs in order to maximize internal efficiency and effectiveness, optimize communications with partners and interact profitably with consumers. Within this multidimensional framework, each tourism enterprise, destination and organization can be one cube in the info-space, which can be defined as the tourism electronic marketplace, or the eTourism area.

The resulting combinations illustrate how strategic marketing and management can be utilized in order to achieve mutual benefits for all stakeholders in a tourism value-added production chain. An ICT-led integration of industry members is therefore evident and is expected to dominate the industry in the near future.

3.10.1 Intra-organizational functions (using intranets)

Most of the literature concentrates on the use of ICTs for maximizing the internal efficiency and effectiveness of organizations. ICTs enhance a number of intra-organizational processes, by supporting a certain level of integration between various functions within organizations. Typically they integrate the front and back offices allowing enterprises to serve customers profitably and undertake their administration work. The aim is to increase efficiency and productivity, as well as to enhance the strategic and operational management of the enterprise. Examples from the tourism industry include:

- property management systems or hotel information systems;
- integrated points-of-sale systems;
- management and strategic information systems;
- accounting and payroll systems;
- food production technology;
- inventory control for tour operators, transportation companies and other principals.

Intranet technology facilitates an internal network by deploying the same technology and presentation tools as the Internet, but restricting access to authorized personnel only. The growth of intranets has been rapid. It is estimated that two-thirds of all large companies either have or soon will have an intranet. Sun (1998) estimated that world-wide server spend in 1997 on intranets was around $6 bn, compared with $3 bn on the Internet, and expected to reach $8 bn by 1998. For years ICT managers have been looking for a better way to deliver information within the organization and almost overnight the intranet technology has opened the door.

3.10.2 Inter-organizational functions through extranets (and the Internet)

Networking can also support communication and interconnectivity between individual organizations. Hence a number of systems and applications emerge to assist communications between tourism enterprises. Extranets emerge to provide a secured interface with trusted partners as they facilitate restricted access and interconnectivity to authorised organizations only. Electronic data interchange also enables organizations to transfer structured data from computer to computer (often hosted by different and remote organizations) using agreed communication standards. This is utilized extensively between tour operators and handling agencies at destinations to transfer passenger lists, invoices and undertake other paperwork, and thus, they maximize the effectiveness of the organizations in the system. Computer reservation systems and global distribution systems have also established both technological solutions and business transaction mechanisms between travel agencies and principals, such as airlines, hotels and car rental firms. CRSs and GDSs offer instant reservations and confirmations to travel agencies and increasingly empower Internet travel portals so they can reach customers directly. In addition, several destination management systems attempt to integrate the management and marketing of independent tourism enterprises at the destination area through secured extranets. In particular, small and medium-sized tourism enterprises benefit from ICT-supported networking as they are able to pool the resources of their partners within extranet developments and compete with their larger counterparts. Electronic mail, the World Wide Web and the **File Transfer Protocol (FTP)** empower interconnectivity and communication between organizations and individuals and hence enhance the productivity of partner organizations.

3.10.3 Consumer and stakeholder interaction over the Internet

The development of eCommerce, often defined as the secure trading of goods, information and services using Internet technologies, assists tourism organizations to communicate directly with consumers and to offer specialized products for their needs. As a result they can provide information and promote their products without the intervention of an intermediary, and are therefore in a better position to interact with consumers. eCommerce also enables them to sell products directly and, thus, to a certain degree can avoid commissions and other expenses such as production and distribution of brochures. The proliferation of CD-ROMs also allows the storage and distribution of memory-consuming multimedia presentations to both individual and institutional customers, improving the promotional function of organizations. Serving consumers electronically also contributes to the cost reduction of enterprises. Sun (1998) estimates that face-to-face banking costs $1 per transaction; call centres cost $0.5, while Internet banking cost merely $0.15 per transaction. Similarly tourism organizations can reduce their costs and improve their competitiveness by serving consumers through the Internet. More importantly perhaps, the development of customer relationship management (CRM) enables organizations to increase interaction with consumers, to record their individual preferences and to develop one-to-one (1-2-1) marketing. This enables them to treat established customers better, reduce untargeted promotional campaigns and maximize their influence through careful segmentation.

Consumers are also empowered to communicate directly with tourism organizations in order to request information and purchase products, as well as to interact with principals. Consumers have access to the Internet from home and can access information about tourism products and organizations instantly, inexpensively and interactively, almost regardless of the physical location of both service providers and themselves. They can do that at any time that can be convenient for them with the company of all people involved in their travel decision-making. They can also make and alter reservations and purchase tourism products through electronic shopping and banking systems. Moreover they often have the opportunity to provide feedback for products and services almost instantly and to tailor their tourism product according to their needs and requirements.

Consumers are able to air their views and even take part in negative publicity for organizations that they claim fail to perform on target and fulfil what they promise. Perhaps the best tourism example is that of United Airlines. Dissatisfied United Airlines passengers have established a web page (**www.untied.com**) in order to share their experiences and urge the company to improve its service and to compensate dissatisfied passengers. Case Study 3.1 demonstrates how consumers use the Internet to advise fellow consumers.

Case Study 3.1

Lonely Planet's Thorntree

Lonely Planet is encouraging feedback to its guides and aims to develop a global community of travellers that contribute to each other's experience. They have launched Thorntree as a free to access service to the travel community. The service has attracted more that 120 000 users in 2002 and participants share experiences and warn fellow travellers about problems that they may face at the destinations as well as provide a variety of tips. For example one traveller demonstrates how to avoid pick-pocketing in a particular airport whilst others give advice on secluded beaches or cultural rituals. "Branches" include specialized discussion groups per geographical region, interest groups (e.g. bikers, divers, homosexuals, travellers with disabilities, as well as various themes such as food, culture and languages. The service is advertisement free and Lonely Planet does not endorse the views of contributors, but controls that comments are civilized, lawful and do not advertise suppliers. Overall there is strong evidence that demonstrates that consumers trust other consumers better than the industry and therefore C2C Internet based discussion forums are expected to rise rapidly.

Source: Based on: **http://www.lonelyplanet.com** and **http://thorntree.lonelyplanet.com/**

Questions

- How can travellers communicate in a C2C environment?
- How can customer interaction online increase consumer satisfaction?
- What are the opportunities and threats for tourism suppliers?

Perhaps the most significant challenge for the tourism organization of the future will be to support its customers on a 365-day/24-hour basis. Given the velocity of response that consumers will expect through the new interactive mobile devices, which will be on permanently, as well as their flexible and unpredictable way of living and shopping, organizations will be required to serve constantly and instantly all customer requirements. Although technological solutions will undertake most of that activity, there will still be a strong requirement for companies to staff calling centres and to support their on-line provision.

3.11 Dynamic partnerships and constant movement

Each organization presented as a cube based on three axes operates within an info-space or the global marketplace where millions of other organizations also perform. Tourism enterprises will have to increase their virtuality by concentrating on their core offerings and outsource peripheral activities to specialist partners. This will allow them to concentrate their resources to their specific market segments and advance their ability to achieve competitive advantage. As a result tourism organizations will have to develop dynamic partnerships with a wide range of other players within the info-space to enable them to perform their business and expand geographically and operationally. Figure 3.8 illustrates that

Figure 3.8 Dynamic tourism partnerships in the info-space

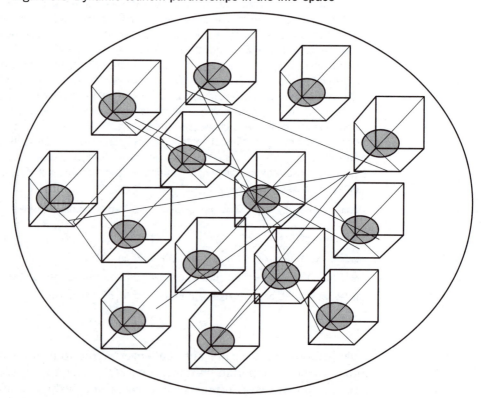

several organizations move within the info-space to position themselves for the best market opportunity. The challenge therefore for any tourism organization will be to identify the 'ideal' partner and to develop and maintain a mutually beneficial relationship. Inevitably most relationships will increasingly be ad hoc and only valid for as long as they serve their purpose within the info-space. Therefore cubes/organizations will 'fly' around and will constantly provide the challenge to develop the right relationship at the right time for the right market segment and conditions.

Although ICTs are presented as 'enablers' and opportunities in this chapter, they should also be regarded as a potential challenge and threat for organizations that ignore these developments and may suffer pivotal competitive disadvantages. One of the major barriers of ICTs' adaptation in the tourism industry is the lack of awareness and understanding of capabilities, especially by smaller players in the marketplace. It is predicted, however, that the adaptation of ICTs will transform not only the competitiveness of smaller organizations but also their ability to survive amid fierce global competition.

Further use of ICTs by tourism suppliers is supported by both quantitative and qualitative factors. Tourism is one of the most information-intensive industries whose growth can only be achieved if there are adequate mechanisms to share and manage information efficiently. The almost 700 million international tourists travelling currently have resulted in a growth of the industry's information requirements. Hence, tourism can no longer be handled without using ICTs. Instant access to information about thousands of destinations, millions of events, facilities and attractions and perhaps billions of schedules, fares, restrictions and regulations make ICTs a critical tool for both the operational and strategic management of the individual organization and the industry as a whole.

3.12 Conclusions: the tourism info-structure and organizational performance

Tourism organizations can enhance their performance by empowering their strategic marketing and management efforts through supporting their functions with advanced ICTs. This will enable them to improve their networking and ultimately to improve their 'virtuality'. The benefits generated by advanced integration of all management and marketing efforts for organizations, within the info-space and info-structure, allows them to support their competitiveness. The multidimensional strategic framework for ICTs in tourism not only demonstrates the dependence of both demand and supply on ICTs, but also illustrates that networking and interactivity will dominate the production and consumption functions. Players who fail to participate in the electronic marketplace, therefore, will face severe competitive disadvantages in the long term and will probably lose considerable market share.

Chapter questions

1 What are the main disciplines that eTourism covers?

2 How can ICTs determine the competitiveness of tourism organizations?

3 Identify innovative tourism organizations and explore their ICT strengths.

4 What are the main ICT applications used in the tourism industry?

5 Why will mobile devices revolutionize the tourism industry once more?

6 How can extranets benefit tourism organizations?

7 What are the synergies between computer reservation systems and global distribution systems?

8 Explain the concepts of info-structure and info-space for tourism.

9 Which tourism organizations will be likely to face competitive disadvantages in the future?

10 Explore how a tourism organization can take advantage of ad hoc networking on the info-structure to serve particular market segments.

Further reading

Buhalis, D. (1998a) Strategic use of information technologies in the tourism industry, *Tourism Management*, **19**(5), 409–421.

Buhalis, D. (2000) Tourism and information technologies: past, present and future, *Tourism Recreation Research*, **25**(1), 41–58.

Cooper, C. and Buhalis, D. (1998b) The future of tourism: information technology, in Cooper, C. et al., *Tourism: Principles and Practices*, Addison Wesley Longman, London, pp. 423–465.

Cooper, C., Fletcher, J., Gilbert, D., Shepherd, R. and Wanhill, S. (eds) (1998) *Tourism: Principles and Practices*, Addison Wesley Longman, London.

Leiper, N. (1995) *Tourism Management*, RMIT Press, Melbourne.

O'Connor, P. (1999) *Electronic Information Distribution in Tourism and Hospitality*, CAB, Oxford.

Poon, A. (1993) *Tourism, Technology and Competitive Strategies*, CAB International, Oxford.

Sheldon, P. (1997) *Information Technologies for Tourism*, CAB, Oxford.

Turban, E., Lee, J., King, D. and Chung, H. (2002) *Electronic Commerce: A Managerial Perspective*, Prentice Hall, New Jersey.

Werthner, H. and Klein, S. (1999) *Information Technology and Tourism: A Challenging Relationship*, Springer-Verlag, Vienna.

Websites

Worldspan: **www.worldspan.com**

Amadeus: **www.amadeus.com**

Sabre: **www.sabre.com**

Galileo: **www.galileo.com**

United Airlines: **www.united.com**

United Airlines complaints: **www.untied.com**

Travel Gate List of web pages: **www.travelgate.co.uk**

News on EyeforTravel: **www.eyefortravel.com**

TRAVELMOLE: **www.travelmole.com**

Carl Marcunsen Trends in Distribution: **www.rcb.dk/uk/staff/chm/trends.htm**

WebTravelNews: **www.webtravelnews.com**

Travel Industry Association: **www.tia.org/home.asp**

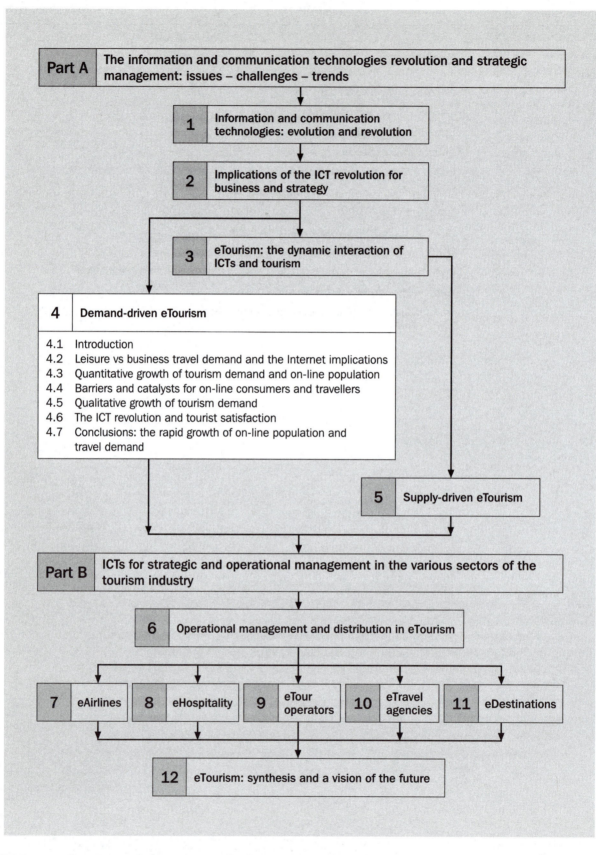

Part A The information and communication technologies revolution and strategic management: issues – challenges – trends

1 Information and communication technologies: evolution and revolution

2 Implications of the ICT revolution for business and strategy

3 eTourism: the dynamic interaction of ICTs and tourism

4 Demand-driven eTourism

4.1 Introduction
4.2 Leisure vs business travel demand and the Internet implications
4.3 Quantitative growth of tourism demand and on-line population
4.4 Barriers and catalysts for on-line consumers and travellers
4.5 Qualitative growth of tourism demand
4.6 The ICT revolution and tourist satisfaction
4.7 Conclusions: the rapid growth of on-line population and travel demand

5 Supply-driven eTourism

Part B ICTs for strategic and operational management in the various sectors of the tourism industry

6 Operational management and distribution in eTourism

7 eAirlines
8 eHospitality
9 eTour operators
10 eTravel agencies
11 eDestinations

12 eTourism: synthesis and a vision of the future

4

Demand-driven eTourism

Chapter objectives

The purpose of this chapter is to explore the growth of the on-line population and demonstrate how this has influenced tourism demand. The chapter argues that consumers are empowered by the new ICT tools and actively seek interaction with tourism organizations. The chapter also aims to demonstrate the main catalysts for facilitating on-line bookings and demonstrates that ICTs will be critical for satisfying the consumer of the future. Thus, the learning objectives may be defined as:

- Demonstrate different types of tourism demand
- Explore how ICTs satisfy the needs of consumers
- Examine the on-line population and the characteristics of the on-line markets
- Identify the factors that would encourage more on-line bookings
- Discuss the relationship between ICT utilization and customer satisfaction

4.1 Introduction

The use of ICTs in the tourism industry is to a certain extent driven by the increase in both the size and complexity of tourism demand. The rapid growth of both the volume and the quality requirements of contemporary travellers necessitates powerful ICTs for the administration of the expanding traffic and forces industry members to adopt ICTs and to expand the volume and sophistication of their products. Hence, on one hand ICTs facilitate the expansion of the industry and the enlargement of the market and on the other the growing volume of demand requires advanced ICTs for the management of tourism organisations. Every tourist is different, carrying a unique blend of experiences, motivations and desires. To an extent the new sophisticated traveller has emerged as a result of experience. Tourists from the major generating regions of the world have become frequent travellers, are linguistically and technologically skilled and can function in multicultural and demanding environments overseas.

The Internet revolutionizes flexibility in both consumer choice and service delivery processes. Increasingly customers are becoming much more sophisticated and discerning, as a result of experiencing high levels of service and also because the standard of living has improved considerably, and thus they enjoy advanced facilities in their everyday environment. Tourists become demanding, requesting high-quality products and value for their money and, perhaps more importantly, value for time for the entire range of their dealings with organizations. This reflects people's shortage of time, evident in Western societies. Having experienced several tourism products and destinations, experienced, sophisticated, demanding travellers rely heavily on electronic media to obtain information about destinations and experiences, as well as to be able to communicate their needs and wishes to suppliers rapidly.

4.2 Leisure vs business travel demand and the Internet implications

Inevitably, frequent business travellers are more familiar with travel arrangements and often have considerable expertise as regards destinations or particular products. Someone who travels from London to Paris on a weekly basis knows, from experience, far more about the Eurostar service and the destination than any travel agency or website will be ever be able to provide. Business trips are often classified into Meetings, Incentives, Conferences and Exhibitions (MICE) categories (Ladkin and Spiller, 2000). The frequency of using a particular travel service and the familiarity with the destination, as well as the time available for non-business-related time spent, determine the information required by visitors. Destination- or service-'naive' tourists require dramatically more information than experienced travellers. In contrast, experienced travellers to a destination may require a much greater depth of information as well as being sure that their needs and particular requirements, based on their previous experience, will be addressed (Snepenger et al., 1990; Fesenmaier et al., 1992). As a result the information requirement as well as the presentation for each of these market segments needs to be assessed accordingly.

Often decisions and bookings are not made by travellers themselves, but rather by their secretaries or travel managers in their organizations. The information required and the distribution channels used for searching and booking travel products vary enormously (Swarbrooke and Horner, 2001; Davidson, 2001). Nevertheless, it is increasingly evident that business travellers use the Internet independently to book their tickets and often to make more complicated travel arrangements. They often compare the **prices** and offers available on-line versus the ones proposed by travel managers and frequently propose an alternative arrangement to the one offered by their organization. This has led to an interesting situation where the user can often find better deals than travel professionals and, thus, save some money on the travel budget of a company. However, when business travellers are able to sort out their own travel arrangements they often disobey the travel policies of their organizations. They also challenge travel managers and spend a considerable proportion of their working time searching for travel products (or 'playing amateur travel agency', as some industry sources refer to this phenomenon) for considerably little benefit. Nevertheless **business travel** represents the highest proportion of on-line travel bookings, not only as it is often fairly straightforward, since most of the variables in terms of times and places are set, but also as the business travellers are better educated, more independent and familiar with computers. The business travel sector is much more lucrative than the leisure market. Predictably, therefore, most organisations that serve this market have developed elaborate Internet interfaces. In addition, B2B transactions between businesses and travel companies also grow at a much faster rate than other sectors of the Internet.

In contrast, leisure travelling has been much slower to take off on the Internet than many industry analysts had anticipated. This is particularly a European issue, as the package holiday still dominates the leisure activity. Not only is a great proportion of leisure travelling based on package holidays but also the recent consolidation of the travel industry means that just a few multinational organizations, namely Preussag, Rewe, Thomas Cook, Kuoni and Airtours, control the leisure industry in Europe, as demonstrated in Figure 4.1 (Bywater, 2001).

Case Study 4.1 clearly illustrates that the vertically integrated organizations control the travel industry in Germany, while about 56 per cent of all turnover in German travel agencies is attributable to package holidays. For a wide range of reasons, the Internet has not yet been explored fully by the leisure market to the level where consumers can use it to book package holidays. These reasons include:

- people that take package holidays often belong to lower economic classes and are less familiar with computers and have a lower Internet penetration;
- the complexity of family holidays create conditions difficult to **program** and model;
- commercial interests of tour operators;
- fairly high degree of substitution between destinations and products;

Figure 4.1 The top European travel and tourism groups, September 2000

Group	Base country	Combined annual turnover in 1999 (euros)
Preussag (TUI/Hapag-Lloyd/Thomson)	Germany	12.27 bn
Rewe/LTU	Germany	5.64 bn
Thomas Cook (ex C&N Touristic inc. Havas and Thomas Cook)	Germany	4.65 bn
Kuoni/Hogg Robinson/Business Travel International	Switzerland	3.50 bn
Airtours	UK	5.52 bn

Source: Based on Bywater (2001)

- high price elasticity of package holidays;
- integrated nature of distribution channel facilitating direct sales;
- low profit margins do not allow great investment in ICTs;
- legacy systems used by tour operators.

However, the independent leisure market dominates North America, southern parts of Europe and other parts of the world. In these regions a much greater percentage of leisure travellers organize their holidays alone or with the assistance of retail travel agencies who package the travel products for them. The Internet has empowered this market dramatically as it has provided access to all information required for purchasing tourism products. Consequently, companies that target independent leisure travellers, such as no-frills airlines easyJet and Ryanair, report that Internet bookings already account for more than 80 per cent of their traffic. The Internet is also increasingly used by small and independent hotel properties that find it easier and more profitable to communicate directly with their clientèle. Perhaps the Internet will gradually enable the independent leisure market to grow faster at the expense of inclusive packages, by assisting consumers to substitute some of the functions and value added currently by tour operators. As a result, the tourism system for these customers will change rapidly and new interfaces with consumers will possibly be required.

Substituting inclusive package holidays with self-assembled leisure products can be more effective for experienced travellers who have been to a destination and feel comfortable with not being looked after by a tour operator or **resort representatives**. This may be more desirable for travellers from southern European countries and North America who have traditionally travelled on their own, as well as for younger and better-educated market segments. There is already a trend for more sophisticated and individualized holidays (Buhalis, 2001), which will be fuelled by ICT capabilities. Increasing the proportion of people booking holidays independently can be achieved if consumers find a better deal on-line and in particular if most of the value added offered by tour operators can be substituted by other members of the channel or technologies available.

Case study 4.1 demonstrates the turnover of the travel market in Germany as an example, and analyses the various types of **travel agency** in operation there.

Case Study 4.1

Size of the German travel market in turnover and travel agencies

	1999		2000	
Total number of travel agencies	15 782		15 700	
Traditional travel agencies	5655		5700	
Travel agencies selling only package holidays	10 127		10 000	
Travel agencies with DB (German Rail) licence	3904		3980	
Travel agencies with Iata licence	4690		4771	
Total turnover of travel agencies including package holidays, etc., air travel including consolidators, rail tickets and miscellaneous travel agency business	DM47.40bn		DM49.04bn	
Turnover on business travel	DM13.91bn	29.34%	DM14.64bn	29.85%
Turnover on private client business	DM33.49bn	70.65%	DM34.40bn	70.14%
Package holidays	DM26.84bn	56.62%	DM27.19bn	55.44%
Air tickets (including consolidators)	DM15.66bn	33.04%	DM16.65bn	33.95%
Rail tickets	DM2.22bn	4.68%	DM2.30bn	4.69%
Miscellaneous travel agency business	DM 2.68bn	5.65%	DM2.90bn	5.91%

Independent travel agencies 36% generating 13% of trade turnover

Tied outlets 64% generating 87% of trade turnover

Note: The term 'travel agency' covers a variety of different operations. In German parlance, there are so-called 'full' travel agencies (Vollreisebüros) holding Iata licences and/or licences entitling them to sell airline and/or rail tickets. Company travel departments and implants are in this category. Apart from these a host of 'travel agencies' simply sell package holidays and related products, while others are part of a wider retail operation (e.g. at mini-markets or lottery ticket sales points).

Source: Adapted from **http://www.fvw.com**

Questions

■ Examine the size of the German travel market and explain what the implications are for the on-line strategy of tourism suppliers.

■ Discuss the difference in consumer behaviour between independent leisure travellers and package holiday makers and explain how this is reflected in their usage of the Internet.

4.3 Quantitative growth of tourism demand and on-line population

The World Tourism Organization's (WTO) Tourism 2020 Vision forecasts that international tourism arrivals are expected to reach over 1.6 billion by the year 2020. Of these worldwide arrivals 1.2 billion will be intra-regional and 377 million will be long-haul travellers. East Asia and the Pacific South Asia, the Middle

East and Africa are forecasted to record growth at rates over 5 per cent per year, compared with the world average of 4.1 per cent. The more mature regions of Europe and America are anticipated to show lower than average growth rates. Long-haul travel worldwide will grow faster at 5.4 per cent per year over the period 1995–2020 than intra-regional travel at 3.8 per cent (WTO, 2000). Tables 4.1 and 4.2 illustrate the anticipated growth per region.

This growth demonstrates a significant increase of traveller volume from previous years and illustrates that about 20 per cent of the world's population will

Table 4.1 Forecast of international tourist arrivals by region (in millions)

	Base year 1995	Forecast 2010	Forecast 2020	Average annual growth rate (%) 1995–2020	Market share (%) 1995	Market share (%) 2020
Total	565.4	1006.4	1561.1	4.1	100	100
Africa	20.2	47.0	77.3	5.5	3.6	5.0
Americas	108.9	190.4	282.3	3.9	19.3	18.1
East Asia/Pacific	81.4	195.2	397.2	6.5	14.4	25.4
Europe	338.4	527.3	717.0	3.0	59.8	45.9
Middle East	12.4	35.9	68.5	7.1	2.2	4.4
South Asia	4.2	10.6	18.8	6.2	0.7	1.2
Intra-regional	464.1	790.9	1183.3	3.8	82.1	75.8
Long-haul	101.3	215.5	377.9	5.4	17.9	24.2

Source: After WTO (2000)

Table 4.2 Forecasted growth of worldwide travel 1995–2010

	Actual					Forecast			
	1985	1995	Annual Growth 1985–95 (%)	2000	Annual Growth 1995–2000 (%)	2005	Annual Growth 2000–2005 (%)	2010	Annual Growth 2005–10 (%)
Volume of travel									
Trips abroad* (million)	307	535	7.4	632	3.6	782	4.8	964	4.7
Trips abroad short-/ medium-haul	272	455	6.7	518	2.7	617	3.8	724	3.5
Trips abroad long-haul	35	79	12.6	114	8.9	165	9.0	240	9.1
Nights abroad (million)	2828	4751	6.8	5518	3.2	6903	5.0	8654	5.1
Spending abroad (US $bn at 1995 prices)	206	393	9.1	516	6.3	686	6.6	922	6.9
Travel characteristics									
Nights per trip	9.2	8.5	–0.8	8.7	0.5	8.8	0.2	9.0	0.5
Spending per trip (constant 1995 US$)	671	735	1.0	816	2.2	877	1.5	956	1.8
Spending per night (constant 1995 US$)	73	86	1.8	93	1.6	99	1.3	107	1.6

* Excludes day trips. Totals may not add up to 100 due to rounding.

Source: After Edwards and Graham (1997)

be travelling. Spending per night and per trip also increases rapidly. So, a greater number of people will be spending more time and money on tourism products; however, the number of nights away has decreased since 1985, as more people take shorter but more frequent breaks. Work pressures, a more active lifestyle and easy access to remote destinations, as well as flexible working arrangements and self-employment, support this trend further. Interestingly long-haul travel is expanding faster than all other forms, as people visit peripheral areas in pursuit of exotic and unspoilt destinations. All these trends require more advanced ICTs in order to enable the industry to service the increasing demand.

4.3.1 On-line population and on-line tourism demand

Nobody really knows exactly how many people are currently connected to the Internet and how many of them buy products electronically. The dynamic nature of the Internet and its rapid development prevents research organizations from illustrating accurate statistics. Although several statistics appear in the press and on-line, they often contradict each other, and thus they need to be treated with caution. It is more important therefore to observe the trends and relationships in these figures, rather than the absolute numbers.

The Computer Industry Almanac estimates that nearly 625 million people or 6.7 per cent of the global population had Internet access worldwide in June 2001. The same source estimates that there were over 400 million Internet users world-wide in 2000 – up from less than 200 million Internet users in 1998. The USA had over 134 million Internet users or nearly 33 per cent of the total in 2000. The Internet is slowly shaking off its American bias and becoming more global. Europe also demonstrates strong demand with the Scandinavian countries leading and with the rest of the developed countries (Germany, the UK and France) following. The top 15 countries account for nearly 78 per cent of the worldwide Internet users at year-end 2000. These numbers include adult Internet users with weekly usage in businesses and homes. An Internet user is defined as being over 16 years of age and using the Internet on a regular or occasional basis. Most notable is the appearance of Russia on the top-15 list of countries. Russia jumped from 1.4 million Internet Users at year-end 1998 to 7.5 million in 2000. That's more than a five-fold increase in the number of Internet users in Russia in only two years. Most Russians do not have their own ISP account, but use the Internet at school and other public places. The Computer Industry Almanac predicts a phenomenal growth with 673 million Internet users worldwide at year-end 2002 and over one billion users by year-end 2005 (www.c-i-a.com).

Tables 4.3 and 4.4 give the latest estimates of the on-line population in the major developed countries, by sheer numbers and by percentage of population. Figures 4.2 and 4.3 also illustrate the absolute and relevant contributions of each country to the on-line population, based on Nua (www.nua.ie). It is evident that the developed world dominates the Internet, with the USA having by far the most significant population of Internet users. Most Internet users are well-educated professionals who travel frequently and therefore should have a higher disposable income. Increasingly more people have access from work or Internet cafes even from countries that are not technologically advanced or wealthy, such

Table 4.3 Ranked top nations in Internet use in 2001 (by size of population)

Country	Month/year	Internet users (million)	Percentage of population
USA	11/2000	153.84	55.83
Japan	11/2000	38.64	30.53
Germany	11/2000	20.1	24.28
UK	11/2000	19.98	33.58
China	7/2000	16.9	1.34
South Korea	10/2000	16.4	34.55
Iceland	7/2000	0.14	52.11
Italy	11/2000	13.42	23.29
Canada	12/1999	13.28	42.8
France	3/2000	9	15.26
Australia	11/2000	8.42	43.94
Netherlands	11/2000	7.28	45.82
Taiwan	7/2000	6.4	28.84
Spain	11/2000	5.49	13.72
Sweden	11/2000	5	56.36
Hong Kong	11/2000	3.46	48.69
Austria	10/2000	3	36.9
Belgium	9/2000	2.7	26.36
Denmark	11/2000	2.58	48.37
Switzerland	9/2000	2.4	33.05
Norway	10/2000	2.36	52.6
Finland	8/2000	2.27	43.93
Singapore	11/2000	1.85	44.58
New Zealand	11/2000	1.49	39.03
Greece	10/1999	1.33	12.42
Ireland	11/2000	1.04	27.5

Source: Nua, How Many On-Line, www.nua.ie/surveys/how_many_online/ (1 June 2001)

Table 4.4 Ranked top nations in Internet use in 2001 (by percentage of population)

Country	Month/year	Internet users (million)	Percentage of population
Sweden	11/2000	5	56.36
USA	11/2000	153.84	55.83
Norway	10/2000	2.36	52.6
Iceland	7/2000	0.14	52.11
Hong Kong	11/2000	3.46	48.69
Denmark	11/2000	2.58	48.37
Netherlands	11/2000	7.28	45.82
Singapore	11/2000	1.85	44.58
Australia	11/2000	8.42	43.94
Finland	8/2000	2.27	43.93
Canada	12/1999	13.28	42.8
New Zealand	11/2000	1.49	39.03
Austria	10/2000	3	36.9
South Korea	10/2000	16.4	34.55
UK	11/2000	19.98	33.58
Switzerland	9/2000	2.4	33.05
Japan	11/2000	38.64	30.53
Taiwan	7/2000	6.4	28.84
Ireland	11/2000	1.04	27.5
Belgium	9/2000	2.7	26.36
Germany	11/2000	20.1	24.28
Italy	11/2000	13.42	23.29
France	3/2000	9	15.26
Spain	11/2000	5.49	13.72
Greece	10/1999	1.33	12.42
China	7/2000	16.9	1.34

Source: Adapted from Nua, How Many On-Line, www.nua.ie/surveys/how_many_online/ (1 June 2001)

as Russia and China. NetValue estimated that in May 2001 there were 13.6 million home Internet users in the UK (or about 27 per cent of the British population). About 27 per cent belong to lower economic classes with a monthly income of less than £600. This illustrates that gradually the Internet is becoming pervasive among all economic classes. Increasingly it will be commonplace for households to have a connected computer and a digital television, just as they currently have a kitchen and a TV set. The phenomenal growth of mobile telephony, in combination with the transformation of mobile devices, will also contribute to the **connectivity** of an even greater percentage of the population.

Not only are more people expected to travel, but also a greater percentage of the population has access to the Internet and therefore on-line tourism products. Slightly less than one-third of Internet users are currently based in the USA, where the penetration is estimated to be 56 per cent of the population. However, Japan, Germany, the UK and even China have more than 15 million users each. Apart from the USA, most of the Scandinavian countries enjoy a penetration level of more than 50 per cent while all the developed countries as well as the English-speaking ones have a penetration level of more than 40 per cent. It is therefore evident that the penetration of ICTs and the usage of the Internet

Figure 4.2 On-line population per country, in millions

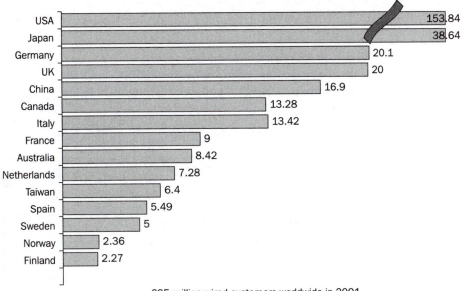

USA	153.84
Japan	38.64
Germany	20.1
UK	20
China	16.9
Canada	13.28
Italy	13.42
France	9
Australia	8.42
Netherlands	7.28
Taiwan	6.4
Spain	5.49
Sweden	5
Norway	2.36
Finland	2.27

625 million wired customers worldwide in 2001

Source: Based on Nua.ie

Figure 4.3 On-line population per country, in percentage

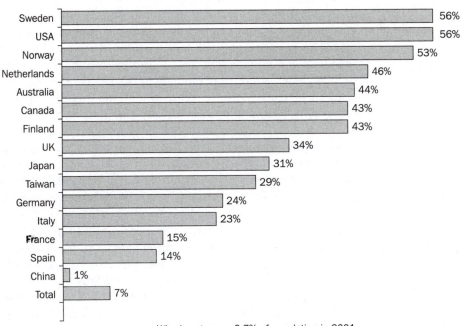

Sweden	56%
USA	56%
Norway	53%
Netherlands	46%
Australia	44%
Canada	43%
Finland	43%
UK	34%
Japan	31%
Taiwan	29%
Germany	24%
Italy	23%
France	15%
Spain	14%
China	1%
Total	7%

Wired customers 6.7% of population in 2001

Source: Based on Nua.ie

Figure 4.4 The rapid rise of on-line adoption

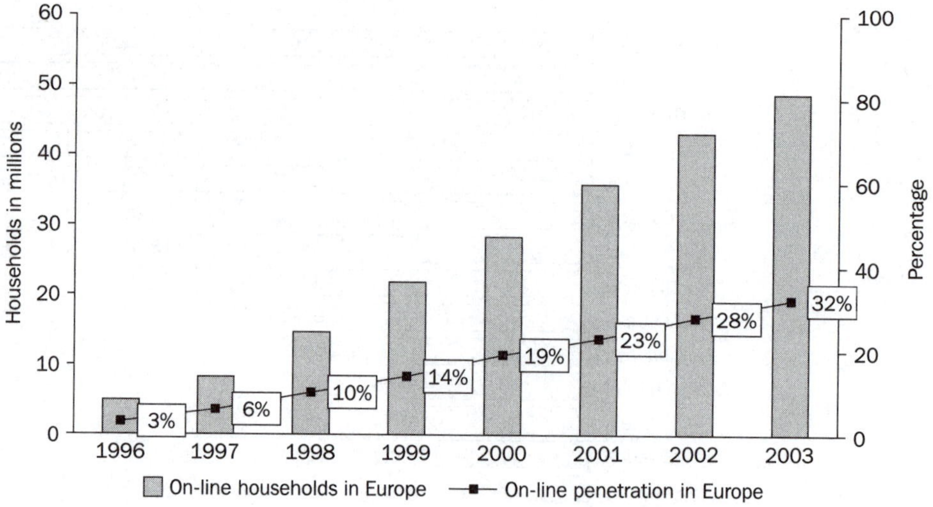

Source: Jones (1999); Jupiter Communications, © Jupiter Research, a division of Jupitermedia Corporation

is a function of the wealth of a country, while English-speaking regions and populations are more advanced as far as the Internet is concerned.

Consumers are attracted to the Internet in order to use a wide range of products and services and there is a high rate of growth, as illustrated in Figure 4.4. In Europe, Jupiter Communication estimates that by the year 2003 there will be an increase of on-line shoppers from 4.7 m in 1998 to 43.6 m, or 11 per cent of the total projected European Union population. This is a growth of almost 1000 per cent in five years (Jones, 1999). European on-line shopping will grow by 2742.5 per cent from 678 million euros in 1998 to 18.6 billion euros in 2003. Scandinavia, Germany and the UK lead the on-line revolution. Jupiter consumer surveys demonstrate that more than 50 per cent of EU on-line users already research purchases on-line before purchasing. About 27 per cent of the research participants claim that they already purchase products on-line and another 32 per cent claim that they collect information about products, compare prices or visit on-line stores, but do not buy on-line. Computer equipment and low-involvement items such as books and music dominate on-line shopping (57 per cent and 48 per cent, respectively), followed by air tickets (45 per cent) and then clothing, automobiles, gifts and other (29–35 per cent). About 86 per cent of on-line shoppers have a specific item in mind to buy when they go on-line and only 10 per cent shop around without a specific item in mind. About 10 per cent visit more that six sites to buy something, 43 per cent between three and five sites, 21 per cent visit two sites and 19 per cent visit only one site.

In Europe it is estimated that over 13 million trips were initiated on the net but booked and paid for off-line in 1999. Only 4 million trips were booked and paid for on-line. Almost 17 m trips taken abroad by Europeans were therefore initiated on the Internet. Surprisingly, 73 per cent of on-line bookings were holidays and only 27 per cent were for business. This is in contrast to the USA where 82 per cent of large companies were predicted to be buying travel on-line in 2001. Trips booked on-line are shorter than trips booked off-line, whatever the kind of trip made, and they are normally initiated at a later stage and close to departure day. Winter sport holidays, events and special trips are popular on-line purchases as consumers tend to be more focused. Internet travellers usually live in large towns, while the 25–34 age group shows a relative favour towards Internet bookings. They are normally better educated, have disposable incomes and may have not started a family yet. This trend is completely reversed in the 45–54 age group as older people often find the Internet demanding and challenging. Household income is the biggest discriminator separating on-line and off-line bookers (World Travel Monitor: www.ipkinternational.com). According to IDC (www.idc.com), the European Internet access market is set to grow at a 30 per cent compound rate up to 2005. The growth will be driven by the number of new users, the success of free services, the falling prices of other services and the emergence of broadband access technologies. Most consumers and small firms will continue to use dial-up connections through to 2005.

Measuring the on-line population growth is a complex task. A number of organizations are performing this service and more often than not they attempt to make informed judgements and measurements. Frequently, one set of statistics contradicts another and there are yet to be established well established Internet metrics. Case Study 4.2 illustrates some of these organizations.

Case Study 4.2

Internet population – catching a moving target

As Internet statistics evolve rapidly there are several research services that provide up-to-date information. They provide estimates, and as all numbers relating to on-line population and usage are expanding constantly they need to be treated with caution.
   These include:

- Jupiter   **www.jup.com/home.jsp**
- Forrester   **www.forrester.com**
- Nua   **www.nua.ie/surveys/index.cgi**

Questions

- Explore the latest predictions for travel growth and discuss whether ICT is one of the key factors determining this growth.

- What are the regional differences in travel demand growth and what are the implications for the on-line strategies of tourism organizations?

- Explore the nua.ie and the www.etcmonitor.com sites to identify trends in Internet penetration. Discuss the impacts for tourism demand.

- Examine travelocity.com, expedia.com, ebookers.com and travelstore.com and
   - explore their main markets;
   - discuss the different approaches for different market segments.

There are several motivators for using the Internet for travel, including:

- the richness and depth of information;
- ease in identifying information;
- self-service and economical;
- available at all times;
- products are offered at discounted prices as suppliers pass distribution savings on to consumers.

It needs to be recognized that older generations and lower socio-economic classes are often technophobic, as they lack training to operate the new machinery. A large proportion of the population does not own a computer and finds it difficult to access one. The Internet is also chaotic and needs some expertise in operating it and benefiting from its content. Finally, there are still security fears for on-line purchases for a large proportion of the international Internet population. Table 4.5 illustrates the top motivating factors for Europeans to purchase more products on-line.

The European market also enjoys a very high penetration of mobile phones. Table 4.6 illustrates the number of mobile phones in Europe and the level of penetration for each country. Europe is the world leader in mobile phones and Scandinavian countries have more mobile than fixed-line phones. However, Japan is actually much more advanced in using mobile Internet through their i-mode system, which generates more activity than the WAP in Europe. Even developing countries are taking advantage, with China having the fastest grow-ing mobile telephone market in the world (Dempsey, 2000). It is becoming increasingly evident that convergence with mobile phones will allow consumers to use mobile devices to access the Internet. Although the level of interaction and **mobile commerce (m-commerce)** based on WAP technologies has failed to reach the expectations of the marketers, it is anticipated that 3G mobile phones will enable travellers to interact with tourism organizations.

The imminent expansion of the bandwidth of mobile communications will accelerate the 'collision' of PCs, phones and entertainment services. Not only will people be able to send and receive text, voice and multimedia messages, but

Table 4.5 Motivation factors for Europeans to purchase more products on-line

■ Better prices	64%
■ Better security for credit card and personal information	56%
■ Ability to return merchandise easily	52%
■ Easier comparison with shops	49%
■ Ability to get answers from merchant	48%
■ Better information about products	48%
■ Greater trust in particular on-line merchants	38%
■ Internet stores use local language	38%
■ Ability of loyalty rewards	37%
■ Easier to order	36%
■ Greater familiarity with the Internet and on-line purchasing	17%

Source: After Jones (1999); Jupiter: Consumer survey; © 2002 Jupiter Research, a division of Jupitermedia Corporation

Table 4.6 Mobile phone usage in European countries

Country	Population (m)	Mobile phones (m)	Penetration (%)
Finland	5.1	3.3	65
Iceland	0.3	0.16	61
Norway	4.4	2.7	60
Sweden	8.8	5.0	56
Denmark	5.2	2.6	50
Italy	57.3	28.4	50
Austria	8.0	3.9	48
Luxembourg	0.4	0.18	46
Portugal	9.9	4.4	44
Britain	58.3	24.1	41
Switzerland	7.0	2.9	41
Netherlands	15.3	6.3	40
Greece	10.4	3.6	35
Belgium	10.1	3.0	33
Spain	39.2	13.1	33
France	57.9	18.0	31
Germany	81.3	21.0	25

Source: Adapted from Lorenz (1999)

they will also be able to download music on MP3 players or short films. This will not only support eCommerce 'on the go' but it will also enable operators to provide location-dependent information and reservations, further empowering consumers.

4.3.2 Demand for tourism on-line and eCommerce

Increasingly consumers become familiar with ICTs and expect that tourism suppliers will have interactive interfaces on-line to support purchasing and discussion about specific requirements. The Internet, in particular, enables travellers to access reliable and accurate information as well as to undertake reservations in a fraction of the time, cost and inconvenience required by conventional methods. Most Internet users are well-educated professionals who travel frequently and therefore should have a higher disposable income, as well as a higher propensity to spend on tourism products. These market segments are targeted by most tourism destinations and organizations, and hence the industry has to reflect on their new needs and ICT-enabled abilities, in order to take advantage of the emerging tools (Smith and Jenner, 1998).

The Travel Industry Association of America has predicted that travel and tourism will be one of the most popular products for on-line purchasing in the emerging electronic marketplace (TIA, 1997). Significant increase of direct bookings by on-line users for airlines, hotels and other travel business is therefore expected to reflect an increase in direct sales by suppliers from 22 per cent in 1997 to 30 per cent of on-line sales in 2002. Although in 1996 less than 1 per cent of all airline ticket revenue came from on-line sources, it is anticipated by the year 2002 it will increase to 8.2 per cent and will be the leading travel purchase on the Internet. Airline tickets accounted for 90 per cent of all on-line travel sales although by the year 2002 the proportion of airline tickets purchased on-line is expected to drop to 73 per cent of all on-line travel sales. Non-airline sales (hotel and car rental) are expected to grow from $31 million in 1996 to $2.2 billion by 2002. Travel organizations will also benefit from selling advertising to other related companies such as destinations, publishers, insurers etc. On-line advertising on travel websites is expected to grow from $2 million in 1996 to $282 million in 2002, and will be the third leading source of revenue for travel-related web sites (TIA, 1997). Leading incentives for consumers to purchase products directly include greater selection of goods and services, better prices, lack of local alternatives, familiarity with company, ease of use, better customer service, and recommendations from friends (Jones, 1999). In 2000, over $13 billion was spent on-line for airline tickets, hotel reservations and car rentals. On average, these travel services make up 28 per cent of *all* on-line purchases. On-line spending for travel services have already surpassed purchases of media (books/music/ videos/software) and is the number one in total spending (Cook, 2001).

The American market is more advanced as far as the use of the Internet and eCommerce is concerned. The Travel Industry Association of America illustrates that the Internet is now used widely by American travellers. Although the number of on-line Americans is still growing, Internet penetration among US households is no longer experiencing the rapid, double-digit gains seen in the late 1990s. Internet use in the USA and travel are highly related. In fact, most (86 per cent) on-line adults claim to be travellers. The market for on-line travellers is estimated to be more than 100 million, a growth of more than 250 per cent, from just 28 million in 1996. Frequent travellers (five or more trips annually) are much more likely to use the Internet (77 per cent). One in six on-line travellers is over the age of 55 and the average annual household income is about $70 100 (TIA, 2001a).

Use of the Internet for travel planning

As the on-line market has expanded, so has the number of on-line travellers who actually use the Internet to plan trips. A majority (68 per cent) consults the Internet to get information on destinations or to check prices or schedules. Among this group, about half (32 million) are frequent travellers taking five or more trips in one year. On-line travel planners carry out a variety of planning activities on the Internet. The most popular are searching for maps or driving directions, searching for airfares/schedules, and looking for places to stay and things to do at the destination, as demonstrated in Figure 4.5. Consumers who plan and/or book leisure trips on-line are a diverse group, reflecting the broadening of Internet access across a wider demographic base. Many travel organizations also find the Internet to be a cost-effective way to deliver this information and to distribute products and services. While eTravel consumers share some common characteristics, there are differences among various subgroups in how they travel and how they plan their travel on-line. On-line leisure travel planners are likely to be quite savvy Internet users, with the majority being on-line for at least 11 hours per week. Half of on-line leisure travel planners are baby boomers between the ages of 35 and 54 while four in ten are under 35 years old. Most on-line planners are college-educated, which may explain why a majority have annual household incomes of $50 000 or more. Given that one of every two

Figure 4.5 On-line pleasure trip planning activities in the USA

Activity	Percentage
Obtained maps/driving directions	59%
Searched for places to stay	54%
Searched for things to do	46%
Searched for airline fares/schedules	45%
Searched for dining/entertainment	36%
Searched local event calendars	34%
Searched for rental car prices/availability	26%
Searched for places to go	22%
Searched for travel packages	13%

Source: Cook (2001)

on-line planners is a baby boomer, it is not surprising that 33 per cent of them are married with children. On average, these consumers take about ten leisure trips per year. About two-thirds of on-line travel planners take five or more leisure trips a year. It seems that the ability to access travel information on-line has reduced the need to use traditional, or off-line, methods of planning leisure trips. Most on-line leisure travel planners claim that since they began planning trips on the Internet, they use phone calls or personal visits to travel agencies, chambers of commerce and tourism offices less often than they used to. In addition, many on-line travel planners make direct calls to airlines, hotels and rental car companies less frequently. Yet word-of-mouth information from friends, family or co-workers is still being used as often or more often by on-line travel planners (TIA, 2001a, 2001b).

Leisure trips planned on-line are most likely to be for entertainment or to visit friends or relatives. More than 50 per cent of trips planned on-line include a car or truck or rental car as the primary mode of transportation while 50 per cent include air transportation. Very few on-line trips involve travel by camper/RV, bus or train. Consumers seek out several types of website content when planning trips on-line. eTravellers most often obtain maps and/or driving directions and search for lodging options and availability. Many on-line planners search for destination-specific content such as things to do at the destination, information on dining and entertainment, or information about local events. About one in five on-line planners uses the web to help them choose a destination in the first place. About 50 per cent of recent trips planned on-line include an on-line reservation or purchase related to the trip. Among these trips, more than half include overnight lodging reservations (55 per cent) and/or booking a flight (54 per cent) whilst 30 per cent included a rental car reservation (TIA, 2001a, 2001b).

As demonstrated in Figure 4.6, search engines are the most popular type of website used for travel, whilst company-owned websites (airlines, **hotels** etc.) are also becoming critical as consumers would like to interact directly with travel

Figure 4.6 Types of website used for planning and booking leisure trips in the USA

Type of website	On-line leisure travellers	
	Travel planning (%)	Travel booking (%)
Company sites	77	77
Destination sites	68	29
On-line travel agency sites	61	60
Search engine sites	59	30
Portal sites	54	30
Travel guide sites	29	10
Special interest sites	20	9
Newspaper or magazine sites	14	7
Community sites	11	6

Source: Cook (2001)

organizations. On-line travel agencies have also grown significantly in popularity and many on-line travel planners also use destination websites. Among frequent leisure travellers (five-plus trips per year), most use the Internet for at least half of their trip planning and they tend to have had on-line access for more than two years. Heavy on-line travel planners also spend more time on-line in an average week and they are particularly likely to use company websites, perhaps because of loyalty programmes or familiarity with the providers. eTravel consumers have varying degrees of experience when it comes to using the Internet for travel planning. About 75 per cent began planning leisure travel on-line within the past two years. Travel guide websites are also more popular among experienced on-line planners, whilst recent planners are much more likely to use search engine web sites (TIA, 2001a, 2001b).

On-line bookings

The growth in the number of Americans planning trips on-line has led to strong growth in on-line travel booking, which may include the on-line booking of an airline ticket, hotel room, rental car or package tour. One-third of all travellers who are on-line and about half of on-line travel planners are now actually booking or making travel reservations on-line. On-line travel booking is still growing at a faster pace than on-line planning, increasing 26 per cent over 2000 and 106 per cent over 1999. Most of those who have booked travel on-line have purchased airline tickets via the Internet (80 per cent) as demonstrated in Figure 4.7. Many on-line travel bookers have reserved a hotel room (62 per cent), and just under half (46 per cent) have made rental car reservations. Tickets for activities such as cultural events (27 per cent), sports events (16 per cent) and amusement parks (14 per cent) are often purchased on-line as well. The most popular type of website used to book travel are company websites that sell directly to consumers. Three-quarters (75 per cent) of travel bookers go to company websites for airline, hotel or rental car reservations while over half (57 per cent) book travel using on-line travel agency sites such as Microsoft Expedia, Travelocity or Priceline. While search engine websites are widely used for travel planning, only about one-third (34 per cent) of on-line travel bookers pay for or make their reserva-

Figure 4.7 Travel products booked on-line

Purchased on-line in past year	Heavy on-line travel bookers	Light on-line travel bookers
Airline tickets	84%	71%
Overnight lodging	78%	63%
Rental car	59%	36%
Tickets for a museum, festival, sports event etc.	33%	21%
Tickets for amusement park	18%	17%
Travel package	17%	9%
Cruise	8%	3%

Source: Cook (2001)

tions using these sites. Travel bookers are more likely to be college-educated and have higher annual household incomes. On-line travel bookers are also younger, with 44 per cent in generations X or Y (18–34 years) (TIA, 2001a, 2001b).

About 60 per cent of on-line leisure travel planners actually purchased travel on-line in the past year. Heavy on-line travel buyers are more likely than light buyers to book travel on most types of website. Company websites, on-line agencies and web portals are the most popular for booking overall. Naturally, destination websites and search engine websites are not as popular for booking travel as for planning it. Nearly 50 per cent of heavy on-line travel buyers are in generations X or Y (age 18–34 years). This compares with only 33 per cent of light on-line bookers, who are more likely to be baby boomers (age 35–54). Because they are younger, heavy on-line bookers are less likely to have children and are more likely to have a college education, and they have slightly higher average annual household incomes than light on-line travel buyers (TIA, 2001a, 2001b).

Although these points refer to US consumers, where a large percentage of consumers is travelling independently and domestically, the European and Asian markets are gradually emerging to take advantage of on-line travel opportunities. The language barrier and the lower ICT penetration may be the cause of delay in this process. It is, however, anticipated that gradually most consumers around the world will increasingly use the Internet for planning and booking their holidays as well as for business trips. It is evident therefore that only tourism organizations and destinations that prepare their presence in the emerging electronic marketplace will be able to gain some of the projected benefits and achieve competitive advantages.

4.4 Barriers and catalysts for on-line consumers and travellers

There are several *barriers and catalysts* for on-line customers. Firstly the cost of access that comprises the fee to the **Internet Service Provider (ISP)**, and then the call to the ISP, which is normally charged at the local rate. The provision of free access to the Internet by ISPs such as Freeserve in the UK encouraged a large number of new computer buyers as well as people who had access to the Internet through their jobs to subscribe from home. However, the relevant high cost of local calls in Europe in comparison with the USA means that consumers stay connected for less time and do not surf on the Internet as freely as the Americans. AOL in a recent survey illustrated that 41 per cent of non-connected UK households would go on-line and stay for longer if phone prices dropped. The average time on-line in the UK is 17 minutes daily while in the USA it is 60 minutes. About 95.6 per cent of AOL's UK customers blame phone charges for not spending more time on line whilst 20 per cent of AOL's customers spend £50–100 per month on phone calls for net access and 13 per cent spend more than £100. It is also estimated that £500 million of British Telecom's recent £4.3 billion profit came from Internet access calls.

A campaign for free local telephone calls or 'unmetered access' is currently under way in the UK and it is anticipated that it will enable Internet users to access Internet pages for free. Several operators including, altavista.com, announced the service and then backtracked. However telecommunication operators such as NTL, BT and AOL are currently offering free Internet access for a flat fee to all their telecommunication subscribers. The argument is that a similar principle applies to customers browsing for free in retail shops. In Italy, Tiscali even pays subscribers in voice telephone time to surf the Internet as advertisers are happy to pay to subsidize this service.

Hitherto, the majority of current prospective tourists use the Internet for collecting information and building their itinerary. However, many Internet users still use traditional intermediaries to book their tourism products off-line. The PhoCusWright Travel eCommerce Survey in the USA illustrated that 44 per cent of the wired American population and 56 per cent of daily Internet users have bought something on-line. As far as tourism is concerned, 80 per cent of Internet users researched on-line for travel products, 58 per cent checked prices and 18 per cent eventually booked on-line. This is a situation that is often referred to in the industry as 'too many lookers, too few bookers'. Jones (1999) illustrated that 45 per cent of European Internet users searched travel and tourism on-line but only 15 per cent have actually purchased something on-line. It is anticipated that by 2003 more than 10 per cent of all tourism products in the USA will be booked on the Internet, generating a total turnover of $17 billion (Jupiter, 1999).

Research has demonstrated that several factors have discouraged people from booking on-line, as illustrated in Figure 4.8. Although these factors deter on-line purchases in the short term it is estimated that consumers will familiarize themselves with the new tools and take increasing advantage of the Internet. Progress is also evident in the design and interactivity of Internet pages as well as the speed, security and reliability of funds transfers. Tourism organizations also realize their benefits and change their business practices to take advantage of on-line bookings. As a result they offer special discounts to on-line bookers, distribute their excess capacity on-line for a fraction of the cost and include telephone numbers with support operators should consumers require assistance.

Nevertheless, it is also quite evident that Internet users who do not book on-line often use other distribution channels to purchase the itinerary that they

Figure 4.8 Reasons that discourage people from purchasing tourism on-line

User/client factors	Internet/business factors
• Plans were not definite • Safety and security of credit cards on network • Cannot see or touch the product • No trust, unfamiliar name • Prefer regular travel agency • Afraid of making mistakes • Did not realize that they could make reservations • Would rather talk to a real person • Plans were not definite • Concerned about privacy of information • Someone else made the reservations • Don't own a credit card	• Takes too long to enter information • Navigation difficulty • Use corporate travel agency • Can't get confirmation • Internet chaotic and difficulty in finding suitable information • Not enough selection available • Internet doesn't give lowest prices/deals • Didn't need to book anything • Internet too slow and takes a long time to find suitable products • Too confusing/complicated • Internet doesn't give up-to-date information

Source: Based on Cook (2001)

organize on the Internet. About 70 per cent of people who researched on-line (lookers) booked directly through airlines (28 per cent), travel agencies (39 per cent) and other means (2 per cent) and finally 27 per cent did not travel. The majority of the bookings goes to fairly simple airline tickets, as out of those booked 83 per cent purchased airline tickets, 40 per cent booked hotels, 32 per cent arranged car rental and 3 per cent purchased holiday packages (Jones, 1999).

4.5 Qualitative growth of tourism demand

It is not only the growing volume of tourists that propels ICT penetration. Tourism demand is undergoing a great transformation and *qualitative* trends are applying more pressure on the industry to use ICTs. Tourists become sophisticated and more demanding, requesting high-quality products. The 'new' tourist is more knowledgeable about tourism destinations and organizations and seeks exceptional value for money and time. Value for time becomes much more significant, as time pressure forces busy people to take fewer holidays and to spend less time organizing them. Having few opportunities to do things that they enjoy propels people to make best use of their time. They constantly compare experiences between destinations and enterprises and have clear views on their preferences. Several web pages encourage consumers to network and exchange experiences and 'horror stories' should companies, destinations or intermediaries fail to deliver. **Holidaysuncovered.com** and **holidaytruths.co.uk**, for example, encourage holidaymakers to report on their package holidays and assess the performance of their resorts against their expectations and the brochure promise.

The Internet has enabled the 'new' type of tourist to become more knowledgeable and to seek exceptional value for money and time. New consumers are more culturally and environmentally aware and they often like a greater involvement with the local society. The Internet provides not only information about the tourism products they can consume but also a whole range of additional data about the resources, history and social and economic structure of destinations. In this sense, certain consumer groups are better equipped to engage in social interaction with locals and to use their travels as an educational experience. Tourists therefore will tend to participate in the experience by being active and spend their time on their special interests. Leisure time will increasingly be perceived as an exploration for both personal and professional development (WTO, 1999).

Poon (1993) has led the debate on the transformation of tourists by suggesting that 'old tourism' is gradually replaced by 'new tourism'. Old tourism is characterized by 'mass, standardized and rigidly packed' tourism with little attention to tourists' personal needs. It follows the Ford model of mass production, low price and lack of differentiation. It has mainly appealed to the mass markets that enjoy cheap holiday packages, based on **economies of scale**. Using charter flights and undifferentiated, inexpensive accommodation, they purchase **packages** from tour operators as commodities. This tourism has primarily served the sun-loving and inexperienced consumer and it has been tailored to their cultural backgrounds, tastes and preferences.

However, since the early 1990s 'new tourism' has been emerging, using new best practices. It is characterized as 'flexible, segmented, customized and diagonally integrated' and recognizes that every tourist is different, bringing a unique blend of experiences, motivations and desires. Thus, the relative importance of package tours, which are often based on low quality/low prices, is expected to decline in favour of independently organized tourism. A relatively new movement towards environmental preservation and appreciation for the local society is also evident. Tourists tend to participate in the experience by being active and by spending their time on their special interests. Leisure time will increasingly be used for **'edu-tainment'**, i.e. the exploration of personal interests for both their personal and professional development. Flexibility in both consumer choice and service delivery processes becomes a key element. The traditional annual family holiday, generally in a Mediterranean beach resort, will change rapidly and will play a less dominant role in the future. Increasingly multi-interest travel replaces part of the industry's present 'bread and butter' products. As a result, most beach holidays will include an element of culture and education, plus pleasure of some kind.

Cooper and Buhalis (1998) suggest that to an extent the new sophisticated traveller has emerged as a result of experience. Tourists from the major generating regions of the world have become frequent travellers, are linguistically and technologically skilled and can function in multicultural and demanding environments overseas. A relatively new movement towards environmental preservation and appreciation for local society is also evident. Tourists tend to participate in the experience by being more actively involved and often spend their time on pursuing their special interests, hobbies and activities. As a result we are moving from a passive attitude to much more involvement and engagement. Flexibility in both consumer choice and the service delivery process is a key element. As leisure lifestyles are increasingly inconsistent and contradictory for individual tourists, in the new millennium tourism organizations will be following the trend towards customization and personalization of products not only according to market segments but also according to preferences, occasions, situations and even moods. Using new technology, the tourism industry is able to offer a much more individualized product to new/experienced/sophisticated/demanding tourists who look for authentic experiences and have an independent and wanderlust attitude (Buhalis, 2001).

As illustrated in Figure 4.9, the traditional 5Ss of the seaside tourism activity (sun–sea–sand–sex–sangria) and the equivalent of urban tourism (short breaks–sightseeing–shopping–shows–scotch whisky) are transformed into sophistication–specialization–segmentation–satisfaction–seduction. Hitherto, the majority of leisure traffic has resulted from holidaymakers from northern countries escaping to the sunny south to 'recharge their batteries' for a heavy winter back home. However, *sea* pollution, health dangers resulting from *sun* exposure, *sand* degradation and modern *sexually* transmitted diseases gradually limit the appeal of these elements. *Sangria* and *Scotch whisky* also symbolize the large amounts of alcohol consumed during holiday periods. In urban and city breaks tourism, consumers have often done all the available sightseeing tours, have seen all the shows and feel familiar with metropolitan regions, and are less interested in shopping as the entire range of products are widely available in their local markets globally, and souvenirs are increasingly standardized.

An increasing demand for more individualized, authentic and enriched travel experiences signify the transformation of the traditional '5Ss' into the five modern ones. Educated, experienced and demanding tourists require *sophisticated* tourism products, which can satisfy their educational, cultural, intellectual and sporting interests. This kind of demand develops tourism into a more sophistic-

Figure 4.9 Tourism demand transformation

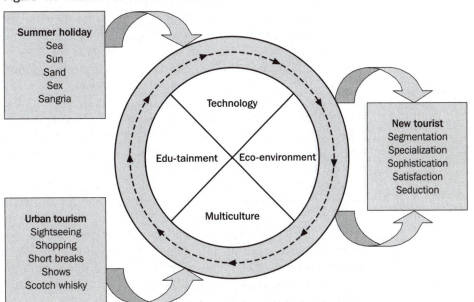

ated marketplace. Since every prospective tourist has almost unique needs and wants, a certain amount of *specialization* is expected to dominate the future tourist product. Thus, the focus is turned to individuals and mini-segments, which can share common activities and desire to experience similar activities. The identification of these mini-markets can only be achieved through detailed market *segmentation*, based on lifestyle variables, rather than on demographics. This process is able to demonstrate the similarities between consumer patterns and can result in the formulation of feasible specialized activities. The ultimate aim for every tourism enterprise and destination should be total customer *satisfaction* throughout the tourist consumption chain, i.e. before, during and after the visit. Ultimately tourism organizations need to be able to seduce consumers and to create a loyal clientèle, which would actively seek to purchase the products of the enterprise or the firm. An integrated approach within the tourism industry is, therefore, required in order to ensure the coordination of the various enterprises and individuals involved in the tourist product delivery. Organizations and destinations that fail to serve and facilitate the transformation of tourism demand will be marginalized and suffer significant losses in their market share (Buhalis, 1994).

ICTs allow the tourism industry to *identify consumer needs* efficiently and to formulate personalized value-added chains for individual consumers. On registration, consumers are required to fill in their profile information and to provide methods for regular interaction. Consumers are empowered through the new tools to search for information and to build their own *personalized tourism products* or to put together their own value chain. The availability of information on everything conceivable enables consumers to package their own bundles of tourism products and to purchase only the most suitable offerings for their own individual needs. Suppliers on the other hand have an unprecedented opportunity to communicate with their target markets globally, to develop their global presence and to establish direct relationships with consumers. This will enable them to evolve their products and make sure that they remain competitive.

ICTs play a critical role in the transformation of tourism demand as they enable consumers to *identify the most appropriate products* for their needs by using the Internet and support their interactivity with tourism organizations. Empowered by the Internet they tend to research their desired products or simply look for last-minute offers. They also use the Internet as an anonymous method of collecting information which reduces their social risk (Poria and Taylor 2001). They use commercial and non-commercial Internet sites for planning, searching, purchasing and amending their travel. Prospective tourists request more specific information on accessibility, facilities, attractions and activities. Before selecting their products, new, experienced, sophisticated, demanding travellers increasingly seek more information about unusual, exotic destinations and authentic experiences. They also expect travel organizations to interact with them in order to satisfy their specific needs and wishes. The contemporary/connected consumer 'is far less willing to wait or put up with delays, to the point where patience is a disappearing virtue' (Rach, 1997). The information currently available on the Internet may sometimes be inaccurate or misleading. However, consumers increasingly develop their evaluation mechanisms and assess the reliability of on-line information.

ICTs enable travellers to access reliable and accurate information as well as to undertake reservations in a fraction of the time, cost and inconvenience required by conventional methods. In fact prospective travellers today have more information and resources than travel agencies only five years ago, and therefore have a much greater ability to judge between products, destinations and packages. Although consumers may not yet buy on-line *en masse* they are well aware of the tourism offerings on a global basis, and the growth of on-line purchasing is remarkable. No-frills airlines report selling 85 per cent of their tickets on-line, whilst hotel group Accor recently announced that 15 per cent of its bookings is made on the Internet by consumers. ICTs can therefore improve the service quality and contribute to higher guest/traveller satisfaction. Improved access to information covering all aspects of tourist activities provides the framework for offering personalized services at price levels comparable to those of standard packages. The key to success therefore lies in using ICT tools for the quick identification of consumer needs and in reaching potential clients with comprehensive, personalized and up-to-date information (WTO, 1988). The Internet has merely empowered this process and has increased its speed and interactivity. Perhaps the growth has been slowed by the fact that several commercial Internet sites are less developed than consumers may have liked, and thus damage the commercial opportunities for their organization. However, it needs to be recognized that buying on-line is often instant and emotional based on moods, personal liking and preference but sometimes even irrational decision.

For example, a family that requires a week's holiday increasingly will not be happy with purchasing their last hotel option out of a range of hotel photos in undifferentiated resorts in the Mediterranean. Typically a holiday booking involves holiday makers selecting properties and resorts that are unavailable and then having to compromise with alternative options. They will incorporate their specific needs and include several additional features to stimulate their interest and to keep them active during the holiday. For example, the experience may include some artistic training for the children, an archaeological research element for the wife and a tennis championship for the husband. They may decide to purchase a package from a tour operator that allows flexibility and then alter/add specific elements. Spending more or less time in resorts and altering the itinerary will be the norm rather than the exception, and organizations such as Kuoni capitalize on this market. Alternatively they can package their personalized product by amalgamating all individually produced offerings. They may travel alone, or arrange to meet people with similar interests that they have met on- or off-line, perhaps negotiating special deals and extra features for their personalized niche segment and group. Having access to all this information and reservation mechanisms, consumers are much better equipped to identify the tourism products that combine all their requirements.

When discussing **consumer** buying **behaviour** in tourism and the impact of ICTs, a clear distinction should be made between experienced and inexperienced travellers. Further distinctions can be made between destination-knowledgeable (have been there several times and have an understanding of the local facilities and culture) and destination-naive (first-timers or uncomfortable with the destination or product) consumers. Obviously the first category feels more comfortable organizing their own holidays, using all the tools available to personalize the product and taking advantage of ICT capabilities to design their package according to preferences. The Internet has really empowered the former type of travellers while inexperienced travellers may still use conventional tourism intermediaries in order to enjoy the feel of security that tour operators offer to their clients. Having organized all accommodation, transfers through a company at the place of origin as well as having local representation from the tourists' country of origin offer an extra level of security that inexperienced tourists appreciate more. As a result, although experienced travellers may go directly to suppliers' Internet interfaces and create their own packages, inexperienced travellers are expected to use the Internet for identifying the best off-the-shelf package.

Nevertheless, ICTs enable tourism enterprises to develop and deliver complex offerings to satisfy specific interests. This supports the segmentation function to specific niche segments. Increasingly success will depend on the quick identification of consumer needs and interaction with prospective clients by using comprehensive, personalized and up-to-date communication media for the design of products. Speed of acknowledging and satisfying enquiries may even be more important than product attributes, as increasingly consumers make emotional decisions, under time pressure. Although competition will be more fierce, as consumers have access to endless numbers of suppliers, providing value for time will be at least equally important to value for money.

4.6 The ICT revolution and tourist satisfaction

ICTs can also improve the service quality and contribute to higher guest/traveller satisfaction. Stipanuk (1993) explores how technology affects tourists' experiences. ICTs are critical for the demand growth experienced in tourism, whilst ICTs often protect and enhance the tourism experience. Schertler, Maier and Rohte (1995) suggest that 'experienced travellers could be "empowered" significantly by ICTs to use travel information and booking systems independently and improve their personal efficiency and competencies'. Timely and accurate information relevant to the consumer's needs is often the key to successful satisfaction of tourism demand (Williams, 1993).

Customer satisfaction depends greatly on the accuracy and comprehensiveness of specific information concerning destination accessibility, facilities, attractions and activities. ICTs can improve customer satisfaction by proving much more content than traditional media and by incorporating realistic videos and pictures of products. In this way the gap between consumers' expectations and perceived experiences will decrease, and thus unpleasant surprises can be minimized. Increasingly, ICTs enable travellers to access reliable and accurate information as well as to undertake reservations in a fraction of time, cost and inconvenience required by conventional methods. Having a greater understanding of what facilities are like and providing accurate information is therefore critical for developing realistic expectations that can be fulfilled by the product. This is in sharp contrast to the conventional marketing practice of over-promising and

Figure 4.10 Customer satisfaction for travellers as a result of ICT tools

- Reduction of the gap between expectations and perceived experience, due to more information and virtual experience before consumption
- Consumers have more information and enjoy greater choice
- Better understanding of consumer needs based on research, interaction and data mining
- Consumers feel empowered to get information on products and services of interest
- Pricing becomes more flexible as organizations are willing to provide great discounts for last-minute, targeted offers and special promotions
- New business models enable consumers to name the price they are willing to pay (e.g. priceline.com)
- New value-added services (e.g. customized in-flight or in-room entertainment and information channels)
- A reduction of the bureaucracy and paper-work frees employee time for better customer service
- Automation of 'boring' operational tasks through ICTs (e.g. in-room TV checkout)
- Personalized services (e.g. telephone operator acknowledges guest by name or waiter knows dietary preferences or requirements)
- Better integration of departments and functions of organizations towards better service
- User-friendly and customized interfaces
- Language barriers increasingly reduced through development of interfaces to serve all target markets and also through automatic translation
- Differentiated and customized services, according to personal lifestyle, preferences and attitudes, rather than socio-demographic segmentation
- Customization of the product and the establishing of 'one-to-one' marketing by using intelligence collected by loyalty schemes (e.g. dietary requirements, product preferences)
- Accurate and much richer marketing research by collecting data from all transactions and enquiries

under-delivering, which maximizes dissatisfaction. In addition, ICTs can provide additional information, in-flight and in-room entertainment. By differentiating products according to individual tastes at an affordable cost, ICTs can maximize the utility of the tourism product. Figure 4.10 illustrates several ICT-facilitated factors that can empower prospective tourists and enhance their satisfaction.

However, ICTs and the Internet, like all other media, can be used unwisely and *reduce customer satisfaction*. When ICTs do not function properly, tourism experiences can be destroyed, especially in products where ICTs play a critical role such as Disneyland (Stipanuk, 1993). The Internet representation of a tourism organization may also affect customer satisfaction negatively, as it is subject to abuse and over-promotion by marketing executives who are keen to show only the positive sides of tourism products. Internet sites also frequently provide inaccurate or out-of-date information, if they are not updated regularly or deliberately broadcast misleading information. Although this is not a new problem in tourism, the availability of information to consumers and the ability of almost everyone to publish their views and interpretations about places and organizations, no matter how biased, may mislead consumers. The global character of the medium, as well as the ability of individuals to publish incorrect material, deliberately or not, without necessarily being accountable makes it much more difficult for consumers to complain formally and request refunds.

Sheldon (1994) asserts 'IT has the potential both to increase the efficiency of travel industry firms, and to make products more accessible to the travel public. Most importantly, when implemented appropriately, information technology can improve the service quality and contribute to higher guest/traveller satisfaction'. Hence, tourism organizations and destinations that would like to satisfy tourism demand and survive in the long term have no choice but to:

- take advantage of the new ICT tools;
- research the requirements of their target markets;
- ensure the accuracy and currency of their on-line information;
- coordinate on-line and off-line branding and pricing issues, in collaboration with partners;
- develop appropriate solutions on-line; and
- enhance their interactivity with the marketplace.

Consumer satisfaction will depend increasingly on the accuracy and comprehensiveness of specific information on destinations' accessibility, facilities, attractions and activities.

4.7 Conclusions: the rapid growth of on-line population and travel demand

The radical usage of ICTs in the tourism industry is driven by the development of both the size and complexity of tourism demand, as well as by the rapid expansion and sophistication of tourism products that increasingly address mini-market segments. Furthermore, current and revolutionary developments in ICTs illustrate that, more and more, the tourism industry will need to be able to take advantage of the emerging potential and re-engineer their marketing, distribution and delivery processes towards pleasing the increasingly discerning customer.

Non-tourism organizations have also identified the emergent opportunity and attempt to serve existing and new market segments by using ICT tools. This is already the case with major ICT providers (e.g. Microsoft have developed Expedia, an electronic travel agency) as well as with newspapers, clubs and associations that develop partnerships with travel organizations for developing suitable tourism products to satisfy tourism demand. It is up to the industry to develop suitable on-line solutions to empower and delight tourism customers. As the market segments that are connected are those that travel more frequently, there are significant synergies between the travellers and Internet users. These will be exploited by the innovative successful organizations of the future.

Chapter questions

1 Which target markets are more likely to book on-line, and why?

2 List the key factors that will encourage more tourism products to be booked on-line.

3 Explain the differences between the information needs of business and leisure travellers.

4 What determines the level of on-line population and the penetration of the Internet in each country?

5 What are the sources of satisfaction and dissatisfaction for the on-line consumer?

6 What non-tourism products/services may enjoy synergies by promoting tourism?

Further reading

Buhalis, D. (2001) The tourism phenomenon – the new tourist and consumer, in Wahab, S. and Cooper, C. (eds), *Tourism in the Age of Globalisation*, Routledge, London.

Bywater, M. (2001) Travel distribution: who owns whom in the European travel distribution industry, in Buhalis, D. and Laws, E. (eds), *Tourism Distribution Channels*, Continuum, London.

Poon, A. (1993) *Tourism, Technology and Competitive Strategies*, CAB International, Oxford.

Schertler, W., Maier, M. and Rohte, S. (1995) The end user acceptance of new information and communication technologies in tourism, in Schertler, W. et al. (eds), *Information and Communication Technologies in Tourism*, Springer-Verlag, Vienna, pp. 46–52.

TIA (2001a) *eTravel Consumers: How They Plan and Buy Leisure Travel Online*, Travel Industry Association of America, Washington DC, USA (www.tia.org).

TIA (2001b) *Travelers' Use of the Internet, 2001 Edition*, Travel Industry Association of America, Washington DC, USA (www.tia.org).

Websites

Statistics on on-line population

European Tourism Commission monitor: **www.etcmonitor.com**

Europe Media: **www.europemedia.net**

Computer Industry Almanac: **www.c-i-a.com**

ACNielsen eRatings Internet measurement service: **www.e-ratings.com**

Forrester: **www.forrester.com**

Gartner: **www3.gartner.com**

GartnerG2: **www.gartnerg2.com/site/default.asp**

Jupiter: **www.jup.com/home.jsp**

NOP Research: **www.nopres.co.uk**

NUA Research: **www.nua.ie/index.shtml**

IDC: **www.idc.com**

Which Net: **www.which.net/surveys**

AllNetResearch: **http://allnetresearch.internet.com**

Travel Industry Association: **www.tia.org**

World Travel Monitor: **www.ipkinternational.com**

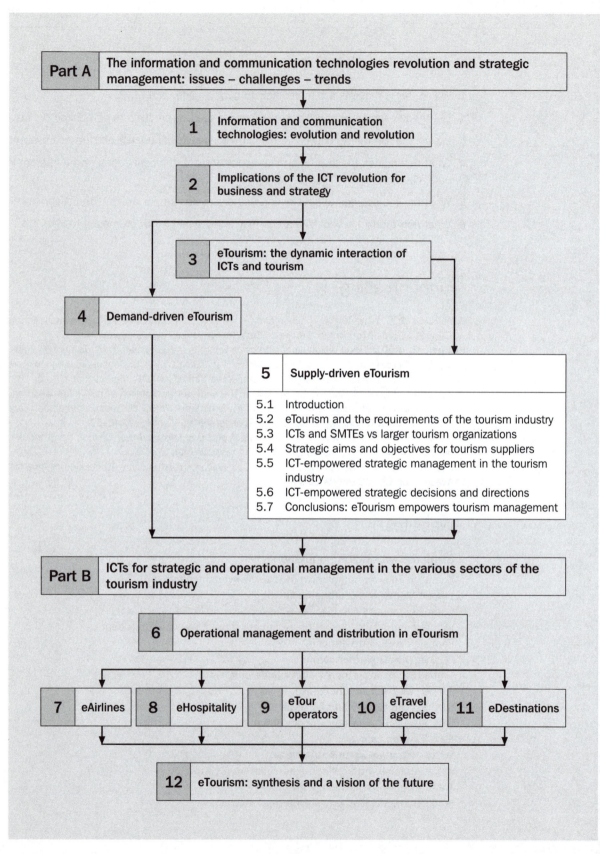

5

Supply-driven eTourism

Chapter objectives

The purpose of this chapter is to explore the strategic implications of ICTs in the tourism, hospitality and travel industries. The chapter also demonstrates how organizations use eTourism to achieve and sustain competitive advantage and illustrates several critical strategic decisions, which are facilitated by technological tools. Thus, the learning objectives may be defined as:

- Elaborate how ICTs can support tourism, hospitality and travel companies to achieve and maintain competitive advantage
- Understand the sources of competitiveness and explore how technology affects them
- Discuss the particular requirements of small and medium-sized enterprises
- Identify critical strategic decisions and directions empowered by ICTs
- Demonstrate the cost and benefit elements applicable for tourism organizations
- Debate the issue of sustainability of ICT-supported competitive advantage
- Explore how ICTs can integrate the entire industry and economy with the tourism value chain

5.1 Introduction

ICTs can provide a powerful tool, which, if properly applied and used, could without doubt bring great advantages in promoting and strengthening tourism industry operations (WTO, 1988, 2001). The tourism industry already uses a wide range of ICT systems. Several tailor-made, internal management applications facilitate the management and marketing of **global organizations**. These systems use databases as well as office automation software for inventory control and for generic administration purposes. **Knowledge management** systems enable organizations to collect information about their functions and to build knowledge on approaches to resolve problems and emerging issues. The Internet provides a window to the world for these organizations and allows them to demonstrate their competencies widely. Increasingly intranets and extranets are used to offer user-friendly access to employees of organizations as well as their authorized partners to use company data in order to perform their tasks.

5.2 eTourism and the requirements of the tourism industry

In addition to tourism demand propelling the penetration of ICTs in tourism, the supply side has also steadily grown to realize the transformation of the industry due to the tools that are emerging. The supply side is defined quite liberally in this book as all those participating in the tourism system, providing services and products and creating value either directly or indirectly for consumption by tourists and travellers. Leiper (1995), Goeldner et al. (2000), Cooper et al. (1998) and Holloway (1989) provide more comprehensive and analytical definitions. This book concentrates on the use of ICTs in private-sector enterprises and elaborates on how ICTs can support the profitability and competitiveness of organizations. In addition, a destination management model is described (in Chapter 11) that provides guidance for **destination management organizations (DMO)**. As already demonstrated, few other industries require as much information and collaboration between actors for delivering their products as does tourism.

The tourism industry has traditionally used ICTs in a number of key strategic and operational functions, as summarized in Figure 5.1. However, it is increasingly recognized that the use of ICTs in tourism is pervasive, as information is critical for both the day-to-day operations and the strategic management of tourism organizations. ICTs support all business functions and are critical for operating the industry as a whole.

The development of the Internet, as well as intranets and extranets in the 1990s, revolutionized the usage of ICTs in the tourism industry and enhanced tourism distribution to a global electronic marketplace. Networking provided the infrastructure for both intra- and inter-organizational cooperation and, consequently, altered the best practices in the industry. There is no better example than that of the development of airline alliances, which now dominate the entire globe.

Figure 5.1 Key strategic and operational functions empowered by ICTs

Key strategic functions	Key operational functions
• Enhance organizational efficiency and effectiveness	• Information distribution and reservation process
• Improve quality of services	• International tourism management and marketing
• Undertake strategic research for new markets and products	• Facilitation of producer–intermediary–consumer interaction
• Follow up competition	• Production and delivery of tourism products
• Penetrate existing and new markets and expand market share	• Organization, management and control of tourism enterprises
• Diversify to new products and services or new markets	• Front office: reservations, check-in, billing, communicating
• Formulate new combinations of tourist products	• Back office: accounting, payroll, procurement, administration
• Differentiate and personalize products and add value at all stages	• Customer entertainment and service
• Reduce cost and achieve cost-competitive advantage by creating value for money	• Communicate with consumers and partners
• Achieve time-competitive advantage by maximizing efficiency for consumers and creating value for time	• React to unexpected events and adopt flexibility and reflective procedures
• Re-engineer business processes and rationalize operations	• Dynamic yield management and adjust price and capacity
• Constantly reinvent new and innovative business practices	• Monitor performance and build in feedback mechanisms
• Outperform competition in the long run	• Control and administration
• Develop partnerships and explore virtual corporations	

The World Wide Web (WWW) enabled the interactivity and networking between computer users by using the Internet to facilitate instant access and distribution of tourism information as well as to support and gradually re-engineer the reservation of tourism organizations (WTO, 1995; Smith and Jenner, 1998). As a result, an electronic marketplace emerged and the vast majority of tourism providers developed Internet interfaces to communicate directly and efficiently with their clientèle and partners. Combining loyalty clubs, guest histories and other information held in operation databases provided airlines and hotel chains with powerful information that enabled them to interact with their existing and prospective clientèle. OneWorld, the Star Alliance and the Qualiflier group incorporate most major airlines and cover all continents. This is only achievable through using ICTs effectively for coordinating and maximizing the efficiency of the system. ICTs have been centrally placed as one of the most critical factors for both the operational and strategic management of the industry.

The networking era enabled easy access to information and ubiquity, and thus enhanced the interactivity between tourism producers or principals (e.g. airlines, hotels), intermediaries (e.g. travel agencies, tour operators) and consumers. In addition, a new breed of intermediaries and tourism enterprises emerged to take advantage of the new capabilities of the Internet. These include electronic intermediaries (e.g. TravelWeb, Expedia) as well as discount and auction specialists who concentrated on selling distressed capacity (e.g. **www.qxl.com**,

www.previewtravel.com, **a2btravel**, **lastminute.com**, **bargain-holidays.com**).
New suppliers also emerged mainly because of the new opportunities that the Internet provided and the capability to reach a large marketplace efficiently and profitably (e.g. **easyrentacar.com**, **iski.com**, etc.). Schmid (1994) warned that tourism
information and suppliers who are not included in the electronic markets will be
unable to address their target markets. He also suggested that the quality of access
mechanisms and product presentation in the global electronic tourism market
are as important as the actual product itself. As a result, ICTs gradually become a
critical determinant of the competence of tourism organizations and destinations.

5.3 ICTs and SMTEs vs larger tourism organizations

Understandably, larger tourism corporations took greater advantage of these
technologies at an earlier stage. Not only do they have the resources and expertise
to do so but also they often have a much more complicated and geographically
spread inventory of products to manage. In contrast, small and medium-sized
tourism enterprises (SMTEs) are more reluctant to introduce technologies and
therefore adopt more traditional management practices. SMTEs are defined by
the European Commission as all enterprises with:

■ fewer than 250 employees (0–10 micro, 11–50 small, and 51–250 medium-sized);
■ less than 40 million euros turnover;
■ less than a quarter of the company being held by a larger firm.

SMTEs are characterized not only by their small size but also by their independence, flexibility, seasonality and often family ownership and management. SMTEs
frequently feature informal organizational structures, with the role of family
members forming a key component within the decision-making process.

It is estimated that more than 90 per cent of hotels are SMTEs and are family-
managed (Shaw and Williams, 1990; Go and Welch, 1991; Sheldon, 1993). This
includes not only primarily tourism enterprises such as hotels and transport companies but also enterprises that serve the local population and travellers, such as
restaurants, bars, leisure centres and cinemas. In addition, it includes organizations that are not normally classified as members of the tourism industry such as
hairdressers, retail shops and Internet cafes as well as other businesses that support tourism enterprises such as accountants, electricians, carpenters, mechanics
etc. SMTEs prevail in the tourism and hospitality sectors throughout Europe and
offer great benefits for regional development and local economies by diffusing
tourist expenditure into local markets. Despite their size, collectively SMTEs are
extremely important to both national and European economies. They provide
stable employment opportunities and support the integration of local economies
in peripheral areas, even during recession periods. Unlike larger chain-based
organizations, they are normally privately owned, are family-run, employ local
people and purchase goods and services from suppliers within the local economy.
SMTEs also give tourists direct contact with the character of the destination.

It is estimated that 99.95 per cent of the existing 1.41 m European HORECA
(HOtel REstaurant CAtering) enterprises employ fewer than 250 employees (EC,

1994). In France for example, the size of tourism enterprises is clearly reflected in research on the microeconomic analysis of the tourism sector, undertaken by The pH Group on behalf of the European Union (The pH Group, 1993). Only 19 per cent of employment is generated within France from enterprises with more than 100 employees. Enterprises employing up to 10 people represent 94 per cent of French tourism firms and 48 per cent of total employment in tourism. Statistics on the accommodation sector confirm this observation. In every European country, small, independent and flexible hotels dominate the market. In Switzerland more than 90 per cent of Swiss hotels have fewer than 50 rooms and only 2 per cent have more than 100 rooms, while in the UK the average hotel has 25 rooms. The average hotel and restaurant establishment in Greece employs 2.5 people while the average number of beds per establishment in the Greek Islands is 63 (Buhalis, 1994).

The rapid developments in ICTs introduce both opportunities and threats for traditional SMTEs. ICTs provide tools for enterprises and organizations to manage and market themselves in a more efficient and effective way as well as develop interfaces with the entire range of their stakeholders. However, the strategic weaknesses of SMTEs are that they often lack the expertise to take advantage of these opportunities and develop their competitiveness. This is often due to the ICT illiteracy of their entrepreneurs, which increases their perceived dependence on trained staff. Moreover, the cost of ICTs is often perceived as prohibitive by entrepreneurs. Thus, SMTEs may therefore find themselves becoming isolated from the marketplace and face severe competitive disadvantages should they fail to appreciate the potential benefits and develop suitable interfaces. As a result, ICTs can be regarded as a major *threat* for SMTEs that fail to invest and capitalize on the new tools.

However, there is evidence that a number of innovative SMTEs appreciate the *opportunity* emerging and can actually enhance their position by using ICT tools for strengthening their competitiveness. Competent tourism and accommodation operators, regardless of their size or location, increasingly perceive the Internet as a major opportunity that will enable them to improve their interactivity with consumers and other stakeholders. Often they are motivated by pioneers in their industry who have taken advantage of new technologies to increase efficiency, reduce operational costs, develop effective interfaces with consumers and partners and also attract new target markets. Consequently, SMTEs have started investing heavily in ICTs in order to improve their efficiency and enhance their presence in the electronic marketplace. Case Study 5.1 (as well as Case Study 2.1) illustrates this point.

The propensity of SMTEs to adopt ICTs in their operations and management is determined by a wide range of *catalysts*. These catalysts can be classified as *push factors* and *pull factors* and influence the degree of ICT adaptation. Catalysts also influence the stakeholders of SMTEs and motivate them to undertake action. Push factors are external forces that oblige enterprises to use ICTs in order to avoid potential threats or jeopardize some of their functions. Enterprises may not have recognized a need that the technology might fill. If the need has been recognized, enterprises may have not matched a particular technology with the fulfilment of that need. Stakeholders seek to promote, garner, support and push a technology. Pull factors provide incentives for enterprises to incorporate ICTs in order to gain benefits in their operation. In this scenario a recognized market need is present and enterprises draw on ICTs to fulfil it. Hence, the difference between push and pull factors is the willingness of SMTEs to undertake action. In the former case, action is forced, while in the latter action is stimulated and desired (Buhalis and Main, 1998).

Case Study 5.1

Hotel Segas

Following the end of a long-standing exclusive arrangement with its tour operator only a few months before the summer season was about to start, Hotel Segas found itself in a very difficult situation: having only 24 rooms and a fairly undifferentiated product apart from superb personal attention, the hotel had no resources and was not in a strong position to approach prospective customers. They could not attract new customers easily at such short notice. Given the limitation of the destination, the lack of funds for marketing activities and the insufficiency of marketing expertise internally, the hotel trusted a willing close relative to develop and maintain a web page promoting the hotel. There was no budget for the development of the site and as a result the hotel could not register its domain name and could only be registered with a free server.

The web design and text developed were significantly different from normal web pages. A much more personal and informal approach was adopted, giving the hotel's life story and introducing members of the host family; emphasis was also given on the destination and the practicalities. The web page went live in September 2000 and was gradually registered with most search engines by March 2001. The lack of funds delayed the registration as multiple submission through free-submit engines was made. Personalized answers to all eMails and booking requests was adopted, communicating with prospective travellers and assisting with all their travel planning rather than just the reservation with the hotel. In the period January–July 2001 the web pages had generated about 1000 viewings from areas as remote as Japan, Nicaragua and Canada. Bookings included an equally diverse background of bookers. A total of £2200 worth of incremental turnover was generated, or about 220 bed-nights, most of which were in the low season. In the first six months of its operation the web page had contributed about 16 per cent of the hotel annual turnover. The cost of developing and maintaining the web page was only the time volunteered by the helpful relative, demonstrating clearly that the Internet can enable even tiny but innovative organisations to maximize their potential.

For more information, see **http://hotelsegas.netfirms.com**

Questions

- What are the key success factors for small tourism enterprises, and how can ICTs influence them?
- What on-line strategies should SMEs have, and how can they take advantage of the emerging distribution channels?
- How can entrepreneurs embrace more ICTs to take advantage of the emerging opportunities?
- What ICT skills will the successful entrepreneur of the future need to have?

Groth (1993) examines the significance of the push–pull factor in harvesting benefit from technology introduction. He defines the pull factor as originating in political, social and economic forces, which 'pull' on the technology, and the push factor as relating to the efforts of the technology's proponents. The push–pull analysis is critical as it illuminates the attitude of enterprises towards ICTs and elaborates on the reasoning for actions undertaken. Inevitably a wide range of push and pull factors is exercised on SMTEs towards increasing their use of ICTs. Figure 5.2 demonstrates some of these push and pull factors and illustrates how they constrain SMTEs to undertake strategic action towards incorporating ICTs in their strategic and operational management.

Traditionally pull factors are related to major opportunities emerging for SMTEs through the development of ICTs. Benefits include an improvement of management and marketing through not only maximizing internal efficiency but also the development of communications and transaction interfaces with all SMTE stakeholders. In contrast, push factors are associated with emerging threats. A wide range of stakeholders increasingly demands certain conditions and prerequisites in order to continue their partnerships with SMTEs. The new 'wired' consumers demand that tourism enterprises be easily accessible on the Internet in order to provide information as well as on-line reservations. In addition, the entire range of partners of SMTEs is also driven towards an increase of efficiency, which can only be delivered by up-to-date ICTs. Increasingly this becomes a prerequisite for further funding and support from sponsoring bodies, such as governments and the European Commission as well as by trading partners. The new generation of tourism and hospitality managers has also gone through ICT training and therefore appreciates the new tools; this generation pushes for a greater utilization of ICTs and for a paradigm shift, which will enable SMTEs to maintain their competitiveness and enhance their prosperity.

Figure 5.2 Push and pull factors determining the introduction of ICTs in SMTEs

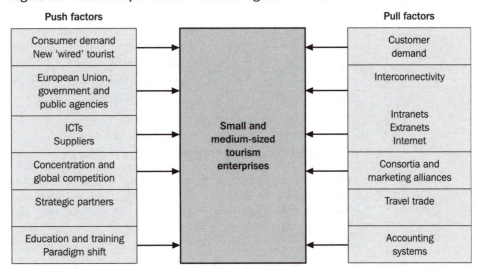

Source: Adapted from Buhalis and Main (1998)

Interestingly, ICTs are also pushed into SMTEs indirectly by the education system, as entrepreneurs' children are introduced to computers at school and wish to practise their coursework or to play electronic games at home. As a result, they often manage to persuade their parents to purchase a home computer, arousing the curiosity of entrepreneurs who in most cases familiarize themselves with the new machines and often learn how to use them for their business too.

Research on Greek, Welsh, French and English SMTEs has demonstrated that once they have acquired basic equipment such as a personal computer, costs can be manageable even for the smallest companies. Entrepreneurs habitually compare their Internet presence with conventional **advertising** in catalogues and brochures. Designing and maintaining an Internet presence can cost as little as £500 per year; this compares favourably with a single advertisement in the travel section of a Sunday newspaper or a single advertisement in one guidebook. The short life expectancy of an advert in a newspaper or a magazine effectively means that there is a much greater possibility of breaking even by advertising on the Internet rather than in conventional media. The rule of thumb in the industry is therefore that SMTEs can break even for a modest presence on the Internet by generating as few as five to ten bookings per year. Enthusiastic Internet and ICT users who appreciate the power of interactivity and electronic marketing generate a much greater number of bookings and gain greater benefits (Buhalis, 1995; Buhalis and Main, 1998; Buhalis and Keeling, 1999).

5.4 Strategic aims and objectives for tourism suppliers

ICTs have had a dramatic effect on the strategic management of tourism organizations. Inevitably different types of tourism suppliers have dissimilar aims and objectives, and as a result are affected differently by ICTs. For the purposes of this book, tourism suppliers are divided simply into private (for-profit) and public (not-for-profit) sectors. Private sector organizations can be subdivided into producers/principals (such as hotels, airlines, train operators, restaurants and bars, sport and leisure facilities) as well as on-line and off-line intermediaries including travel agencies, tour operators, incoming agencies or handling operators. It is recognized, however, that increasingly these lines are blurred as public sector organizations are often briefed to generate funds in order to maintain their operations.

5.4.1 Private and for-profit tourism organizations

Private-sector tourism organizations, similarly with other enterprises, aim at increasing their profitability in the long term by maximizing the difference between their turnover and cost. In order to achieve this, they need to develop their activities in a way that ensures that they can increase their turnover, spread their risk and expand gradually to optimize their resources. Maximizing profitability and reducing costs across all their activities often requires organizations to formulate a portfolio of several strategic business units (SBUs) and to manage them accordingly. SBUs are entities of their own, have their own management and operate with a certain degree of autonomy from the mother organization. For example, Whitbread Corporation operates a wide portfolio of SBUs, including Marriott, Courtyard by Marriott and Travel Inn Hotels; pubs including the Brewers Fayre brand; restaurants and bar chains, such as TGI Friday's, Bella Pasta, Pizza Hut, Dragon Inns, Café Rouge, Mama Amalfi, Costa Café, Potters and Beefeaters; and finally the David Lloyd health and sports clubs. All these enterprises are managed individually at a corporate and individual unit level as SBUs, but also contribute to the corporate profitability.

The financial value of organizations is determined by two main factors, namely operational profit (turnover minus costs) and company value when traded in the stock exchange or when assessed by independent evaluators. Given the significance of the two methods of raising the value of an investment and the recent experiences with dot.com companies, they need to be evaluated with equal significance.

Operational profit

In order to increase their profitability organizations need to maximize their yield (price × units sold) and at the same time minimize their costs. Thus, in airlines both the average fare and load factors need to be maximized. Similarly, accommodation establishments need to maximize their REPAR (REVenue Per Available Room), not only by achieving highest possible average room rates and occupancy, but also by incorporating potential revenue from other departments, such as food and beverage and conferences. Identifying market niches enables tourism enterprises to develop suitable products and marketing mixes in order to attract the custom of both individual consumers and intermediaries. In addition, managing resources rationally enables them to keep costs under control and achieve maximum difference between income and expenditure. ICTs offer tools for forecasting demand levels and for adjusting provision and pricing in order to maximize yield, as well as for communicating with consumers and promoting the product. In the longer term, ICTs enable the growth of the market to be assessed and investment plans evaluated for altering capacity by, for example, adding more rooms in a hotel or more planes on a route.

Company value

Public companies and corporations can increase their value and ultimately their profitability by attracting the interest and confidence of investors in the stock exchange. Privately owned organizations can also increase their value in the marketplace. Investors with confidence in the profitability prospects of a corporation will purchase shares and equities in anticipation of high dividends. In this way investors increase the value of corporations. Several recent examples demonstrate that newly established tourism intermediaries have managed to raise significant amounts when launched on the stock exchange. Perhaps the most famous example is the case of lastminute.com, which managed to raise £800 m on its flotation in May 2000, having been established only 18 months before, employing 200 members of staff and demonstrating an operational loss of $30 m in six months in 2000. The value the company attracted in the stock exchange was comparable with W.H. Smith, the newsagents, a company with a 100-year history, more than 800 outlets in prime locations, a significant operational profit and an employment record of about 42 000 staff in the UK. However, the last-minute.com price share was rapidly devalued soon afterwards, leaving investors disappointed. Maximizing the return on investment in a private tourism organization aims at increasing the profitability and value of the organization; ICTs can play a critical role in both.

5.4.2 Public and not-for-profit tourism organizations and destinations

Not-for-profit and most public-sector organizations may have different strategic objectives and agendas. Not-for-profit organizations in tourism often operate culture, arts and heritage attractions. Destinations bodies such as national, regional and local **tourist boards** (NTBs, RTBs and LTBs) aim at bringing together and coordinating all local players (Buhalis, 2000b). Typically, unique and treasured heritage resources, such as Stonehenge in the UK, the Acropolis in Greece and the Pyramids in Egypt, are operated by public-sector organizations or trusts that concentrate more on conservation and sustainability rather than on the profitability of the monument or the site. However, income generated through visitation often covers part of the maintenance and preservation costs, and hence it can no longer be neglected. Thus, in most cases, even not-for-profit organizations have financial and profitability targets to ensure that they have sufficient funds for achieving their objectives. In addition, public-sector organizations in some countries operate tourism-related companies. For example, airlines such as Air France, Olympic and Air Portugal, or hotel chains such as the Paradores in Spain, the Posadas in Portugal and the Astir Hotels in Greece, are public-sector owned and managed. These enterprises may primarily support the policies and political priorities of the respective governments. However, they may need to be profitable or at least break even and remain competitive.

Destinations are more challenging entities to manage and market as they are amalgams of all products provided locally, offering an integrated experience to consumers. They can include tangible assets such as man-made attractions, facilities and resources, but also intangible resources such as landscapes, images, atmospheres and perceptions. Destinations represent the entire range of tourism resources, products and services, consumed under the brand name of the destination. For example, Paris as a destination includes the landscapes, urban environment and heritage monuments as well as the atmosphere, accommodation establishments, restaurants and bars and conference centres available in the city.

For the purpose of this book, destinations are considered to be a defined geographical region with a political and legislative framework for tourism marketing and planning. This definition enables destination management organizations (DMOs) to be accountable for the strategic management of regions and to have the power and resources to undertake action towards achieving their strategic objectives. National, regional and local tourism organizations aim at promoting the tourism activity in their area. They are normally subsidized by the public sector and in some cases aim at reducing public subsidy by selling value-added tourism information and products and souvenirs or by undertaking tourism product reservations for a commission. Destinations are extremely difficult to manage and market, mainly due to the complexity of the relationships of their stakeholders, namely local people, tourists, private enterprises, public sector and intermediaries.

Destination management and marketing organizations should act as catalysts for achieving a complex range of strategic objectives. Ultimately, they need to satisfy the needs and wants of all their stakeholders. Four key generic strategic objectives should be addressed by DMOs, as illustrated in Figure 5.3. Hence, destination management and marketing should be regarded not only as a mechanism for attracting more visitors to a region and for maximizing profitability for local enterprises. Instead, they should operate as a tool for facilitating regional development objectives and for rationalizing the provision of tourism in order to ensure that the strategic objectives of destinations and the optimization of tourism impacts are achieved. Strategic management should also ensure equitable returns on resources utilized for the production and delivery of tourism products, as well as the regeneration of these resources in order to ensure the sustainability of destinations. It should also provide suitable gains to all stakeholders involved in the tourism system. Hence, destination strategic management should be used as a coordination mechanism, ensuring equitable returns on resources utilized, rather than as a sales tool (Buhalis, 2000c; Cooper and Buhalis, 1998).

ICTs are critical for coordinating destinations, as illustrated in Chapter 11. By developing a destination info-structure, NTOs are capable of communicating efficiently with the entire industry and coordinating the sales and development functions, providing on-line availability and enabling eCommerce through a destination management system. NTOs emerge as neural networks of the entire destination system.

Figure 5.3 Strategic management and marketing objectives for destinations

- Enhance the long-term prosperity of local people

- Delight visitors by maximizing their satisfaction

- Maximize profitability of local enterprises and maximize multiplier effects

- Optimize tourism impacts by ensuring a sustainable balance between economic benefits and socio-cultural and environmental costs

5.5 ICT-empowered strategic management of the tourism industry

Both public- and private-sector organizations can benefit greatly from the technological revolution. ICTs support the strategic management of tourism organizations by empowering long-term decision-making and by providing a platform and the info-structure for collaboration and transactions between suppliers. Few other industries rely on so many partners to collaborate closely for delivering their products and few other value chains are as elaborate as that for tourism. As

Chapter 3 illustrated, all interactions take place within an info-space, which helps the entire industry to operate. This is achieved by empowering internal processes and coordinating partners, as well as interacting with prospective travellers and the general public. The recent ICT developments have revolutionized the entire system and have profound implications for both the strategic and tactical management of tourism organizations.

Early adopters, including both well-established and newly founded tourism enterprises, identified a clear opportunity. They invested heavily in order to develop their on-line brand name and capture a significant market share. Pioneers included established airlines, such as American Airlines, which invested in SABRE, and Bratthens, Ryanair and easyJet, which adopted the Internet from the early stages and even painted their aircraft with their Internet addresses. Hotel chains such as Marriott launched their websites before most other competitors. They also strengthened their partnerships with Switch companies such as THISCO, distributing their products electronically to both consumers and the travel trade. Some travel agencies and intermediaries took advantage of the emerging technologies to enhance their distribution mechanisms and also their research and development processes. Thomas Cook and TUI, for example, established their electronic presence early enough to protect their market shares.

However, the rapid development and innovation of many electronic intermediaries, such as expedia.com and lastminute.com, continue to challenge traditional players and may force the disintermediation and re-intermediation of the distribution channel. Most travel organizations have introduced ICTs internally and have tried to rationalize and re-engineer their production processes in order to enhance their efficiency and effectiveness. However, a number of organizations have failed to take full advantage. Many organizations that have invested heavily in ICTs may not have made a direct profit. However, in most cases they have supported and probably enhanced their competitiveness and profitability in the long term by maintaining or expanding their market shares and safeguarding their position. Others have managed to raise the value of their companies through the stock exchange mechanism as investors anticipate that 'clicks and mortal' companies will surpass traditional 'bricks and mortar' companies in the near future.

Other competent, but less adventurous, tourism organizations have carefully observed developments before spending considerable amounts of money investing in ICTs and eCommerce. In some cases, this has allowed them to learn lessons from others' mistakes and experiences. In other cases, organizations have developed partnerships with pioneers in the ICTs or purchased significant amount of shares and benefited from their success. For example, American Express purchased the Internet Travel Network (ITN), reaping the rewards of their experience and technological infrastructure.

However, a large percentage of suppliers, and particularly small and medium-sized enterprises, often located in peripheral and remote destinations, have failed to follow developments or respond accordingly. As a result, they are left out of the current growth and their market share is endangered. This is already evident for traditional intermediaries and smaller travel agencies, who are threatened by the vertical integration of leisure organizations, capping of their **commission** by scheduled airlines and the emergence of electronic intermediaries who gradually increase their market share. Smaller principals that have failed to incorporate the Internet, such as family-run hotels and local enterprises, will probably lose their market share gradually and may suffer in the long term.

The influence of ICTs on tourism organizations is pervasive, as information is critical for both day-to-day operations and the strategic management of tourism organizations. ICTs support all business functions and are critical for operating the industry as a whole. On the strategic level, tourism organizations need to continuously assess all elements of their external environment, as well as their competition and customer needs, and consequently, reinvent themselves in order to enhance their competitiveness. Using ICTs, tourism organizations can differentiate their product by using their core product as the basis and then by customizing the final product by adding value and products according to individual requirements. For example, a tour or a cruise operator may theme a holiday to appeal to a niche market. Several themes can run in parallel if they do not conflict with each other. Although the core elements of the product can remain the same (essentially transportation and accommodation), attracting special-interest consumers – for a cooking week in an Italian village, for example – can add value to the product and provide some unique attributes to the product. ICTs provide the tools to search for meaningful and profitable niche market segments, to identify value-added components for the product and to promote the differentiated product through specialized media to particular market segments that would be interested. Cost effectiveness and flexibility are critical assets contributed by ICTs in this process, as they assist cost reduction and efficiency maximization.

5.5.1 Monitoring the environment and dynamic response: proactive management and neural organizations

Interoperable information platforms enable tourism organizations to integrate all their systems and monitor and control both their internal processes and external trends. Tourism organizations need to take advantage of existing data in the organization and use knowledge management, expert systems, artificial intelligence and **neural networks** in order to develop neural and proactive organizational management. This will enable them to monitor their external environment and take the most beneficial action. They can take advantage of neural networks to recognize and capture patterns and elements in a sea of data, coming from both the internal and external environment of organizations and assist decision makers to design appropriate responses (Gupta, 2000).

For example, a hotel can monitor its reservations and expected REVPAR (REVenue Per Available Room) and take appropriate action, based on guest histories, data from previous years and forecasted demand for the region. The hotel management can monitor the prices and offerings of competitors, the development in attractions and activities at the destination, and elements of the external environment such as the weather, flight schedules or the political situation locally. A proactive schedule of events, activities and products can therefore be planned and executed accordingly. If demand levels are satisfactory and a high occupancy level is predicted the hotel will need to maximize its profitability by adjusting its pricing policy. The hotel can identify associations and similarities between bookings from previous years and develop add-on services from previous experience. If, for example, a group celebrates a particular occasion, such as a football match of the national team of guests, a themed party may allow one of the quiet hotel outlets to generate additional activity and revenue.

If demand levels are not satisfactory, neural networks can identify demand patterns that may be useful for the property. Demand for an area nearby, for example, may reveal a special attraction and the hotel may be able to place an attractive package, including transportation, there. The hotel may also decide to offer some special last-minute deals, to arrange for an on-line auction, to organize additional activities and event attractions or to accept lower-margin local business, which may not be a priority under different circumstances. If everything else fails, the hotel may decide to rationalize its resources by, for example, giving a day off to employees, reducing its suppliers, concentrating guests to lower floors so they can economize on heating and energy for elevators, closing some outlets and minimizing personnel and other variable costs.

In addition, on-line connections may provide information platforms that allow partners to follow the operational developments of each other. They can then prepare for consequences and alter their operational planning dynamically. For example, airline management would appreciate knowing that there is a hotel or catering capacity available for their stranded passengers should one of their flights be delayed or cancelled. Equally a hotel would be able to identify passengers arriving late due to a delayed flight and make alternative arrangements for dinner, should their kitchen be closed after a certain time. Tour and coach operators on their way to a property can identify how many rooms are unavailable for check-in due to late check-outs. They can then perhaps decide to make a stop-over before arriving at the hotel, to allow time for rooms to be prepared rather than arriving early and having to deal with several unsatisfied customers. Not only can these suggestions improve the operational elements of an organization but, perhaps more significantly, they can contribute to their strategic management, as they will influence the choice of partners, re-engineering of processes and most importantly customer relationships and satisfaction.

Neural organizations constantly monitor and control their external and internal environment, identify patterns, trends and developments, and take proactive measures to advance their interests. Interconnected processors and networks may run in parallel and interact dynamically with each other in a way that develops knowledge and procedures for dealing with issues and problems before they arise (O'Brien, 1996). This enables them to manage their resources efficiently and to communicate with their consumers and external partners proactively and re-actively in order to improve their competitiveness. Time increasingly becomes more critical, as both consumers and partners are bombarded with information. Providing the right total solution, at the right time, will be one of the most significant generators of competitive advantage. The strategic benefit emerges from the development of the neural network and the constant update of the system.

The emerging capabilities of ICTs enable the constant collection and analysis of information, enabling tourism and hospitality decision-makers to adopt a very dynamic management, or to 'manage by wire' (Haeckel and Nolan, 1993). They can redesign and repackage tourism products instantly, according to consumer desires, trends and fluctuations. Adding value and specializing tourism products in response to external developments or internal challenges can increase their profitability and explore new market segments efficiently and effectively. The strategic benefit is associated closely with constantly monitoring the external environment and acting proactively and reactively for maximum benefit.

5.5.2 Building and maintaining competitive advantage using ICTs

As explained in Chapter 2, Porter (1985a) demonstrates clearly that competitive advantage can be achieved through either product differentiation or cost advantage either for the entire marketplace or for particular market segments (focus). To the degree that ICTs enable organizations either to differentiate their products or reduce their costs, and therefore their price, they can assist them to achieve competitive advantage, and hence have strategic implications. ICTs are often a major factor in achieving product differentiation and/or cost advantage, directly affecting an organization's competitiveness. In the former case organizations aim to attract a high profit margin but a relatively lower volume of transactions, while in the latter they aim at attracting high volumes but low profit margins. Ultimately organizations are keen to maximize their total profitability and select strategies according to market conditions, competition, their strengths and weaknesses as well as future opportunities and threats.

Meeting the needs of each individual consumer through differentiation increasingly becomes easier as on the one hand technology enables efficient collaboration between suppliers and on the other ICTs empower consumers to identify and include desirable elements in their shopping basket. Customer relationship management (CRM) supports organizational initiatives to develop a dialogue with consumers and to customize their products. Reducing cost is often a result of great efficiency, reduction of the cost per unit and minimizing waste in the process. ICTs particularly assist the distribution process as they reduce dramatically the levels of commission paid and the cost of administering reservations. This is achieved through outsourcing a number of functions, such as product identification and itinerary building, back to the consumers and saving significant labour costs.

Competitive advantage through pricing and cost

Pricing in tourism has been used as a strong source of competitive advantage as discounting often attracts consumers seeking a bargain. Tourism, being one of the luxury and high-income-elasticity but also prestigious products, is often sold on price. It is critical to establish whether and how ICTs can contribute to the ability of organizations to manage and minimize their costs better than their competitors and thus achieve competitive advantage. ICTs contribute to both sides of the balance sheet and can be equally beneficial and costly.

It is difficult to assess objectively whether ICTs can contribute to cost reductions and to enable tourism organizations to reduce their price accordingly, in order to achieve cost advantage. Each tourism enterprise and destination operates within a distinctive environment. Nevertheless, there are several factors that can influence the ability of an organization to achieve cost advantage, as a result of their ICTs. Therefore a **comprehensive feasibility study** based on rational cost-and-benefits analysis should be undertaken for each player. This should take into consideration the entire range of ICT cost and benefit factors, as illustrated in Figure 5.4 (p. 155).

Mass production, enabled by the Industrial Revolution at the beginning of the twentieth century, and mainly in the post-war era, allowed organizations to manufacture mass products and to dramatically reduce their cost per unit. Similarly in tourism, mass destinations have developed especially since the 1970s to deal with the emerging demand for holidays and tourism products in an industrial way by taking advantage of economies of scale. The development of **mass tourism** destinations around the world, and in particular in Mediterranean destinations, has allowed organizations to take advantage of economies of scale and minimize the price per unit, often at the expense of the local environment. In addition, the development of larger and more economical aircraft and hotel facilities enabled even the lower socio-economic classes to take annual holidays for a very reasonable price.

ICTs have encouraged mass tourism by enabling the handling of large amounts of information that support large-scale operations. Consequently, ICTs have enabled the reduction of the price per unit taking advantage of economies of scale and minimal marginal costs. Only ICT-supported enterprises can increase the operational size of hotels, airlines and intermediaries to capacity levels. Large hotels with more than 250 rooms would be almost impossible to fill without advanced technological solutions, while airlines with more than a few aircraft or tour operators with more than few thousand passengers would be simply impossible to run. Technology enables the further vertical and horizontal integration of the tourism system, which consequently enhances economies of scale, operational efficiencies and intra-channel negotiation power, all of which contribute to price reductions. As a result, a large proportion of the tourism industry and particularly the package-holiday market sells products on price. In addition, price is also used for selling distressed inventory through last-minute deals or auctions. Again ICTs facilitate this function by maximizing efficiency and enabling consumers to purchase tourism products literally hours before consumption.

Costs are likely to include the cost of purchasing hardware, software and communication packages as well as the training cost of users. Although technology becomes more affordable and easier to use, ICT investments are often quite substantial and it is frequently one of the most critical costs of travel intermediaries. The short life cycle of ICTs means that regular upgrades need to take place, which increases costs. The design and construction of web pages as well as hosting the site on a reliable server, while enabling organizations to develop their Internet presence, will also contribute to their costs. Keeping a web presence current is critical, and there is therefore a strong requirement for ongoing maintenance and regular updating. Typically on-line promotion costs only a fraction of off-line promotion. Thus, a reduction of promotional cost and brochure waste can assist organizations to reduce their costs. Registration of domain names is relatively inexpensive provided that an organization has registered its name early enough and does not have to buy back from one of the individuals or companies that register names and then sell them for a premium.

Although registering on-line domains is relatively easy and inexpensive to achieve through the Internet, developing a brand on- and off-line still requires both on- and off-line promotion and marketing, which may also contribute to the costs, especially in the beginning and for new start-up companies. Advertising fees for banner representation and strategic alliances with search engines and other portals as well as TV commercials may also contribute to the cost. For example, lastminute.com uses board advertisements as well as on-line banners to generate sufficient traffic to its website. The development of on-line presence also requires a re-engineering of all procedures and practices for an organization. For example, customer service call centres, operating on a 24-hour basis, can be required to support consumers and partners that need help through telephone or eMail. Finally on-line purchases through intermediaries such as Expedia, Travelocity or thomascook.com are also commissionable and perhaps more intermediaries may be involved, increasing the cost of distribution.

Large organizations, however, that design comprehensive websites pay considerable amounts of money. For example, in February 2000 British Airways announced that it would be spending £100 million on its on-line strategy within two years. In 1999 BA spent £12 million on developing a technological framework for its eCommerce platform that links bookings, check-in and flight details, enabling the airline to accumulate historical data on what happens to each customer across the Internet, ITV, WAP and eventually any mobile device (Simmons, 2000).

On the other hand, several important *benefits* can be identified that can enable organizations to reduce their cost or increase their profit margin. ICTs enable organizations to reduce all inefficiencies and to re-engineer their processes in a way that maximizes their effectiveness. This includes the automation of manual procedures as well as the design of management information and decision support systems. Currently, for example, a package holiday booking needs to be recorded no less than six times, multiplying the administrative costs and the error possibilities. ICTs reduce the time for each process to be completed and thus minimize the labour cost but also improve both the interactivity and reflexes of the organization while reducing the possibility for error.

One of the most common motivators for tourism organizations to develop their Internet presence is to accept direct bookings (eCommerce), and thus to reduce or eliminate commissions, booking fees and other distribution costs. As a result, organizations can, if they wish, pass on savings to consumers, and thus reduce their price accordingly, achieving price-competitive advantage. This strategy also enables them to communicate directly with their customers.

Developing a cost-efficient eCommerce application and global distribution of multimedia information and promotional material on a 365/24 basis is also very attractive, as ICTs enable organizations to be permanently available to their markets. The low cost of providing and distributing timely updates of information also provides great flexibility and interactivity with consumers and partners. This cannot be achieved through traditional marketing methods and is critical for reducing the time required for transactions and for the ability of organizations to offload their distressed capacity in last-minute promotions. Once the Internet presence of an organization is established, the marginal cost of serving additional consumers and users is minimal, enabling the organization to benefit from economies of scale and to expand rapidly. The Internet presence also has a better durability in comparison to the limited life-span of press, radio and TV advertisements. TV commercials last only a few seconds, while advertising in the printed press and magazines normally has a maximum life-span of one week.

The active role of consumers and information seekers in asking for information also ensures that the information targets people with a genuine interest in the product. As a result generic and untargeted campaigns can be eliminated, enhancing the cost efficiency of marketing. For example, prospective travellers would only access information related to their chosen destination. Perhaps one of the less discussed benefits of ICTs for tourism enterprises is their support of their **marketing intelligence** and product-design functions. Organizations can easily develop targeted mailing lists through people who actively request information and to segment them according to their interests, background site usage and consumer behaviour. Organizations can collect marketing information from all enquirers. By registering users, tourism enterprises can develop extensive databases of consumers and their preferences and target them according. By tracking the identity of the user as well as what they do once they visit the web page, valuable **market research** information can be collected.

Niche marketing as well as great interactivity with existing and prospective customers therefore become easily achievable, affordable and cost effective in comparison with other marketing initiatives. In addition, organizations can use ICTs to monitor their competitors and identify opportunities and challenges accordingly. Consumers who feel appreciated take ownership of tourism products and often contribute to their long-term prosperity by generating a community feel for current users and prospective customers. By developing strategic partnerships organizations can provide added-value products and services before, during and after the travel experience. Effective interactivity with partners can also enable organizations to reduce their communication costs and enhance their efficiency. This is particularly true at the destinations where seamless connections between local partners can enhance the local product and total consumer experience.

Figure 5.4 illustrates a comprehensive framework of all ICT-related costs and benefits. An elaborate balance sheet should be developed for each organization demonstrating the potential costs and savings achieved by using ICTs. The elements identified are some of the most critical for the determination of the contribution of ICTs to the bottom line. It is noticeable that the majority of the costs and benefits identified are management- and marketing-based, rather than ICT-based. This is because most of the costs and benefits emerge through the re-engineering and the redesign of the organizational processes, rather than as isolated costs. Assessing costs and benefits holistically is therefore critical. Hence competent and innovative organizations will find ICTs more beneficial than their counterparts who lack marketing or management skills, abilities and knowledge.

Cost advantage can be achieved by using ICTs to serve the maximum number of travellers through economies of scale, negotiation with partners and maximizing load factors. This is particularly evident in the tour operator business in Europe, where ICTs play an instrumental role in expanding and managing the

Figure 5.4 Cost- and-benefit analysis for incorporating ICTs and developing on-line presence

Costs	Benefits and potential savings
• Cost of purchasing and customizing hardware, software and communication package • Training cost of users • Design and construction of Internet presence • Cost of hosting the site on a reliable server • Ongoing maintenance and regular updating • Marketing the Internet service and registration of domain • Advertising fees for representation in search engines and other sites • Reduction of promotional cost and reduction of brochure waste • Development of procedures for dealing with Internet presence • Commissions for purchases on-line by intermediaries • Interconnectivity with travel intermediaries such as TravelWeb and Expedia	• Reduce all inefficiencies and administrative labour cost • Eliminate mistakes from manual procedures • Maximize efficiency through sharing files and data across the organization • Re-engineer processes in a way that maximizes effectiveness and efficiency • Customers spend their own time finding the right product and typing the booking request rather than the time of company employees • Direct bookings, often intermediaries and commission-free • Global distribution of multimedia information and promotional material • Low cost of providing and distributing timely updates of information • Global presence on the Internet, 24 hours a day, 365 days a year • Durability of promotion (in comparison to limited life of printed advertising in press) • Ability to cross-promote to relevant sites • Ability to evaluate effectiveness of promotional campaigns • Great degree of attention by visitors to website as visit generally intentional • Reduction of time required for transactions and ability to offer last-minute promotions • Low marginal cost of providing information to additional users • Support of marketing intelligence and product design functions • Development of targeted mailing lists through people who actively request information • Great interactivity with prospective customers • Niche marketing to prospective consumers who ask to receive information • Interactivity with local partners and provision of added-value products at destinations • Ability to engage and generate a community feel for current users and prospective customers

inventory as well as for moving to other geographical regions. Pressaug currently serves about 10 million holidaymakers in Europe, with attractive products and prices. Serving such a number of customers can only be realized through using ICTs to expand and manage the customer basis.

Differentiation advantage: customizing the tourism product

Differentiation strategies aim to develop unique products and added value. Differentiation advantage emerges when organizations develop and specialize their products/services to meet the specific requests of consumers. They can enhance the unique attributes of their products and increase the perceived value of a product. Providing a specialized and better overall offering than the competition and addressing the specific requirements of consumers enable organizations to attract and maintain a loyal clientèle that appreciates the uniqueness and quality of their product and as a result is willing to pay premium prices. ICTs provide endless opportunities for packaging customized tourism organizations and experiences, as well as for developing specific services and niche products.

Through the Internet, tourism organizations can develop and incorporate content on the specific specialisms and also develop partnerships with other players in the area. Identifying the entire range of services, information and products required for niche markets can enable organizations to develop comprehensive and integrated offerings to support that market. There are endless niche markets waiting to be explored in tourism. They can be segmented according to activities (e.g. skiers, scuba divers, birdwatchers etc.); age groups (e.g. young and active: 18–30, families, golden age 50+); specific interests and life-style (e.g. philatelists, historians, wine enthusiasts, motor sport fans etc.). ICTs provide the opportunity to bring people with special interests together at an affordable cost; using the Internet they can request to be kept informed about developments. Partnerships with clubs and associations, as well as with specialized press and suppliers, can also enable tourism organizations to target their membership. The Internet has enabled tourism firms to develop global specialisations and to target their markets regardless of their location at an affordable cost. For example, unmissable.com targets a specific market that concentrates on experiences, adventures and special occasions by mediating between suppliers and incentive and corporate travelling companies to offer unique products. ICTs have also enabled the development of partnerships with complementary service providers and the establishment of comprehensive value chains, by offering services before, during and after the tourism experience. It would be extremely time-consuming and uneconomical to develop and maintain a relationship with their target markets off-line as consumers are scattered around the globe, making it extremely difficult to target and approach. Developing a community and coordinating its activity interactively can be very profitable for tourism organizations.

For example, a golf-specializing hotel or tour operator in Bali, Indonesia, can provide an interactive Internet page, which can allow guests to undertake a whole range of golf-centred activities; this would maximize their revenue, as demonstrated in Figure 5.5. They can serve their clientèle globally at almost no extra cost. Developing partnerships with golf-specialist companies and establishing strategic alliances with partners can strengthen their market and enable tourism organizations to add value to their products. Eventually a vertical portal (vortal) can be established based on the different elements brought together.

Specialized information becomes a product in its own right and allows specialist operators to enhance the value of their products. Differentiation should be evident in all operational and strategic elements of the enterprise. All aspects of the product can be specialised and targeted, from interior design and decorations to dinner menus. The product can eventually become the background to the themed experience. For example, a Club Med experience is similar in all 130 villages around the world.

Tailor-made tourism products are not a new marketing technique. However, the emergence of the Internet and the ability of organizations to reach the entire marketplace electronically and cost-effectively provide unprecedented opportunities for differentiation strategies. Establishing a global **brand** name and identity in a niche market is relatively easier in the on-line era and can be achieved with

Figure 5.5 Potential golf-related activities and products offered by a specialized provider

- Organize tournaments and championships
- Follow the news of the sport on a global basis
- Discuss recent developments
- Organize training or special events
- Arrange for trips to golf courses and tournaments
- Organize specific promotions and discounted rates on golf equipment

a fraction of the resources required in the off-line world. Consumers from all over the world use the Internet and wait to be impressed by service providers. Providing a comprehensive, valuable and pleasurable experience becomes the key criterion for success; it secures consumers, and increases their willingness to pay and their brand loyalty.

However, specialized tourism organizations can easily be imitated. There are several vortals targeting skiers, for example. Thus, a differentiation-competitive advantage is difficult to maintain unless a programme of constant innovation is implemented. International competition intensifies and tourism organizations that fail to constantly reinvent themselves and focus on the needs of their customers will be unable to survive in the long term. Similarly, however, organizations can reduce the differentiation advantage of competitors by using ICTs to identify what is on offer, market gaps and opportunities. Undertaking such research before carrying out detailed cost and benefit analysis can enable organizations to develop counter-offerings. They can then develop offensive strategies to capture market share or new market segments if they can outperform their competitors. Developing a marketplace is easier, cheaper and more rapid on-line than off-line.

Focus advantage for particular market segments

Porter (1985a) illustrates that the **focus strategy** offers differentiation advantage or cost leadership for specific market segments. In essence, focus uses one of the two previously discussed strategies for a specific part of the market. Segmentation can be based on customers' location, demographics, consumer behaviour, lifestyle and life-cycle etc. (Middleton and Clark, 2001; Horner and Swarbrooke, 1996). By identifying the unique characteristics and needs of a particular segment, organizations can develop suitable offerings and aim to be competitive either through differentiation or cost advantage. Segmenting the market and identifying feasible market segments becomes increasingly easy with the use of ICTs.

Perhaps this is one of the most critical contribution of ICTs, as it makes the identification, development and servicing of mini-market segments feasible at a fraction of the cost and time required by off-line marketing. Armed with responses from on-line questionnaires and promotional campaigns, as well as tracking website navigation patterns, enables organizations to cross-reference this information with consumer behaviour from real data. This can support them to develop data warehouses and to bring together and manage their knowledge. Every time consumers log into the system, organizations can collect useful information about their needs and preferences, and factors affecting their behaviour. Adjusting interfaces, web pages and offerings, and enhancing their interactivity, organizations can determine the most critical factors that influence consumer behaviour. Being able to cross-tabulate data and analyse them against the behaviour of individual consumers can provide an unprecedented wealth of information that can enable organizations to develop mini-segments and customize accordingly. For example, looking into the frequency of checking particular flights, the affiliated products examined and the booking behaviour of users may enable an airline to add a new route or to develop innovative packages, or even to target the market segment of one by adding individualized value to their offering.

Market segments can be defined and targeted much more precisely than before. Traditional segmentation based on demographics and location can gradually be replaced with more subjective and qualitative criteria such as taste, interests, moods, life-style, usage of ICTs and personal preferences.

The focus strategy can be a powerful tool for yield management at both tourism principal and destination levels. Theming the tourism offering and developing differentiated products with unique attributes and characteristics enable organizations to attract different market segments. This may enable them to maximize their revenue by attracting high profit margin and yield consumers. However, during the low season, when organizations are desperately looking for consumers to increase their occupancy and keep the facilities functional, low-profit-margin but large-volume market segments may be targeted based on cost advantage. For example, tourism facilities in the Seychelles would inevitably be much busier during school holidays. Thus, they can adjust their products and attract market segments that have a lower ability to pay, but greater time flexibility during their off-peak periods. Pensioners, young couples and people with special interests, such as scuba divers or marine biologists, may be suitable target markets. Approaching them through electronic media with a suitable proposition can be cost efficient and inexpensive in comparison to all other methods. In addition, event attractions and specific events can be organized to stimulate demand. It is critically important to match markets with complementary seasonality patterns, needs, requirements and budgets in order to make best use of different strategies during different seasons.

Ideally tourism providers need to develop a unique product for each one of their clients and undertake **one-to-one marketing**. In practice, however, most organizations have hitherto failed to develop one-to-one offerings because of the costs involved. Identifying unique needs, designing and most importantly delivering unique tourism product propositions are extremely time- and resource-consuming. Thus, individualization of tourism products has mainly been used by celebrities and people who enjoy receiving royal treatment and are prepared to pay for it. Organizations therefore often have to settle for niche products that have certain attributes and can attract specific market segments. Soon, however, they will be able to use intelligent agents to identify the unique characteristics of consumers and to match them with individually designed or packaged products.

Focus as a strategy assists organizations to identify consumer needs; however, the emergence of mobile devices as Internet terminals will mean that consumers can be offered specialized products interactively. Location-dependent technologies will recognize the position of consumers and will provide local products suiting not just the location and local conditions but also the pre-defined preferences of the consumer. Activities, food and clothing that match the profile and preferences of the consumer as well as local weather conditions, for example, may be offered on a daily basis at each location visited by that consumer. New business models, such as priceline.com, effectively allow consumers to declare what they wish to purchase and at what price, and then identify potential suppliers willing to offer that product. In this sense, ICTs empower consumers to develop the **marketing mix** of the products they wish to purchase, and search the marketplace for suitable suppliers.

Competitive advantage through time

Time becomes another source of competitive advantage, as consumers short of time increasingly appreciate value for time and efficiency in the process often more than differentiation or cost advantages. Thus, consumers appreciate saving time during the information-seeking and reservation process through efficient and interactive mechanisms. It is argued here that time should be added as a source of competitive advantage. Time will eventually overtake both cost and differentiation for several market segments as a critical factor for purchasing products. Simplified and at the same time comprehensive websites that enable consumers to complete a transactions in a few minutes and within a few clicks already enjoy great competitive advantages and thus their organizations emerge as winners of the electronic battle.

Visiting expedia.com or ebookers.com, for example, consumers can have access to a one-stop shop for all their travel requirements such as flights, hotels, car rentals, holidays and business trips. Everything is bookable in a few clicks and travel documents are sent to the appropriate address within a few days or are collected from the airport. Several added-value services are also readily available such as airport guides, currency converter, World Guide and access to the Rough Guides, arrivals and departures of airlines, fare tracker, flight timetables etc. Although the prices charged at these sites are not the cheapest possible in the market and the products are not differentiated greatly, the fact that the sites offer an efficient mechanism for dealing with most of the requirements of the customer has developed them into major players.

Although many organizations have yet to develop suitable interactive interfaces, increasingly ICT improvements suggest that fairly simplified products, such as a return flight or a hotel reservation, can be undertaken on-line in a fraction of the time required to visit a retail outlet. The emerging mobile devices will foster this issue further, as consumers on the road will wish to undertake complete transactions almost instantly. This is predicted to change consumer behaviour dramatically as travellers will be less prepared to book in advance and will purchase tourism products as they go at the destination. They will be able to take advantage of the entire range of offers communicated to their mobile devices as well as being able to purchase according to their preference, mood and situation at the time, rather than months in advance. This trend will dramatically alter the business model of tourism organizations, forcing them to interact constantly with consumers in real time.

5.5.3 Using ICTs for sustainable competitive advantage

Research in both large and small organizations illustrates that achieving competitive advantage for a short period of time is possible. Organizations can use technology to achieve one of the aforementioned competitive advantages and they can capture a market by communicating their offerings effectively. However, product and price transparency facilitated by the Internet enable competitors to monitor organizations closely and to compare and improve their offerings. In addition, the introduction of the euro and its circulation in January 2002 in most European countries can only intensify price transparency, causing products throughout the European Union to compete fiercely. The most notable example of this was the launch of the Consumer Association car Internet site, which forced British motor manufacturers and dealers to reduce their prices to Continental levels. Both on-line and off-line organizations are therefore forced to reassess their position constantly. Organizations that innovate and proact will increasingly be able to lead the race while the rest will be forced to follow their lead.

Sustaining competitive advantage over the long term, however, is one of the most difficult challenges organizations have to face. New players that use modern marketing and new technologies threaten even some of the most established organizations, such as Thomson and Marks & Spencer. Mobile phones and cable companies challenge organizations such as British Telecom, which was until recently a monopoly and had a major market. By applying interactive interfaces new competitors can communicate constantly with their clientèle and become much more respondive than traditional firms. Retailers such as amazon.com and expedia.com embrace much more interactive interfaces and evolve dynamically, threatening established retailers globally. By identifying customer preferences and needs, they adopt a much more individualized, sophisticated and proactive style of marketing that enables them to address a range of market segments globally.

Increasingly tourism organizations should not only aim at achieving competitive advantage but also develop mechanisms to sustain it in the long term. They can only achieve that by adopting dynamic and innovative practices that will enable them to constantly outperform their competitors. Competitor tactics as well as demand trends can increasingly be monitored on-line, in real time. Organizations can take advantage of the instantaneous interaction facilitated by the Internet and electronic mail and address the need of their clients at the right time. The emergence of pan-European tour operators, as well as the strengthening of hotel and travel agency chains, will intensify competition and will force smaller and inflexible players to lose considerable market share. Several established suppliers and other principals, such as Marriott, have already developed their global presence on the Internet and taken advantage by not only arriving there before other competitors but also sustaining their lead through innovation and constant development. Newcomers, such as lastminute.com, expedia.com, qxl.com and priceline.com, challenge all tourism intermediaries and suppliers as they introduce new and flexible business models and gradually increase their market share dramatically. The emerging ICT tools introduce new capabilities, which consequently provide new opportunities as well as major challenges for all players.

One of the most difficult challenges for tourism organizations is deciding when to enter the competitive arena and how much to spend on their on-line strategy. Pioneering technological solutions often mean that organizations take greater risks and have to explore a fairly difficult field. In return they can hope to establish a market share that will enable them to increase their profitability in the future. In contrast, being a latecomer may be less risky in terms of investment and ICTs but more complex to attract customers and develop relationships once those are established with other organizations. These dilemmas are not unique in tourism, as mobile telephony and the providers of 3G mobile technologies discovered when several services failed to take off despite huge investments in their technologies and marketing.

Developing interactive interfaces that support efficient and effective communication will enable tourism organizations to keep in constant contact with consumers and serve them at every opportunity. Although hitherto this has only been demonstrated by altering the prices according to the rules of demand and supply, a much more comprehensive interaction will need to be evident. Organizations will need to manage their demand in a much more interactive way and evolve all elements of their supply. By constantly monitoring and predicting market trends, tourism organizations should aim to constantly reinvent themselves, offering suitable products and outperforming their competitors. This is particularly difficult for organizations with fixed assets, such as hotels, which are difficult and expensive to alter in the short and medium term. In contrast, intermediaries, transportation companies, event attractions and other organizations with less fixed assets can redirect their resources even in the short term to satisfy the needs of their customers or to take advantage of more profitable routes, locations and events. Organizations that respond instantly both at the tactical and strategic level can therefore maximize their performance and achieve sustainable competitive advantage.

5.5.4 Using ICTs to avoid competitive disadvantage

In addition to trying to achieve competitive advantage, organizations also need to ensure that they can avoid competitive disadvantage. As competitive advantage is based on constant innovation, speed and ability to differentiate or reduce the cost of products, relationships between all competitors are dynamic and continuously evolving. Ignoring and under-utilizing ICTs can create strategic vulnerability and competitive disadvantage (Bradley et al., 1993). Tourism organizations need therefore to constantly monitor their competitors and ensure that they outperform them.

Several major sources of competitive disadvantage can be identified. Firstly, the emergent electronic market gives rise to newcomers who are taking advantage of the new technologies and increasing their market share. For example,

Microsoft launched expedia.com to capture part of the travel market, while other newcomers such as travelstore.com target the business travel market segment. easyJet is a good example of a newly established airline, which adopted the Internet as a prime method of communication and distribution and managed to receive more than 80 per cent of its bookings through the Internet by late 2001. Secondly, established players that adopted new technologies early enough captured a significant market share. For example, Marriott Hotels established their on-line strategy and presence before other competitors and generated significant bookings. SABRE launched and developed Travelocity, as a consumer interface and virtual travel agency, into one of the top 25 travel agencies in the USA before other GDSs had realized the Internet challenge. Thomas Cook and American Express travel agencies as well as TUI and Kuoni tour operators also managed to increase their market share at the expense of organizations that failed to follow the race for on-line presence.

Ultimately, organizations are threatened by their own internal weaknesses. Competitive disadvantages emerge from their inability to serve their customers properly and to match or exceed the performance of competitors. Often this is routed back to internal problems, lack of resources and suitable personnel. Perhaps more importantly it demonstrates a lack of understanding of recent developments as well as a lack of long-term vision by management. As the electronic presence of organizations becomes critically important for their competitiveness and profitability, no action is not an option for established players. Tourism organizations therefore need to develop their ICT vision and adopt realistic and expanding implementation programmes that will enable them to keep up to date with industry developments, competitors' moves and both operational and geographical expansion.

Using ICTs as a stand-alone initiative is both inappropriate and ineffective. ICT usage has to be coupled with a long-term strategy, which should incorporate the re-engineering of all business processes as well as the redesign of organizational structures and control systems. **Market research** and consumer requirements should be incorporated into robust business models, which need to use ICTs as dynamic tools for their implementation. ICT-based strategies can be fruitful, only if certain prerequisites are satisfied, namely:

- *long-term planning and strategy*, whereby ICTs are viewed as a competitive weapon, critical for the organizational competitiveness; investment in an online presence is thus inelastic. However, business models rather than ICTs should lead;
- *innovative business processes re-engineering* is required to redesign all processes and procedures based on the new tools and opportunities emerging;
- *commitment of top management* is critical as ICTs become the backbone of every strategy implementation. Thus, top management should have overall responsibility for the development and implementation of the on-line strategy, rather than delegating to the ICT department;
- *continuous training throughout the hierarchy* will provide decision-makers with tools and methodologies for the dynamic and innovative management of tourism organizations.

Perhaps the greatest challenge is to identify and train managers who will be effective and innovative users of ICTs and can lead technology-based decision-making towards quantifiable gains and advantages. This is particularly challenging for the tourism industry, which is dominated by SMTEs, lacking in trained managers and expertise. Intellect, therefore, becomes one of the major assets of organizations, while continuous education and training are the only methods of developing and maintaining this asset. Provided rational and innovative planning and management are exercised constantly and consistently, ICTs can support the success of organizations.

5.6 ICT-empowered strategic decisions and directions

The nature of the tourism industry increases the importance of ICTs in several directions, tourism being part of the service sector that requires a higher propensity and quality of information. The fragmented character of the industry as well as the long distances and unfamiliar environments involved make information and technology essential ingredients for the competitiveness and prosperity of suppliers and destinations. The perishability and seasonality of tourism products also generate particular ICT requirements not evident in other industries. Hence ICTs are critical for a number of strategic decisions and directions, including:

- strategic alliances and partnerships;
- scope of operations: geographic and operational expansion;
- **outsourcing;**
- distribution strategies;
- brand-building, protection and enlargement;
- **direct marketing;**
- customer relationship management dynamic marketing (loyalty boosters);
- portfolio management;
- tactical planning and operational management.

5.6.1 ICT-empowered strategic alliances and partnerships

ICTs are instrumental in a wide range of other strategic decisions, including franchising agreements, alliances and partnerships. Increasingly the ability of tourism organizations to cooperate by sharing information, attracting the same target market, establishing similar quality standards and contributing different parts of the value chain determines their competitiveness. As a consequence, several multinational organizations have developed from integrating organizations horizontally or vertically or both.

Horizontal integration and expansion are evident in hotel chains where multinationals such as Bass expand their portfolio by developing properties in remote destinations and also by engaging with several partners on franchising agreements. ICTs enable them to keep a close control on the operational performance of their properties, to interact dynamically with all properties and at the same time to expand their marketing, distribution and sales networks to the global marketplace. *Vertical integration* enables different contributors to the tourism value chain to come together and deliver complete products to their clientèle. The Airtours example in Case Study 5.2 illustrates an organization developing a network of SBUs in several countries offering complementary services to their customers and reaping the benefits of synergies. In other instances independent suppliers may come together and provide service networks by using ICTs. For example, a tour operator may have an established partnership with an inbound operator, several airlines, transportation and taxi companies, as well as with a range of accommodation establishments. All this can be administrated through interactive networks, which can facilitate and control the entire system of service delivery. Achieving interoperability between the great variety of systems and integrating systems to work together are significant challenges for the ICT communities. Fierce global competition also forces enterprises to concentrate their efforts and use ICTs in order to avoid being left behind and suffering from competitive disadvantages (Go and Welch, 1991; Buhalis, 1998).

By using ICTs, it becomes increasingly easier to develop partnerships in order to cover a wider geographical area and to provide consistent service to consumers and vice versa. Because organizations need to offer consistent service they use more ICTs and, consequently, they can expand and take advantage of branding and consistency in more locations and industries. This is particularly evident in airlines and hotel chains where few alliances dominate the global provision. Airlines have realized that by harmonizing their schedules and delivering quality standards they can streamline their routes and concentrate only on those that offer them competitive advantage. They can also expand their network to an international scale and support their clientèle globally. Because of **code sharing** they gain preferential ranking on GDSs as well as on Internet sites. This means that their flights are displayed in a higher position on the display, enabling them to promote and manage their schedules seamlessly. Sharing information and developing joint promotional campaigns also assist their marketing function. All these activities could only take place because of powerful ICT tools, which support inter-organizational communications. Without ICT tools these developments will be uneconomical and inefficient to the degree that would jeopardize objectives.

The new ICT capabilities therefore offer the opportunity for principals to develop strategic alliances, partnerships and franchising agreements, enabling them to coordinate the products and to offer similar services on a global scale. By outsourcing non-core functions to specialist organizations they can reduce their inefficiencies and concentrate on the elements in which they can outperform their competitors. Through extranets, partners can have access to all relevant information and perform operations from distant geographical locations. For example, the accounting department of a New York hotel can be located in India, where both accountancy and ICT skills are highly developed and cost a fraction of that in the USA. Several calling centres for global companies are based in Mauritius, for example, to take advantage of the multilingual staff available at a very competitive labour cost. Outsourcing also blurs the borders of organizations as it enables tourism organizations to establish ad hoc relationships with other suppliers and intermediaries when needed. As a result, they can expand their value chain considerably to accommodate specific needs and requests without necessarily expanding their infrastructure and fixed assets. In this way satisfying consumers' needs is not only much easier but also efficient and effective.

5.6.2 ICT-empowered scope of operations: expansion and portfolio management

Global concentration and horizontal integration of tourism organizations have developed multinational companies, offering services in several geographical regions. For example, the Bass organization operates more than 3000 hotels in more than 100 countries under the Intercontinental, Holiday Inn and Crown Plaza brand names. In addition, vertical integration has increased the concentration of complementary organizations to a few multinational and multi-sector companies. This has enabled them to strengthen their own position, as they can control several stages of the value chain and spread their risk to several markets and destinations. They have also created conditions in the marketplace that influence the competitiveness of their rivals. This is illustrated in the Airtours example in Case Study 5.2.

Both ICTs and tourism propel developments in each other's field. On the one hand, tourism expands rapidly to become one of the most dominating industries internationally, and as a result requires better quality and efficiently transmitted information. On the other hand, ICTs offer new tools and mechanisms for information management and dissemination. Multinational organizations and global delivery of tourism products can only be implemented if a sufficiently robust info-structure is in place to support the global superstructure of facilities and networks required for the delivery of tourism.

Thus, the globalization experienced in the tourism industry can be attributed partly to the emergence of new ICTs and to the fact that globalization and expansion of the tourism industry generate new demands and requirements from ICTs. As a result, tourism organizations develop their portfolio of activities and strategic business units according to their ability to manage and control them. ICTs play a critical role in identifying the available opportunities and providing the management tools for this activity.

5.6.3 ICT-empowered distribution strategies

Distribution became the battlefield for marketing activity in the 1990s, as the concentration of retailers and wholesalers had significant impacts on the ability of suppliers to access their consumers. Intermediaries increasingly use more sophisticated research tools as well as data collected through loyalty clubs and other interactions with consumers and have a much better idea of their needs and requirements. Consumers are increasingly aware of intermediaries' brand names. As a result, suppliers seem to become the background of the marketplace and often play a less significant role in consumers' travel choices. The development of major European tour operators means that a large proportion of the leisure market relies on tour operator brands, almost ignoring the realities of

Case Study 5.2

The Airtours business and strategic business units

Airtours, a UK tour operator, has expanded its business dramatically to include travel agencies, charter airlines, hotels and cruise ships in addition to its ever-expanding tour operating business. Airtours employs 20 000 people and organized 10 million holidays in 1998. Its global portfolio includes tour operators, travel agencies, hotels, cruise ships, and an airline (Airtours, 1999). Vertical integration is used widely in order to control the quality of the products offered as well as for maximizing the profit margin throughout the value chain. To coordinate an organization of this magnitude and to deliver profitable results throughout each SBU, Airtours needs to keep communication channels and control mechanisms dynamic. ICTs provide the info-structure that such a large organization requires in order to be managed profitably.

Tour operators	UK: Airtours Holidays, Tradewinds, Eurosites, Panorama, Direct, Cresta Holidays, Bridge Travel
	Scandinavia: Ving, Spies, Saturn, Globetrotter
	Belgium/Holland/France: Sunair, Marysol, Traveltrend, Voyage Conseil
	Germany: FTI, Berge & Meer, Sport Scheck
	North America: Vacation Express, Suntrips, Sunquest
Travel agencies	Going Places, Travelworld, Advantage, Ving, Allkauf, FTI, Flugborse, v5F, Maretours
Cruises	10 cruise ships: Sun Cruises, Costa Crusies, Direct Cruises
Hotels	46 resort properties: 18 Sunwing-Airtours, 6 Blue Bay, 19 Siva, 3 Tenerife Sol
Airlines	42 aircraft: Airtours International (UK), Premiair (Scandinavia), Air Belgium (Belgium/Holland/France), Fly Fti (Germany)

Source: Based on Airtours (1999)

Questions

■ How can a vertically integrated travel organization use ICTs to manage its operations?

■ What are the synergies emerging through an integrated on-line strategy for a vertically integrated tour operator?

■ What other organizations compete with Airtours/MyTravel, and what are their on-line strategies?

supplier holidays and often the destination. Business travellers too find the distribution critical for their products as on the one hand airlines develop alliances through code sharing agreements and on the other independent hotel companies join international consortia to communicate their product (Buhalis and Laws, 2001).

However, the development of the Internet has provided unique opportunities for direct communication between suppliers and consumers, and thus has threatened the disintermediation of the distribution channel. Each supplier could, at least in theory, target each consumer and offer a uniquely designed product, based on the enhanced interactivity offered through the Internet. Opportunities to add value through customer relationship management and the design of personalized services have also emerged. In reality, though, only a few large suppliers with strong brand names have been in a position to partly disintermediate their channel with consumers confident enough to trust the supplier and purchase directly from them. Strong financial incentives were introduced as suppliers were prepared to share some of their savings from commissions with consumers. For example, British Airways and easyJet offer a £5 incentive for all passengers booking their tickets on-line. At the same time, suppliers have taken a more drastic approach to benefits for intermediaries, often providing disincentives for selling their product. Commission capping started in the USA, where major airlines reduced the commission paid to travel agencies from about 10 per cent to 5 per cent and introduced a maximum of $50 for each booking. European carriers followed similar patterns while some low-cost carriers refused to distribute their products via global distribution systems (e.g. easyJet and Ryanair), making sales through travel agencies much more complicated and non-commissionable. As a result, the business model of several tourism players has been altered significantly. For example, travel agencies have to deal with reduced commission rates and commission caps, as well as competition from principals' Internet representations through electronic intermediaries. Moreover, the new ICT capabilities have introduced several new distribution strategies and practices, including 'reverse auctioning' and 'guess your price' as well as 'last-minute' special deals that target consumers directly and aim to maximize the yield of tourism organizations.

Distribution becomes one of the most critical success factors and tourism organizations will need to have much better control and understanding in order to realize their full potential (Buhalis and Laws, 2001). Principals need to protect and develop their brands both on- and off-line by using ICTs dynamically. They also need to add value at each stage of the process and seduce their customers by interacting constantly in order to avoid losing them to competitors.

5.6.4 ICT-empowered building and protecting of brands on-line

Branding is the dynamic process of developing a name, term, sign, symbol, design or a combination of these elements that is intended to identify the goods and services of a seller and differentiate them from those of competitors. This is a particularly important process for services and intangible products as it provides a clearer idea of what the product is about and the value that can be added for the consumer (Kotler et al., 1996; Horner and Swarbrooke, 1996).

The development of the Internet, electronic markets and eCommerce has raised a whole range of new issues for branding. Firstly, the Internet has provided an unprecedented medium for *brand enforcement, enlargement and expansion* as it has allowed millions of people all over the world to access information on any product and even purchase it. Marriott hotels, for example, had the opportunity to reach a much wider audience than any of their advertisements could have potentially reached. People who were aware of the Marriott brand anticipated that it would have an on-line presence consistent with its off-line brand values and qualities. They also anticipated they would be able to interact with the organization, gain more information and perhaps value and be able to undertake on-line transactions. Having almost unlimited space to elaborate on the brand qualities and the product attributes is a major benefit introduced by ICTs. A typical example of brand enlargement is Virgin, which uses its key brand values and communications mechanisms to promote anything from airline, train and balloon journeys to music and beverages.

Unfortunately, however, only a few tourism organizations appreciated the power of the new medium early enough to gain major benefits. The majority failed to take advantage and registered their brand name late, providing limited content mainly from their off-line brochures and failing to interact with their consumers and partners. A lot of organizations were caught unaware that their brand name or a close variation was already registered by technology experts who then demanded a great amount of money for releasing that brand name. Organizations that registered a 'theirfirm.com' often found out that other similar domain names (e.g. 'theirfirm.co.uk' or 'theirfirm.net') were registered. *'Cyber-squatters'* were taking prospective customers to sites that had no relationship with the branded product and potentially had offensive and damaging content. Famous examples include MacDonalds who had to buy the domain 'macdonalds.com' back from the person that registered it, whilst they still have to fight the Maclibel action in the courts and on-line to limit the damage. Cyber-squatting (which will be dealt with in more detail in Chapter 11) has been detrimental to the brands of a wide range of tourism organizations.

In addition, the issue of *consistency* emerged. Would the on-line marketing mix of products and services be exactly the same as the off-line one? On the one hand, it makes sense to differentiate the marketing mix according to market segment. To the degree that a tourism organization can target a much wider audience on-line than off-line, it makes sense to differentiate the branding of products and services. On the other hand, though, brand consistency is critical if people are to believe the stated attributes. Therefore a differentiation can potentially damage the brand. This is more evident on pricing decisions. Should on-line pricing be consistent with off-line pricing, or should organizations take advantage of the unique opportunities of the Internet and vary their prices considerably, according to their yield management? Different organizations follow different practices. For example, no-frills airlines such as easyJet and Ryanair use the Internet to discount their products heavily and frequently sell flights for less than £10. Schedule carriers, such as British Airways, are much more reluctant to do so. Instead they use consolidators and electronic intermediaries such as priceline.com and lastminute.com to promote their discounted seats and do not disclose the identity of the company until the purchase has been completed. This practice not only allows them to protect their brand and mainstream revenue, but also excludes their competitors from knowing the level of pricing charged by the carrier.

Similarly recent research (O'Connor and Horan, 1999; O'Connor and Frew, 2000) has demonstrated that hotel companies have been prepared to negotiate prices over the phone while being reluctant to publicize discounted rates on the Internet, despite such a course of action costing them much more in communication and administration costs. Ultimately it is anticipated that ICTs and the euro will force organizations to adopt a more transparent policy, based on simple demand-and-supply economics, instead of the consumer trying to guess the price for travel products if certain restrictions and conditions apply. It is also expected that a more interactive process, which informs the consumer on their alternative choices and costs, will rationalize the pricing of tourism products.

The Internet has enabled several *new organizations* to be developed and thus has introduced several new brands. Companies such as expedia.com, last-minute.com, iglu.com, ebookers.com and trainline.com emerged from scratch and had to develop their credibility in the industry and their brand for con-sumers. Some of the most prominent organizations spend considerable amounts of money on establishing their position, in anticipation of capturing a significant share of the electronic market by which they will be able to attract sufficient reservations and become profitable. While some organizations have used their off-line brand (e.g. marriott.com and thomascook.com), others have separated their on-line provision and developed new brands for their on-line presence (e.g. Thomson launched the firstresort.com web site and Airtours mytravelco.com). By the end of 2001, none of the new on-line travel intermediaries had become profitable, having had to spend considerable amounts of money on not only the technology but also developing their brand through on- and off-line advert-ising. They anticipate that they will be able to break-even within the next two to three years and naturally their main concern is to raise adequate capital to survive during this period.

5.6.5 ICT-empowered customer relationship management and dynamic marketing (loyalty boosters)

Customer relationship management (CRM), or one-to-one marketing, aims at establishing, maintaining, enhancing and commercializing customer relation-ships through a better understanding of customer requirements and promise fulfilment. It implies that organizations segment their market into specific mar-ket niches and attempt to dominate them by developing highly appropriate products and services. It involves a two-way interactive and dynamic communica-tion, which ensures that consumers and suppliers interact dynamically towards achieving their goals. Ultimately consumers are involved in the product design process and assist the development of products suitable for themselves. Organ-izations should therefore encourage consumers to declare their interests and to interact with them in order to provide feedback and develop a relationship. Relationships should be based on adding value to the product on offer and on providing greater satisfaction for consumers. Organizations need to adapt and constantly monitor, analyse and interact with their environment in order to appreciate the dynamic developments and update their products constantly to satisfy the entire range of their stakeholders. Consumers need maximum satis-faction from the product and enterprises to achieve their objectives and financial targets. Organizations such as amazon.com have illustrated how consumers can be identified and acknowledged as individuals and how the organization can use data to take a proactive approach, suggesting books and other products that fit to their customer profile (Grönroos, 1990; McKenna, 1993; Strauss and Frost, 1999; Chaffey et al., 2000).

Customer relationship management and dynamic marketing can use knowledge about consumers to add value to their offerings and to differentiate their products constantly, in order to address the market segment of one – the unique customer. Using several research techniques, organizations can identify critical factors that can drive consumers to purchase products and test the most effective marketing tools. Developing a global presence, distributing products, testing and tracking consumer behaviour on-line enable organizations to collect information and undertake research. This would be enormously more expensive and time-consuming off-line. Remaining competitive and avoiding competitive disadvantage become core functions for every organization. Instant response and customer gratification will be critical for achieving that. The ICT revolution intensifies this process by propelling globalization and worldwide competition; increasingly tourism organizations will need to serve their customers at all times, at all places, using all available equipment. By using CRM, brands can be augmented and enlarged to offer seamless services to consumers. This will assist converting lookers into bookers and the appreciation of individual preferences for each individual consumer at each particular moment. Circumstance marketing that addresses particular situations and personal characteristics, such as taste, mood, peer pressure etc., provide unique challenges for the tourism organization of the future.

Traditionally few data were kept by tourism organizations and were rarely used for interacting with consumers. Some hotels kept guest histories but they were rarely used proactively to make customers feel special. The growth of loyalty clubs during the last decade has enabled more tourism organizations and airlines and hotel chains in particular to know more about the consumer patterns of their customers. Airlines classified passengers into gold, silver and blue card-holders to illustrate the frequency and value of their custom, but they rarely went further to appreciate individual needs and wants. Increasingly, however, travel intermediaries are starting to offer relationship marketing and proactive functions based on consumer profiles. The new intermediaries such as expedia.com and lastminute.com lead the field in this.

Although one-to-one marketing is an expensive process, tourism products are ideal for customization. Not only are they bundles of individually produced products and services, but they are also consumed under unique-by-customer circumstances. There is a great volume of information available through each reservation and consumers are generally happy to provide more information about their preferences when they interact with members of the industry. Using knowledge management technologies a hotel may, for example, collect information about consumers during the entire duration of their visit and share it between different departments or even properties to enhance customer satisfaction. Technological developments have made the recording of elements of individual taste easier; tourism enterprises that are prepared to capitalize on this information will be able to achieve competitive advantage through adding value to the core products.

5.7 Conclusions: eTourism empowers tourism management

In conclusion, ICTs provide strategic tools for tourism organizations by enabling them to achieve competitive advantage through cost, product or time differentiation or via focus strategy. On the one hand, ICTs determine the scale and scope of business and define the potential for geographical and operational expansion of a tourism organization. On the other, business requirements generate more demand for ICTs. This puts pressure on technology experts to develop suitable applications that meet the industry challenge. This is a dynamic step process, which moves both the ICT and tourism industries forward at a rapid pace.

Increasingly ICTs are closely related to a number of strategic decisions for tourism organizations and they are gradually one of the key strategic considerations for tourism planning and development at both the micro and macro levels. This is reflected in the promotion of ICT directors to the board of tourism corporations. It is critical, however, to ensure that ICTs support and serve the business plans and models of tourism organizations, rather than the other way around. It is equally important that ICT capabilities and opportunities inform business models and plans. Only a close integration between ICT potentials and business models will allow the tourism organization of the future to realize its full potential and to avoid strategic perils.

Chapter questions

1   What are the key strategic and operational functions supported by ICTs for a tourism organization of your choice?

2   What are the main opportunities and challenges for SMTEs through ICTs?

3   Try to book a domestic trip on the Internet and identify SMTEs offering services on-line.

4   Explain the key factors that influence SMTEs to adopt new ICTs.

5   What are the main differences between for-profit and not-for-profit tourism organizations as far as ICTs are concerned?

6   Why do tourism organizations need to be proactive and reactive, and how do ICTs assist this process?

7   Can ICT-related competitive advantages be sustainable? What are the main conditions for achieving this?

8   What can a tourism organization do when competitors imitate their ICT provision or their on-line representation?

9   Explain the main sources of ICT-related competitive disadvantages, and discuss how to avoid them, for an organization of your choice.

10   What are the ICT-related challenges for managing tourism brands?

Further reading

Buhalis, D. (1998) Strategic use of information technologies in the tourism industry, *Tourism Management*, **19**(3), 409–423.

Ingold, A., McMahon-Beattie, U. and Yeoman, I. (2000) *Yield Management*, 2nd edn, Continuum, London.

O'Connor, P. (1999) *Electronic Information Distribution in Tourism and Hospitality*, CAB, Oxford.

Porter, M. (1985) *Competitive Advantage*, Free Press, New York.

Porter, M. (1989) Building competitive advantage by extending information systems, *Computerworld*, **23**(41), 19.

Porter, M. and Millar, V. (1985) How information gives you competitive advantage, *Harvard Business Review*, **63**(4), 149–160.

Sheldon, P. (1997) *Information Technologies for Tourism*, CAB, Oxford.

Smith, C. and Jenner, P. (1998) Tourism and the Internet, *Travel and Tourism Analyst*, no. 1, 62–81.

WTO (2001) *E-Business for Tourism: Practical Guidelines for Destinations and Businesses*, World Tourism Organisation, Madrid.

Websites

American Airlines: **www.aa.com**

Six Continents: **www.sixcontinents.com**

Priceline: **www.priceline.com**

Expedia: **www.expedia.com**

Who Owns Whom: **www.fvw.com**

EyeforTravel: **www.eyefortravel.com**

Wardell's Library on eTourism: **www.wardell.org/publicat.htm**

Travel Industry Association: **www.tia.org/home.asp**

Accenture: **www.accenture.com**

European Commission IT and Tourism Report by Luis Costa: **europa.eu.int/comm/enterprise/services/tourism/workinggroups/finalreporte_june2001_en.pdf**

Jewell, G., Williamson, B. and Kärcher, K. (1999) The Airtours Cruise Intranet: streamlining the distribution of information, knowledge and money, presented at the 6th ENTER Conference, Innsbruck, Austria, January 1999. **www.genesys.net/karcherenter_0199.pdf**

Part B

ICTs for strategic and operational
management in the various sectors
of the tourism industry

Introduction to Part B

The proliferation of the Internet and the expansion of networking have revolutionized the tourism industry and have altered the core business for a wide range of organizations. By networking tourism players globally, innovative operators have realized that a number of major opportunities and challenges emerge. Principals are empowered to communicate directly with consumers and to develop customer relationship management programmes to facilitate their interaction efficiently and profitably. Principals use ICTs primarily to reduce operational and distribution costs, by establishing powerful tools for on-line direct contact with consumers. As a result, distribution channel members are threatened with dis-intermediation. They need to refocus their core business in order to be able to survive in the future. A trend for re-intermediation demonstrates that innovative players who take advantage of the emerging ICT tools, developing appropriate products and services, can add value in the process. Destinations emerge as umbrella brands that represent, coordinate and promote the entire range of local attractions and services. Inevitably therefore they develop interfaces with consumers and travel trade partners to communicate their offering and to promote the local inventory. All tourism players therefore should rearrange their entire business and partner relationships in order to take advantage of ICT tools and survive in the future. Innovative operators that will manage to achieve cost or product differentiation will be able to strengthen their position and to gain significant competitive advantages.

Part B of the book examines the key developments for most of the key sectors of the tourism industry. It adopts Leiper's (1995) tourism system, as demonstrated in the figure overleaf, to explain the interrelationships between partners in the industry. Chapter 6 provides an overview of the industry structure and distribution channels and explores the generic ICT requirements for the management of the tourism organization. Each of the following chapters explores briefly the history of ICT developments for each sector. This provides some insights into the technological and business requirements that have propelled the adaptation of ICTs. These developments, to a certain extent, explain the current technology utilization and explore the function of legacy systems.

Part B follows the conceptual framework developed in Chapter 3 and structures industry requirements around internal systems/intranets, partner systems/extranets and the stakeholder interaction systems/Internet. Although many organizations have instigated a system migration to Internet Protocol (IP) systems, the vast majority of the tourism industry still operates on legacy systems. Several key factors are responsible for the slow migration process, mainly:

■ low profit margins in the industry, which results in a reluctance to invest in ICT;

Figure B.1 The tourism system

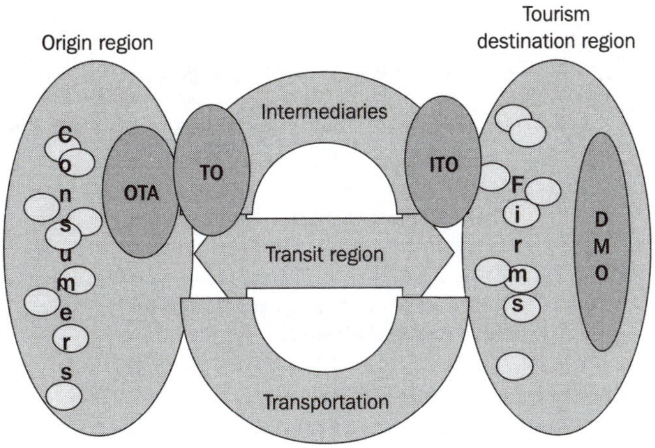

Origin region

Tourism destination region

Consumers

OTA

TO

Intermediaries

ITO

Firms

DMO

Transit region

Transportation

Source: Based on Leiper (1995)

- a volatile environment, with ICT technology developing faster than the industry is able or willing to follow;
- small players find it difficult to invest and develop systems further;
- there is a low degree of interoperability and standardization across the value chain;
- there have only been a small number of IP-based systems in the marketplace hitherto.

Some of these issues are explored in further detail in the following chapters. Complete migration of systems to IP solutions will require all members of the value chain to follow this development. Failing to do so can create more barriers to communication and prevent organizations from distributing products through partners. Currently, therefore, major players such as airlines, hotel chains and integrated tour operators have adopted a gradual upgrade approach, which allows them to develop multi-channel strategies. This aims to support all systems that partners operate and at allowing parallel interaction on different technological platforms. However, as supporting obsolete technological solutions implies a high cost and investment, it is likely that key players will gradually adopt the new technological standards and require all their partners to migrate to the new info-structure platforms.

Part B focuses on the business ICT requirements for each of the main tourism industry sectors separately. A number of operational and strategic requirements are examined within the intranet, extranet and Internet frameworks. The book deliberately avoids explaining particular software solutions or systems and describing technical requirements. Technological evolution provides new tools and these are absorbed to fulfil the need of the business requirements. Hence, creating a vision for the tourism industry of the future is far more important and it is attempted here. The following chapters therefore identify business operational and strategic ICT needs and explore some of the strategic issues for each sector. The chapters also provide a forecast of the development of the new systems that will facilitate close interaction, innovative development of tourism products and achievement of competitive advantage.

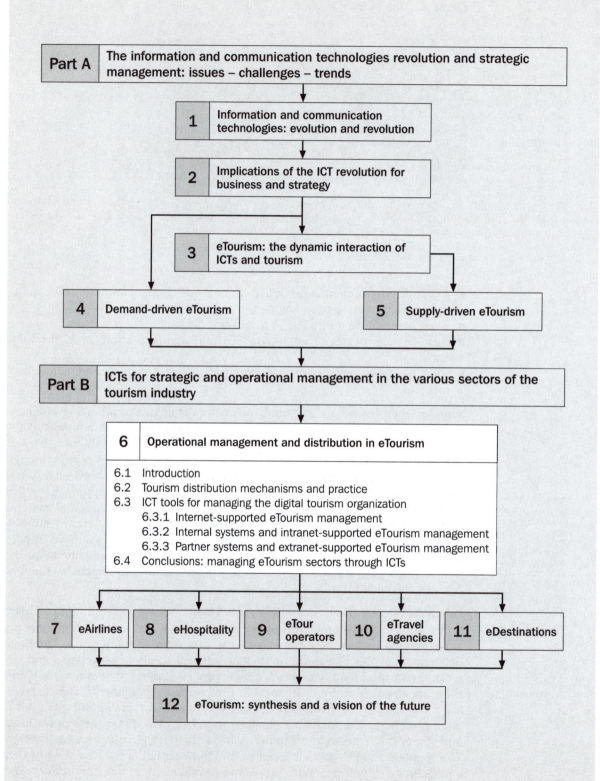

Part A | The information and communication technologies revolution and strategic management: issues – challenges – trends

1 | Information and communication technologies: evolution and revolution

2 | Implications of the ICT revolution for business and strategy

3 | eTourism: the dynamic interaction of ICTs and tourism

4 | Demand-driven eTourism

5 | Supply-driven eTourism

Part B | ICTs for strategic and operational management in the various sectors of the tourism industry

6 | Operational management and distribution in eTourism

6.1 Introduction
6.2 Tourism distribution mechanisms and practice
6.3 ICT tools for managing the digital tourism organization
    6.3.1 Internet-supported eTourism management
    6.3.2 Internal systems and intranet-supported eTourism management
    6.3.3 Partner systems and extranet-supported eTourism management
6.4 Conclusions: managing eTourism sectors through ICTs

7 | eAirlines   **8** | eHospitality   **9** | eTour operators   **10** | eTravel agencies   **11** | eDestinations

12 | eTourism: synthesis and a vision of the future

6

Operational management and distribution in eTourism

Chapter objectives

The purpose of this chapter is to explain the mechanisms and operational requirements of the tourism industry. A brief analysis of tourism systems and the distribution channel of tourism in particular provide the basis for understanding the ICT needs of each industry sector. The chapter then introduces the analysis framework by examining the generic requirements for internal/intranets, partner/extranets and the stakeholder interaction/Internet systems. Thus, the learning objectives may be defined as:

- Establish a level of understanding of the tourism system
- Demonstrate the distribution mechanisms in the industry and the role of each major player
- Appreciate the ICT applications required by organizations within an internal/intranet, partner/extranet and the stakeholder interaction/Internet system framework
- Explore the requirement for an integrated approach between the different systems in the organization
- Demonstrate the generic eBusiness principles that are applicable to all sectors
- Identify the need for integrated managerial solutions within the tourism industry context

6.1 Introduction

ICTs continue to change the strategic, operational and tactical management of tourism organizations. On the tourism supply side, ICTs play a critical role in the *production, marketing, financial, operational and distribution functions* of both the private and public sectors. This is clearly demonstrated within tourism systems, and particularly in the distribution channel of tourism. An understanding of the distribution channel mechanisms allows us to appreciate the interconnection and ICT requirements for tourism organizations. This also assists us in judging objectively whether ICTs can disintermediate the distribution channel and what the conditions are for re-intermediation. This chapter also illustrates the general principles of how tourism organizations use ICTs to manage their communications and interaction with the external world (Internet), internally (intranet) and with trusted and regular partners (extranet). Using the internal/intranets, partner/ extranets and the stakeholder interaction/Internet system framework, as demonstrated in Chapter 3, a number of issues are raised. The generic eBusiness principles are also discussed in the following paragraphs and these are applicable to all sectors.

6.2 Tourism distribution mechanisms and practice

Perhaps few other industries have experienced the effects of the Internet, extranets and intranets as much as tourism distribution. ICTs have gradually re-engineered the entire range of business processes in the distribution channel and all players need to re-evaluate their position and core competencies. Understanding the role of each actor of the distribution channel within the tourism operational management framework will be critical for appreciating the range and nature of the changes emerging. This will also allow us to appreciate the interaction with principals and destination management organizations.

Distribution becomes one of the most critical factors for the competitiveness of tourism organizations and destinations. Setting appropriate distribution channels effectively allows principals to build bridges with consumers, address their needs and provide mechanisms for purchasing tourism products. Inclusion in the distribution channel mechanisms determines whether they can be included in the set of decision-making models of prospective consumers. The globalization of the industry intensifies the information required for all tourism transactions, and thus more effective communication and distribution channels are required in order to provide sufficient information and to undertake a transaction. To the degree that distribution channels provide this information and facilitate the transactions, they extensively influence the prosperity of both tourism enterprises and destinations all over the world. Distribution channels often influence both consumer behaviour and the ability of the industry to respond to consumers' requests efficiently. Hence, they determine the competitiveness of suppliers and destinations (Buhalis and Laws, 2001).

ICTs have revolutionized tourism distribution channels dramatically, as they have introduced a wide range of opportunities and challenges. The technological revolution has demonstrated that several additional players, such as computer reservations systems (CRSs), global distribution channels (GDSs) and destination management systems (DMSs), have emerged to facilitate the distribution of tourism products. As tourism intermediation is mainly about handling information and facilitating transactions, ICTs play a critical role in the operation of intermediaries. The proliferation of the Internet has strengthened the role of electronic intermediaries and developed their position to a strategic one for tourism suppliers. Electronic intermediaries have developed to a degree that they can potentially threaten traditional distributors. Not only do they facilitate distribution but they also affect the other marketing-mix 'Ps' elements. They increasingly determine the *price* by assessing real-time demand and available supply. They also manipulate and formulate tourism industry *products* by combining and specializing products, according to customers' needs and wishes. Finally they facilitate *promotion* by targeting specific markets and establishing communication. They also transform the business model for several organizations by introducing new distribution strategies such as creating or co-branding Internet portals, auctions, name-your-price and other innovative distribution strategies. To a certain extent electronic tourism distribution channels dictate the choice of product as the difference between products becomes secondary to the eases of completing an entire transaction (Buhalis, 1998, 2000b, 2000c). Gradually, therefore, ICTs change the function of distribution from facilitation of information exchange and reservations to a much more sophisticated mechanism of adding value and providing service. In addition, to the degree that a great number of new players provide tourism and regional information, there is a rapid expansion of intermediaries in the marketplace.

The primary distribution functions for tourism are information, combination and travel arrangement services. Wanhill (1998) suggests that 'the principal role of intermediaries is to bring buyers and sellers together, either to create markets where they previously did not exist or to make existing markets work more efficiently and thereby to expand market size'. Moreover, Middleton (1988) proposes that 'a distribution channel is any organized and serviced system, created or utilized to provide convenient points of sale and/or access to consumers, away from the location of production and consumption, and paid for out of marketing budgets'. Most distribution channels therefore provide information for prospective tourists, bundle tourism products together, and also establish mechanisms that enable consumers to make, confirm and pay for reservations. In tourism the position of the distribution sector is much stronger than other trade intermediaries. Travel agents and tour operators as well as charter brokers, reservation systems and other travel distribution specialists have a far greater power to influence and to direct demand than do their counterparts in other industries. Since they do, in fact, control demand, they also have increased bargaining power in their relations with suppliers of tourist services and are in a position to influence their pricing, their product policies and their promotional activities. Thus, distribution starts to assume a much more central position in the strategy of most tourism organizations and destinations, as illustrated in Figure 6.1 (WTO, 1975).

Figure 6.1 Functions and benefits emerging through the tourism distribution channel

- Facilitation of access to often remote tourism products, for both bookings and purchasing
- Provision of information by using discussions, leaflets, maps, brochures, video, CDs
- Consumers' guidance/consultation for particular packages or products
- Undertake pre- and post-experience marketing research on consumers' needs and experiences
- Assemble tourism products from different providers according to tourists' expectations
- Facilitate selling process of tourism products, by reserving and issuing travel documents
- Ameliorate inventory management by managing demand and supply
- Issue of travel documentation, i.e. ticketing, vouchers etc.
- Utilize a clearing system where each channel member receives payments for their services
- Spreading the commercial risk involved between tourism distribution channel members
- Arranging details and ancillary services, such as insurance, visas, currency
- Promotion of particular products or packages, in cooperation with principals
- Complaint handling for both customers and industry

Two different types of intermediaries are normally used in order to access and purchase products, namely outgoing travel agencies (retailers) and tour operators (wholesalers). In addition, incoming (handling) travel agencies often offer support to tour operators in developing and delivering products based at destinations but do not come in contact with consumers.

The tourism distribution channel is illustrated in Figure 6.2. Consumers may purchase various components directly from producers, while numerous

Figure 6.2 Tourism distribution mechanism

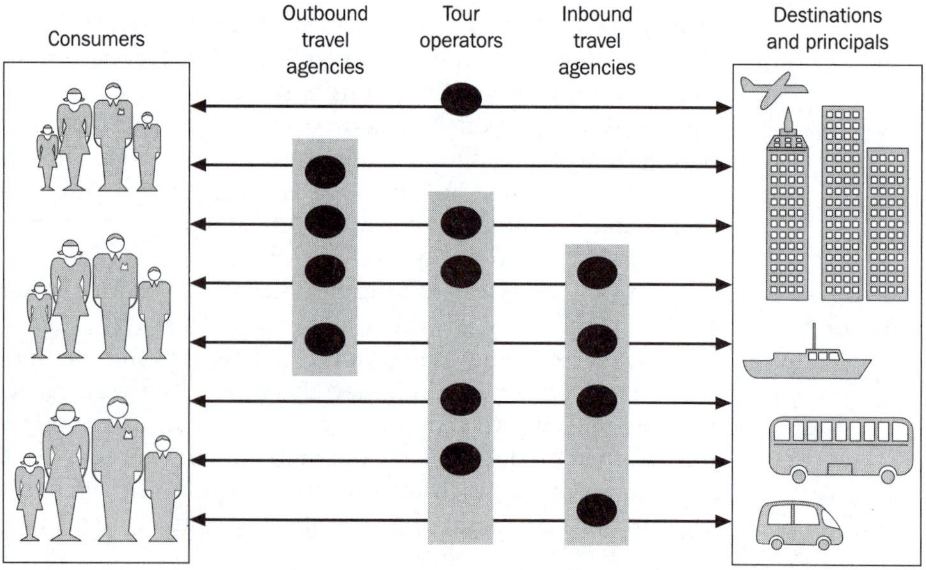

distribution and sales intermediaries are involved in promoting the tourism product. Prospective tourists may also use more than one category or tourism distribution channel for one trip.

A general trend for horizontal and/or vertical integration can be observed in the tourism industry. Horizontal integration takes place at the same level of any tourism distribution channel and essentially enables homogeneous enterprises to distribute their products more efficiently and effectively. Vertical integration emerges when organizations at one level in the tourism distribution channel merge with members from other levels to achieve economies of scale, better cost control, coordinated brand management, more channel control and increased bargaining power. Mergers between tour operators and outgoing travel agencies, airlines and accommodation establishments are typical examples of vertical integration (Buhalis and Laws, 2001; Cooper et al., 1998; Gee et al., 1989; Mill and Morrison, 1998; Middleton, 1994).

Each tourism distribution channel member has different needs and wants, as illustrated in Figure 6.3. Unfortunately, some of these needs are conflicting and antagonistic, and therefore a degree of **channel conflict** is inevitable. This

Figure 6.3 Tourism distribution channel member's needs and wants

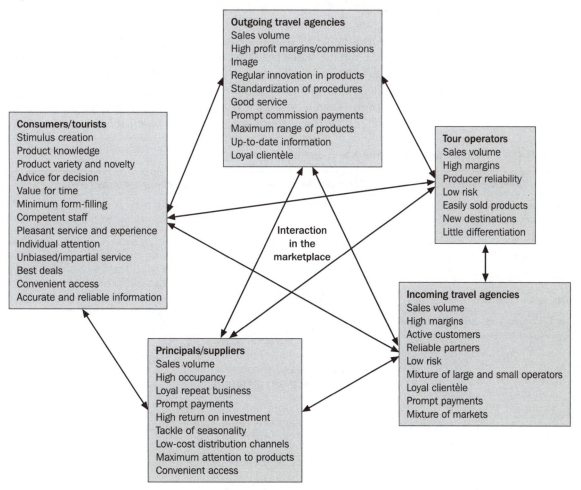

occurs particularly when **oligopsonio** or **oligopolio** situations emerge in the market place. Conflict emerges mainly due to the natural tendency of each player to maximize their profit margin at the expense of their partners, as consumers are prepared to pay a fairly fixed amount for their products. Power distribution within the tourism distribution channel affects channel control and leadership, while organizations often need to redesign their channels in order to resolve these conflicts. Tourism distribution channels require detailed analysis before their ICT needs and developments are examined.

6.3 ICT tools for managing the digital tourism organization

Gradually digital firms manage all their business processes and relationships with customers, suppliers and employees electronically, while increasingly coordinating their key corporate assets through digital means (Laudon and Laudon, 2002). This is more critical for tourism principals who own perishable inventory, and hence depend for their profitability on their ability to coordinate all their assets efficiently. Hence, ICTs are placed in the centre of their tactical planning and operational management, as illustrated in Figure 6.4.

The terms 'intranets' and 'extranets' are used in a wider context in this and following chapters to include all internal and partner systems respectively, regardless of whether or not they are based on the Internet Protocol (IP). Although this may not be technically accurate, as often there are legacy systems, it is increasingly evident that gradually most tourism ICT applications will migrate to IP-based solutions. Therefore, legacy systems are progressively either replaced with IP-based systems or they are interfaced with IP-based solutions. Therefore

Figure 6.4 ICT-enabled tactical planning and operational management

Internet/stakeholder-wide systems	*Extranet/partner systems*	*Intranet/internal systems*
Network of networks interconnecting everybody in the world	*Private intranet accessible to authorized outsiders*	*Internal network based on Internet and World Wide Web technology and standards*
■ Selling and eCommerce ■ Brand building ■ Loyalty clubs and affiliations ■ Communication and interacting with all stakeholders	■ Communications and interacting with partners ■ Interacting with stakeholders ■ eBusiness functions • eSales and marketing • eProduction and manufacturing • eProcurement • eAccounting and eFinance • eHuman resources outsourcing	■ Operational processes • Control inventory • Dynamic pricing • Check-in and billing procedures • Routing and scheduling • Coordination of production ■ eBusiness functions • eSales and marketing • eProduction and manufacturing • eProcurement • eAccounting and eFinance • eHuman resources • eManagement ■ Knowledge management

legacy systems will be increasingly interfaced with other systems available in the industry to support interoperability and interconnectivity.

6.3.1 Internet-supported eTourism management

Tourism organizations use ICTs to communicate with all stakeholders and to manage and control their inventory. They use the Internet extensively for eCommerce and for selling products directly to their consumers. Increasingly, Internet presence is part of the **promotion mix** for both tourism enterprises and destinations. Most tourism organizations have their own web page, with information and reservation capabilities, allowing consumers to search for availability and prices before making their bookings on-line. This allows organizations to communicate directly with different market segments and to adapt their offerings according to developments in the external world. They can also adopt dynamic pricing according to demand and supply. Increasingly, tourism organizations communicate their brand values and allow consumers to familiarize themselves with elements of their offering. The Internet provides endless opportunities to communicate with all stakeholders and to interact dynamically. Theme parks, for example, often introduce the different rides on offer, allowing consumers to appreciate the nature of their product before visiting. Disneyland Paris provides an opportunity to sample the product before arrival, offering practical information and the chance to pre-book tickets, and updating the programme of activities on a regular basis (www.disneylandparis.com).

In addition, a number of organizations aim to increase interaction and partnership with loyal customers and thus maximize **customer loyalty**. Airlines have pioneered loyalty clubs and several examples can be seen on the Internet (e.g. www.ba.com, www.united.com). Not only do they develop exclusive parts of their websites for their loyal clientèle, offering special privileges and benefits, but they also assist customers to manage their rewards, air miles and other benefits by automating this process. Developing interactive facilities enables consumers to offer feedback to enterprises and to communicate dynamically.

Apart from customers, tourism organizations support other stakeholders, such as local residents, environmental groups, travel agencies and tour operators, in exploring their offerings and perhaps their policies with regards to environment, commissions, recruitment etc. The largest tour operator in the world, TUI, for example, provides information on its environmental analysis and monitoring of destinations as well as its entire range of initiatives and projects (www.tui-environment.com). Employment and human resources management is also empowered through the Internet as increasingly tourism organizations rely on the Internet for advertising vacancies and recruitment. British Airways advertises and manages its recruitment drive on-line (www.britishairwaysjobs.com) maximizing efficiency, allowing candidates to submit their CV on-line, filling positions faster and reducing recruitment agency fees.

6.3.2 Internal systems and intranet-supported eTourism management

Perhaps more importantly, managing internal resources effectively and efficiently and enabling everybody within the organization to have access to a wealth of information are some of the most significant contributions of ICTs. Internal systems and intranets in particular facilitate a number of operational decisions and processes, support business functions and allow organizations to coordinate their resources through integrated enterprise systems (Laudon and Laudon, 2002). Principals, such as airlines, trains, ferries, hotels, car rental companies, theme parks etc., are particularly keen to control their inventory effectively. Similarly with all services, tourism products are perishable, and therefore it is critical for principals to sell most of their inventory on time, as there is no opportunity to sell the product at a later stage.

Controlling inventory supports principals proactively and reactively in anticipating and managing demand for their products. Reservation systems help them sell tourism products through multi-distribution channels simultaneously. In some cases they are capable of manipulating the level of supply by reducing or diverting their inventory. For example, airlines may decide to consolidate flights with hotels to operate only the number of floors they require, and train companies may use only a limited number of cars. Transportation companies often adapt their planning of routes and equipment to maximize the yield of their resources and to match demand with supply. However, as the fixed costs are quite high for the tourism industry, principals often use dynamic pricing that takes into consideration the time available for selling a product as well as historical data and other elements of the external environment to manipulate demand with the pricing of the tourism products.

Finally, intranets are used extensively for managing the production process and for coordinating departments within organizations. Information is critical for the production and operation of most tourism products. Hence, timely sharing of all data can be critical for the production process and consequently for the quality of the service and satisfaction levels. In hotels, for example, housekeeping can inform the front office that rooms are serviced and available to be sold. In the airline business, sales and ticketing are in contact with the check-in, gate management and dispatch departments to inform them of late sales and late boarding of passengers. Both can be critical for delays that may affect customer satisfaction, as well as for selling available products at the last minute, affecting the bottom line. Coordinating the entire production and ensuring the smooth running of multi-department tourism organizations, operating under time and budget constraints, require extensive inter- and intra-organizational networking and intensive as well as time-critical communications. The geographical spread of many of the tourism products as well as the multi-cultural environment within which the industry operates makes the role of ICTs more critical for effective communications.

In addition, intranets are widely used to re-engineer, automate and facilitate the entire range of *eBusiness functions*. eMarketing and eSales enable tourism organizations to develop their **marketing management** as well as their strategies and tactics by sharing all data digitally. Being connected to their eCommerce applications on the Internet, eSales can have up-to-date information on demand and supply. Altering the product, price, distribution channels and promotion accordingly can be critical for the profitability of the organization. eManufacturing in tourism refers to the coordination of all processes and people involved in the production. For example, coach drivers can report their position electronically in order to optimize routes and prepare attractions or hotels for their exact arrival time. Similarly, waiters using handsets can send their order straight to the kitchen for preparation as well as to the point of sale for debiting customers' bills. One of the areas in which intranets have been used extensively is eProcurement, stock management and control. Tourism organizations can control all their input and re-engineer their processes by automating parts of the process and by developing links with their suppliers. Purchasing material through specialized portals, such as zoho.com, provides the opportunity for tourism organizations to streamline their purchasing processes, maximize efficiencies and coordinate all actors involved. By constantly monitoring the marketplace for better deals and by taking advantage of electronic auctions, tourism organizations can also reduce their costs.

eAccounting and eFinance refer to the digitalization of all accounting and financial management processes for the tourism organization. Developing budgets and regular financial reports, monitoring cash flows, and invoicing are supported through the use of intranets. Similarly, crediting and debiting internal departments (such as bars and restaurants), customers (both individual and corporate) and properties/branches are empowered by intranets, maximizing efficiencies. eHuman resources management (eHRM) also assists tourism organizations in managing their human resources. As the tourism and hospitality industries are very labour-intensive and at the same time experience a high level of labour turnover, recruiting, organizing and managing human resources are critical for an organization's success. ICTs allow tourism organizations to promote vacancies across the Internet, to manage applications and recruitment by using their intranet. Once employees are in employment, tourism organizations can organize departments, as well as deal with all issues associated with personnel, including salaries and payroll, pensions, training, appraising, job transfers and promotions (Laudon and Laudon, 2002). This is more critical for international hotel and tourism organizations, where employees operate in several countries and there is high staff mobility.

eBusiness and eManagement refers to the coordination of all *management functions* for tourism organizations, including the ePlanning and eStrategy functions. ICTs are seen as tools for achieving the business model of tourism organizations (i.e. enabling them to fulfil their mission and strategy). ICTs are also seen as the key ingredients of the informing and facilitating the eStrategy (i.e. determining what is possible and in what direction the organization has decided to head). For example, hotel chains use ICTs to manage their properties and ensure that their business models and the key indicators, such as occupancy, REVPAR, profitability, expansion, productivity etc., are coordinated and achieved.

The availability and technical capabilities of ICTs inform and determine their business models, and therefore influence property expansion, mergers and alliances, mission statements and expected outcomes. eOrganizing involves the departmentalization of organizations into coherent and management units that assist them to achieve their objectives efficiently and effectively. Intranets may facilitate the process of developing and managing departments, as the way that data, information and knowledge are handled internally determines the need for internal structures. Similarly with eHRM, eStaffing looks after the labour input requirements and the skills required for the organization. eLeading allows tourism organizations to share their vision and strategy and influences their employees towards contributing to the organizational goals. For example, providing generic guidelines for the service quality and standards and making employees adopt the service philosophy of a tour operator service is critical for delivering satisfactory programmes and also reinforcing the brand. Finally, eControlling assists tourism organizations in measuring and correcting individual and organizational performance to ensure output optimization. This may involve indicators such as sales figures, average fares, load factors, productivity measures, and questionnaires for travellers. Intranets have improved the ability to access control information instantly and to monitor it automatically. As a result, tourism organizations are increasingly able to take corrective measures 'on the flight' (i.e. very soon after an event happens), and therefore are able to address the issue.

Finally, intranets enable tourism organizations to take advantage of *knowledge management* in order to collect and disseminate the insights, understanding and practical know-how that employees possess. On one hand, knowledge management systems use ICTs to systematize, enhance and expedite the intra- and inter-firm **knowledge** and expertise of the organization's human capital. On the other, they organize, interpret and make widely accessible this knowledge to help the organization maximize its collective efficiency and effectiveness, as well as to cope with labour turnover, rapid change and downsizing (Leidner, 1999; Augier et al., 2001; Bollinger and Smith, 2001). This is particularly important for the tourism and hospitality industries, where soft aspects of the product are vital for customer satisfaction. Hotel employees, and concierges in particular, often understand and serve the personal requirements of their guests; this makes these employees into an incredibly powerful force for customer satisfaction. Hotel chains that operate in a global environment can also benefit by sharing understanding and knowledge of consumers globally. In addition, all employees usually have a number of methods, trade secrets and techniques that influence the operation of their property. Being able to collect and disseminate this information throughout the organization allows a hospitality firm to develop an intelligence network and optimize its operations.

6.3.3 Partner systems and extranet-supported eTourism management

Partner systems and extranets enable close cooperation between partners by giving access to dedicated parts of each other's systems. For example, authorized tour operators can access a dedicated part of a hotel company's intranet to see corporate rates and availability for their guests or to update rooming lists and manifests. By using extranets, tourism partners achieve a certain degree of transparency and interactivity, and thus can increase the efficiency and productivity of the entire value chain. However, firewalls are used to authenticate users and to ensure that access to internal data is restricted and secure. Therefore, extranets contribute to the cordination of the value chain without compromising the security and confidentiality of each partner. Extranets can improve interactivity between all tourism production and distribution partners, integrating the entire value chain and supporting closer cooperation towards the provision of seamless products.

Extranets are particularly useful for all eBusiness functions, especially when several partners are involved in the management of a process. In eSales and eMarketing tourism partners can work together closely to maximize their occupancy/load factors and average price. Appreciating the operational requirements and the key profitability considerations for hotels, for example, and having access to inventory on-line can empower travel agencies to promote properties and create special/last-minute offers. Business travel agencies also benefit by providing access to reservation suites and specialized services for their regular clients, maximizing their efficiency and reducing communication costs for both.

Since the early 1970s, ICTs have supported the distribution mechanisms and functions of eTourism. The World Tourism Organization (WTO) acknowledged that computerized networks, and in particular airline computer reservation systems (CRSs), have been leading dramatic structural changes since the early 1970s. Most larger tourism organizations have been utilizing CRSs to manage and distribute their capacity since the 1960s. CRSs were first developed for airlines in order to manage their reservations and seat availability before expanding to global distribution systems (GDSs), as illustrated in Chapter 3, in the early 1980s; this effectively developed them into electronic travel marketplaces and business-to-business (B2B) systems. GDSs gradually expanded their geographical and operational coverage by integrating both horizontally with other airline systems, and vertically by incorporating the entire range of principals, such as accommodation, car rentals, train and ferry ticketing, entertainment and other provisions (Truitt et al., 1991; Kärcher, 1996; French, 1998; WTO, 1995).

Although GDSs, as earlier extranets, could not take advantage of the World Wide Web technologies, they were still effective enough in allowing partners to share operational data and to exchange information, orders and funds. CRSs and GDSs enabled tourism providers to control, promote and sell their products through the entire range of partners and suppliers in the international market. They also helped them to increase occupancy/load factor levels and to reduce seasonality by managing their demand and supply better. GDSs also serve the travel trade (intermediaries) as they allow quick and firm responses to customers' enquiries by making tourism products instantly accessible. Therefore they contribute directly to the ability of tourism organizations to distribute their products widely and therefore, to their profitability.

Tourism principals realized that their presentation on travel agencies desktop screens was critical for their ability to attract bookings. Hence, they developed interfaces to enable them to communicate directly with intermediaries through CRSs. Switch companies such as THISCO and WIZCOM also emerged to facilitate interconnectivity between dedicated or internal hotel systems and GDSs (Emmer et al., 1993; O'Connor, 1995, 1999b). In addition, destination management systems emerged to provide integrated solutions for destinations and SMTEs excluded from the major systems, as well as to amalgamate all local systems and providers under one brand name (Buhalis, 1994, 1997). However, it was the introduction of the World Wide Web and the Internet that really revolutionized tourism distribution and empowered the networked tourism enterprise.

As far as eProduction and eManufacturing are concerned, extranets are extraordinarily useful in coordinating all the players involved in the value chain; such coordination is critical for the seamless production and delivery of the tourism product. Extranets can be used for allowing external partners to serve consumers. As increasingly tourism organizations will take advantage of virtual corporations and rely on outsourcing for vital functions, eProduction will be critical in the tourism industry for performing the core business. For example, most airlines rely on external in-flight catering business companies for providing meals on board. Customers require more choice for cultural, religious and health reasons, and can book their meals on-line, making catering on board extremely complex. For example, Air India allows passengers to book from a range of more than 25 different types of meals (www.airindia.com/meal.htm). Communicating this information efficiently to catering partners, enabling them to check on-line the number of passengers booked and the types of meals reserved, will be critical for system efficiency and customer satisfaction. Similarly, a hotel may have arrangements with a local company for the delivery of take-away food or for arranging the installation of in-room computers and other equipment. Using an extranet system helps them to optimize their collaboration. For example, taxi companies can communicate with airlines to arrange limousine service for passengers and do most of the check-in procedures during the transfer to the airport. Similarly, airlines can communicate with hotels and advise them of early or late arrival of guests.

eProcurement and eSupply management are probably the most popular function of extranets. Purchasing products in a B2B environment is one of the most successful applications of the Internet globally. Many tourism and hospitality organizations enjoy the benefits of extranets by ordering ingredients and inputs on-line, as demonstrated in Case Study 6.1. Developing closed partnerships with their suppliers has allowed them to streamline their stock control, invoicing and payment processes. Automating stock control and determining operational practices, criteria and desirable levels of storage, enables organizations to communicate automatically with suppliers and digitalize the entire process.

eAccounting and eFinance assist partners to transfer money between accounts and to follow up the process of payments. In addition, they allow organizations to follow exchange rates and also provide financial information for shareholders and other stakeholders. For example, British Airways communicates information about its shares and develops a relationship with shareholders on-line (www.bashares.com). This is applicable to all members of the tourism value chain. In addition, eAccounting allows tourism organizations following payments from and to partners, developing relationships with financial institutions and investors, as well as interacting with the external financial environment of the tourism organization. As transactions frequently involve several countries and partners, often based on different time zones and speaking different languages, coordinating the system efficiently is of critical importance.

Finally, eHuman resources management (eHRM) also enables tourism organizations to develop partnerships with recruitment agencies or sources of casual staff in order to deal with labour turnover. Recruiting on-line and managing the relationship with all employment-related partners such as social security agencies and trade unions through extranets can also be beneficial. ICTs assist tourism organizations to promote vacancies across the Internet, to manage applications and recruitment by using their intranets. eHuman resources is of particular use

Case Study 6.1

The Biz2Biz Hospitality Marketplace

The Biz2Biz Hospitality Marketplace is an eProcurement system with over 30 000 suppliers and thousands more buyers already in place. It simplifies the industrial purchasing process to a radical degree by helping companies to reduce costs through better pricing and enforced corporate purchasing policies. Biz2Biz Hospitality Marketplace delivers a targeted buying audience to the hospitality industry. The company provides buyers and suppliers with tools, offering an intermediation mechanism in the marketplace. Products include beds, linen, tableware, china, uniforms, ice-making equipment, lobby accessories, fittings, railings, bell carts, luggage carts, bathroom amenities, hotel stationery, framed art, mirrors, compact refrigerators, commercial laundry equipment, vended copiers, security hardware, signs, room air conditioners, amenity baskets, amenities, bed frames and thousands more products for the hospitality industry. Biz2Biz Hospitality aims to offer a complete B2B eBusiness solution for the hospitality industry.

For more information, see **www.biz2bizhospitality.com**

Questions

■ How can eProcurement support other business functions in the tourism industry?

■ Who are the current key players for eProcuremet in the hospitality industry?

■ How can the hospitality industry change as a result of eProcurement?

when parts of the tourism operation are outsourced. For example, when hotels contract part of their housekeeping or catering to external providers, partners can follow the operational requirements of the property in order to have the latest updates. They can then adapt their provision accordingly. Extranets also support the recruitment process, when travel companies outsource this function to specialized agencies and communicate with them digitally for the shortlisting, selecting and appointing process.

6.4 Conclusions: managing eTourism sectors through ICTs

The tourism distribution channel is a complex system involving travel agencies, tour operators and incoming travel agencies. The channel facilitates ad hoc relationships between partners that perform the development and delivery of tourism products and services. eTourism principles and the Internet, extranet and intranet framework outlined in this chapter can apply to almost all sectors of the tourism industry, including transportation, hospitality, catering, entertainment and value-added services. In addition, they provide the info-structure and the distribution mechanism for the entire industry. The following chapters provide a brief discussion of the level of ICT utilization in the different industry sectors and provide case studies to support the arguments. First we investigate the implications of ICTs for principals such as airlines and hospitality organizations. Then we explore the developments in the distribution channel partners, including travel agencies and tour operators, before examining the eIntermediaries of the future. Finally, an analysis of destination management organization systems brings together the utilization of ICTs at the destination level.

Chapter questions

1 Who are the main players in the distribution channel of tourism?

2 Explain the role of tour operators and travel agencies, and explore their interaction with other partners in the tourism industry.

3 Discuss the coordination of ICT systems in the tourism industry (e.g. CRSs, GDSs, DMSs, PMSs etc.).

4 Examine where ICT systems in the tourism industry fit within the distribution channel framework.

5 What are the main uses of the Internet for a tourism organization of your choice?

6 Explain how extranets facilitate B2B transactions and applications.

7 What is the relationship of intranets with the entire range of internal and computerized systems for an organization of your choice?

Further reading

Buhalis, D. and Laws, E. (2001) *Tourism Distribution Channels*, Continuum, London.

Cooper, C., Fletcher, J., Gilbert, D., Shepherd, R. and Wanhill, S. (eds) (1998) *Tourism: Principles and Practice*, Longman, London.

Goeldner, C., Ritchie, B. and McIntosh, R. (2000) *Tourism: Principles, Practices, Philosophies*, 8th edn, J. Wiley and Sons, New York.

Mill, P. and Morrison, A. (1998) *The Tourism System*, 3rd edn, Kendall/Hunt, USA.

Sheldon, P. (1997) *Information Technologies for Tourism*, CAB, Oxford.

Werthner, H. and Klein, S. (1999) *Information Technology and Tourism – A Challenging Relationship*, Springer, New York.

Websites

ConnectedInMarketing, Chartered Institute of Marketing: **www.connectedinmarketing.com**

CISCO on eCommerce: **http://resources.cisco.com/app/tree.taf?asset_id=48266**

CISCO Internet economy: **http://newsroom.cisco.com/dlls/tln/economy.html**

eCommerce: surveying the digital future, UCLA: **ccp.ucla.edu/pdf/UCLA-Internet-Report-2001.pdf**

BTA tourism industry tips: **www.tourismtrade.org.uk/home.htm**

Who Owns Whom: **www.fvw.com**

News on EyeforTravel: **www.eyefortravel.com**

News on eTid: **www.e-tid.com**

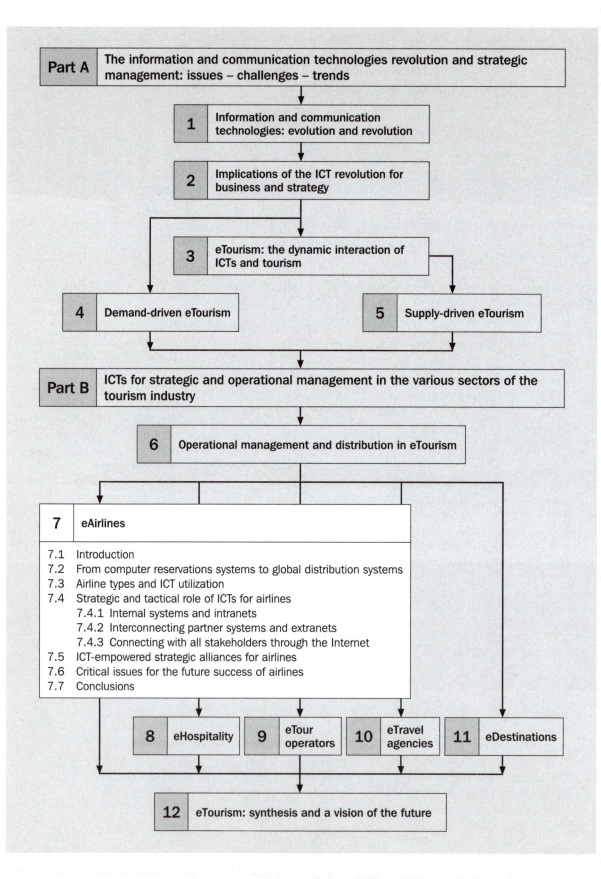

Part A The information and communication technologies revolution and strategic management: issues – challenges – trends

1 Information and communication technologies: evolution and revolution

2 Implications of the ICT revolution for business and strategy

3 eTourism: the dynamic interaction of ICTs and tourism

4 Demand-driven eTourism

5 Supply-driven eTourism

Part B ICTs for strategic and operational management in the various sectors of the tourism industry

6 Operational management and distribution in eTourism

7 eAirlines

7.1 Introduction
7.2 From computer reservations systems to global distribution systems
7.3 Airline types and ICT utilization
7.4 Strategic and tactical role of ICTs for airlines
    7.4.1 Internal systems and intranets
    7.4.2 Interconnecting partner systems and extranets
    7.4.3 Connecting with all stakeholders through the Internet
7.5 ICT-empowered strategic alliances for airlines
7.6 Critical issues for the future success of airlines
7.7 Conclusions

8 eHospitality

9 eTour operators

10 eTravel agencies

11 eDestinations

12 eTourism: synthesis and a vision of the future

7

eAirlines

Chapter objectives

The purpose of this chapter is to explore the strategic implications of ICTs for airlines. The chapter illustrates the different types of airlines and their levels of ICT utilization. It explores the competitive drivers in the airline business and demonstrates that ICTs become critical for the strategic and operational management of airlines. A number of systems that enables airlines to maximize their internal efficiency as well as their collaboration with partners are demonstrated. The chapter illustrates several critical strategic issues that will determine the competitiveness of airlines in the future. Thus, the learning objectives may be defined as:

- Demonstrate how ICTs can support airlines in their strategic and operational management
- Understand the sources of competitiveness and explore how technology influences them
- Illustrate how airlines use ICT systems internally and externally to communicate with partners and consumers
- Present critical strategic and operational decisions and directions empowered by ICTs
- Explore how ICTs can integrate the airline industry and strengthen its competitiveness
- Discuss the development of strategic alliances and the role of ICTs
- Identify critical trends and developments for the airline industry resulting from ICT developments

7.1 Introduction

Airlines realized fairly early on the need for efficient, quick, inexpensive and accurate handling of their inventory and communicating with travel agencies and other distributors. Airlines have been investing heavily in ICTs since the early stages of their development. Originally, in the 1950s, reservations were made on manual display boards, on which the passengers were listed. Travel agencies had to locate the best routes and fares for their customers in a manual such as the Official Airline Guide (OAG) or the World Airways Guide ABC, and then phone for availability, reservation and confirmation before issuing a ticket manually. In 1962, American Airlines introduced its SABRE computer reservation system (CRS), a project that was then described as 'a technical marvel representing a programming task that surpassed the coding effort required for NASA's Project Mercury', as an alternative to expanding its Boeing 707 fleet by 50 per cent (from 8 to 12 aircraft) (Feldman, 1987; Hopper, 1990; Boberg and Collison, 1985). By the mid-1970s SABRE was much more than an inventory-control system. Its technology provided the base for generating flight plans for the aircraft, tracking spare parts, scheduling crews and developing a range of decision support systems for management (Hopper, 1990; Knowles and Garland, 1994).

Although many years have passed since then, ICTs continue to play a critical role in the strategic and operational management of airlines. In the 2001 Airlines IT trends survey it was revealed that airlines are moving fast to Internet protocol (IP)-based systems, having either to modernize legacy systems or to invest in new technological solutions. Getting closer to customers and cutting costs are the key drivers for ICT projects; 20 per cent of carriers have already moved to IP-based systems and are experiencing the business and cost benefits. Another third is expected to join them in the next couple of years while over 90 per cent of the carriers are reported to have started the migration to IP. Just 6 per cent of tickets are currently sold on-line using web-based services, and airlines see their own websites as the most important distribution channel. It will probably take until 2007 for on-line sales and eTicketing to become the major distribution mechanisms worldwide (O'Toole, 2001).

7.2 From Computer Reservations Systems to Global Distribution Systems

Most airlines have been developing and implementing ICT systems for several decades. The growth of air traffic as well as the US air transportation deregulation in the 1970s enabled airlines to change their routes and fares as frequently as desired. This generated a great demand for flexibility as well as for internal and external communications. As a result, it stimulated the introduction of the first CRSs, which expanded rapidly to form gigantic computerized networks. CRSs on the one hand aimed at organizing airlines internally, by offering them a tool to manage their inventory, and on the other aimed to allow distributors and partners to access information about availability and prices. As prices, schedules and routes were liberated, airlines could change them indefinitely, while new airlines entered the markets. 'Fare wars' complicated the fares structure and increased the computing and communication needs (Boberg and Collison, 1985). These systems were initially regarded as tools for improvement in productivity and efficiency but there soon followed a more integrated approach to the utilization of CRSs in administration.

CRSs allowed airlines to compete fiercely by adapting their schedules and fares to demand. The sophistication of CRSs expanded in order to distribute up-to-date information to all potential customers worldwide and to support the operation and administration of airlines. This development also resulted in the development of CRSs into marketing and distribution systems, as they contributed significantly to the competitiveness of vendor/host airlines. They became strategic business units (SBUs) in their own right, due to their ability to generate income and boost airlines' sales at the expense of their competitors. CRSs introduced three major financial benefits for vendor airlines, namely a wide distribution network and CRS services; revenues generated from services to third parties; and incremental benefits through directional selling to the parent carrier (Sheldon, 1997; Sloane, 1990; Truitt et al., 1991; Freedman, 1991; Wheatcroft and Lipman, 1990; Feldman, 1987; Levine, 1987; Copeland, 1991; Copeland and McKenney, 1988; Wardell, 1987a).

Carriers used the newly emerging computer technology to manage reservations and fare data more accurately and efficiently. In addition, the remote printing of travel documents such as tickets and boarding passes, itineraries and invoices as well as the sales settlements between airlines and travel agencies, and the partnership marketing through **frequent flyer programmes**, were invaluable benefits. Eventually, every airline developed or purchased its own system, which was run domestically and primarily served its national market (Mietus, 1989; Wardell, 1987a; Hanlon, 1999).

Each airline still runs an internal CRS, which manages its inventory and supports its needs. However, CRSs increasingly use intranets to make the system widely available internally in order to maximize their efficiency. They also act as the backbone of the digital airline. By integrating their external links, through extranets and the Internet, they offer eCommerce opportunities as well as interaction with partners.

In the mid-1980s, CRSs developed into much more comprehensive global distribution systems (GDSs), offering a wide range of tourism products and providing the backbone mechanism for communication between principals and travel agencies. Single CRS systems, such as SABRE, developed their databases to include itineraries and inventory from other airlines, while two groups of scheduled airlines emerged in Europe to develop the **Galileo** and **Amadeus** systems (WTO, 1995; French, 1998). It is estimated that the American SABRE holds 45 million fares in a database with up to 40 million changes entered every month. Moreover, 500 000 passenger name records are created every day while the system handles nearly 2000 messages per second (Hopper, 1990). 'Each seat is sold, on average, 2.5 times (and cancelled 1.5 times) during the three months prior to departure' (Adam, 1990).

The development of CRSs into GDSs, with the integration of comprehensive tourism services, utilized the CRSs' infrastructure and provided value-added services for their core products. As a result, GDSs provide one-stop customer service at both the point of departure and the destination. GDSs have effectively become travel supermarkets offering information and reservation capabilities for the entire range of travel products, including accommodation, car rentals, schedules for non-air transportation etc. GDSs are at the heart of scheduled airline operational and strategic agendas as they control and distribute the vast majority of airline seats.

Strategic alliances, consolidations, mergers and interrelations between CRSs increase competition in the CRS industry. Four major GDSs, namely Amadeus, SABRE, Worldspan and Galileo, currently compete fiercely in the recruitment of travel agencies and penetration of the marketplace (Kärcher, 1996). As demonstrated in Case Study 7.1, GDSs emerge as the main technology suppliers for a wide range of tourism organizations, reinventing yet again their strategic objectives and aiming at developing solutions that will enable them to provide the info-structure for a number of industry players.

The cost of GDS representation and distribution increased considerably in the 1990s and airlines find it difficult to control. It is estimated that on average airlines spend 25–30 per cent of their turnover on distribution. This is a greater problem for smaller and regional airlines, which find it difficult to pay GDS fees and in-house technology expertise. As a result, airlines tend to recognize the need for re-engineering the distribution process and costs in order to maximize the efficiency and effectiveness of both their marketing and operational functions. Developing relationships with their clients and encouraging them to purchase tickets directly on the carrier's website by offering special discounts are gradually changing the distribution mechanism in the airline industry once again.

Case Study 7.1

Amadeus: global travel distribution

This case study analyses the development and operation of Amadeus, one of the four main GDSs and a main technology provider in travel and tourism. Amadeus is a neutral and global distribution system. It provides a wide range of solutions, which contribute to the virtualization of the tourism industry. It was founded in 1987 by Air France, Iberia, Lufthansa, SAS and Continental Airlines and begun operations in January 1992. Amadeus (and its competitor Galileo) emerged as a European response to the US CRSs' sophistication and expansion plans in the mid-1980s. Most European national airlines had developed their own reservation systems, which served the respective national markets. However, imminent air transportation deregulation in Europe and competition with American carriers made it imperative to create a distribution system able to distribute airline seats in Europe and globally, as well as to establish direct links with travel agencies. Amadeus's mission was to replace existing airline reservation systems, mainly in the markets in which its owner/partner airlines operated, with a system that would provide a totally neutral distribution system through leading technology. Amadeus also aimed to increase efficiency in airline bookings and to give equally comprehensive access to car rental and hotel services, in order to create a global system and allow interactivity with all types of tourism principals and intermediaries.

Currently Amadeus operates one of the world's most extensive electronic marketplaces. It supports travel agents and travel service providers in marketing and selling travel to corporate and consumer end-users in over 200 markets around the world. In addition, its technology is used by over 100 airlines and other travel service providers to optimize their internal operational requirements. Their core business has expanded and they currently serve many different travel companies – whether airlines, travel agents, hotel operators or car rental firms – by providing technology that moves the travel industry. Through the Amadeus system, over 182 000 travel agency terminals in 59 200 travel agency locations and almost 8500 airline sales offices around the world are able to make bookings with around 500 airlines, representing more than 95 per cent of the world's scheduled airline seats. In addition, 58 500 hotel properties and some 50 car rental companies, serving some 24 900 locations, are represented in the system. A number of other travel provider groups (ferry, rail, cruise, insurance companies and tour operators) are also accessible and bookable. Amadeus is also the owner of vacation.com, one of the leading US marketing networks for leisure travel. The company has been a publicly listed company since 1999 although the three founder airline shareholders still hold 59.92 per cent of the company: Air France (23.36 per cent), Iberia (18.28 per cent) and Lufthansa (18.28 per cent). The remaining shares are held publicly. Amadeus headquarters are in Madrid, Spain while its data centre is in Erding (near Munich), Germany, and its development offices are located in Sophia Antipolis (near Nice), France. The company has over 3950 employees worldwide. Amadeus has regional offices in Bangkok, Buenos Aires and Miami. The company has a network of National Marketing Companies (NMCs) globally. e-Travel, the Amadeus eCommerce business unit, has key operational sites in the US, Europe and Asia-Pacific.

Apart from serving travel agencies, which are still the core users of the system, the Amadeus system is one of the leading technology solutions suppliers in the marketplace. e-Travel is a global provider of online travel technology. It provides eCommerce solutions for airlines, corporations, travel agencies and other online travel businesses, and is dedicated to its customers' net success. e-Travel serves customers in over 90 countries, including corporations such as Airbus, Daimler Chrysler, Gateway Inc, Ingersoll-Rand company, Oracle and Philip Morris, as well as travel suppliers such as Air France, Iberia and Qantas, and online agencies such as Opodo. It is a significant provider of information technology and an enabler of eCommerce for the travel industry globally. Amadeus offers airlines the ability to use the system not just for distribution but also for making bookings at airport ticket offices (ATOs) and city ticket offices (CTOs). Amadeus is developing new and sophisticated tools that go beyond its traditional role as application service provider of sales and reservations systems to embrace the outsourcing of airlines' other strategic systems, most especially in the areas of inventory and departure control. Over 100 airline customers use the system, with more than 80 206 Amadeus terminals installed. It also provides the powerful booking engine behind the web pages for over 2100 travel agencies, 173 corporate sites, 18 hotel sites and 128 websites serving 39 airlines. Additionally, it provides similar eCommerce solutions for partners including Terra Lycos (Spain, Portugal and Latin America). Amadeus's corporate travel management solutions allow business travellers to book arrangements from their desktop.

More information about Amadeus is available at **www.amadeus.com**

Questions

- What is the influence of the Internet on Global Distribution Systems?

- Several authors have argued that GDSs will disappear as a result of the Internet. Discuss this, giving arguments for and against this possibility.

- How can GDSs compete against cooperative airline web pages, such as Opodo and Orbitz, and what are the strategic implications for GDSs?

7.3 Airline types and ICT utilization

There are several different kinds of airlines, which can be characterized mainly by type, ownership and routes. Different types of airlines use ICTs differently and have a different emphasis on their on-line presence, although most of them take advantage of the basic ICT modules.

- *Scheduled carriers*, such as Air France and United Airlines, offer a full service to their clientèle through regional, national, international and intercontinental services. They are often **flag carriers**, belonging to their national government and are mainly used by business travellers. **Scheduled** airlines were the first to invest heavily in ICTs and were instrumental in developing CRSs and GDSs. They primarily targeted business travellers purchasing their tickets through travel agencies, hence developing a sales network and facilitating on-line ticketing was critical for them. Increasingly their on-line provision aims to attract customers and bookings directly to reduce travel agencies' dependency and commission costs. Airlines such as Air France and British Airways develop interfaces with consumers through the Internet, but also support a wide range of alternative distribution channels.

- *No-frills or low-cost carriers*, such as easyJet, Ryanair and South West Airlines, provide a fairly limited service on-board and passengers have to purchase any in-flight catering. They offer lower prices and more flexible ticket regulations. No-frills airlines normally fly national and short-haul international routes, with a high percentage of both leisure and business travellers. No-frills airlines emerged in the 1990s primarily for low-budget, independent, leisure travellers. Therefore, being able to communicate with their clientèle directly, reducing commission fees and enabling consumers to purchase their products there and then were critical for their business models. At the end of 2001, more than 90 per cent of easyJet's seats were booked on-line on the Internet.

- *Charter airlines*, such as Britannia Airways, provide a major service to holiday makers and leisure travellers in Europe. Owned by tour operators, they offer a full service to package holiday makers by flying short-haul international routes, mainly within Europe. **Charter** airlines, in contrast, are less pressurized to sell directly to consumers as most of their inventory is sold as part of a package through tour operators or through charter flight consolidators (such as **www.avro.com**). Therefore, they are not connected to GDSs and they only offer value-added services on the Internet, such as selecting seats or pre-booking meals (see, for example, **www.britanniaairways.com**).

7.4 Strategic and tactical roles of ICTs for airlines

As with all other businesses and as discussed in previous chapters, airlines use ICTs for a wide range of business functions as well as for tactical and strategic management. Airlines depend on ICTs for their strategic and operational management. From a strategic point of view, airlines use technology to manage their business model as well as to undertake revenue analysis and forecasting, to perform yield management, to monitor competition, to maintain historical data, to predict demand, to design desirable products and to decide the routes they fly. ICTs are critical for monitoring and forecasting the performance of SBUs and deciding which markets airlines should penetrate and how. Route planning, frequency of service and strategic partners are functions supported by ICTs. Similarly strategic pricing and **yield management** are also supported by running complex algorithms on computers in order to establish optimum performance and profitability levels. Branding and communication of principles are also critical for airlines at a strategic level, as managing communications with all stakeholders including investors, press, employees and customers is of paramount importance. ICTs are also a prerequisite for developing partnerships and alliances with other airlines as well as for monitoring competitors.

On the operational side, ICTs are critical for managing the inventory of carriers by assisting their reservations management and ticketing. Increasingly eTicketing instigates paperless transactions, while offering significant savings. Tactical pricing, yield management and special offers and promotions are all facilitated by constantly assessing demand and supply and by taking both proactive and reactive measures. There are several operational management requirements, including check-in procedures, allocation of seats, the generating of a number of reports and orders, such as flight paths, weather forecasts, load and balance calculations, manifests for airports, in-flight catering orders and crew rotas. ICTs also facilitate eProcurement and management of suppliers and partners on a regular basis for maximum efficiency. In addition, as airlines have bases and distributors globally and particularly at destinations they serve, they need efficient coordination and communications with stations, branches, distributors and customers globally. Interaction with travel agencies and other distributors can determine levels of sales whilst efficient invoicing and revenue collection are critical for both cash flow and profitability. Finally, airlines have been investing in customer relationship management programmes in order to manage their loyalty clubs. ICTs are particularly significant for a number of functions, as illustrated in Figure 7.1.

The critical role of ICTs in airlines is demonstrated by their investment volume. In the IT trends survey, O'Toole (2001) shows that the average planned ICT expenditure for 2001 was 2.8 per cent of the airlines' revenues. Figure 7.2 reveals that 24 per cent of the respondents had planned to spend more than 4 per cent of their revenue on ICT investments. This critical role is also evident by the fact that 29 per cent of the carriers surveyed have started pilot studies using wireless and mobile technologies, while 60 per cent of airlines now have ICTs represented at board level.

7.4.1 Internal systems and intranets

Airlines use a wide range of internal systems and intranets to coordinate their activities. A number of information management and decision support systems support their core business processes and operational management. Airlines aim to maximize their profitability by optimizing their total yield. This is based on appropriate scheduling, managing of crew and aiming for peak operational efficiency. The process is facilitated by a number of integrated systems that operate

Figure 7.1 eAirlines' ICT functions

Strategic functions
■ Strategic business unit management ■ Route planning and market assessment ■ Monitoring of competitors ■ Strategic pricing and yield management ■ Branding and communication of principles ■ Partnerships and alliances ■ Capacity and aircraft decisions
Tactical planning and development and running the business
■ Networking and schedule development ■ Scheduling, operational management and control ■ Critical incident management and corrective mechanisms ■ Crew management and control ■ Maintenance management and control ■ Cargo management, reservations and revenue support ■ Baggage handling and monitoring ■ Procurement of materials and equipment ■ Coordination of stations and hubs ■ Weather, fuel and rota reports and manifests ■ Inventory management and distribution of tickets ■ Check-in, gate management and reporting to authorities ■ Management of in-flight catering ■ Airport passenger handling and baggage management ■ Pricing, ticketing, revenue and yield management ■ Coordinating with partners and alliance members
Interface with consumers, partners agencies, other distributors and ticketing
■ Management of inventory and bookings through GDSs and the Internet ■ Reservations management, ticketing and electronic ticketing ■ Operational management, check-in procedures and allocation of seats ■ Tactical pricing, yield management and special offers and promotions ■ eProcurement and management of suppliers and partners ■ Communications and transactions with stations, branches distributors and customers globally ■ Invoicing and revenue collection ■ Customer profiling, customer service and communication with consumers ■ Managing loyalty clubs and customer relationships management
Generic management
■ Employee productivity and crew management (rota, training etc.) ■ Relationships with partners and alliance integration ■ Business management and reporting ■ Safety and security procedures

in parallel to facilitate and coordinate a number of critical airline functions. These are on top of generic business functions, such as accounting, financial management, human resources etc.

Planning and operations departments use integrated *flight schedule management systems* to support airlines to plan their schedules. Planning processes need

Figure 7.2 Planned ICT investment as percentage of airlines' revenue in 2001

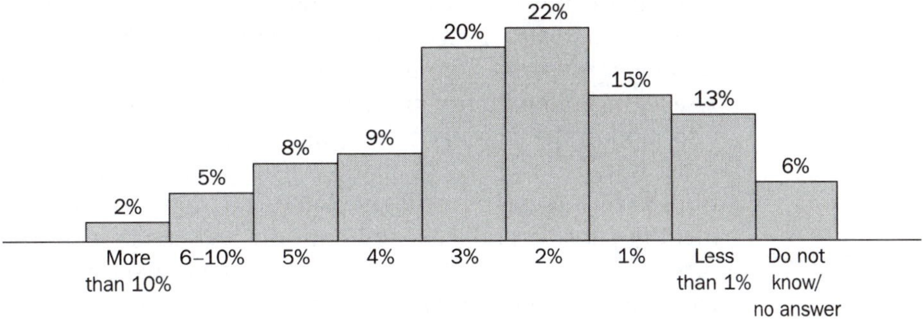

Source: O'Toole (2001)

to optimize network performance by taking into consideration the technical and operational characteristics of equipment, human resources availability and regulations, demand for traffic, as well as government regulations and operational constraints such as air traffic control rules. Planning ranges from long-term strategic issues, such as which routes to maintain and the level of competition required for particular regions, to day-to-day operational schedules for equipment, staff and market segments. These systems examine historic traffic data and previous load factors as well as forecasted demand figures. Scheduling implies deciding the number of connections between airports as well as their timing and choice of aircraft equipment. As hub and spoke systems become more important in air transportation, scheduling departure waves and coordinating flights between regions in order to increase the load factors of long-haul flights is of critical importance (Hanlon, 1999). As any single schedule can have radical implications for the entire network, flight schedule management systems allow airlines to test numerous scenarios and what-if situations. This also includes unplanned situations such as delays, weather conditions and other unpredictable circumstances that can disrupt airline schedules. Scheduling systems need to provide seamless integration with all other systems available, including operations control, reservations and revenue management, maintenance control, and crew management.

Crew management systems assist in the creation and maintenance of duty rosters by ensuring that they are efficient, complete, legal, economic and fair. They handle the process from crew planning to crew control. Crew management needs to be coordinated with all associated activities such as flight scheduling, operations control, crew contact, flight briefing etc. These systems can also undertake a number of routine tasks, such as checking legalities, publishing rosters and notifications, and administrating hotel accommodation, dead-heads and pick-up services. Crew management systems use comprehensive crew databases to undertake pairing construction, roster generation and crew control in order to optimize the human resources performance. Communicating scheduling information with crews is also critical and a number of intranet solutions facilitate this process. To enable crew control to monitor the completeness of crews, each crew member must register with the controllers when starting and finishing duties. In addition, crew members can print out their duty plan, as well as information about changes to their work schedule (notifications) or about the next duty period (briefings). This information may cover, for example, flight load or crew composition, as well as aircraft and airport details (Konig and Strauss, 2000).

Operations control systems enable airlines to plan their operations and to analyse all incoming information. The functionality and processes of these systems also support the automatic calculation and distribution of flight plans as well as other features, such as automatic consideration of all valid aeronautical restrictions in the process of the flight plan calculation. Operation control systems also identify possible problems and critical situations by performing a flight watch procedure, collecting and displaying vital information such as booking figures, passenger transfer information, critical weather conditions, crew rotations, airport limitations etc. These systems often generate alert messages and update all other operational systems, such as flight scheduling, reservation, maintenance and crew control systems, in order to take reactive action and rectify problems. For example, a delayed transfer passenger can be booked on an alternative onward flight or a new aircraft and crew may replace one that arrives late for its next flight. Automatic communications with air traffic control, with stations, using standard IATA protocols, and with reservations and revenue management ensure that all information is constantly updated and all members of the value chain are informed about the dynamic developments.

Aircraft maintenance commercial and operational requirements need to be coordinated through maintenance control systems. As equipment requires regular technical support as well as scheduled and unscheduled service, monitoring the time of service and ensuring that aircraft remain out of service for as little time as possible are critical for airline profitability. Hence, airlines aim to maximize fleet utilization by improving maintenance, repair and overhaul performance, and by optimising the supply chain network, aircraft downtime and materials management. These systems therefore perform maintenance check planning and control due dates or flight hours. They also manage ad hoc maintenance requirements and associate all this information with flight schedule and operation control systems, trying to schedule maintenance work during low-demand periods. Often these systems are integrated with eProcurement systems, to allow airlines to order parts and consumables on-line, while engineering systems may be integrated for providing on-line manuals and technical support. Technical documentation management systems often create, distribute and manage complex technical data and documents.

Station control systems monitor all kinds of connections on a hub in an airline's network. These include aircraft turns, crew connections, passenger connections and cargo connections. Station personnel can retrieve detailed information about each connection, such as transfer passenger names and baggage. Critical connections are identified and all related systems are updated. In addition, these systems combine the planned and actual movements and calculate the amount of resources needed for check-in and handling. This assists the station to open adequate check-in desks or to ensure that enough baggage handlers or cleaners are in place to service the flight, supporting gate and resource management.

Airline *Computer Reservation Systems* offer an integrated solution for managing reservations, sales, ticketing and accounting. These systems support administration, accounting and passenger handling by coordinating inventory management, marketing and sales, yield and revenue management, ticketing and departure control. They are often interfaced with GDSs and with the Internet in order to distribute their inventory globally. Electronic ticketing issues electronic tickets, links with the GDSs, and exchanges e-tickets with multiple carriers worldwide, promoting increased revenue and superior customer service. Many airlines use *cargo reservation and revenue support systems*. These systems link all partners in the handling process, automate procedures and support a smooth communication flow. Integrating new technologies such as electronic scales, stacker systems, handheld terminals and bar coding reduces time and effort and thus cuts costs significantly. The simplification of the handling process eliminates redundant work, and supports precise tracking and tracing and automatic generation of documents.

Airports and airlines work together to reduce aircraft turnaround times and shorten passenger connection times. *Baggage handling and monitoring systems* allow airlines to increase their efficiency and to track every bag as it moves through the system. This also ensures that no baggage is transported without its owner, as per the International Civil Aviation Organization (ICAO) regulations. The systems support reconciliation procedures of checked passenger baggage and enable airlines to ensure security, reduce operating costs and improve passenger satisfaction without compromising punctuality.

Finally, *decision support systems* allow airlines to monitor traffic and bookings on computer reservation systems in order to identify customer behaviour, traffic flows or trends, as well as the performance of partners and sales agencies. These systems also enable airlines to measure themselves against the performance of their competitors and to adopt proactive and reactive decision making. A broad information base leads to more suitable decisions for core airline strategy and operational activities, such as marketing and sales, schedule planning, yield management or pricing. It is the coordination of all these systems that ensures that airlines enjoy operational efficiency and at the same time allows them to design and implement their long-term strategy.

7.4.2 Interconnecting partner systems and extranets

There are few other organizations in tourism that rely as heavily on external partners for their operations as airlines. All airlines need *airport infrastructure* for their operations. Hence, they need to develop suitable systems to interact with airport and air traffic control systems for requesting landing slots and docking gates, informing about arrivals and departures, altering slots should there be delays, declaring flight paths, and coordinating their operations. As mentioned already, a number of airline operational systems flag out this information and relay it to responsible personnel. In most cases this information is transmitted manually between carriers and airport authorities. Printed manifests and passenger lists are often submitted to airport authorities. As is the case with other players, airlines are reluctant to invest in IP extranet systems and they rely heavily on legacy systems for their operations. However, a number of airlines are gradually developing or adopting electronic environments for data exchange with the customs and airport authorities in their main stations. These extranets assist them to develop reliable and direct connections to customer and airport systems and help them to maximize their efficiency.

Airlines also interact with a number of organizations that provide *handling services* for aircraft and airlines at airports. These services include maintenance, refuelling, security, baggage handling, load and dispatch, lounge provision, catering and cleaner services. In most cases these services are provided by a number of companies at each location. Developing B2B applications and interconnecting extranet systems will help both airlines and their partners to streamline these processes and improve their turnaround time at the airport and to minimize administrative costs, supporting efficiency. Case Study 7.2 demonstrates the in-flight catering system extranet and shows how significant the improvements in efficiency are. In addition, handling a large amount of baggage on a daily basis between a number of airlines and airports is very complex and is facilitated by extranets such as the WorldTracer, demonstrated in Case Study 7.3.

Procurement marketplaces have become highly significant, economically. Besides their cost-saving potential in the purchase of supplies, they are backed by intelligent logistics concepts allowing companies to downsize their inventories. This is because eProcurement makes markets more transparent, allowing companies to bundle their procurement volumes and, most importantly, to realign customer–supplier relations through their supply chains.

Within this context eProcurement is also a major force for extranets in the airline business. As airlines regularly purchase products and services from partners, such as fuel, aircraft parts and catering, B2B applications allow them to benefit from great cost savings. Lufthansa, for example, has three types of procurement tools in operation or in planning:

- an on-line catalogue system for ordering general supplies like computer hardware, forms and office furniture. This is the AirPlus 'ProNet' product, which is already up and running;
- an Internet marketplace, which puts all types of orders out to tender. This self-developed tool (**www.fairpartners.com**) has been used by Lufthansa and other German companies since mid-2000;
- an airline industry on-line trading exchange, which offers industry-specific goods and services, ranging from special screws to aero-engines. The 'AeroXchange' marketplace is being set up by Lufthansa in cooperation with most of the Star Alliance partners as well as Northwest, Japan Airlines, KLM, Cathay Pacific and FedEx.

Similarly, airlines often appoint *General Sales Agencies (GSAs)* in all regions that do not operate a branch to handle their reservations and distribution locally. General sales agents were appointed by international airlines to secure business from IATA and non-IATA agents in markets where agency networks were yet to get fully automated and airlines needed financial security to cover business risks. In addition, consolidators pre-purchase seats in bulk and then distribute them to their local markets at discounted rates. Developing extranets with these players and ensuring that they support their onward distribution chain, providing adequate tools to interact with all departments of the airline and managing their revenue collection on time are also critical for airlines' profitability.

Case Study 7.2

The British Airways in-flight catering system extranet

In-flight catering is increasingly becoming a complex and mission-critical process. Across the industry, an estimated US$250 million is wasted each year on redundant stock, representing up to 8 per cent of all stock holdings. With a fleet of 300 aircraft, BA's inventory control system has to ensure the availability of 10 million stock items daily, from 160 different catering stations around the world. Considering this level of activity, it is imperative for BA to match worldwide inventory levels against passenger bookings when planning the production of 70 million meals a year. The Heathrow-based headquarters of British Airways' catering division is responsible for supplying the company's catering stations around the world. All branded catering equipment used on BA's planes, including trays, trolleys, crockery, napkins, soap and tissue paper, is supplied to the catering stations that service BA's 700 daily flights, so it is essential to ensure that its caterers never run out of these items. Traditionally, BA's caterers held excess stock to ensure that they always had sufficient available. Catering stations manually faxed inventory forms to BA's head office, or relied upon internal mail carried on flights. Once these arrived at Heathrow, the catering division staff keyed the handwritten information into their stock control system, which was a time-consuming process.

BA spends up to $600 million per annum on its catering operation. Unused catering supplies therefore need to be kept at a minimum. BA introduced a leading-edge forecasting and planning system to reduce the levels of stockholdings worldwide and to improve its supply chain systems. This necessitated the replacement of paper-based administrative processes with a global means of electronic data capture to provide accurate stock information on a daily basis. This led to the development of the CONEX (Catering Online Extranet) project, which extended BA's supply-chain applications over an extranet.

CONEX provides BA with low-cost access to its supply chain applications using PC-based software located at each caterer's site, with a dial-up connection to a local node on a SITA global extranet. IMI's System ESS – the BA logistics application responsible for operations planning – is connected to the CONEX Extranet via a SITA data clearing-house facility. This minimizes any changes to BA's systems, and insulates BA from any change control issues that may arise from its caterers' systems. When BA needs up-to-date stock level information, or wants to notify caterers of impending deliveries, ESS sends a structured message, which passes through CONEX and is downloaded to the caterer's PC. The CONEX software, developed by Equant, processes these messages and presents the information as a form via a standard browser. The user completes the form, and the CONEX software converts the information into a structured message and transmits it back to BA's central system. The entire process is completed in a few minutes – a sharp contrast to the hours, or even days, taken previously. The new process is also more accurate: as the information is entered just once, at source, there are no re-keying errors.

For more information, see **www.sita.net** and **www.ifcanet.com**

Questions

- Using the value chain framework, explain how airlines can integrate their functions and processes through ICTs.
- How can airlines use ICTs to provide value-added services?
- Discuss and demonstrate how airlines can gain competitive advantage through the use of ICTs.

Case Study 7.3

WorldTracer – the mishandled baggage system

Every day, thousands of baggage pieces go missing within the airline and airport systems. WorldTracer is a comprehensive airline information management system for mishandled property that enables airlines and airports to trace missing baggage. Co-sponsored by SITA and IATA, WorldTracer was introduced to assist in the rapid recovery of misrouted passenger baggage, allowing information exchange within a given airline as well as between airlines worldwide. The system is used by 300 airlines at over 2200 airport locations. The system maintains a large worldwide database of on-hand and forwarded baggage information and has a sophisticated matching mechanism based on external and internal baggage characteristics. The Management module also offers a subscriber the ability to maintain a log and find unchecked articles left in an airline's facility, such as a book left in an airplane seatback pocket or an umbrella left in the gate area. The system also offers a Claims Investigation module that acts as a data repository of baggage claims that are pending, settled or closed as a result of a passenger's bag being lost, damaged or having had contents stolen. This module gives members the ability to monitor files and match with other files from their airline or other member airlines where a claim payment has been made. SITA recently developed an Internet interface to enable airline passengers to obtain the most current information regarding their mishandled baggage without having to contact the airline directly.

For more information, see **www.sita.net** and **www.worldtracer.com**

Questions

- What are the critical information flows for airlines, and who are the main recipients of information? Elaborate on how ICTs can assist the formulation of partnerships between airlines and other organizations.
- How can airlines use ICTs to reduce theft and compensation demands?
- What are the key technologies that airlines can share for enhancing their collective performance?

In addition, *cooperation between two or more airlines* is increasingly common. This may include code-sharing agreements, alliances and other business arrangements. Being able to communicate records electronically between different airlines through extranets is critical for their ability to collaborate efficiently. Extranets can allow the on-line exchange of schedule information and consolidation, while they can help them to settle accounts on-line. In addition, they can credit each other's loyalty schemes and allow passengers to change their seating or meal requirements on-line by accessing each other's systems.

7.4.3 Connecting with all stakeholders through the Internet

The development of the World Wide Web (WWW) in the mid-1990s has been one of the most challenging opportunities for airlines. By 1998 most airlines already offered websites, which not only informed consumers but also supported itinerary building, fare construction and reservations. This enabled the interactivity with consumers and to build up relationship-marketing strategies. It also helped airlines launch another communication and purchasing channel in order to reduce the power and costs of conventional intermediaries. Hitherto, it is reported that there are still far more 'lookers' than 'bookers' on the Internet. It is estimated that on-line bookings contribute less than 5 per cent of the total bookings globally. However, innovative carriers take advantage and sell a great percentage of their seats on-line. British Airways' Internet site (www.britishairways.com) currently achieves 1.5 million visits per month, whilst the average growth of on-line bookings has been 11 per cent per month. The figures often quoted for American carriers are significantly greater, as a result of the penetration of the Internet. Airlines' Internet sites attract consumers directly and assist the bypassing of travel agencies and their commissions. easyJet was advertised as the web's favourite airline and currently achieves more than 90 per cent of its bookings on-line, as demonstrated in Case Study 7.4.

Case Study 7.4

easyJet on-line

easyJet (www.easyjet.com) in the UK is one of the pioneers of the Internet and has capitalized fully on its potential. Stelios Haji-Ioannou was persuaded to invest an initial £15 000 on the Internet and monitored the growth of the bookings to the dedicated telephone number. Having seen the increasing number of bookings taken on that particular number the airline was persuaded to invest in eCommerce and to develop the transaction side of the site. The airline sold its first seat through the Internet in April 1998. In 1998, easyJet sold 13 000 seats via the Internet in 24 hours following a campaign with *The Times* newspaper and for most of the year it achieved 10 per cent of its bookings electronically. In just three and a half years it reached 12 million seats sold, selling almost 90 per cent of all its inventory through its website by September 2001. The airline uses the phrase 'the web's favourite airline' to promote its own on-line offering. Booking on-line is quick, easy and secure and the airline offers a £5 discount for passengers booking on-line.

easyJet passenger and Internet statistics

	September 2001	September 2000	Year
Passengers	680 383	534 913	7 115 147
Load factor	83.16%	83.03%	83.03%
Internet sales	91.0%	77.8%	86.5%

Source: Based on **www.easyjet.com**

Questions

- What are the key ICT success factors for no-frills airlines?
- What added-value services are offered on-line by no-frills airlines, and what are the implications for the tourism industry?

As a result of the Internet representation of airlines and their ability to communicate directly with consumers, several structural changes came about in the industry. Initially in the USA, and increasingly globally, airlines reduced their commission rates significantly (from 10–12 per cent to 7–10 per cent), while also introducing 'commission capping' (e.g. $50 per ticket). Major airlines quote savings of several million dollars. In addition, electronic ticketing and ticket-less travel gradually reduce both distribution and labour costs, while increasing the efficiency of airlines. Continental Airlines is often quoted as an example of an airline that reduced its costs by $20 million simply by reducing commissions to travel agencies and by introducing electronic ticketing. Perhaps the most useful feature introduced through the Internet is the ability to promote distressed capacity at discounted rates at the last minute. Most American airlines have been promoting heavily discounted fares via electronic mail and auctions, as illustrated by Southwest Airlines in Case Study 7.5. As a result, they manage to sell a significant proportion of their perishable seats contributing directly to the bottom line. Industry experts explain that this should be regarded as direct profit, as unless sold at the last minute airlines would have lost this revenue.

Airline tickets accounted for 90 per cent of all on-line travel sales in 1996, generating $243 million in revenue. The Travel Industry Association of America predicts that by the year 2002 airline tickets purchased on-line will account for $6.5 billion. Although in 1996 less than 1 per cent of all airline ticket revenue came from on-line sources, it is anticipated that by 2002 it will have increased to 8.2 per cent and will be the leading travel purchase on the Internet (TIA, 1997).

Case Study 7.5

Southwest Airlines on the Internet

Southwest was the first airline to establish a home page on the Internet and recently reported that approximately 30 per cent, or $1.7 billion, of its passenger revenue for 2000 was generated by on-line bookings via southwest.com. Southwest's cost per booking via the Internet is about $1, while the cost per booking via a travel agent is between $6 and $8. The cost per booking to Southwest via the airline's reservations agents lies somewhere in between. Initially, five employees comprised Southwest's website development team, and the site took about nine months to create. Now there are more than 60 full-time employees on the airline's marketing automation team, with about half of them working on the software development team. More than 3.3 million people subscribe to Southwest's weekly Click 'N Save e-mails. Southwest Airlines' website has been named the top-ranking website for customer satisfaction among major travel sites according to research conducted by Nielsen/NetRatings and Harris Interactive. Southwest Airlines scored a rating of 8.62 out of 10, with its website attracting 4 million unique visitors during March 2001.

For more information, see **www.southwest.com**

Questions

- Compare and contrast the pricing between no-frills airlines and national carriers, and demonstrate which type of airline offers better value for money. Explain how ICTs are influencing pricing.
- Discuss the cost and benefit implications of the no-frills airlines' on-line strategy.
- Explain how the no-frills airlines have revolutionized the airline industry and the role ICTs play in this process.

7.5 ICT-empowered strategic alliances for airlines

Distribution is well recognized as one of the most important elements of airline marketing strategy and competitiveness for the future. Not only does it influence airline costs, but it also determines the ability of airlines to access consumers directly. Increasingly distribution determines: air fares (*price*), as commission costs and reservation fees dictate a significant part of operational costs; the *product* itself, since CRSs facilitate the development of hub and spoke systems as well as code-share agreements; and finally the *promotional* campaigns undertaken by airlines. One-to-one and relationship marketing are widely used by airlines establishing new methods of communication with consumers and partners.

ICTs are also instrumental in the current globalization of the airline industry. The global alliances such as OneWorld, Qualiflyer, Star Alliance and others are only possible because of the coordination that can be achieved through harmonized ICT systems or through effective interfaces. In effect consumers receive a seamless service, collect frequent-flyer miles and enjoy privileges from different carriers in all continents simply because ICTs provide the info-structure for close collaboration. Hence, ICTs will not only formulate all elements of the marketing mix of airlines in the future, but they will also determine their strategic directions, partnerships and ownership.

Almost half of the airlines within alliances are already sharing some systems with their partners and another 20 per cent planned to do so by year-end 2001 to help offer customer seamless services. Outsourcing increases across all airlines to cover more and more IT services and 85 per cent of carriers have already outsourced all or parts of their IT functions (O'Toole, 2001).

The launch of Internet portals such as Orbitz and Opodo (see Case Study 7.6) by competing airlines demonstrates clearly that airlines appreciate the need to cooperate with competitors (co-opete). They develop links through alliances and industry bodies such as IATA and SITA to develop common platforms for eCommerce, eProcurement and facilitating all their business and operational functions. There are two major challenges in this process, namely technological and business considerations. Technological issues need to be resolved before airlines can expand their interoperability further. They have been prevented from doing so by the dominance of legacy systems, which operate on proprietary protocols and platforms. This prevents airlines from communicating with each other and also makes it difficult to develop extranet applications and protocols for electronic exchanges with trusted partners such as airports, distributors, catering and handling companies. A certain degree of technological standardization will therefore be required in order to support airlines in expanding their electronic exchanges and achieving maximum operational efficiency of the entire system.

In addition, business issues related to partnership need to be resolved. Currently airlines compete and collaborate with all other airlines simultaneously. In reality, the existing strategic alliances, such as OneWorld and the Star Alliance, have failed to develop services and collaboration beyond code-sharing and a degree of loyalty club collaboration. However, airlines need to develop stronger

Case Study 7.6

The Opodo travel portal

Following the introduction of Orbitz in the USA, nine of Europe's leading airlines (Aer Lingus, Air France, Alitalia, Austrian Airlines, British Airways, Finnair, Iberia, KLM and Lufthansa) created the Online Travel Portal Limited as a new on-line travel portal. Later they changed its name to Opodo, which stands for 'Opportunity to do' and reflects the personal on-line service that will open the doors to a world of new and inspiring travel experiences. The creation of Opodo was a reaction of airlines to the consumer requirements for more transparency between travel information as well as complete reservation functionality for more than one airline. The system also reflected the fear of airlines that a few electronic travel agencies, such as Expedia and Travelocity, will dominate the electronic distribution and airlines will be forced to accept their terms.

Opodo offers an unbiased and competitively priced on-line travel service for world travel, with access to flights from over 480 airlines, 54 500 hotel properties and car rental from over 23 500 locations worldwide, as well as travel insurance and a number of value-added services. Opodo aims to offer a more comprehensive travel service tailored for the European consumer. This will include abundant travel information including destination guides and interactive maps, and a large range of recognized travel brands tailored for each country market. Opodo will have local independent sites serving each European market.

It is supported by a number of established suppliers, including Amadeus, Galileo, TRX Inc., Energis and Sapient. Amadeus will provide the country-specific booking system for Opodo customers. Galileo has offered Opodo two of its leading Applications Programming Interface (API) solutions, EDIFACT Select and XML Select. With XML Select, Galileo customers can build an on-line presence and seamlessly integrate bookable travel content into a new or existing website. Based on XML (extensible mark-up language), XML Select helps to reduce costs and contributes to a flexible distribution strategy. The effort and specialized knowledge required for development is minimal, and at the same time access to a range of new distribution channels, including digital TV and wireless applications, is possible. EDIFACT Select provides access to Galileo's CRS from any popular business platform (UNIX, IBM, DEC, Data General etc.). It also provides multi-session capability and is platform-independent. As with all of Galileo's 'Select' products, both XML Select and EDIFACT Select uses structured data. The systems will be launched initially in Germany, the UK and France and later across Europe during 2002 and 2003. Customer service and fulfilment centres, in several countries, will be staffed by travel experts with 24/7 website support and booking facilities.

For further information, see **www.opodo.com**

Questions

- What are the structural impacts that airline cooperative sites (such as Opodo and Orbitz.com) have on the tourism industry?
- Is Opodo competing with the direct distribution channels of its individual member airlines?

alliances and meaningful wealth-creation networks if they are to survive global competition in the future. ICTs will play a critical part in this process. To date, airlines have given confusing signals. Carriers that originally supported either Galileo or Amadeus now support Opodo, while some airlines from the Star Alliance and some from OneWorld support this venture. Unless airlines coordinate their info-structure and develop competitive on-line systems that help them improve their internal processes, as well as collaborate with partners and develop electronic windows to the world through the Internet in a consistent and coherent way, they will be unable to capitalize on the increasing potential of ICTs. Business strategies and alliances management will therefore need to refocus and include ICT solutions as part as their core competencies, their collaboration info-structure and brand drivers. Only then will alliances be able to maximize their contribution to airlines and their impact in the marketplace.

7.6 Critical issues for the future success of airlines

Technology will assist airlines to *integrate* their operations and to control and coordinate all their business and management functions. Implementing enterprise resource planning enables airlines to integrate all facets of the business and maximize internal efficiency and effectiveness. In addition, using the Internet and extranets can support productive interaction with all stakeholders. Although further ICT developments and applications will be required for most airlines to run their business successfully, at the same time it is gradually becoming evident that this technology will be managed by specialized experts. More airlines are outsourcing components of their operational systems to trusted partners and a number of specialized **Application Service Providers (ASPs)** have emerged to serve this particular market.

The eAirlines' futures will be determined by their ability to use ICT strategically for achieving their vision and mission. Although great progress has been achieved in the last few years, there are several obstacles that prevent airlines achieving their ICT strategy. These include lack of skilled ICT personnel, lack of investment, lack of ICT personnel with airline experience, resources concentrated on legacy systems, lack of board-level supervision, poor outsourcing experiences, and technology not yet ready to support the range of airline requirements. In addition, a number of business issues considered critical by airlines in association with their on-line travel sales include security, customer relationship management, lack of industry standards, revenue management and protection of the brand integrity, itinerary changes and cancellations. These challenges will be crucial for the ability of airlines to maximize the ICT potential and achieve their strategic and operational management objectives (O'Toole, 2001).

Airlines around the world face a wide range of challenges and ICTs provide several tools to help them to address these challenges. Firstly, following the 11 September events, *safety* and *security* have emerged as being the most critical challenges for airlines. Detection security systems are expected to assist airlines to prevent hazardous material being taken on board and to identify defects at an early stage. In addition, tracing material, luggage and passengers through ICT will increase efficiency and reduce theft and accidents.

Airlines also aim to improve the entire customer travelling experience. Frequent travellers demand speedier check-in processes and a higher degree of flexibility and control over their own travel arrangements. More passengers therefore prefer self-service check-in rather than queueing up in overcrowded terminals. eTicketing and paperless communications are expected to improve customer service and experience by reducing the level of bureaucracy involved in travel arrangements, by increasing flexibility and speeding up all processes. Providing self-service through kiosks and wireless technologies can mean operational and productivity gains, improved customer satisfaction and reduced costs. Self-service *kiosk* applications support travellers to make travel reservations, check-in, receive boarding passes, select seats, check frequent-flyer miles, request upgrades, purchase a ticket, print eTicket receipts or check bags – all without waiting in line for a check-in agent. This helps airlines to reduce check-in times and to minimize check-in unit costs. It also enables flights to depart and arrive on time, increasing customer satisfaction. Several airlines, including Alitalia, Air Canada, Ansett Australia, British Airways and US Airways, use self-service kiosks to serve their customers.

With wireless solutions, airlines can offer their passengers the ability to purchase through a handheld device virtually anywhere, at any time. Travellers being able to adapt their itinerary on the go is expected to be one of the most widely used services for mobile devices; 29 per cent of carriers have already started pilot studies using wireless and mobile technologies, while another 16 per cent will be able to do that by the end of 2002 (O'Toole, 2001). Increasingly consumers require instant access to their travel itineraries, regardless of their location. This is particularly important for frequent business travellers.

Mobile phones, **Personal Digital Assistants (PDA)** *and other wireless devices* are already used for searching and booking flights, altering flight arrangements, retrieving updated arrival and departure information, and checking in quickly and selecting seats directly. Flight alerts through SMS (short message service), message pagers or eMail as well as notification from either the airline or travel agency can be sent when changes occur mid-travel and new reservations must be made. In addition, vouchers in the form of bar-code SMS can be sent for meals or accommodation when flights are delayed. Wireless technologies will also be used for communications between airline partners, and wireless networks are currently being implemented in several airports. An integration between wireless LAN solutions that will allow connections with the wired LANs will support airlines, airports and consumer applications (SITA, 2001). In-flight entertainment, communications and constant interaction and customer service will also be critical in the future. ICTs will therefore be used dynamically before, during and after the travel experience to serve passengers and to reinforce the airline brand.

Developing successful extranets will also mean airlines can develop effective collaboration channels with all their partners. Managing the entire supply chain electronically enables all partners to benefit by allowing them to reduce costs, increase their transaction accuracy and optimize their efficiency. There is evidence therefore that eProcurement is developing rapidly and it seems that other extranet applications will soon emerge to facilitate communications and interaction with customs, immigration, airports, air traffic control and civil aviation authorities around their stations.

Further integration and *consolidation of the airline business* seems inevitable. This process enables airlines to establish global networks serving multiple airports and countries worldwide. They also support the integration of their frequent flyer programmes and benefits, provide access to business lounges and allow endorsement waivers to switch between airlines, should a passenger need to be transferred to a more convenient flight. From the business point of view, consolidation supports code sharing, optimization of capacity and yield as well as a certain level of collaboration between competitors (**co-opetition**).

7.7 Conclusions

Just as ICTs will become more critical to their operations and strategy, it can be predicted that technology will also facilitate and support the successful airlines of the future. It is also likely that technology may provide a major motivation for merger and collaborations. ICTs are instrumental in rearranging airline alliances and concentrations. Code sharing and ranking in GDSs was one of the prime factors that initiated alliances; then, the development of GDSs in several continents brought airlines close together and forced them to collaborate. The launch of the Orbitz and Opodo portals, incorporating several airlines that also belong to different alliance groups (e.g. Star Alliance and OneWorld) or that support different GDSs (e.g. Amadeus and Galileo), shows that carriers are prepared to constantly re-group themselves around business opportunities.

Chapter questions

1 What are the main purposes of airline CRSs?

2 What is the difference between airline CRSs and GDSs?

3 Will GDSs be disintermediated in the future?

4 Explain the main functions of GDSs.

5 Why have GDSs not moved to IP protocols?

6 Explore the different kinds of airlines, their distribution networks and their ICT utilization.

7 What are the key strategic ICT functions for airlines?

8 Explain why ICTs are critical for the operational management of airlines.

9 Why is integration of airlines' internal systems significant for their business management?

10 What ICT requirements and challenges emerge as a result of alliances and partnerships?

11 How can airlines increase their direct bookings from consumers?

12 What new initiatives are taken to manage distribution better in airlines?

13 Discuss wireless applications for the airline of the future.

14 What information do airlines need to communicate with ground stations and airports, and how can this be facilitated?

15 How can airlines use ASPs in the future, and what are their main advantages and disadvantages?

Further reading

Collier, D. (1989) Expansion and development of CRS, *Tourism Management*, **10**(2), 86–88.

Copeland, D. (1991) So you want to build the next SABRE System, *Business Quarterly*, **55**(33), 56–60.

Copeland, D. and McKenney, J. (1988) Airline reservation systems: lessons from history, *MIS Quarterly*, **12**, 535–570.

French, T. (1998) The future of global distribution systems, *Travel and Tourism Analyst*, no. 3, 1–17.

Hopper, L. (1990) Rating SABRE – new ways to compete on information, *Harvard Business Review*, **68**(3), May–June, 118–125.

Kärcher, K. (1996) The four global distribution systems in the travel and tourism industry, *Electronic Markets*, **6**(2), 20–24.

Knowles, T. and Garland, M. (1994) The strategic importance of CRSs in the airline industry, *Travel and Tourism Analyst*, no. 4, 4–16.

Konig, J. and Strauss, C. (2000) Rostering integrated services and crew efficiency, *Information Technology and Tourism*, **3**(1), 27–39.

Marcussen, C. (1999) The effects of Internet distribution of travel and tourism services on the marketing mix: no-frills, fair fares and fare wars in the air, *Information Technology and Tourism*, **2**(3/4), 197–212.

O'Toole, K. (2002) Airline IT Trends Survey 2002, *Airline Business*, August. http://www.sita.net/index.asp?activeDir=Home/News Centre/Airline IT Trends 2002/&activeFile=Foreward.html/

SITA (2001) Wireless applications for airports. http://www.sita.net/Home/Resources/collateral/wirelessairport.pdf?activeDir=/Home/Resources/collateral/

Truitt, L., Teye, V. and Farris, M. (1991) The role of computer reservation systems: international implications for the tourism industry, *Tourism Management*, **12**(1), 21–36.

Wardell, D. (1987a) Airline reservation systems in the USA: CRS agency dealerships and the gold handcuff, *Travel and Tourism Analyst*, no. 1, January, 45–56.

Websites

GDSs and IT providers

Sabre: **www.sabre.com**

Worldspan: **www.worldspan.com**

Amadeus: **www.amadeus.com**

Galileo: **www.galileo.com**

Airline systems

IBM: **www.ibm.com/solutions/travel**

Lufthansa: **www.lsyna.com**

LIDO: **www.lido.net**

SITA: **www.sita.net**

Jane's: **www.janes.com**

International Air Transportation Association (IATA): **www.iata.org**

Inflight Catering Association: **www.ifcanet.com**

Airport Technology: **www.airport-technology.com**

Airlines

Comprehensive list: **www.travelshop.de/english/airlines-e.html**

Aer Lingus: **www.aerlingus.ie**

Aeroflot: **www.aeroflot.org**

Air Canada: **www.aircanada.ca**

Air France: **www.airfrance.com**

American Airlines: **www.aa.com**

Austrian Airlines: **www.aua.com**

British Airways: **www.british-airways.com**

British Midland: **www.iflybritishmidland.com**

Canadian Airlines: **www.cdnair.ca**

Cathay Pacific: www.cathaypacific.com

China Airlines: www.china-airlines.com

Continental Airlines: www.continental.com

Delta Airlines: www.delta.com

easyJet: www.easyjet.com

El Al: www.elal.co.il

Emirates: www.ekgroup.com

Finnair: www.finnair.fi

Iberia Airlines: www.iberia.com

Icelandair: www.icelandair.is

Japan Airlines: www.jal.co.jp/e/index.html

KLM: www.klm.nl

KLM UK: www.klmuk.com

Lauda Air: www.laudaair.com

LOT Polish Airlines: www.lot.com

Lufthansa: www.lufthansa.com

Malaysia Airlines: www.malaysia-airlines.com

Mexicana: www.mexicana.com

Northwest Airlines: www.nwa.com

Olympic Airways: www.olympic-airways.gr

Qantas Airways: www.qantas.com.au

Ryanair: www.ryanair.com

SAS: www.scandinavian.net

Saudia Airlines: www.saudiairlines.com

Singapore Airlines: www.singaporeair.com

South African Airlines: www.saa.co.za

Southwest Airlines: www.iflyswa.com

Swissair: **www.swissair.com**

Turkish Airlines: **www.turkishairlines.com**

United Airlines: **www.united.com**

Virgin Atlantic Airways: **www.fly.virgin.com**

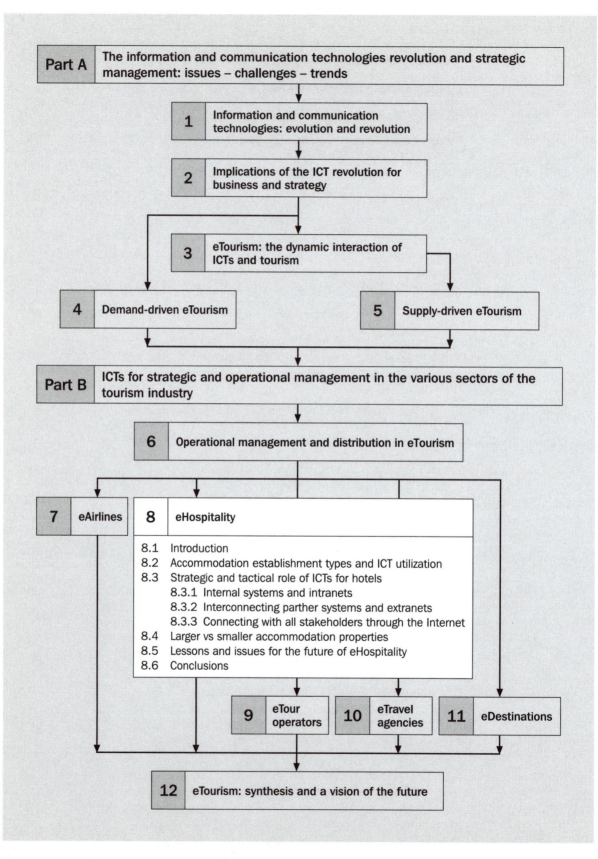

Part A The information and communication technologies revolution and strategic management: issues – challenges – trends

1 Information and communication technologies: evolution and revolution

2 Implications of the ICT revolution for business and strategy

3 eTourism: the dynamic interaction of ICTs and tourism

4 Demand-driven eTourism

5 Supply-driven eTourism

Part B ICTs for strategic and operational management in the various sectors of the tourism industry

6 Operational management and distribution in eTourism

7 eAirlines

8 eHospitality

8.1 Introduction
8.2 Accommodation establishment types and ICT utilization
8.3 Strategic and tactical role of ICTs for hotels
    8.3.1 Internal systems and intranets
    8.3.2 Interconnecting parther systems and extranets
    8.3.3 Connecting with all stakeholders through the Internet
8.4 Larger vs smaller accommodation properties
8.5 Lessons and issues for the future of eHospitality
8.6 Conclusions

9 eTour operators

10 eTravel agencies

11 eDestinations

12 eTourism: synthesis and a vision of the future

8

eHospitality

Chapter objectives

The purpose of this chapter is to explain the role of ICTs in hotels and similar accommodation establishments as well as restaurants and catering organizations. The chapter illustrates how the hospitality business uses ICTs to improve internal efficiency and to communicate with partners and customers. The chapter makes a distinction between large hotel chains and small independent hotels and demonstrates that ICTs can benefit both. Thus, the learning objectives may be defined as:

- Understand the sources of competitiveness for hospitality organizations
- Explore how technology can support hotels and restaurants to improve their efficiency and effectiveness
- Demonstrate the key technology applications as well as the main software used for their operations
- Explain the importance of integrating intranet, extranet and Internet applications
- Discuss the particular requirements of small and medium-sized enterprises
- Debate some key issues for the future of hospitality and the role of ICTs

8.1 Introduction

Accommodation establishments are beginning to employ ICTs to manage their inventory and control their assets. ICTs are penetrating at a fast pace, by integrating the hotel operation, reshaping the marketing function, improving total efficiency, providing tools for marketing research and partnership building, and enhancing customer services while providing strategic opportunities. In addition, consumers increasingly expect ICT facilities in their rooms, and thus Internet access from the television set as well as data ports have become standard for higher hotel categories. More importantly, recent evidence from the USA demonstrates that there is a dramatic shift in hotel reservations away from telephone sales through toll-free numbers towards GDSs and the Internet. Thus, hotels will be unable to perform their operations profitably without using technology extensively. ICTs are recognized as a means of achieving competitive advantage for the hospitality industry.

The Internet has improved hotel representation and reservation processes dramatically. A wide range of distribution and reservation mechanisms is offered on-line proving reliable and adequate service as well as instant confirmation to both consumers and the travel trade. Hotels are able to develop their own presence and to collaborate with distributors in order to present multimedia information on their properties, facilities and services. They can also provide on-line reservations and interaction with consumers and partners. Booking through the web is particularly convenient for customers who frequent the hotel as it provides an efficient and effective communication mechanism.

It is evident therefore that the emergent ICTs provide unprecedented opportunities for hospitality organizations, as they assist the promotion of properties to a wide range of institutional and individual buyers around the world. However, ICTs introduce a wide range of new challenges that hoteliers need to consider if they are to be successful in the future.

8.2 Accommodation establishment types and ICT utilization

As there are endless variations of hotels and accommodation establishments, their technological needs vary enormously. Understanding the variables characterizing a hotel property can therefore help us to appreciate their ICT requirements (Figure 8.1). There is a great range of hotel types and categories (Jones and Lockwood, 1989; Teare and Olsen, 1992; Jones and Pizam, 1993; Jones, 1996), resulting in a wide range of ICT applications being used.

Generally, larger, luxurious and more central properties, catering mainly for business travellers who stay for a short period of time and usually change their travel itinerary frequently, are in greater need of ICTs. Equally, hotels with many departments and outlets, such as restaurants, bars, fitness centres and entertainment facilities, as well as those that are part of a hotel chain, tend to have a higher level of ICT usage. Independent, smaller and peripherally based properties,

Figure 8.1 Variables characterizing accommodation establishments

Factors	Examples
Location	Urban/metropolitan/peripheral/seaside/alpine/rural
Size	Small/medium/large properties
Ownership and affiliation	Family-run/chains/franchising/consortia/state-owned
Price	Exclusive/expensive/affordable/inexpensive
Activities	Sports/all-inclusive/clubs/farmhouses
Services	Hotels/B&B/rooms to let/self-serviced apartments
Reasons of visiting for travellers	Leisure/business/conference/seminars/incentives
Reasons of visiting for locals (non-residential customers)	Functions/special occasions/using F&B entertainment and leisure outlets
Proximity to transportation terminals	Airport/port/railway/roadside
Primary market	Youth hostel/university and school accommodation/hospices

cater mainly for leisure travellers who stay for longer periods of time, and may require fewer technological facilities. Naturally, therefore, larger properties and hotel chains have been using technology for longer and in more processes. The majority of smaller and medium-sized properties continue to use low-level technology, relying more heavily on manual processes.

Therefore, the greater the capacity, number of departments, transactions, arrivals and departures and reservations, the greater the need for technologies to facilitate these processes. Equally, the greater the number of properties in a hotel chain/company, the more sophisticated the technology required to manage and control all remote properties.

8.3 Strategic and tactical role of ICTs for hotels

In general, the **hospitality industry** has been reluctant to use ICTs, and the great benefits the web can offer to the hospitality industry are yet to be implemented at property level. The lodging industry is the most under-automated segment of the international travel industry. Most reservations are still rooted directly to the property or through central reservation offices often by subsidized toll-free phones, while the percentage of bookings emerging from GDSs and the Internet is still fairly low. Expensive technology and large amounts of time are top of the list of challenges holding up the process. This is partly due to the difficulty the industry experiences in describing, standardizing and managing rationally the hospitality product electronically and in communicating the entire range of information required for consumers to make a transaction on-line.

The critical role of ICTs in hospitality, however, is demonstrated by the ICT investment evident in the industry. In *Hotels* magazine's 'Technology trends

Figure 8.2 Planned ICT investment as percentage of hotels' revenue in 2001

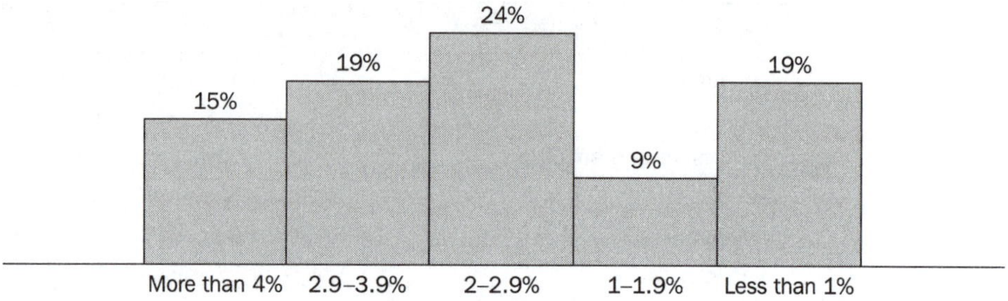

Source: Based on Marsan (2001)

survey', Marsan (2001) demonstrates that the average planned ICT expenditure for 2001 was 2.6 per cent of the hotels' gross revenue. Figure 8.2 demonstrates that 15 per cent of the respondents had planned to spend more than 4 per cent of their revenue on ICT investments, while only 19 per cent invested less than 1 per cent.

Nevertheless in the last decade, hotels have also capitalized on the newly available ICT tools. Hospitality organizations increasingly use computerized systems in order to improve their inventory management, communicate with their clientèle and maximize their profitability. The Internet has allowed them to increase their interactivity with consumers and reduce some of their operational costs (Marsan, 2001; O'Connor and Horan, 1999; O'Connor and Frew, 2000; Beldona et al., 2001; Van Hoof et al., 1999; Murphy et al., 1996).

8.3.1 Internal systems and intranets

Larger hotels introduced systems to manage their inventory, while hotel chains introduced group-wide systems as early as in the 1970s. These systems focused on the in-house management for single hotels, as well as their distribution through electronic distribution channels, such as airline CRSs and GDSs. *Property Management Systems (PMSs)* were introduced to facilitate the front office, sales, planning and operation functions. This was achieved by running a database with all reservations, rates, occupancy and cancellations, and thus, managing the hotel inventory (O'Connor, 1995, 1999b; Frew and Horam, 1999). Critical to the PMS for each hotel property and chain is therefore the computer reservation system managing the hotel inventory. Most hotel CRSs and PMSs tend to share a number of objectives, while they serve several business functions, namely:

- improving capacity management and operations efficiency;
- facilitating central room inventory control;
- providing last room availability information;
- offering yield management capability;
- providing better database access for management purposes;
- supporting extensive marketing, sales and operational reports;
- facilitating marketing research and planning;
- providing travel agency tracking and commission payment;

- tracking frequent flyers and repeat hotel guests;
- direct marketing and personalized service for repeat hotel guests;
- enhancing handling of group bookings and Frequent Individual Travellers (FITs).

In addition, a number of electronic distribution options have emerged to allow hotel reservations to be made from an ever-increasing variety of sources. These include direct bookings to the hotel, hotel chains' own reservation central offices, independent reservation agents, hotel representation and consortium groups, airline CRSs and GDSs, the Internet and destination management systems. A variety of CRSs is used by hotels at different levels, as demonstrated in Table 8.1. The first chain CRS was the HOLIDEX system of Holiday Inn, which in 1987 comprised rooms in over 1900 hotels worldwide, effectively dealing with 30 million room nights a year. Similar systems were established and developed by almost all the big hotel chains: Ramada (RENOIR), Marriott (Marsha), Crest (Crestar II), Intercontinental (Global II), Hilton (Hilton), Forte (Travelodge) and Sheraton (Reservator IV) (McGuffie, 1994; Wardell, 1987b; Hickey, 1988). Case Study 8.1 demonstrates how Active Hotels can assist properties and hotel chains to enhance their onward distribution.

Two integral components of hotel CRSs and PMSs play a significant role in their operations, namely yield management and guest history. The *yield management* concept consists of the ratio of actual revenue to potential revenue. In essence, yield management forecasts, accepts, rejects or redirects demand. It attempts to maximize both occupancy and **average room rate** simultaneously in order to maximize the total revenue of the property. As the system forecasts demand, based on previous experiences and anticipated events, a great variety of input is required, such as time series of sales and external factors influencing demand. Appropriate prices for particular time periods are then suggested, by optimizing room demand and supply, while marketing strategies are drawn to target different market segments. Increasingly, yield management takes into consideration other departments in the hotel and aims to maximize the total revenue or the revenue per available room (REVPAR) (Ingold et al., 2000; Lieberman, 1993; International Hotel Association, 1992; Lattin, 1990; Orkin, 1988; Rowe, 1989).

Table 8.1 Typologies and examples of hotel computer reservation systems

In-house CRSs and PMSs e.g. Micros/Fidelio OPERA	Facilitate the inventory control and reservation function for an individual hotel
Hotel chain CRSs e.g. Intercontinental's Global	Operated by hotel chains, these aim to increase the yield across all hotel units and to coordinate central reservation offices in booking all properties, and also to distribute hotel rooms through GDSs and the Internet
Independent reservation systems e.g. Utell	Representation systems enabling smaller and independent hotels or hotel chains to participate through their system to GDSs and the Internet
Strategic alliances and consortiums e.g. Best Western's STAR	Representation systems allowing consortium members to distribute their inventory centrally though the consortium CROs as well as GDSs and the Internet

Case Study 8.1

Active Hotels

Active Hotels is a Cambridge based company providing profitable and cost effective distribution, marketing and payment solutions for thousands of European hotels, including both independents and chains. With over 15 000 web sites and 84 000 travel agencies through whom a hotel might sell its rooms, Active Hotels essentially provides a very simple solution that enables hotels to maintain centralized inventory that is automatically distributed to web sites and agencies. Inventory is either updated through the hotel CRS/PMS or availability and prices can be updated directly by the hotel through web based software. In addition, extensive descriptive information is collated for each property to enable effective marketing of the hotel to consumers. This hotel information and inventory is then fed to web sites and agencies via the most appropriate interface and technology. Examples include XML data feeds, ASP search facilities or hyperlinks to individual properties web sites. At the time of writing, Active Hotels charges a one-off connection fee of £270 + VAT (waived if you commit for three years) and a £30 + VAT monthly service charge (redeemable if they do not generate the same amount in room revenue after one year). They also charge a low commission fee for each reservation they generate. The one-off connection fee covers the initial cost of collecting and uploading hotel information and images, creating a website, training reservation staff and integrating property with the distribution partners. The monthly service fee covers the ongoing cost of managing information and placement with distribution partners, search engine placement and web hosting. It also enable hotels to place special offers with selected partners. Active Hotels have set up a payment network to ensure commissions are paid efficiently and on-time to all the parties involved in the transaction. The simplicity of the systems has enabled independent hotels as well as group hotels successfully to utilize electronic distribution, with over 2000 properties utilizing the system in the UK alone at the end of 2002.

Source: Contributed by Andrew Phillips, CEO, Active Hotels. For more information see http://www.activehotels.com/

Questions

- What are the advantages and disadvantages of hotel representation services?

- How can small hotels enhance their distribution mechanisms?

- What should Active Hotels do to maximise the productivity of their services for hoteliers?

Moreover, hospitality CRSs often incorporate a *guest history* function, an early CRM software, which maintains data on past guests. It is widely used to assist sales and front-office personnel to identify consumers' preference and price range, as well as to identify lucrative frequent guests. A certain degree of personal service can also be facilitated, as hotels can easily recognize guests' requirements. In addition, substantial time is saved as customers' personal details and credit card numbers are known. A number of additional internal systems have also emerged to support hospitality organizations to improve their organizational performance (Ference, 2001).

PMSs have integrated back-office operations and improved general administration as well as specific functions such as accounting, marketing research and planning, yield management, payroll, personnel management, and purchasing at individual properties. Similarly, hotel chain-wide systems also support groups of hotels in coordinating their activities and maximizing their collective performance. Understandably, hotel chains, in particular the multinational ones, have gained more benefits from PMSs by introducing a unified system for planning, budgeting and control for all their properties. Eventually, though, both hotel chains and independent properties have introduced PMS software packages to facilitate their operation. Increasingly these functions move on *intranet* platforms, improving interfaces and allowing easier employee training. Several software houses have developed suitable applications for properties, including MICROS-Opera and HIS (Hotel Information Systems), as demonstrated in Case Study 1.1. In addition, revenue and yield management systems ensure that hotels optimize their revenue, by taking into consideration past and forecasted performance, as well as a wide range of additional factors. Revenue management systems are critical, particularly for large properties with numerous outlets and departments, as demonstrated in Case Study 8.2 (Peacock, 1995; Buhalis and Main, 1998; Go and Welch, 1991).

8.3.2 Interconnecting partner systems and extranets

Hotels have also realized the need to establish wide distribution networks in order to access their clientèle by demonstrating their availability and rates worldwide. This was more imperative for hotel chains, which needed to manage their inventory for all their properties globally. They therefore established central reservation offices (CROs) with sales agents that had access to the hotels' CRS. CROs allowed both individual customers and the travel trade to make reservations over the phone as sales agents had access to accurate information on availability and rates and could make and confirm reservations instantly.

The developments of GDSs forced central reservation offices to adapt new technologies and inevitably to develop automated hotel CRSs that could connect electronically with GDSs (Emmer et al., 1993). As a result, not only were the availability and rates of rooms displayed globally, but a higher degree of integration was achieved with GDSs. Being able to confirm reservations on-line and within a few seconds was critical for the integration of hotels in the GDSs. Further integration between PMSs and hotel CRSs also improved efficiency, facilitated control, reduced personnel and reduced the response time to both customers and management requests. In addition, it offered the opportunity to introduce a more personalized service and relationship marketing, as agents had access to guest histories and could recover information for individual customers and agencies (O'Connor, 1995; Robledo, 1999; Chervenak, 1991, 1993; Braham, 1988).

Interconnectivity and interoperability between hotel CRSs and GDSs was a major problem, as each hotel and GDS system has its own communication protocols and functions. As a result, two major *Switch companies* emerged, namely WizCom and THISCO, to provide an interface between the various systems and eventually to allow a certain degree of transparency. WizCom, the first switching service of the hotel and car rental industry, was founded in 1987 to provide GDS

Case Study 8.2

Revenue management system at the MGM Grand Hotel, Las Vegas

MGM Grand Hotel and Casino, 'The City of Entertainment', is a huge hotel and leisure complex in Las Vegas. It offers approximately 4.2 million square feet of space for a diversity of gaming, entertainment and recreational facilities. Its four 30-storey towers soar 280 feet above downtown Las Vegas and contain more than 5000 guest rooms. In addition to hotel accommodation and gaming opportunities, the MGM Grand features the 17 157-seat Grand Garden Arena, the 1700-seat EFX Theatre, which hosts the $45-million stage spectacular EFX, 16 signature restaurants, a 380 000-square-foot conference centre, a 6.6-acre grand pool and spa complex, as well as two wedding chapels and a nightclub.

In January 2000, the hotel completed installation of an advanced software-based revenue management system, in partnership with OPUS 2 Revenue Technologies, a subsidiary of MICROS Systems Inc. A consulting team from OPUS 2 worked closely with revenue management and MIS specialists at the MGM Grand to execute what is described as a record-breaking installation. TopLine Prophet is a Windows-based yield management system designed to maximize revenue and boost overall hotel property profitability. The system brings together sophisticated tools for forecasting, analysis, and rate quotation in a fully integrated, easy-to-use format. Interfaces to most property management systems (PMS), as well as sales and catering systems (SCS), are available. The software guides both transient reservation agents and group sales managers in offering rates and dates that maximize revenue for higher profits.

Source: Adapted from **www.hotel-technology.com** and **www.mgmgrand.com**

Questions

- Discuss the advantages and disadvantages of revenue management systems and yield management.
- Explore the qualitative factors that need to be considered by yield management systems.

and Internet connectivity, CRS and information services to the hotel, car rental and tourism industries. As a wholly owned subsidiary of Avis Rent A Car System from 1987 to 1996, WizCom used the framework of the Avis Wizard Reservation System to develop its suite of products. WizCom is now a wholly owned subsidiary of Cendant Corporation and is the world leader in reservations transactions processing for the hotel and car rental industries. Pegasus Solutions was founded in 1989 for the hotel industry as The Hotel Industry Switch Company (THISCO). Its mission was to develop a universal electronic reservations switch to connect hotel reservation systems to the major GDSs, such as SABRE and Galileo, that travel agents use to book travel electronically. The establishment of Switch companies minimized both set-up and reservation costs and maximized the number of reservations, as it enabled hotel CRSs to be distributed through GDSs (Emmer et al., 1993; McGuffie, 1994; Chervenak, 1993; Lindsay, 1992). Effectively these systems are managed through *extranets* that facilitate inter-organizational communication, allowing partners to share information and processes.

8.3.3 **Connecting with all stakeholders through the Internet**

The proliferation of the Internet in the late 1990s and the revolution of technologies have introduced a wide range of new marketing tools. Although GDSs currently dominate hotel bookings, the Internet emerges as the prime medium for receiving travel bookings from individuals. O'Connor and Frew (2000) suggest that using GDSs to distribute hotel products is problematic for three main reasons:

- GDSs allow only a fairly limited number of rates to be displayed due to their database architecture. Potentially a hotel can price each room individually for each day.
- Abbreviated and truncated descriptions cannot do justice to the properties of the rooms.
- GDSs take an unacceptable amount of time to update data as they are more geared up for regular airline updates.

Therefore, the Internet is much more suitable for promoting hotel rooms and inventory while it provides the tools to increase revenue at a fraction of the traditional cost of booking. A greater number of hospitality establishments take advantage of the opportunities emerging through the Internet. Most large and medium hotels and virtually all hotel chains have developed their web presence, most with suitable eCommerce solutions allowing on-line transactions. A great number of hotels surveyed in 1998 was already receiving bookings through the Internet. The majority of the remaining properties were developing their facilities in order to be able to receive Internet bookings in the near future, as illustrated in Figure 8.3 (Hensdill, 1998). The follow-up survey of the *Hotels* magazine at the end of 2000 demonstrates that virtually every hotel surveyed receives reservations through the Internet, as demonstrated in Table 8.2.

On-line bookings are showing dramatic growth, according to PhocusWright.com. The gross value of Internet hotel reservations was US$2.6 billion in 2000,

Figure 8.3 Use of the Internet for reservations by accommodation establishments

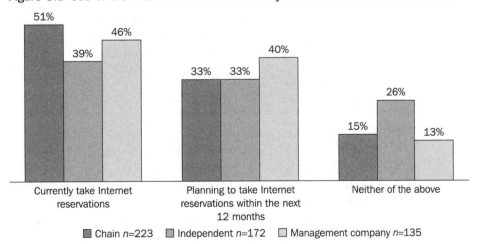

Source: Adapted from Hensdill (1998)

Table 8.2 Hotel Internet reservations in 1997 and 2000

	USA hotels 1997 (n = 308)	International hotels 1997 (n = 257)	USA hotels 2000 (n = 172)	International hotels 2000 (n = 161)
Currently take Internet reservations	43%	48%	78%	70%
Planning to take Internet reservations within 12 months	34%	39%	13%	22%
Neither of the above	22%	12%	4%	5%

Source: Based on Marsan (2001)

up 136 per cent from 1999. Of that, 55 per cent of bookings came from hotel-branded websites and 45 per cent from on-line travel agencies such as Travelocity and Expedia. Internet bookings were projected to reach US$4.6 billion in 2001, with 53 per cent being booked through hotel websites.

Case Study 8.3 demonstrates that Accor receives one booking every 17 seconds and explains that the on-line bookings are growing rapidly. One of the best examples of driving traffic to a website is Marriott International. Dennis (1998) illustrated that innovative and advanced hospitality organizations can benefit enormously from their Internet presence. The on-line performance of Marriott has not only increased the revenue and market share of the company, but has also reduced its distribution, promotion and marketing costs, contributing directly to the bottom line. Revenue through marriott.com had more than doubled, reaching US$150 million, or 3 per cent of its total sales, in the first quarter of 2001, and was expected to have doubled its web revenue in 2001. Of the total web bookings, two-thirds of revenue come from marriott.com.

Straight, clear and transactional websites facilitate on-line bookings. Much of Marriott's increase is a result of its newly redesigned website, which was relaunched in 2000, featuring its own booking engine. In addition to displaying photos of amenities and locations, it focuses on generating transactions by offering visitors the ability to store content for personal profiles. eCommerce has also helped hotels to reduce their costs significantly. Since its inception, Marriott has been able to save US$2 per Internet booking using its own booking engine instead of an outside source. Other hotels have realized similar savings through Internet bookings. According to PhocusWright, Hilton, for example, saves US$25 on each website booking (compared with a traditional travel agency booking). Hyatt's cost for an on-line booking is US$3, compared with US$9 to book via the call centre. Looking for other ways to improve e-business, Marriott has begun to partner with large corporations to bring its website into their intranet's travel pages, creating a B2B environment and enhancing electronic collaboration. The strength of its brand, and the fact that consumers have always relied on booking directly through the hotel instead of intermediaries, are playing a critical role (Oliva, 2001).

Perhaps the second most successful application of the Internet for the hospitality industry is *eProcurement*. As hotels are highly dependent on regular supplies of good quality and cost-efficient materials and ingredients, this function is

Case Study 8.3

Accor hotels on-line

Accor's portal (accorhotels.com) had 12 million visitors during the year 2000. In the second quarter of 2001, accorhotels.com recorded 70 000 visits a day – a figure more than double that at the end of 2000. Across the world, every 17 seconds, a room-night is reserved via the Internet in an Accor hotel. Over a million room-nights were reserved in the first half of 2001 and via its on-line, real-time hotel reservation service, thus already exceeding its results for 2000 as a whole.

From January to July 2001 Accor recorded almost 15 million visits for its hotel sites as a whole (the accorhotels.com portal and its hotel brand sites: sofitel.com, novotel.com, mercure.com, coralia.com, thalassa.com, ibishotel.com, etaphotel.com, hotelformule1.com, motel6.com and redroof.com), i.e. an annual average of 78 000 visitors per day. The number of consultations per day has in fact increased rapidly in recent months: from 50 000 visits per day in January to 100 000 early in July. It is estimated that by the end of 2001 the reservations made over the Internet should have passed the 2 million room-night mark. Over 15 per cent of the total room nights are currently reserved via central reservation systems. Internet reservations are over 15 per cent of the reservations made via the central channels (telephone reservation centre, Internet, GDSs, voice servers and Minitel). Total turnover via the hotel sites in 2000 amounted to 45 million euros. For 2001, taking into account the tendencies observed since the beginning of the year, it could climb to, or even exceed, the forecast total of 100 million euros.

In addition, Accor recently launched an affiliation programme for partners. Accorhotel Affiliates allows Internet site partners to include a link on their web pages directing Internet users towards accorhotels.com. Partners include those close to the group's business activities (for example, sites focusing on travel, family, senior citizens, golf, sport in general, weather etc.). In this way, with a single click, surfers can access the real-time, on-line worldwide reservation service for the group's 3500 hotels. This helps to increase the visibility of Accor's hotel offering on the Internet and to multiply sales opportunities. The ultimate goal is to achieve 20 per cent of sales from accorhotels.com via the affiliation platform. Each affiliate is remunerated on the number of room-nights generated (6 euros for Sofitel, 3 euros for Novotel, 3 euros for Mercure, 1 euro for Ibis). A site wishing to join Accorhotel Affiliates registers on-line under the heading Become Affiliate of accorhotels.com. After its registration has been confirmed, it then receives a password and access code for downloading the accorhotels.com link. Each affiliate can consult its reporting, on-line and in real-time, with the details of the nightly reservations generated and the amount of remuneration.

For more information, see **www.accorhotels.com**

Questions

- How can multi-brand hotel chains use ICTs to maintain their brand integrity?

- What are the synergies emerging through a unified representation of all properties, and what are the shortfalls of this approach?

- Explore which decisions are transferred to the head office as a result of an on-line strategy and what the implications are for the management and marketing of individual properties.

critical for their operational efficiency. eProcurement pledges to end the hurdles of an inefficient buying system through cost controls, fully automated order processing and corporate power to require properties to be compliant with purchasing policies. Eventually hotel eProcurement will integrate all aspects of the purchasing process electronically. As soon as the level of demand can be predicted, from reservation levels and past data/experience, orders can be generated automatically, authorized by departmental heads, delivered and paid with little human involvement.

eProcurement may require a certain level of up-front investment to integrate processes and partners. Again, cooperating with competitors (co-opetition) may be critical for enabling industry partners to develop suitable platforms for eProcurement. Although in theory significant savings can be made in the process, labour and cost of goods, there is still little concrete evidence demonstrating the level of savings in each of those areas. eProcurement can enable hospitality organizations to streamline the purchasing process, leveraging volume and enforcing purchasing agreements. As stock management and ordering takes a considerable amount of employee time, digitizing the process can free time and help employees to manage the process better.

As a result, a number of B2B applications and companies emerged to serve this demand. For example, Avendra, a procurement company, was founded in early 2001 by Marriott International, Hyatt Hotels Corp., Club Corp, Six Continent Hotels and Resorts and most recently Fairmont Hotels and Resorts as an independent company providing the largest, most comprehensive procurement network for the North American hospitality and related industries, a market estimated at $80 billion annually. Ultimately Avendra aims to integrate systems of sellers and buyers in the hospitality industry in order to automate the entire purchasing process.

Despite being in its infancy stage, there are benefits of electronic B2B purchasing which offer time and cost savings to individual properties. At full integration, when broken down, a hotel that saves 10 per cent using on-line purchasing will see 5 per cent of that coming from price controls, 3 per cent from standardization of volume and quality of goods, and 2 per cent saved on the payment end, or integration, according to Accenture. However, the industry has been fairly slow in adopting eProcurement, as a very low percentage of its properties practises eProcurement currently. This is attributed to lack of capital investments in wiring the necessary components, lack of up-to-date technology and the fear of change. In addition, training employees, loading catalogues and other integration issues contribute to the lag in implementation. To be successful, eProcurement must be comprehensible to the end-user, eliminating challenges such as slow dial-up service and creating employee incentives to spur more usage.

Apart from eCommerce, eSales, eMarketing and eProcurement the Internet also assisted hospitality organizations to develop their value chain and to enhance a wide range of their *business functions*. Increasingly eFinance and eAccounting enable hotels to use information and data from operational processes in order to automate most of their functions. In addition, eHRM enables them to recruit and manage all their human resources issues on-line. By using the Internet they can attract employees and explain their policies, training programmes and promotion opportunities. Marriott, for example, provides comprehensive information for employees and allows them to submit their CV electronically for consideration (www.careers.marriott.com). In addition, intranets are frequently used for managing employee relationships and for regularly distributing information, while extranets are often established for communicating with recruitment partners, social security, insurance and pension organization. Six Continents, for example, have outsourced part of their recruitment to HCareers and use a specialized section on their website for their recruitment (sixcontinents.hcareers.com/jobs).

8.4 Larger vs smaller accommodation properties

Larger accommodation establishments gradually seem to capitalize on the new ICT tools and improve their competitiveness. However, the vast majority of properties are *small and medium-sized tourism enterprises (SMTEs)*, independent, seasonal and family-run. Much of the success of Internet bookings comes from knowing how to market a hotel's website, a luxury many independent hotels cannot afford. These properties often lack the expertise and resources to adopt the emerging ICT tools and in many cases are left behind, jeopardizing their future prosperity (Buhalis, 1999). The majority of SMTEs are reluctant to introduce new technologies, and as a result become increasingly marginalized, mainly due to:

- the ICT illiteracy of their entrepreneurs;
- lack of marketing and technology understanding;
- the cost of ICTs being perceived as prohibitive for entrepreneurs;
- inability to control the equipment;
- perceived dependence on trained staff;
- lack of standardization and, often, professionalism;
- seasonality and limited period of operations in resorts;
- insufficient training and established organizational practices;
- small size multiplies the administration required by CRSs to deal with each property;
- the unwillingness of SMTEs to lose control over their property.

Morrison (1994) explains that for SMTEs to participate in the global marketplace three types of participation expenses are required, namely economic (in commission and fees), operational (as a degree of autonomy to be sacrificed), and flexibility and individuality of SMTEs (rules and sanctions). Hence, SMTEs and independent properties are the weakest and most vulnerable parts of the hotel industry, which are at risk of losing substantial market share. As a result, SMTEs are placed at a major disadvantage and jeopardize their future existence (Buhalis, 1999; Cooper and Buhalis, 1992; Go and Welch, 1991; Go, 1992).

SMTEs cannot afford to sit by, watching the rapid developments of ICTs with apathy. SMTEs failing to develop their Internet presence and hence unavailable in the electronic marketplace will be inaccessible to consumers and intermediaries; their future prosperity will therefore be jeopardized. Independent properties can easily lose considerable market share, increase their dependence on intermediaries and undermine their profitability if they do not develop their Internet presence and interactivity as part of their marketing strategy. As technological expenditure and knowledge become inelastic, SMTEs will have no alternative but to incorporate modern technologies in order to serve the markets adequately. Hence, the argument that SMTEs cannot afford the cost of ICTs gradually becomes irrelevant, as ICT expenses become part of the core product, operational practices and investment (Buhalis and Main, 1998; Buhalis and Cooper, 1998; Morrison et al., 1999b). Moreover, as computers become smaller, quicker and cheaper, even the smallest companies can afford some basic systems. As Poon (1988) states, 'there will be no place for the small stand alone participants, but the world can become the oyster for the small, innovative, flexible and networked enterprises'.

Conversely, there is evidence suggesting that there are more innovative small operators taking advantage of the situation and profiting accordingly. Small properties that advertise their offerings and offer on-line bookings are reported to achieve as much as 60 per cent of their reservations through the Internet (Buhalis and Keeling, 1999). If small independent hotels use ICTs, and the Internet in particular, to confront their marketing challenges, they can survive in the future, as demonstrated in Table 8.3 (Morrison et al., 1999a; Anckar and Walden, 2001). Provided that they develop credible and accurate websites and ensure that they are promoted both on-line through search engines and off-line through

Table 8.3 Internet opportunities for innovative SMTEs

Internationalization	■ Small hotel can target a much more international market, with potential access to guests from all around the world at a very marginal cost ■ Time difference is not an issue any more, as Internet is available on a 24-hours-a-day basis ■ Web materials can be translated into a variety of languages ■ Machine translation, available freely on the Internet, can help translation of web pages and eMails
Differentiation	■ Niche and specialist interest markets can be pursued more effectively by small hotels on the Internet ■ Differentiation can be demonstrated and 'tangibilized' through photos, text, graphics, testimonials, awards and other means ■ Regular themed events can be advertised on-line and through targeted eMails ■ Developing collaboration with specialized associations, publications and interest groups can differentiate products, and creating specialized Internet pages for them is worthwhile
Adding value	■ Provide special offers and deals to visitors of website ■ On-line club of regulars to facilitate interaction of loyal and repeat guests ■ Facilitate the entire value chain on-line ■ Providing additional services through partnerships with other local providers, e.g. taxi transfers, restaurant meals etc. ■ Follow all leads ■ eMail visitors regularly and establish communication channels ■ Offer additional information on the local area, events and attractions
Interconnection and distribution	■ Develop digital alliances on the web through reciprocal hyperlinking ■ Expand network through representation companies that do not require fixed costs or expensive technologies (e.g. worldres.com) ■ Develop links with small travel organizations from around the world and interconnect smallness
Embracing technology	■ Embrace technology through developing an Internet site ■ Provide extra technological assistance for technologically advanced travellers through modem sockets and plug-and-play systems

Source: Based on Morrison et al. (1999a, 1999b)

stationery, conventional advertising and partners' cooperation, they will be able to attract consumers and maintain their competitiveness. By developing close relationships with other members of the tourism value chain, locally and internationally, small hotels can enhance their virtual size and develop virtual organizations in which each partner concentrates on its core business and establishes co-destiny. Interconnecting with representation organizations, such as worldres.com, helps SMTEs to maximize their interconnectivity. This is achieved by allowing them to distribute their product through a wide range of distribution mechanisms, as demonstrated in Case Study 8.4. Several innovative entrepreneurs have taken advantage of the Internet and gained benefits that they would have never be able to achieve off-line, as demonstrated in Case Studies 2.1 and 5.1.

Case Study 8.4

worldres.com, the hotel reservation network

WorldRes was founded in 1995 to provide an on-line hotel reservation network for leisure travel. Built specifically for the Internet, WorldRes uses the latest technology to provide a cost-effective alternative to reservation services that rely on the global distribution system (GDS) and other legacy systems. For hotels, WorldRes offers an effective, low-cost way to market and sell accommodations via the Internet. Hotels pay a commission on the bookings received through the system. WorldRes provides a cost-effective way for all properties to create a worldwide Internet sales and marketing strategy, or supplement an existing one. With just a PC and Internet access, any property can join WorldRes – from independent one-room B&Bs to international hotel chains. Membership in WorldRes is non-exclusive so properties that already participate in other on-line marketing and distribution services can also join WorldRes.

WorldRes offers comprehensive property pages with photos, detailed information, and real-time, confirmed reservation capabilities and empowers SMTEs to achieve a presence – including real-time reservation capabilities – on all applicable websites and call centres in WorldRes's international partner network. Hotels enrol in the system at a very low cost and WorldRes charges a small percentage transaction fee for each reservation made via a WorldRes partner site and a 4 per cent fee for a reservation made via the hotel's own website. The system has more than 20 000 member properties and over 2000 distribution partner websites and call centres through which reservations are made. As key distribution points, WorldRes also owns the consumer travel website, placestostay.com, and operates a wholly owned subsidiary, bedandbreakfast.com, the leading supplier of information about B&Bs. For distribution partners, WorldRes offers rich content on a range of unique properties, plus a share of revenues generated by room reservations that are made through partner websites and call centres.

For more information, see **www.WorldRes.com**

Questions

- Explore the factors that determine the successful representation of individual hotel properties on-line by representation companies.
- What are the costs and benefits of hotel on-line representation companies for individual properties?

In addition, *collaborating at the destination level* can help SMTEs to pool resources and share development and operation costs in order to achieve **economies of scope** (Buhalis and Cooper, 1998; Buhalis, 1999). Networks of shared costs, resources and information can assist small hotels in alleviating some of the constraints of their size and enable them to obtain more benefits from scale economies. This cooperation needs support by local, regional, national and international public tourism organizations and tourist enterprises/hoteliers' associations. **Cooperative strategies** and **cooperative marketing** are ideal for smaller properties. SMTEs' cooperative participation in the expanding destination management systems can also enable SMTEs to develop their global presence and to be able to attract visitors to their properties. This is expected to benefit the prosperity of both local enterprises and destinations. This will allow them to compete effectively in order to increase the market share of their destinations and consequently their own benefits. Destination-oriented systems emerge to support the competitiveness of SMTEs by coordinating the local supply, establishing value chains and enabling SMTEs to distribute their products through GDSs and the Internet (Buhalis, 1994; Archdale, 1993; Poon, 1989).

8.5 Lessons and issues for the future of eHospitality

There are several key trends in eHospitality and they will shape the future of the hospitality industry. First of all the industry is gradually realizing the ICT revolution has changed best operational practices and paradigms, altering the competitiveness of all hospitality actors in the marketplace. Many large hospitality corporations have already revised their info-structure dramatically and have gradually integrated their back and front office into a framework that takes advantage of the capabilities of the Internet as well as of intranets and extranets. Several generations of web designs have been introduced since the 1990s, gradually re-engineering several business processes and integrating the entire organization.

Convergence of all technological devices gradually empowers greater connectivity, speed, transparency and information sharing. As a result, hospitality organizations gradually focus more on knowledge-based competition and on the need for continuous innovation, forcing the management to stay abreast of the dynamic developments in the marketplace (Connolly et al., 2000). Gradually, large hospitality organizations attempt to increase their on-line bookings by promoting their Internet presence more aggressively and by capitalizing on partnership and collaboration marketing. As a result, *multi-channel strategies* are required to assist hotels to interconnect with the wide range of distributors in the marketplace. It is currently estimated that there are 35 000 websites from which consumers can book a hotel room. There are many ways in which a hotel company can manage its Internet distribution channels. Some issues to consider when managing Internet distribution are rate integrity, brand perception and market segments, in order to protect the value of the long-term customer versus the financial gain of the last-minute one. Therefore, a number of challenges emerge through this evolution. On the one hand, suitable business models need to be developed to allow all partners to gain equitable returns on their resources and investments. On the other, the lack of standardization in most systems available, legacy systems in particular, prevents the interoperability and interconnectivity of systems.

Perhaps the interoperability issue can be resolved through standardization of software hosted by *Application Service Providers (ASPs)*. ASPs will increasingly be more involved in hosting a number of business applications for hospitality organizations. Hotels will 'rent' the same software for a fee and will use it across the Internet. For example, some hotel firms may 'rent' their PMS software application from supplier Micros/Fidelio. Rambler and McGrew (2000) suggest that ASPs are ideal for hotels, especially for small to middle-sized ones that 'want to leverage the best vertical and enterprise support applications on the market without having to deal with the technology or pay for more functionality than needed'. As they do not have extensive ICT departments and expertise, they can easily access up-to-date applications and benefit from the collective knowledge accumulated by ASP providers without having to invest extensively in technology or expertise building. In general, ASP benefits can be classified into two categories: bottom-line and top-line benefits. Bottom-line benefits assist organizations to manage their resources better and to reduce their costs. By sharing research and development costs with others, small hotels can maintain up-to-date systems at an affordable cost. Top-line benefits create further value, improve customer service, and support the organization to improve its service provision and to add value to its provision. These benefits can improve the competitiveness and profitability of an organization (Paraskevas and Buhalis, 2002).

Customer care and recognition become central for the successful hospitality organization of the future. Customers demand more and are increasingly difficult to satisfy. They also compare their experiences from a wide range of service providers around the world. To please them, hotels need to appreciate customer motivations, circumstances and even mood and should work harder and differently every time. Integrated customer relationship management solutions allow the collection of information from operational transactions for more accurate profiling of consumers. Gradually each consumer will be addressed as a market segment, enabling personalization of communications and service. Emerging wireless and identification technologies are expected to facilitate this process. Several tourism and hospitality organizations have already started experimenting with wireless services, as illustrated in Case Study 8.5.

Stemming from the Internet are wireless devices, *Bluetooth* technology and biometrics, all of which promise to be 'the next big thing' in hotel operations. Bluetooth technologies will empower mobile devices, such as mobile phones, PDAs and even electronic digital jewellery (e.g. rings and necklaces), to communicate with hotel systems and undertake a number of functions automatically. In addition, products that include voice, handwriting and other biometric recognition devices are frequently listed as key trends emerging for hotel technology. The ability to recognize guests and have access to guest data via biometrics would help to improve the levels of service. For example, upon arrival at the hotel, guests with a Bluetooth-enabled device will be able to speed up their check-in

Case Study 8.5

Six Continents hotels use wireless devices

Six Continents Hotels & Resorts, a global leader with more than 3000 hotels in close to 100 countries, recently launched the industry's most comprehensive wireless services for locating hotels and making room reservations. Working with Air2Web, the leading mobile Internet platform provider, Six Continents Hotels & Resorts guests can now easily obtain hotel information from wireless devices including the Palm VII, web-enabled phones and digital text messaging phones. Guests who are members of the Priority Club, Six Continents Hotels & Resorts' frequent-guest programme, can also make reservations on mobile devices with a minimal amount of effort. As a Priority Club member, stored room preferences and credit card information are used to offer personalized reservations and streamline the process. Guests can register on any Six Continents Hotels & Resorts branded website to select their device and customize their profile. Air2Web has tailored links for more than 260 wireless devices based on manufacturer and specifications. According to the Yankee Group, the number of wireless Internet users today in the USA is one million, compared with 150 million PC users. By 2005, there should be 177 million wireless web users, compared with 200 million PC users. Furthermore, Forrester Research predicts that by 2005, one in 10 households in North America is expected to have a PDA (personal digital assistant) and four out of five people will have a net-enabled mobile phone.

Questions

- What are the major value-added hospitality services that can be offered on mobile devices?
- Explore the costs and benefits of wireless services in the hospitality industry.

process. A server in the lobby will recognize the device and send a welcoming message back to the device asking whether the guest wants to check-in automatically. A guest keying a number ('9' for yes, perhaps) will be told the room number via the device and will be directed to the correct room. Once within the range of the door, a message will ask whether the guest wants the door unlocked by punching a pin number selected when the hotel reservation was made. This technology is expected to provide additional services for guests and particularly to reduce the time for checking in and out. Communications during the visit can also be enhanced as hotels will be able to notify guests of special events, promotions and received messages. Obviously, this technology may not suit all hotel guests. More regular guests will perhaps be able to benefit more from these technologies and reduce the administrative tasks.

In addition, hotel rooms will increasingly offer more ICT capabilities to provide *in-room entertainment* as well as *working facilities*, emulating the 'home away from home' and 'office away from office' principles. In the recent *Hotels* survey on TV-based Internet access, eMail, multiple phone lines, on-demand movies and games, TV-based shopping and tourism information, and computers with Internet were on the top of the shopping list of hoteliers in 2000 (Marsan, 2001).

Although ICTs aim primarily to reduce staffing levels and to minimize costs in general, the hospitality industry must realize the significance of the entire process. It is therefore 'high tech – high touch' that consumers of the future will require; they will want to deal with human beings who possess up-to-date information and will therefore be able to understand their needs and wants instantly. Hotels must cultivate relationships with their customers as the value of the lifetime customer is higher than owning a large piece of market share. This will be more critical in the future and hospitality organizations may need to shift to enterprise transformation to achieve it. This shift implies a reinvention of work from a structured environment to a customer-centred and task-focused environment. Technology needs to simplify the way project teams work and to integrate all functions to look after the customer's every need.

8.6 Conclusions

Technological developments have created a number of significant tools for the integration of the hotel operations. By coordinating all departments and services in a hotel, as well as coordinating all properties in a hotel chain, they allow business to run more efficiently. The Internet has contributed unprecedented tools for communicating with consumers and partners and this has radical implications for hotel distribution. Innovative smaller properties are gradually developing their on-line presence, enabling them to communicate their message to the world. Larger hospitality organizations benefit from economies of scale, multi-channel distribution strategies and from streamlining their operations through eProcurement. Strategically ICTs will be pushing hospitality organizations towards either small and unique properties with specific value attributes or towards global hospitality players. In both cases ICTs and the Internet will be critical for their competitiveness.

Chapter questions

1 Why do different types of hotels have dissimilar ICT needs and uses?

2 Which hotel types use more technological solutions, and why?

3 How do ICT investments compare with other expenditure in the hotel business?

4 What entertainment and value-added services should be added to the hotel room of the future?

5 Why do hotel systems need to be integrated?

6 Explain the differences between a PMS and a hotel CRS.

7 What is yield management, and why is it critical for the hotel business?

8 How can hotel properties that charge a standard price (such as Travel Inn) apply yield management?

9 What is eProcurement, and why is it critical for hotels?

10 How can affiliate programmes with other organizations boost productivity?

11 Is interfacing with GDSs important for hotels?

12 What distribution channel should be utilized for the successful hotel of the future?

13 Explore the issue of branding integrity for on-line hotel promotions.

14 How can ASPs assist hotels in the future, and what will be the conditions for their success?

15 Can customer relationship management enhance brand loyalty in hospitality?

16 Will small properties around the world be able to survive in the future, and what are the conditions for developing their competitiveness?

17 Explore the opportunities for using wireless technologies in hotel properties and assess their feasibility.

18 Does technology promote further concentration in the hospitality industry?

Further reading

Anckar, B. and Walden, P. (2001) Introducing web technology in a small peripheral hospitality organization, *International Journal of Contemporary Hospitality Management*, **13**(5), 241–250.

Braham, B. (1988) *Computer Systems in the Hotel and Catering Industry*, Cassell, London.

Collias, G. and Malik, T. (1999) *Hospitality Information Technology*, Kendall/Hunt, Iowa.

Connolly, D., Olsen, M. and Allegro, S. (2000) The hospitality industry and the digital economy, *IH&RA Visioning the Future: Think Tank Event*, Report, International Hotel and Restaurant Asscociation, Paris.

Connolly, D., Olsen, M. and Moore, R. (1998) The Internet as a distribution channel, *Cornell Hotel and Restaurant Administration Quarterly*, **39**(4), 42–54.

Ference, G. (2001) Improving organizational performance using survey-driven databases, *Cornell Hotel and Restaurant Administration Quarterly*, April, 12–27.

Frew, A. and Horam, R. (1999) eCommerce in the UK hotel sector: a first look, *International Journal of Hospitality Information Technology*, **1**(1), 77–87.

Hensdill, C. (1998) Hotels technology survey, *Hotels*, February.

Jones, P. and Lockwood, A. (1989) *The Management of Hotel Operations*, Cassell, London.

Jones, P. and Pizam, A. (1993) *International Hospitality Management – Organizational and Operational Issues*, Pitman, London.

Marsan, J. (2001) Hotels technology survey, *Hotels*, February, 78–94.

Morrison, A., Taylor, S. and Morrison, A. (1999) Marketing small hotels on the world wide web, *Information Technology & Tourism*, **2**(2), 97–113.

O'Connor, P. (2000) *Using Computers in Hospitality*, 2nd edn, Cassell, London.

O'Connor, P. and Frew, A. (2000) Evaluating electronic channels of distribution in the hotel sector: a Delphi study, *Information Technology and Tourism*, **3**(3/4), 177–193.

O'Connor, P. and Horan, P. (1999) An analysis of web reservations facilities in the top 50 international hotel chains, *International Journal of Hospitality Information Technology*, **1**(1), 77–87.

Peacock, M. (1995) *Information Technology in Hospitality*, Cassell, London.

Teare, R. and Olsen, M. (1992) *International Hospitality Management – Corporate Strategy in Practice*, Pitman, London.

Websites

Hotel technology providers and associations

www.hedna.org
www.hotel-technology.com
www.wizcom.com
www.pegs.com
www.avendra.com
www.hotelsmag.com
www.micros.com
www.utell.com
www.worldres.com

Hotel websites

Best Western: www.travelweb.com/best.html
Choice Hotels: www.hotelchoice.com
Concorde Hotels: www.concorde-hotels.com
Corinthia Hotels: www.corinthia.com
De Vere Hotels: www.devere.com
Embassy Suites: www.promus.com/embassy.html
Grand Heritage: www.grandheritage.com
Hilton Hotels Corporation: www.hilton.com
Holiday Inn Worldwide: www.holiday-inn.com
Hyatt Hotels & Resorts: www.hyatt.com
Intercontinental: www.interconti.com
Kempinski hotels: www.kempinski.com
Leading Hotels of the World: www.lhw.com
Luxury Hotels of the World: www.slh.com/slh
Marriott International: www.marriott.com
Novotel: www.novotel.com/welcome
Pan Pacific Hotels and Resorts: www.panpac.com/hotels
Posthouse: www.posthouse-hotels.com
Radisson Hotels: www.radisson.com
Relais & Chateaux: www.relaischateaux.fr
Sandals: www.sandals.com
SuperClubs: www.superclubs.com
Thistle Hotels: www.thistlehotels.com
Travel Inn: www.travelinn.co.uk
Travelodge: www.travelodge.co.uk
Westin Hotels and Resorts: www.westin.com

Hotel directories

London Hotel Net: www.demon.co.uk/hotel-net
Travel Web: www.travelweb.com
Expotel: www.expotel.net
Paris Hotels: www.parishotels.com
Official Hotel Guide International: www.ohgionline.com
Old English: www.oldenglish.co.uk

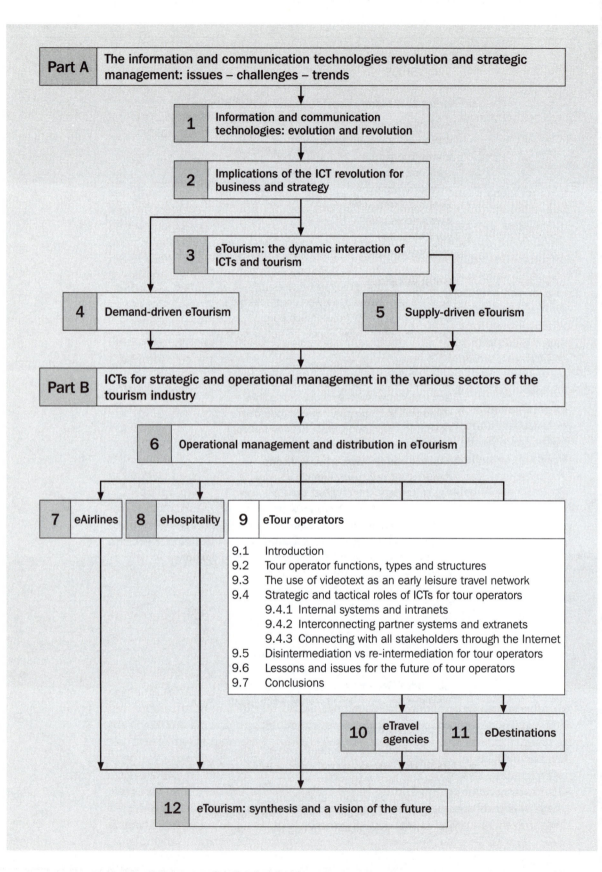

9

eTour operators

Chapter objectives

The purpose of this chapter is to explain the role of ICTs in tour operating. The chapter explains the basics of the tour operating business in the European context and elaborates on the differences between small and larger players in tour operating. The chapter illustrates the use of ICTs by tour operators and the ways that ICTs support tour operators' efficiency and promotions, and enable them to communicate effectively with their partners. The chapter also examines the threats for disintermediation in the industry. Thus, the learning objectives may be defined as:

- Explore how technology can assist the business of tour operators
- Illustrate the strategic and tactical aspects of the ICT utilization
- Demonstrate how ICTs allow tour operators to communicate with all their partners for the development and delivery of packages
- Demonstrate the key technology applications as well as the main software used for their operations
- Understand the sources of competitiveness in the tour operating business
- Explain the importance of integrating intranet, extranet and Internet applications
- Discuss the issues related to disintermediation and re-intermediation in the distribution channel
- Debate the key issues for the future of tour operating and the role of ICTs

9.1 Introduction

The most significant contribution of tour operators in the distribution channel is the package tour. A combination of different products is assembled together into 'tourism packages' or '**inclusive tours**'. Packages are selected travel and tourism products, marketed under a particular product or brand label, and sold at an inclusive price (Middleton, 1988). Tour operators are therefore organizers, who put together packages and sell or offer them for sale, directly or through a retailer. Packages are pre-arranged combinations of transport, accommodation and other tourist services, sold or offered for sale at an inclusive price (EC, 1990). ICTs have been changing the business of tour operators dramatically as they have revolutionized communications and interactivity with all stakeholders.

In northern European countries, where tour operators dominate the leisure travel market, traditional airline and hotel CRSs and GDSs are used less frequently for arranging leisure travel. Tour operators' packages still account for a large amount of the leisure travel products and the ICT systems they use are therefore critical for distributing these products.

9.2 Tour operator functions, types and structures

As tour operators make bulk reservations on various tourism products, before distributing them through outgoing travel agencies, they are often regarded as wholesalers. A great variation between tour operators' practices and strategies can be observed in various countries. However, northern European tour operators have, to a certain extent, standardized packages due to the horizontal integration experienced. In contrast, southern European tour operators predominately concentrate on short breaks/sightseeing/shopping/shows in European capitals, as most of their clients are residents or neighbours of sunny destinations (Buhalis and Laws, 2001).

Tour operators undertake a wide range of activities in order to negotiate with suppliers as well as to prepare and sell their packages to consumers. They normally pre-reserve and sometimes pre-purchase a number of travel services and set up a package at a single price. Packages are standardized and repetitive and they normally offer transport and accommodation, while sometimes they include catering, entertainment, attractions, other facilities and services of scale. Tour operating is a process of combining aircraft seats and beds in hotels (or other forms of accommodation) in a manner that will make the purchase price attractive to potential holidaymakers. Buying in bulk generates immense discounts and economies. Product packages are marketed to the general public, directly or through retail travel agencies at a published, inclusive price, in which the costs of the product components cannot be identified separately.

There are several ways of describing the type of tour operator, but there is a clear distinction between large/mass operators, covering a very wide range of destinations and tourism products, and small/specialist operators who normally provide holidays for a few destinations and/or specialize in themed or activity holidays. In the UK, the former normally belong to the Federation of Tour Operators (FTO), while the latter are often members of the Association of Independent Tour Operators (AITO). Smaller tour operators tend to concentrate on differentiation and value-added strategies, while the majority of large tour operators attempt to achieve cost advantage and thus to increase their market share and turnover rather than their profit margin. The high horizontal integration of tour operating means that most of the larger British and German organizations now operate throughout Europe (Bywater, 2001). Traditionally large/mass tour operators concentrate their effort on increasing their sales volume, often at the expense of their profit margins. Smaller operators tend to address niche markets and normally charge premium prices for specialized services.

9.3 The use of videotext as an early leisure travel network

In the early 1980s, tour operators realized that they had to capitalize on ICTs and use more effective distribution methods. They wanted to enhance their productivity, improve their holiday-capacity management, reduce the labour cost of telephone operators and provide a better service to both agencies and consumers. The transformation of the British travel industry from telephone to electronic reservation using videotext systems was initiated by Olympic Holidays in 1980. However, it was really established by Thomson's Open-line Programme (TOP), which developed its first real-time computer-based central reservation office in 1976, introduced direct communication with travel agencies in 1982, and announced that reservations would only be accepted through TOP by the end of 1986. Gradually, all major tour operators developed or acquired databases and established electronic links with travel agencies, aiming to reduce their information handling costs and increase the speed of information transfer and retrieval. They also utilized available market intelligence data arising from the systems to adjust their supply to the demand fluctuations, as well as to monitor the booking progress and productivity of travel agencies (Kärcher, 1996; Hitchins, 1991; Bennett, 1993).

Consequently, tour operators developed direct links with travel agencies via videotext networks. This enabled travel agencies to have interactive access to tour operators' reservation systems and allowed them to search their databases, to enquire availability of packages and to make bookings. Videotext networks also benefited travel agencies, since they provided the opportunity for low-cost bookings, improved communications, increased the speed of booking procedures and improved customer service. The establishment of videotext terminals and the familiarity of travel agencies with this technology prompted other tourism suppliers, such as ferry operators, railways and travel insurance companies, to develop connections with these systems and benefit accordingly. Moreover, the balance of power between retailers and wholesalers shifted towards the latter, as they were in a more privileged position to manipulate the availability and prices appearing on the videotext systems more efficiently. Hence videotext networks were the most popular method of communication for leisure travel agencies for most of the 1990s (Inkpen, 1998; Bennett and Radburn, 1991; Feeny, 1988; Deng and Ryan, 1992).

9.4 Strategic and tactical roles of ICTs for tour operators

As a result of their function in the marketplace, tour operators need to constantly interact with the all their partners, including accommodation and transportation principals, travel agencies and consumers. Coordinating the simultaneous movement of large numbers of travellers, often in many different countries and continents, represents a major operational management challenge in which ICTs have a crucial role.

ICTs are also critical for the distribution of tour operators' packages. Traditionally tour operators distribute their products by displaying brochures of their packages in travel agencies. A pre-printed form is normally provided, to be completed by travel agencies in order to request a holiday from a tour operator (Wanhill, 1998). Travel agencies search tour operators' databases and make bookings through videotext booking systems. The introduction of the Internet as well as intranets and extranets as strategic tools has a number of critical benefits for tour operators.

The *emergence of the Internet, extranets and intranets* has introduced a wide range of great opportunities and perhaps threats to tour operators. They have facilitated the distribution of electronic brochures and booking forms to both travel trade partners and consumers taking advantage of multimedia presentations about tourism destinations and packages.

9.4.1 Internal systems and intranets

Intranets offer strategic and operational tools for tour operators to coordinate their departments and to improve their internal efficiency. Similarly to principals, tour operators need to manage their inventory. This is particularly important for products that they have pre-purchased, which normally include charter flight seats and accommodation contracted on commitment. Being able to maximize the occupancy on all pre-purchased inventory is critical for the profitability of the tour operator. Products purchased as part of **allotment** contracts or on allocation also need to be managed in order to support tour operators in maximizing their yield. Monitoring performance per travel agency, market target, region, airport catchment area as well as resort, principal, destination, employee etc. will also assist tour operators to maximize their efficiency, to address problems systematically and early enough and to reward high performance and achievement. More importantly, this information provides the basis for longer-term strategic decisions and ultimately determines the focus of tour operators' business. Case Study 9.1 provides an example of such integrated systems for tour operators.

In addition, tour operators need to manage their operations in all resorts where they send holiday makers. As the actual delivery of the product takes place at the destination, a number of tour operators' employees are based there.

Case Study 9.1

Anite's PowerRes system

PowerRes is a fully integrated reservation, ticketing, marketing, administration and accounting system designed to meet the specific business needs of tour operators and airline consolidators. Based on open technology, PowerRes provides integrated functionality, distribution capabilities and connectivity to a third-party reservations system. It is used by traditional package tour operators, consolidators, tailor-made and long-haul specialists. The system is also used by charter and scheduled flight-only operators, city-break, fly-drive, ski, diving, adventure and escorted tour holiday operators. In-house users can access the system using either the traditional character-based screens or a browser front-end specifically tailored and branded for each individual client. Customers implementing the browser interface can present their users with the opportunity to switch between displays, enabling them to use the character-based display or the browser-based presentation.

As tour operators should provide access to real-time inventory over every channel of distribution, PowerRes enables operators to significantly reduce costs through on-line distribution. This includes a move from traditional travel agent technology, such as viewdata and GDS, to an agent-based Internet model. The system can also be used in all the traditional channels to distribute travel products, and represents a platform specifically designed to allow clients to take advantage of new distribution channels. These include:

- in-house call centres;
- external call centres (using browser technology);
- Internet booking system (consumer and agent sites);
- XML-based messaging for integration into emerging distribution channels;
- viewdata/videotext.

The system provides a comprehensive integrated accounting suite by enabling clients to get a much closer financial control of their business through integrated accounting functionality. Benefits include immediate booking profitability, strict cost control, multi-currency purchase ledger, comprehensive reporting and operational monitoring through simplified month-end procedures. Anite continually enhances and improves the functionality of the system to help its customers to reduce costs wherever possible. A continual programme of process review and optimization is also employed to identify any opportunity for improvements in efficiency.

For more information, see **www.anitesystems.co.uk**

Questions

- What is the future of videotext technology, and what are the factors that prevent it from being replaced?
- How can tour operators integrate their operations through ICTs?

Coordination and exchange of timely information are critical for them being able to coordinate activities, ensure that customer requirements are communicated to all principals delivering the tourism product and for resolving potential problems. The ability of tour operators' employees to communicate with their head office or other parts of their organization is often critical for the performance of the operator, customer satisfaction and relationship with partners. A delayed flight, for example, can aggravate holiday makers, who will reasonably demand regular updates and also the opportunity to remain at the destination for longer, rather than wait at an airport. Efficient communication with the head office is critical for representatives to be able to update all people involved and organize emergency plans such as extension of check-out times, extra meals and alternative transfer timetables. As tour operators' products are based on human interaction between holiday makers (who often feel vulnerable away from home) and principals (based on a multi-cultural environment), employees overseas require constant interaction based on information and agility. Success in dealing with the constantly changing external environment can be rewarding for tour operators. Failure can create customer dissatisfaction, raise requests for compensations and refunds, and damage relationships with partners. Hence, ICTs provide critical tools for the operations of tour operators.

Tour operators also need to manage all their business functions, such as accounting, finance, human resources, marketing and sales etc. In an industry that is characterized by tiny profit margins, dynamic and volatile international environment, very high labour turnover and currency fluctuations, being able to manage business functions electronically is of paramount importance. Financial management needs to ensure that foreign currency is purchased at the right price to maximize profitability (Moon, 1994). In addition, tour operators experience a very high level of labour turnover, especially as far as overseas representatives are concerned. Hence, being able to recruit staff on-line and to use ICTs for training purposes are significant. Controlling all internal resources, such as inventory, labour force and assets, requires advanced ICTs. This is particularly the case for larger tour operators working in a multi-national environment.

9.4.2 Interconnecting partner systems and extranets

The development of extranets between tour operators and travel agencies as well as hotels and other suppliers is critical for their operations. Developing seamless systems that enable tour operators to communicate with all their partners is critical for the efficiency and effectiveness of the entire value chain. Electronic transactions of bookings, invoices, rooming lists, manifests and other documents help tour operators to digitalize all their dealings with their suppliers and customers and to ensure that all the routine transactions are undertaken through automated procedures. Technological developments are driven by tour operators themselves as well as by technology suppliers who seek to increase the value added to their customers. For example, Imminus in the UK promotes an electronic commerce platform that integrates the front-end applications with the back office procedures, not only for tour operators but for all the partners involved in transactions (Edwards et al., 1998; Jewell et al., 1999).

The dominance of *videotext systems* in the UK leisure travel market means that many tour operators still support low-technology viewdata traffic. Despite attempts by key network providers to upgrade videotext to computer systems, communicating through their Internet protocol by developing their web-style travel trade portals (e.g. Telewest's is Endeavour and X-TANT's is Traveleye), a large percentage of retail travel agencies as well as tour operators has failed to upgrade their systems. These portals can combine a real-time booking capability with the 'added value' of useful information, while migrating to Internet protocol (IP) solutions will enable the systems to increase speed and make far more efficient use of the networks. However, the initial investment has acted as a major deterrent for many organizations. Tour operators have also feared that if they upgrade their systems they will be unable to communicate with travel agencies who do not have IP technology, and thus they will jeopardize bookings.

One of the most difficult issues in developing successful electronic interoperability between systems is *standardization*. As there is a wide range of systems available in the marketplace, it is difficult for tour operators (and all other tourism organizations) to develop fully functional links with each of these entities. Therefore they find it difficult to develop fully functional extranets that will enable them to undertake transactions on-line. There is a major business requirement therefore for standardization of system protocols and interfaces, which will empower systems to function seamlessly. The Extensible Markup Language (**XML**) and the Internet provide an opportunity for the travel industry to communicate across multiple channels using a common language; this can also expedite the flow of information and facilitate transactions. Developing common specifications provides a standard format for exchanging data between and among travellers and travel-related businesses. These specifications encourage development of interoperable systems that can help create and promote new collections of travel services. Moreover, supporting commonly accepted communication processes, by using well-accepted Internet standards such as XML, can assist the tourism industry to transform into a global marketplace, where all key players will be able to interconnect and trade their products and services. The European Commission aims at encouraging the interoperability and interconnectivity of tourism systems. One of the major European Commission projects therefore in the tourism area leads these developments, as illustrated in Case Study 9.2. In addition, a number of initiatives have emerged in the industry to instigate standardization, including the Open Travel Alliance, the Hospitality Industry Technology Integration Standard (HITIS), and others. Most of these initiatives will be critical for the travel industry to take full advantage of the near-universal access to the Internet and also for developing their extranet provision. Ultimately, tour operators will require their partners to use open systems that will allow them to 'plug and play', enabling flexible and seamless interaction and transactions.

Strategically extranets and ICTs also play a critical role for tour operators. Vertically integrated travel organizations that own both travel agency and tour operator businesses often use information from retailers for *market intelligence* as a basis for strategic decisions, such as mergers and acquisitions as well as hostile take-overs of retail units. They also use data for forecasting market trends and to adjust their offerings according to demand fluctuations or preferences. By being able to access up-to-date information on a number of key indicators such as bookings, average expenditure, preferred products and destinations from their retail outlets as well as from their competitors, they can support their decision-making processes.

Case Study 9.2

The European Commission Harmonise project

The tourism industry essentially is an information business in which data interoperability exchange is necessary to create a more dynamic market and to foster cooperation. The absence of a widely adopted methodological and technological standard in European tourism hampers the efficient B2B exchange of information. Indeed, many substantial participants in the fragmented tourism industry have developed or currently develop their own system or standards. Harmonise, in coordination with other initiatives and with the involvement of international tourism organizations (ETC, IFITT, NTOs etc.), aims at establishing bridges between existing and emerging on-line marketplaces. This project will enable these marketplaces to cooperate with each other, and will create the necessary conditions for a new European marketplace.

Harmonise, in order to reach interoperability, will allow the reconciliation of different standards moving to XML, providing a reconciliation and mediation tool between different standards and providing the minimum ontology to formally describe the domain of reference. This reconciliation tool will support the harmonization of semantic and technological differences existing among data structures, which will allow providers and users to communicate, while keeping their proprietary data formats. That is, individuals in the market will be able to 'move' from one standard to another without having to change their technological architecture. The ontology provides a shared and common understanding of a domain that can be communicated between people and across application systems. This is a key asset in information exchange. Harmonise will bring together the different market participants and domain experts to ensure a broad acceptance of the reference model, creating an interoperable network of information systems and services. Therefore, Harmonise will set up, within six months from inception, the Tourism Harmonization Network (THN), which major tourism experts and the major standard owners will be invited to enter taking the role of external participant, along with Harmonise partnership.

The Harmonise mission

The Harmonise mission is to eliminate the gap between technology evolution and market needs, as well as eliminate the interoperability gap still existing in the European tourism market, allowing enterprises to interoperate with different operators using different industry standards. In this way, it empowers small and mid-size tourism enterprises entering the European tourism market, giving to 'big' players the opportunity to enter growing and high-quality local tourism markets. This will reinforce the integration process of the tourism sector, fostered by the European Commission (EC).

The Harmonise approach is based on some key elements:

- identification of the relevant tourism standards, analysing their contents (Ontology) and their underlying methodologies (Meta Ontology);
- supporting the integration of the main tourism standard owners, promoting a consensus process among them (Tourism Harmonization Network);
- definition of an Integrated Meta Ontology (IM), containing an agreed kernel of modelling constructs;
- definition of an Interoperable Minimum Harmonization Ontology (IMHO); that is, a minimum set of concepts defined according to the IM;

■ definition of a method of modelling that allows each provider to describe its offering (based on XML); definition of a set of reconciliation rules (based on XML technology, e.g. XSLT or RDF) and a reconciliation engine (obtained as the sum of the reconciliation rules and the standard browser functions).

Harmonise will develop a data mediator approach to solve the interoperability problem. A data mediator is a computer program that translates data between two systems with different data schemas. The difference between this mediator and other approaches is that the mediator automatically generates data translations from descriptions of the data in the source and the receiver schemas. This approach depends on a shared, conceptual reference schema, the ontology of the domain.

The Harmonise approach is based on four technological key elements:

1. A common minimum ontology (IMHO).
2. A modelling method to allow each service provider to describe its offerings (based on XML), according to the concepts specified in the IMHO.
3. A set of reconciliation rules (based on XML technology).
4. A reconciliation engine/tool (obtained as the sum of the reconciliation rules and the standard browser functions).

Interoperable Minimum Harmonization Ontology (IMHO)

An ontology represents a shared understanding of some domain of interest (the way we see the world). It is organized as a domain vocabulary; that is, a set of terms (for relevant concepts in the domain) with their definitions, enriched with a set of semantic relationships (e.g. generalization and specialization, or part-of and has-part). An ontology provides a shared understanding of a domain that can be communicated between people and across application systems and it becomes something vital, a key asset in information exchange. The goal of an ontology is to reduce conceptual and terminological confusion. The construction of the Harmonise ontology will start with the identification of the relevant standards that have been proposed within the tourism domain, and analysis of their contents (ontologies) and their underlying methodologies (meta ontologies). In this way it will be possible to analyse, compare and evaluate the differences and similarities among standards, and to create an exhaustive classification of them. This method will expose the overlapping and conflicting concepts. The next step will be the definition of an Integrated Meta Ontology (IM), containing an agreed kernel of modelling constructs. Then an Interoperable Minimum Harmonization Ontology (IMHO), a minimum set of concepts defined according to the IM, will be established. It will provide definitions for general-purpose terms and a structure for compliant lower-level domain ontology. Therefore, the IMHO will be developed to provide the base for the mapping/reconciliation tools. In other words, it will be followed by an approach to services, data and events that will allow providers and users to move from one standard to another. This open-source mapping/reconciliation tool will not require any changes in the existing technological architectures.

The modelling method and reconciliation rules

The proposed harmonization method will avoid any restructuring or re-implementation of existing systems/standards. However, if a TIS (Tourism Information System) wants to enter the 'harmonization space' and to cooperate with another TIS, it needs to acquire the IMHO and evaluate the 'distance' between the system and the harmonization ontology.

Case Study 9.2 *continued*

This distance will be bridged by a number of reconciliation rules, to be constructed in accordance with the Harmonise methodology. Once a TIS has been 'harmonized', it can enter the 'harmonized space' and freely cooperate with the other players in such a space. At system level, the cooperation will take place by using XML technology to encode information to be exchanged.

Reconciliation tool

In order to reach interoperability, Harmonise will create a reconciliation tool that will enable communication between partners. This will allow them to keep their specific standard and proprietary data formats and simultaneously allow interaction among them, acting as a mediator module between the different tourism data provided in the market. This open tool will not be mandatory but will be the only one able to cope with different existing standards and to create a mapping among them, without imposing constraints. The mapping/reconciliation tool will follow an open source licence, which will result in highly reliable software that evolves more rapidly and is 'reviewed' by a large community of developers. This approach will assure complete reliability and advanced features with a low overhead development cost. This reconciliation tool will give to the user and end-user new entries, the chance to decrease their dependency from key actors (and their standards) and the chance to operate better in the imperfect tourism market.

The Harmonise project, developing a data mediation approach for the interoperability of TISs and mediating the data standardization process, will supply the missing parts of the solution towards system interoperability. This approach will provide a flexible, cost-effective mechanism for satisfying the information exchange requirements of all types of TIS, giving access to the next level of information sharing for the service providers of the European tourism market.

Source: Based on discussions with Harmonise Project Coordinator Hannes Werthner and **www.harmonise.org**

Questions

- Why is interoperability critical for tour operators?
- Explain how interoperability can enhance the competitive advantage of tour operators.
- Who are the key actors that tour operators would like to enhance their interoperability with, and what are the main factors for success?

9.4.3 Connecting with all stakeholders through the Internet

The Internet also provides unparalleled opportunities for tour operators to research destinations and develop their products on-line. Using the Internet as a database, tour operators can access information on local products, design packages and provide much better information for product managers and contracting employees. In addition they can enrich their products by offering a whole range of additional value-added services such as financial and loan facilities, weather forecasts, shopping opportunities etc. (Marcussen, 2000).

In addition, being able to *interact closely with consumers*, tour operators have the opportunity to understand the needs of their clients better, to alter elements of the marketing mix according to the market conditions and to improve the level of flexibility they offer. In addition they can demonstrate pictures and videos of accommodation and they can offer opinions of previous customers as well as many more added-value services. Tapestry Holidays (Case Study 9.3) has developed such a website. Kuoni allows consumers to alter their tourism packages on-line and to build their own itineraries by making it possible to extend the trip, change accommodation, meal plans and add value-added services such as car rentals, scuba diving lessons etc. By enabling consumers to search by the brochure reference, Kuoni also strengthens its off-line and on-line marketing drive. Often consumers are willing to pay a premium for customized products with a greater degree of flexibility, and tour operators who facilitate this process will gain considerable benefits.

Larger tour operators increasingly realize that they need to address the needs of particular market segments and *niche markets*. In particular, activity holidays such as skiing, diving, parachuting etc. have been neglected by all major tour operators. The practicalities and economics of developing specialized brochures and distributing them through travel agencies have been prohibiting them for doing

Case Study 9.3

Tapestry Holidays offers a virtual tour on its website

Tapestry Holidays, a small tour operator specializing in Greece and Turkey, introduced its website in 2000. The site aimed at improving and personalizing service for their loyal guests (approximately 60 per cent of whom have travelled with them previously). Marketing research has demonstrated that the more information Tapestry provided before guests' departure, the better chances they had to increase customer satisfaction. The website enabled them to introduce a room-by-room booking service allowing consumers to select individual rooms. A natural progression of this service was to provide as many visual references as possible. The operator developed the site further to provide as many images of each and every room, as well as the view from each balcony, as has been practical to collate. In addition, they developed 360° panoramic images from various points within almost all the properties featured and several destination regions too. It also includes a search engine locating destinations according to criteria, comments from previous customers for each property as well as a loyalty card scheme. Together with many other features, the website provides the easiest means to discover at a glance all the new properties and ideas incorporated in the brochures. In addition, the operator has launched a separate web page for Travel agencies (**www.tapestryagents.com**), which omits all contact details in order to support their sales and at the same time to avoid an antagonistic relationship.

For more information, see **tapestryholidays.com**

Questions

- How can tour operators use the Internet effectively for promoting packages?
- What will be the main contribution of digital television to the tour operating industry?
- Can/should tour operators bypass travel agencies by using ICTs?

so. However, the Internet enables them to gradually develop web pages specializing in these particular market segments. The World of TUI in Case Study 9.4 demonstrates many of the above points and how TUI and Thomson are gradually specializing their product to attract particular market segments.

The Internet has also proved particularly significant for *smaller and specialist operators*. Smaller operators have been experiencing difficulty in accessing consumers through the vertically integrated travel agencies as they have frequently refused to rack their brochures and facilitate bookings. Smaller operators have traditionally had a very loyal clientèle and their main promotional support was word of mouth from satisfied clients. Most small operators have established their Internet presence and to the degree that they have developed differentiated products and provide considerable value they have been able to expand their markets and to attract clients from markets that were previously inaccessible. For example, specialized operators offering unique holiday themes, such as big game safari, whale, dolphin and polar bear watching, ornithological tours and elephant treks, frequently attract interest from international customers and are able to expand their global operations. Being able to bring together resources through the Association of Independent Tour Operators (www.aito.co.uk) enables them to develop their virtual size and to combine forces in order to cover a bigger range of holidays, regions and activities.

Eventually ICTs can assist tour operators to reduce the costs involved in *brochure* printing and distribution (estimated to be about 5 per cent of the package cost or £25 per package sold). Brochure costs are a massive financial burden on operators, one that they are continually seeking to reduce. Perhaps more importantly, only 50 per cent of the brochures printed reach consumers, as they frequently become out of date and have to be disregarded. Dynamic pricing may also mean that prices may no longer be printed in brochures; they may only be offered on-line to reflect the changes as well as the demand and supply in the marketplace. Adventure tour operator, First48, is the first tour operator in the UK or USA to have stopped producing brochures, concentrating solely on producing a good website (www.first48.com). First48 is still happy to take bookings from agents but it is not concerned about having its brochures racked. However as people inherently like to browse paper-based information, perhaps generic brochures will be replaced by individualized virtual brochures. A smaller and tailor-made brochure specific to customer requirements could perhaps be made available electronically or as a print-out. This would allow a customer walking into a travel agency to find, for example, a holiday in a 4-star hotel in Majorca and walk out with a 10- or 20-page brochure, rather than five 100-page brochures with a whole raft of holidays that are of no interest. This would entail agents being able to download brochure content through broadband network access and high-speed colour printers to produce a brochure quickly for a waiting customer. However, the cost in equipment, time and change management of such developments may discourage both travel agencies and tour operators from going down that route. As consumers get used to searching for travel on the Internet and digital TV, operators are expected to divert funds from brochure production to these channels. Fewer brochures will therefore be made available to travel agents and more operators are likely to follow First48's lead (Richer, 2000).

Case Study 9.4

Thomson and World of TUI on-line in the UK

Thomson recently launched a fully functional Internet presence allowing consumers to search and book holidays on-line. The UK's number-one holiday company has revamped its direct booking service to offer customers unique access to a range of expert, convenient information that is tailor-made for their holiday needs. Holiday makers have exclusive access to the opinions of others who have visited their resort via customers' satisfaction scores. This covers everything from food to accommodation, to location, to entertainment. The insiders' information is revised every season so all details are completely up to date. Thomson Holidays is also reassessing its package design by rejecting the 'one size fits all' package holiday to provide more tailor-made experiences for every individual. A direct booking telephone service supports the web page and reflects their approach, offering holiday makers a friendly, personal and expert information service so they can make exactly the right choice for them. A number of specialized websites have also be launched for particular market segments, including skiers, snowboarders and 'free-stylers'. Links to other TUI UK sites include:

URL	Brand properties
www.thomson.co.uk	Thomson's on-line booking and information
www.portland-direct.co.uk	The UK's number-one direct holiday company – on-line booking available
www.just.co.uk	Just a holiday and that's it. The Med, Canaries, long-haul and Florida Flydrive
www.clubfreestyle.co.uk	Club Freestyle is about independence and the desire to get out there and do it!
www.thomson-snowboarding.com	Thomson is the UK's leading snowboarding operator with more learn-to-ride packages than anyone else
www.thomson-ski.com	View every single one of the resorts featured on the website
www.thomsonlakesandmountains.com	Fresh air, relaxation and a world of choice with the UK's no. 1 in lakes and mountains
www.thomsonbreakaway.co.uk	Cities and short breaks – for specialist knowledge and expert advice
www.lunnpoly.com	The UK's number-one travel agent for last-minute deals, cheap flights and holiday packages
www.skydeals.co.uk	Thousands of flights on one site, from cheap tickets to first-class airfares. Book your tickets on-line
www.britanniaairways.com	Britannia Airways

For more information, see **www.thomson.co.uk** and **www.tui.com**

Questions

- How can tour operators differentiate their products through ICTs?
- What should tour operators do to maintain brand integrity through their on-line presence?
- Discuss whether ICTs reduce or increase the negotiation power of tour operators with suppliers.

9.5 Disintermediation vs re-intermediation for tour operators

Internet developments illustrate two major trends: on the one hand, tour operators aim to disintermediate travel agencies, and on the other, tour operators are threatened with disintermediation themselves. Ultimately, the more players in the distribution channel, the more commissions and fees need to be generated, increasing the price of the final product. Organizations have been trying for years to reduce the dependency on partners to promote their products and ICTs offer suitable tools for that to happen.

The Internet provides the tools for tour operators to communicate directly with consumers and to target specific specialized and niche markets. This allows tour operators to bypass travel agencies and to promote holidays directly to consumers, making significant savings on commissions paid to travel agencies (which tend to vary between 10 and 18 per cent), as well as reducing the costs of incentives, bonus and educational trips for retailers. Thus, a significant proportion

---

Case Study 9.5

On-line and eCommerce for tour operators in Scandinavia

Sweden's Fritidsresor tour operator web page, **www.fritidsresor.se**, represents 6 per cent of total Internet sales turnover in Sweden during 2001. Fritidresor belongs to the World of TUI. By comparison, all Sweden's mail-order firms represent 10 per cent of total turnover. fritidsresor.se sells 15 per cent of the total volume of tour operator inventory in Sweden. Gran Canaria, Tenerife and Cyprus are the top-three booked destinations via the site. Additional resources will be added soon. New web-based information films will be presented on the site. First to be presented are Gran Canaria, Tenerife and Lanzarote. Sister company star tour.no sells 9 per cent of the total volume in Norway while fritidsresor.fi and finnmatkat.fi represent 17 per cent of the total volume in Finland. Top tour operator brands have gradually reached 20 per cent of sales through the web in the Nordic region. The annual turnover is over 100 million Euros, probably making on-line sales of tour packages the biggest eCommerce operation in the Nordic area.

There are many benefits of on-line distribution. Internet selling systems create an effective sales channel that is additional to the well-established ones. The cost including development, marketing and discounting is less than 3 per cent, in comparison to the average distribution cost in normal channels of 6 per cent. Once the system has been developed the cost of incremental sales is close to zero and currently less than 0.5 per cent. Web sales are by far the cheapest channel when threshold volume is achieved. However, brand is important for driving volumes and giving reassurance, and therefore click-and-mortal strategies are more successful.

Source: Based on Holst (2001). For more information, see **www.fritidsresor.se**

Questions

- What are the factors that determine the level of purchasing of packages on-line?
- What are the opportunities for decompartmentalization of package tours as a result of ICTs?

(about 20 per cent) of the package price can be saved when the development and distribution costs of electronic brochures are deducted. As demonstrated in Case study 9.5, the cost of developing the Internet presence is considerable, but once the web page is developed and established the marginal/incremental cost per sale and inquiry is minimal. This can be offered to the public in order to achieve cost advantage or to increase tour operators' profit margin. However in Chapter 10, we explore the forces for and against their disintermediation.

Tour operators are also threatened with disintermediation, as the Internet enables consumers and travel agencies to build their own personalized packages and purchase them on-line. Figure 9.1 demonstrates a number of arguments for and against the disintermediation of tour operators from the distribution channel. Most of the arguments refer to large and vertically integrated operators, rather than small and specialized ones. However, it is quite evident that tour operators will need to shift their focus from information provision and the reservation mechanism to a more strategic role of adding value to the product and the

Figure 9.1 Arguments for and against the disintermediation of tour operators

Arguments for the disintermediation of tour operators	Arguments against the disintermediation of tour operators
■ Tour operators add little value to the tourism product, as they act primarily as aggregators	■ Tour operators offer professional travel services and develop tourism packages by aggregating packages from disparate services, offered by individual principals
■ Tour operators manage information and package products in a unified and mass approach	■ Many holidays allow a degree of flexibility and are sometimes themed
■ Tour operators often 'pile products high and sell cheap', often at the expense of quality	■ Tour operators develop packages based on extensive research and experience
■ Often tour operators operate in environmentally downgraded areas and contribute to the mass development of resorts	■ Tour operators manage to reduce the total price of the packages by operating charter airlines and by negotiating prices with principals
■ Ultimately principals have the responsibility for serving tourism products	■ The Internet is still inadequate and unreliable, especially for destination-naive or inexperienced travellers
■ Tour operators often offer biased advice and direct consumers to principals who offer override commissions and higher profit margins or to in-house companies	■ It is difficult and riskier to organize holidays for people with health problems or with young families
■ Experienced travellers are much more knowledgeable than many tour operators and now have the ability to research and develop individualized packages for their needs	■ Tour operators offer representatives that speak the local language and can deal with the local conditions
■ Tourism packages are often not inexpensive, as tour operators need to add administration and marketing costs	■ A large part of the market is computer-illiterate
■ Often the terms and conditions of packages are unfavourable for consumers and principals	■ Tour operators reduce the insecurity of travel, as they are responsible for all arrangements and can compensate consumers should products fail to reach specifications
■ There is an increase for demand of independent holidays, especially by young, experienced and educated travellers	
■ Technology enables consumers to undertake most functions from the convenience of their armchair	
■ The re-engineering of the tourism industry and particularly the development of no-frills airlines facilitates disintermediation	

process. Different market segments will have dissimilar requirements. For example, younger and experienced travellers will probably be looking for better value added through negotiated rates or for themed packages for niche markets. Older generations and people who travel infrequently may require a larger degree of comfort and assistance during the trip.

Tour operators, therefore, will need to reassess their core values and identify specific market segments that they will be able to satisfy in future. It seems that eventually there will be two distinctive forms of tour operators: on the one hand, multinational, large and vertical integrated organizations will take advantage of economies of scale, wide distribution and a global network. On the other hand, small, niche and differentiated operators will be concentrating on a particular region, theme or activity and will be attracting niche markets with particular interests. Inevitably the former type will be based on a high-volume, low-profit-margin strategy and the latter on a low-volume and high-profit-margin strategy.

Nevertheless an ICT plan, driven by the marketing strategy, should support operators regardless of their type to develop tools, such as customer relationship management, in order to develop interactivity with clients and to adopt proactive and reactive mechanisms in the marketplace. Understanding the entire range of distribution channels and strategies and capitalizing on new technologies such as interactive digital television will be crucial for tour operators who wish to remain competitive in the future.

9.6 Lessons and issues for the future of tour operators

Until recently tour operators tended to be reluctant to focus on ICTs for their operational planning and management. Few of them seemed to realize the radical changes in ICTs as well as the paradigm shift experienced in the tourism industry. They tended to regard ICTs exclusively as facilitators of their current operations, since efficient technology reduces certain administration costs. Legacy systems dominated their operations and they virtually ignored the strategic significance of the Internet developments (Kärcher, 1997; Edwards et al., 1998). There was little evidence of them actively seeking to develop tools to position themselves in the emerging tourism marketplace. This is attributed to the small scale and limited scope for smaller operators, as well as the cost orientation and reluctance to invest in 'unnecessary technology' by larger ones. In addition, they were reluctant to upset travel agencies by developing direct channels of communication with consumers. Thus, they seemed to ignore the potential long-term strategic benefits that could assist them to maintain their position in the new era of tourism.

However, since early 2000 a wide range of initiatives have emerged, demonstrating a change of direction for many operators. This change is attributed to a number of issues. Firstly, the further concentration of the tour operating business, in particular following the acquisition of Thomson by TUI/Preussag (Bywater, 2001), demonstrated that tour operators become global businesses with assets that need close management, and as a result ICTs will be critical in the future.

Secondly, the announcement in May 2000 of Airtours' eCommerce strategy and the launch of www.mytravelco.com made a considerable impact in the industry. Airtours' eCommerce strategy pledged to establish a holistic approach, which integrated distribution and customer relationship management with appropriate content and product. The strategy encompassed the multitude of distribution channels, which consumers may access to buy holidays and travel products, including interactive TV, mobile technology, the Internet, call centres and the high street. Airtours also announced that one of mytravelco's unique features was its ability to personalize the experience for every user regardless of channel. This feature could enable Airtours to target product and value-added services to its customers based on their individual preferences. Several months later Airtours rebranded itself as MyTravel Group plc, demonstrating that its on-line strategy was gaining a central role. This particular initiative forced many of its competitors to rethink their ICT strategies.

It is becoming increasingly evident that only very large vertically integrated groups and small, niche, specialized and personalized operators will be able to survive in the future. In the first case ICTs are critical for coordinating all aspects of the business for each strategic business unit and for developing interactivity with partners, suppliers and customers. Smaller operators already depend on the Internet for their presence, promotion and marketing, as they find it difficult to penetrate the market through vertically integrated travel agencies. Being able to promote specialized travel products allows them to expand their catchment area and also to collaborate with other operators in order to cover more types of holidays and regions globally.

9.7 Conclusions

To the degree that ICTs will determine the competitiveness of tour operating in the future, a wide range of changes is anticipated in business practices and roles in the future tourism distribution channel. The leadership and power of major tour operators may be challenged, should other members of the channel or newcomers utilize the newly available ICTs more effectively to reach and attract consumers. Consumers are also able to acquire information and build their own packages by accumulating individual elements on the Internet. Therefore tour operators will need to re-examine their core products and to develop suitable solutions to ensure that their packages offer value for money and time. Although a partial disintermediation seems inevitable, there will always be sufficient market share for tour operators who can add value to the tourism product and deliver innovative, personalized and competitive holiday packages. Hence, innovative tour operators will be able to take advantage of the emerging ICTs and establish interactive platforms for their partners and customers. Adopting a multi-channel strategy will also support promotion and trade of tourism products on the Internet, mobile devices and digital television. It is anticipated that digital television will replace, to a certain extent, the significance of the brochure as it will enable tour operators to provide multimedia content about destinations and tourism products. This will empower them to add value, maximize their efficiency and expand their market base. The development of new electronic intermediaries and portals, based on value-added products and supported by ICTs, will perhaps assist tour operators to take a major part in the re-intermediation of the distribution channel.

Chapter questions

1 Why are ICTs critical for the operational management of tour operators?

2 What key technologies are used by tour operators?

3 Why do different types of tour operators have different ICT needs and requirements?

4 Why do tour operators still support videotext-based solutions?

5 Explore why standardization and interoperability are more critical for tour operators than other tourism actors.

6 Explain why tour operators need to be integrated for supporting their operational management.

7 How can tour operators of the future take advantage of ICTs strategically?

8 What is a multi-channel strategy, and how can it be beneficial for a tour operator?

9 What are the advantages and disadvantages of a multi-channel strategy?

10 Explore the impacts of interactive digital television for tour operators.

11 How does the concentration of European tour operators influence their ICT requirements?

12 How can small tour operators take advantage of the Internet?

13 What strategies should be followed for medium-sized tour operators?

Further reading

Bennett, M. and Radburn, M. (1991) Information technology in tourism: the impact on the industry and supply of holidays, in Sinclair, T. and Stabler, M. (eds), *The Tourism Industry: An International Analysis*, CAB International, Oxford, pp. 45–67.

Buhalis, D. and Laws, E. (2001) *Tourism Distribution Channels*, Continuum, London.

Bywater, M. (2001) Travel distribution: who owns whom in the European travel distribution industry, in Buhalis, D. and Laws, E. (eds), *Tourism Distribution Channels*, Continuum, London.

Edwards, G., Dawes, C. and Kärcher, K. (1998) The Imminus travel and tourism intranet, in Buhalis, D., Tjoa, A.M. and Jafari, J. (eds), *Information and Communications Technologies in Tourism*, ENTER 1998 Proceedings, Springer-Verlag, Vienna, pp. 190–201.

Inkpen, G. (1998) *Information Technology for Travel and Tourism*, 2nd edn, Addison Wesley Longman, London.

Kärcher, K. (1997) *Reinventing the Package Holiday Business: New Information and Telecommunications Technologies*, DeutscherUniversitatsVerlag, Gabler, Germany.

Marcussen, C. (2000) Tour operators in Scandinavia and Finland on the Net: a European perspective, *Anatolia*, **11**(1), pp. 6–21.

Moon, D. (1994) Deployment of computer networks in leisure packaged tour marketing in the USA, *Journal of Vacation Marketing*, **1**(1), 43–60.

Websites

Tour Operators Directory: **www.travelgate.co.uk**
Association of Independent Tour Operators: **www.aito.co.uk**
Federation of Tour Operators: **www.fto.co.uk**
European Tour Operators Association: **www.etoa.org**

Tour operators

TUI: **www.tui.com**
Thomson: **www.thomson.com**
Airtours: **www.airtours.co.uk**
Bridge Travel Services: **www.bridgetravel.co.uk**
Cosmos: **www.cosmos-holidays.co.uk**
Cresta: **www.crestaholidays.co.uk**
Crystal Holidays: **www.crystalholidays.co.uk**
Kuoni: **www.kuoni.co.uk**
Olympic Holidays: **www.olympicholidays.co.uk**
Sunvil: **www.sunvil.co.uk**
Kirker: **www.kirkerholidays.com**
KeyCamp: **www.keycamp.co.uk**

Specialist holidays for skiers

Iglu: **www.iglu.com**
Complete Skier: **www.complete-skier.com**
Ski Chalets: **www.skichalets.com**
I Ski: **www.iski.com**

Standardization and interconnectivity issues

www.harmonise.org
www.opentravel.org
www.hitis.org

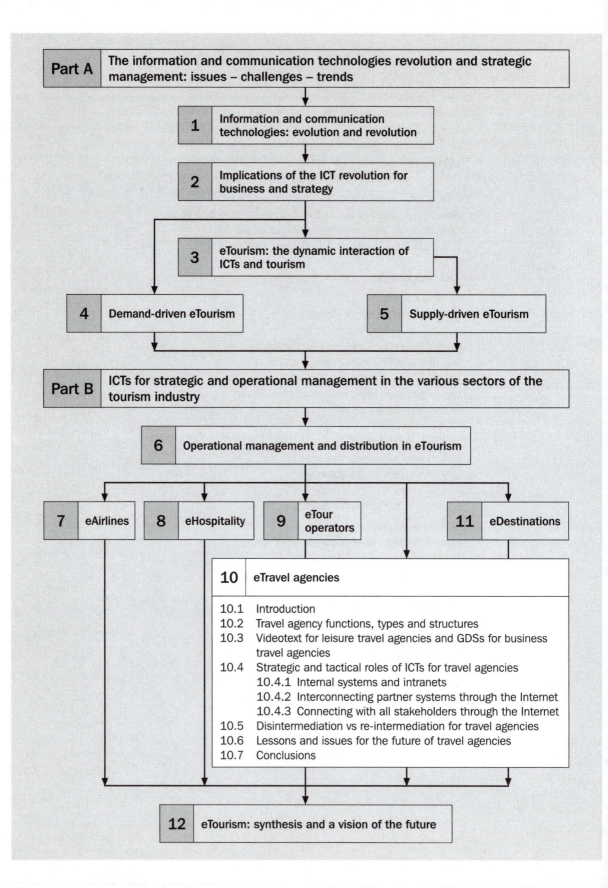

10

eTravel agencies

Chapter objectives

Travel agencies are the main distributors of the tourism product. The purpose of this chapter is to explain the role of ICTs in travel agencies and to illustrate the opportunities and challenges emerging. The chapter examines the different types of travel agencies and explores their ICT utilization. ICTs have revolutionized the role of travel agencies and this chapter demonstrates that the new tools are prompting them to redesign their function. The chapter examines the threats for disintermediation of the travel agencies and the opportunities for re-intermediation. Thus, the learning objectives may be defined as:

- Explore how technology has changed the travel agency function
- Illustrate the strategic and tactical aspects of ICT utilization in travel agencies
- Demonstrate the key technology applications as well as the main software used for their operations
- Understand the sources of travel agency competitiveness and illustrate how ICTs support the strategic and operational functions
- Demonstrate how travel agencies use ICTs for communications and bookings
- Explain the importance of integrating intranet, extranet and Internet applications
- Discuss the issues related to disintermediation and re-intermediation in the distribution channel
- Debate the key issues for the future of travel agencies and the role of ICTs

10.1 Introduction

Outgoing travel agencies often act as an interface between the tourism industry and outbound consumers. A clear distinction between inbound and outbound agencies is made here, although agencies in several countries are likely to undertake both activities. Holloway (1989) suggests that 'the main role of agents is to provide a convenient location for the purchase of travel. At the locations they act as booking agents for holidays and travel, as well as a source of information and advice on travel services. Their customers look to them for expert product knowledge and objectivity in the advice offered'. In addition, outgoing travel agencies provide ancillary travel services such as travellers cheques, foreign currency, provision of passports and visas, as well as travel insurance (Beaver, 1993; Renshaw, 1992). Retail travel agencies are essentially intermediaries who serve as sales outlets for tourism principals and wholesalers. As such, they do not own the services and cannot stock travel products. Instead, they only stock travel information in the form of brochures, leaflets and data, as well as calling on the personal expertise of travel consultants. Consequently, agencies carry limited financial risk, as they do not purchase tourism products in advance. They only reserve/confirm/purchase/issue travel documents, i.e. tickets and vouchers, on customer request (Beaver, 1993).

ICTs provide a wide range of *tools for travel agencies*, by providing the mechanism for information exchange and tourism product distribution. ICTs enable agencies to build complicated travel itineraries in minutes, while providing up-to-date schedules, prices and availability data. The proliferation of CRSs and GDSs has also provided an effective reservation mechanism that helps travel agencies to get information, make reservations and issue travel documents for the entire range of tourism products, both efficiently and in a fraction of the time required by manual processes. Therefore travel agencies use ICTs to access tourism suppliers' databases, to verify availability and rates, and to confirm reservations (Sheldon, 1997; Inkpen, 1998).

10.2 Travel agency functions, types and structures

Outgoing travel agencies take part in several channel configurations. They are approached by prospective tourists (individual or group) who normally enquire about a very wide range of information, including rates, schedules, location, facilities and services, availability, booking procedures, issuing of tickets/vouchers, travel insurance, currency, transfers and travel formalities. Consumers may also ask for a recommendation for a forthcoming trip. Consequently, outgoing travel agencies need to search through their files/brochures/directories/databases/CRSs/GDSs/Internet in order to identify tourism products that satisfy consumers' particular needs and requirements. Outgoing travel agencies can sell individual tourism products or packages, while designing a customized product for customers' special needs, by contacting principals directly or **incoming tour operators** at destinations (Buhalis, 2001).

Outgoing travel agencies can be classified into numerous categories depending on several variables such as the geographical spread, size, type of business and appointment. A great degree of differentiation can be observed between outgoing travel agencies in various countries. Firstly, their geographical coverage of activity is a variable for classification to multinational, national, or regional outgoing travel agencies. Only a few outgoing travel agencies operate globally, and they are mainly business travel agencies such as American Express operating a network of franchisees. Secondly, they can be characterized as multiples (more than 100 retail outlets), mintiples (10–100 retail outlets), miniples (fewer than 10 retail outlets) or independents. Thirdly, a distinction between leisure and business outgoing travel agencies is essential in most countries, as they often serve totally different products and markets. Fourthly, outgoing travel agencies can be characterized according to the organization that has appointed them (Renshaw, 1992). It is estimated that about 40 000 outgoing travel agencies operate in Europe, while another 32 400 outgoing travel agencies function in the USA. The magnitude of this sub-sector is demonstrated by Smith and Jenner (1994), who suggest that over 200 000 people are employed in outgoing travel agencies, an average of six people per outlet, while a £50 billion combined annual turnover is estimated.

10.3 Videotext for leisure travel agencies and GDSs for business travel agencies

Travel agencies need to establish powerful tools for communicating with principals in order to build itineraries for their customers efficiently. They need to be able to complete an average transaction in 20–30 minutes if they are to make a profit. Therefore, travel agencies have been using ICTs for interacting with their partners. Although telephone communications still dominate the travel trade, fax, telex and computers have been widely used. The type of travel agency and its main clientele determine the type of technology it uses. Most travel agencies around the world operate some kind of a *reservation system*, mainly through videotext networks or/and GDSs, which enables them to check availability and make reservations for tourism products. Business travel agencies tend to use terminals, which give them access to search GDSs efficiently. Leisure travel agencies use a higher proportion of videotext systems, which allow them to connect with tour operators' databases and reservation systems. Many agencies that serve both the leisure and business markets often operate both GDS and videotext systems simultaneously.

Business-focused travel agencies mainly need to contact scheduled airlines and business/city hotels that are often operated by hotel chains. They therefore have GDS terminals that give them access to one or more of the major global distribution systems, namely SABRE, Worldspan, Galileo and Amadeus. The two former systems dominate travel agencies in America, while the latter two are the market leaders in Europe. GDS terminals provide travel agencies with access to a wealth of information about scheduled airlines, hotel chains, car rentals and a variety of ancillary services. Each GDS has several advantages and disadvantages depending on the location of the agency, volume of traffic, target markets and types of products. Most travel agencies subscribe to one GDS. There are several incentives for doing so, including minimum thresholds for maintaining equipment for free, as well as training and updating courses. Paradoxically smaller and independent travel agencies tend to subscribe to more reservation systems and thus increase their overheads. Smaller agencies tend to offer a wider range of tourism principals and information and therefore constantly compare prices and products across systems. Hence they need access to more than one network in order to provide a more comprehensive and personalized service for their clients, rather than to multiples, which tend to concentrate on the mass and standardized markets.

In contrast, leisure agencies use videotext networks primarily to access tour operators' databases, as well as for a wide range of other tourism products, including airline tickets. The establishment of videotext terminals and the familiarity of travel agencies with this technology has prompted other tourism suppliers, such as airlines, ferry operators, railways and travel insurance companies, to develop connections with these systems and benefit accordingly. Videotext systems are relatively inexpensive, require little staff training and expertise and are fairly reliable. However, they are slow to use and proprietary, as operators have to log in to one principal's database each time; they therefore have to re-enter all customer requirements for each database they access. It is estimated that 97 per cent of travel agencies in the UK have access to videotext, while an average of three sets per outlet is the norm (ABTECH, 1993).

Although many industry leaders have been challenging videotext technology for more than 10 years, there is a hard core of agencies and operators still using this technology. Despite offering inexpensive and relatively easy access to tour operators' and airlines' databases, it is increasingly recognized that videotext is a very slow, non-secure, unreliable and inflexible communication medium. They possess less sophisticated ticket issuing/back-office systems and they can suffer from slow connection. The reservation process is time-consuming, as every time a travel agent accesses another CRS to check availability, all travel requirements need to be retyped, slowing down their operation and causing consumer dissatisfaction. Hence, videotext-operated travel agencies under-utilize the available technology and jeopardize their efficiency. Moreover, videotext technology does not allow integration between front and back offices, and thus increases agencies' workload. There is an urgent need to replace the videotext sets with quicker and more reliable PC terminals, capable of supporting and integrating the operational, marketing and management functions of the travel business and also accessing the Internet. It is predicted that once major tour operators, such as Thomson, take the risk and disconnect videotext access and interactivity, travel agencies will be forced to move to more advanced IP-based systems. The efficiency improvements as well as the savings from the more efficient use of the networks are expected to compensate for the initial investment for this upgrade (Inkpen, 1998; Hitchins, 1991; Vaughan, 1995; Bennett, 1993).

10.4 Strategic and tactical roles of ICTs for travel agencies

Different types of travel agencies have different ICT requirements. Business agencies need to access information and reservation systems efficiently, as they often need to serve a market with dynamic and constantly changing needs. As business travellers often book their trips a short period before travelling and change their itineraries frequently, the ability to access information, build itineraries and issue tickets efficiently is critical for the competitiveness of agencies. Leisure travel agencies need to have access to a very wide range of information in order to support consumers at the 'inspire me' stage when they have not decided the destination, timing or budget of their holidays. Then they need to be able to undertake reservations on a wide range of products in order to fulfil customer requirements. In both cases, integration of the entire business is critical for the profitability of the organization. Being able to manage cash flow to ensure that commissions are paid on time and that employees can devote more of their time to customer care determines the productivity and ultimately the profitability of an agency. The more of these processes that can be supported through ICTs, the more tools travel agencies have to undertake for bookings and for coordinating their operations effectively and the more they can support their competitiveness.

10.4.1 Internal systems and intranets

ICTs introduced major improvements in the internal organization of travel agencies. Internal systems and intranets are instrumental in maximizing the efficiency of travel agency administration. By integrating their back office (e.g. accounting, commission monitoring, personnel) and front office (e.g. customers' history, itinerary development, ticketing and communication with suppliers) travel agencies have achieved significant synergies, efficiencies and cost savings. A number of commercial organizations have developed specialized software. Case Study 10.1 demonstrates the comprehensive Via Voyager travel agency solution, illustrating the range of solutions offered by these programs.

Multiple travel agencies in particular experience more benefits by facilitating branch control by their headquarters. As transactions made in branches can automatically be reported back to the head office, there is tighter financial control. In addition, transactions provide invaluable marketing research data, which can almost instantly report market movements and ameliorate tactical decisions. At the individual level, CRM systems support agencies tracking the activity of their clients and allow them to provide a customized service. At the regional level, information emerging from transactions can enable travel agencies to decide on expansion strategies, opening hours and appointment policies as well as the specialization or distribution mechanisms they may want to pursue. Hence, travel agencies increasingly rely on computerized systems not only to respond to travel inquiries but also to facilitate both their tactical and strategic management and marketing functions (Inkpen, 1998; Bennett, 1993; ABTECH, 1993).

Integrated systems based on Internet and intranet technologies can provide advanced technological solutions to manage and control travel procedures by

Case Study 10.1

Via Voyager travel agency solution

The Voyager system offers a comprehensive management tool for travel agencies. Via Voyager is the latest product offered by the company that is based on a Network Managed Solution (NMS). Via Voyager aims to provide the very best in technology available with an affordable cost that is so important in the travel industry due to ever-decreasing gross margins and continued discounts.

Via Voyager includes the following four modules:

- Voyager 2000: Retail Travel Agency Management System
- Corporate Traveller: Corporate Ticketing and Business House
- Travelbank: Bureau de Change
- Median–Central Control: a real-time central payments, management, reporting and tactical program

Voyager 2000 was designed for retail travel agencies, telesales and homeworkers. It provides a full front- and back-office system, which controls sales from the initial booking stage through payments to completion. It is scaleable for companies of different size. Transactions are on a real-time basis whether at a retail travel location, head office or off-site. The Voyager 2000 section of VIA includes:

- Viewdata integration
- CRS integration
- Teletext integration
- Insurance integration
- Tailor-made booking facilities
- ATOL-approved documentation
- Tactical campaign management
- Holiday club module
- Campaign and loyalty schemes
- Word processing and spreadsheet
- Enquiry database
- Powerful diary
- Balanced accounting
- Client history and profiles
- Cheque production
- BSP and BACS reconciliation
- Rail, coach and insurance returns
- Daily and weekly audit reports
- Management reporting historic analysis
- Full mailing program

The *Median–Central Control* allows head office to control all branch payments, management facilities, reporting and tactical campaigns. This facility allows reporting week on week and year on year for each branch, by region, by budget centre and for the company as a whole. All transactions are on a real-time basis, whether at a retail travel location, head office or off-site. The Median–Central Control section of VIA includes:

- Central accounting cheque production
- Batch payments reconciliation of operator statements
- View booking for all branches
- Comprehensive reporting module
- Tactical campaign management
- Real-time control of all areas of business

For more information, see **www.voyager-ap.com**

Questions

- How can travel agencies integrate their operations by interconnecting internal systems with the Internet?
- What are the main costs and benefits emerging through the use of ICTs for travel agencies?

adopting an open, knowledge-based architecture. Integrated systems running on intranets significantly reduce the time spent on data entry and the possibility for errors, allowing travel agencies to capture detailed financial data that can support their future policies (Minghetti and Mangilli, 1998). To facilitate this process almost all GDSs offer internal travel agency management systems. Sabre, for example, offers eVoya, a travel agency system that helps agencies to work smarter, reduce costs and boost business while providing more value to customers. Products and services are grouped into four components – desktop, delivery, content and tools.

10.4.2 Interconnecting partner systems and extranets

Interconnectivity between all members of the value chain provides major benefits for travel agencies. Specific extranets therefore allow agency staff to access dedicated parts of principals' or intermediaries' systems. Agencies can have access to on-line availability and reservation functions for all products and services as well as to manage financial transactions such as invoices, payments and contracts. Moreover, to the degree that GDSs develop Internet-based interfaces with agencies, they will be able to develop extranet solutions. By using extranets, travel agencies can reduce the cost of bookings, improve communications and efficiency, increase the speed of booking procedures and enhance customer service.

In addition, travel agencies can develop extranets for their corporate clients. Enabling corporate customers to utilize specialized sections of their on-line provision also helps agencies to expand the value chain and to provide tools for their corporate customers to undertake part of the process themselves. Customers with extranet facilities are able to search for and identify travel products in a protected and efficient environment, which allows corporate deals and other value-added services to be displayed. Perhaps more importantly, they are able to enforce travel policies, monitor expenses, manage corporate deals and settle all financial transactions electronically.

Integration between front- and back-office systems of all members in the travel agency value chain improves the operations of agencies by strengthening their efficiency and control, while enabling them to increase their competitiveness. Storing information in data warehouses can also assist them in developing proactive marketing tools in order to target individual customers with specialized products. This can help them increase the value-added services offered to each customer and also to defend themselves against disintermediation.

10.4.3 Connecting with all stakeholders through the Internet

The proliferation of the *Internet* has introduced major opportunities and challenges for travel agencies. As far as opportunities are concerned, agencies can develop their Internet presence and interact with their clientèle, partners and other stakeholders through their website, eMail and all other ways of *communication*. By developing their Internet presence, travel agencies can communicate with consumers from all over the world, attract more customers, promote special deals and interact constantly. This opportunity effectively revolutionizes agency marketing communications opportunities and allows them to get their message across on a global scale. Providing the right type of content to the right kind of customer is of critical importance. The Internet allows agencies to develop specialized sites for their distinctive markets. Business markets can be segmented further and particular information, deals and suggestions may be offered, for example. Structuring the content according to their needs is critical as this encourages them to engage with the website. The ability to expand the Internet provision through adding more information and pages enables agencies to build scalable solutions and to expand by reacting to the needs of the marketplace. Updating the Internet site constantly, agencies can be reactive to market trends, customer feedback and new offers from principals, as they do not need to wait for printed material to be finalized. In addition, communicating efficiently through eMail and calling centres supports dynamic and personalized interaction with consumers. eMail also instigates targeted marketing campaigns as well as vital marketing opportunities, helping agencies to communicate their messages interactively with consumers. Often consumers request eMail updates for products, prices and special offers, which also enables agencies to put their message across. Perhaps the most significant opportunity emerging through the Internet is the cost-efficient communication mechanism. As the cost of communicating is negligible, many agencies have taken advantage and strengthened their position. Case Study 10.2 demonstrates that a multi-channel distribution and communication strategy will be increasingly important for successful travel agencies for the future.

In addition, a web presence allows agencies to develop their *brand name* both on-line and off-line; they can communicate their mission, principles, aims and objectives as well as their brand values. By doing so they encourage consumers, partners and other stakeholders to interact more closely. Coordinating the on-line and off-line brand in a consistent and coherent way is significant for every successful agency. However, the brand conception, properties and manifestations need to be developed in a manner that will facilitate both on-line and off-line design to work for the agency. Developing close associations with partners such as principals, destinations etc. may support mutual reinforcement of brands and can allow organizations to develop beneficial links.

Sales generation and fulfilment are ultimately what most travel agencies aim to achieve. Providing opportunities for eCommerce on-line allows consumers to purchase travel products. Organizing the content properly, ensuring the reservation process operates efficiently for users and enabling customers to contact agencies should they experience problems can maximize sales potential. This process can institute major sales efficiency, as it requires minimal if any face-to-face interaction with travel consultants. Mutually supportive partners are imperative in the eCommerce and sales generation and fulfilment processes. Providing sufficient incentives to partners may generate significant sales leads and can support travel agencies to trade through their interfaces. For example, the bookings part of the *Daily Telegraph* travel website (**www.travel.telegraph.co.uk**) is fulfilled by the Online Travel Company (**www.otc-uk.com**), a travel agency founded in January 1998 to provide travel and travel-related services through the Internet for the leisure and corporate traveller in the UK.

Case Study 10.2

Thomas Cook on-line

Following the acquisition of Germany's C&N, Touristic AG acquired Thomas Cook UK in 2000 and consequently rebranded its entire operation to Thomas Cook AG at the end of June 2001. The British travel group Thomas Cook Holdings Ltd, London, is the country's third largest vertically integrated travel group with annual revenues of about £1.5 billion, 3.5 million customers and a workforce of 16 000 people. The portfolio of brands includes the JMC, Club 18–30, Neilson, Style, Skiers World, Thomas Cook Holidays and Time Off tour operator brands. Thomas Cook also owns JMC Airlines, the UK's second largest charter airline, operating a fleet of 29 aircraft.

The sales network consists of 1800 travel agencies worldwide, including some 700 Thomas Cook travel shops in the UK. In addition, Thomas Cook leads the UK market in direct selling both via four Thomas Cook Call Centres employing over 1000 staff (Thomas Cook Direct) and over the Internet (thomascook.com). Thomascook.com offers over two million holidays and flights from hundreds of airlines, all of which can be booked on-line. The site is split into four sub-sites – sun, flights, snow, late deals – with a different look and feel to each one. Users can download free travel guides, supplied by Rough Guides and complemented by the company's own guidebooks. The site also offers real-time information on hotel booking, car hire, travel insurance, weather and snow reports. Foreign currency ordering is available on-line too. In 2001, thomascook.com was one of the most visited UK travel websites, and was regularly getting 35 000 visits a day. Thomas Cook has developed a truly multi-channel strategy with customers having access to its products and services across five platforms: travel shops, telephone, Internet, WAP-enabled technology and interactive TV.

For more information, see **www.thomascook.com**

Questions

- Explain how traditional travel agencies can take advantage of ICT tools and improve their business functions.
- What are the key advantages and disadvantages for travel agencies that have both on-line and off-line offerings?

The *challenges* are also significant. Agencies not only have to match the availability of information and reservation capabilities of the Internet; they also need to provide great value when servicing consumers who have access to most of the *available information*. Availability of information through a wide range of media as well as price and product transparency through the Internet means that agencies need to work harder to earn the respect of their clients. In addition, as consumers become more experienced, they gradually require more specialized information and expect their travel agency to provide it. The level of Internet usage in travel agencies is still minimal, with even major and innovative travel agency chains, such as Thomas Cook, not having installed Internet access in their outlets by the end of 2001. However, the utilization of advanced ICTs such as intelligent assistants can enable travel agencies to improve the methodology of matching travellers' preferences with product and destination attributes (O'Brien, 1999).

Moreover, traditional travel agencies need to compete with several *ICT-based newcomers*, such as Expedia, Travelocity and lastminute.com, which allow consumers to have access to information and make on-line bookings (Buhalis, 1998; Wardell, 1998). Choosing the right technological platform and suppliers as well as integrating the Internet provision with legacy systems can also be tricky for uninitiated travel agencies. It becomes increasingly evident, therefore, that only a few innovative agencies have developed platforms for communications with suppliers and customers. The majority of the agencies, however, jeopardize their competitiveness by ignoring many of these developments and by failing to prepare for the new industry challenges. Inevitably ICTs and the Internet support further integration and concentration in the industry, as only a few brand names will be able to survive as global players in the market place.

10.5 Disintermediation vs re-intermediation for travel agencies

The Internet is also expected to change dramatically the role of tourism intermediaries, and travel agencies in particular. Hitherto, travel agencies have been the major brokers of tourism services and the interface of the industry with

Figure 10.1 Developments and trends in the marketplace affecting travel agencies

- Tourism principals and suppliers are anxious to control distribution costs as well as to improve their communication function and therefore attempt to bypass travel agencies by developing Internet-based interfaces with consumers
- Commission capping or termination by airlines around the world
- Development of no-frills airlines that perform most of their reservations on-line
- The majority of the consumers that are capable and able of travelling gradually become computer-literate, set up connections with the Internet, and feel empowered to search and amalgamate their tourism products themselves
- Availability of net rates/fares on the Internet
- Publication of contact details and Internet sites on tour operators' brochures
- Emergence and rapid development of electronic intermediaries (e.g. Expedia, Travelocity)
- Development of new business models, including auctions (e.g. qxl.com) and name-your-price sites (e.g. priceline.com)
- Expansion of customer relationship management systems and their gradual integration with loyalty schemes
- Principals use a wide range of consumer incentives through relationship marketing, aiming to establish a direct partnership with consumers
- eTicketing eventually will enable the entire process of making reservations and purchasing tourism process paperless
- Traditional intermediaries (such as Thomas Cook) re-engineering their processes in order to update their offering, improve customer satisfaction and remain competitive
- Tourism destinations develop regional systems to enhance their representation, boost their image and attract direct bookings

consumers. Often agencies are reduced to being booking offices, rather than travel counsellors, and often the consumers are more knowledgeable than staff members (Richards, 1995). However, as the Internet on the one hand allows principals and destinations to promote their products on-line and on the other enables consumers to develop and purchase their own itineraries on-line and unaided, the future of travel agencies looks questionable. The high dependence of travel agencies on information and communication in order to perform their role, in combination with their reluctance to take advantage of the emerging technology, places traditional agencies in an extremely vulnerable position. A threat for disintermediation is therefore evident (Buhalis, 1998). This is also reinforced by a number of recent developments and trends in the marketplace, as illustrated in Figure 10.1.

Figure 10.2 demonstrates the most prominent arguments for and against disintermediation of the tourism distribution channel. In reality, different market segments will use dissimilar distribution channels for selecting and purchasing their tourism products. For example, older generations and people who travel

Figure 10.2 Arguments for and against the disintermediation of travel agencies

Arguments for the disintermediation of travel agencies	Arguments against the disintermediation of travel agencies
■ Travel agencies currently add little value to the tourism product, as they primarily act as booking offices	■ Travel agencies are professional travel advisers and offer valuable services and advice
■ Travel agencies merely manage information and undertake reservations	■ Travel agencies use expertise to save time for consumers
■ Travel agencies are biased, in favour of principals who offer override commissions and in-house partners	■ Technology is difficult to use and expensive to acquire for individuals
■ Experienced travellers are much more knowledgeable than travel agencies	■ A large part of the market is computer-illiterate and unwilling to improve its skills
■ Visiting travel agencies is inconvenient, time-consuming and restricted to office hours	■ The more complex computers and the Internet become, the more people need experts to use them
■ Commissions to travel agencies increase the total price of travel products ultimately	■ Travel agencies offer free counselling services and add value by giving advice
■ Personnel in travel agencies are often inadequately trained and inexperienced	■ Electronic intermediaries primarily serve the business market and are more expensive
■ There is a gradual increase in independent holidays and a decrease in package holidays	■ There is currently limited provision for the organized inclusive tourist on-line
■ Technology enables consumers to undertake most functions from the convenience of their armchairs	■ Travel agencies can achieve better prices through the right channels and deals and by buying in bulk or through consolidators
■ Electronic travel intermediaries offer a great flexibility and more choice	■ Travel agencies offer a human touch and a human interface with the industry
■ A number of themed/specialized web portals emerge to serve niche markets	■ Travel agencies reduce the insecurity of travel, as they are responsible for all arrangements
■ The re-engineering of the tourism industry (e.g. electronic ticketing, no-frills airlines, airline commission capping, loyalty schemes) facilitates disintermediation	■ Internet transactions are not secured or reliable yet and consumers are not willing to provide credit card details

Source: Based on Buhalis (1998)

infrequently will probably continue purchasing tourism products from traditional travel agencies. These are travellers on low budgets, however, and may not
provide sufficient business for travel agencies to survive. The more lucrative, business and frequent traveller markets may use on-line providers to arrange their
itineraries and eventually purchase their tickets either on-line or off-line. This
will depend on the security of Internet transactions, the reliability and quality of
information available on the Internet, and the convenience of the entire process.
The future intermediation of the tourism distribution channel will therefore be
quite different from the current situation. The competitiveness of travel agencies
will depend on their ability to re-engineer their core product and demonstrate
that they can add value to the process and the final product.

Traditional travel agencies, therefore, will need to reassess the developments
in the marketplace and decide which market segment they would like to concentrate on. Adequate ICT equipment, training and service will be of paramount
importance, however, to maintain their competitiveness in the long term. Travel
agencies' ability to develop a **click-and-brick** strategy and focus their operations
on service excellence, which will support customer loyalty, gathering of market
intelligence, creating custom-made travel products and addressing niche markets
will be critical for their future survival (WTO, 2001; Van Rekom et al., 1999).

10.6 Lessons and issues for the future of travel agencies

Hitherto, despite using ICTs for some years now, the vast majority of travel agencies have not yet managed to take full advantage of ICT capabilities. This is a
result of a certain shortage of strategic vision in ICTs, as well as a failure to invest
in new technology. Low profit margins and a traditional reluctance to invest in
assets have deprived agencies of a wide range of critical tools, preventing them
from taking full advantage of the emerging ICTs. This results in a relatively low
level of technology integration, and thus less information is available to support strategic and tactical decision-making. In addition, it results in a low level of
management and operational integration, preventing agencies from capitalizing
on information for efficient operations, integrated customer service and development of partnerships with suppliers and institutional buyers.

Agencies often ignore the opportunities emerging through the Internet as well
as extranets and intranets. Thus, only a few agencies have managed to improve
their communications with consumers and take advantage of the synergies.
Expedia, the electronic travel agency of Microsoft, managed to develop its position to being one of the top 10 US travel agencies in less than four years from its
establishment. As demonstrated in Case Study 10.3, lastminute.com emerged as
a major lifestyle travel agency and has attracted a considerable market share in a
fairly limited time. This clearly demonstrates that agencies will increasingly be
challenged by innovative organizations. Unless they take counter-action they
will lose significant market share. In addition, the launch of dynamic Internet
sites by airlines, hotels and other suppliers who are willing to offer flexible/real-
istic prices as well as discounts for direct bookings will also challenge one of the
core benefits once offered by agencies – price.

Case Study 10.3

lastminute.com

lastminute.com was founded by Brent Hoberman and Martha Lane Fox in 1998. Their website was launched in the UK in October 1998. lastminute.com aims at creating the one-stop shop for all last-minute needs. Using the Internet they match suppliers' distressed inventory with consumer last-minute demand at short notice. lastminute.com carries almost no inventory risk, selling perishable inventory for its suppliers, and, where appropriate, protects suppliers' brand names until after purchase. Their mission statement – 'lastminute.com encourages spontaneous, romantic and sometimes adventurous behaviour by offering people the chance to live their dreams at unbeatable prices!' – clearly defines their business as a lifestyle portal offering a wide range of products and services to people who purchase on impulse. Although tourism products dominate the site, several additional products are available, including meals delivered at home, gifts including electronics and underwear, and insurance.

lastminute.com seeks to differentiate itself by generating some of the lowest prices for many travel and entertainment deals, and by packaging and delivering products and services, such as restaurant reservations, entertainment tickets and gifts, in convenient, novel and distinctive ways. It also aims to inspire its customers to try something different. Since 1998 the company believes that it has developed a distinctive brand, which communicates spontaneity and a sense of adventure, attracting a loyal community of registered subscribers who use lastminute.com's website and have submitted their eMail addresses and other data in order to receive lastminute.com's weekly eMail. In September 2001 the company had over 4.2 million registered subscribers in Europe. lastminute.com aims to be the global marketplace for all last-minute services and transactions. Following the success of the UK site, localized versions of the website have since been launched in France, Germany, Sweden, Italy, Spain, the Netherlands, Australia, New Zealand and South Africa. This growing multinational presence will give the company the ability to develop and further strengthen the lastminute.com brand.

To achieve this it is vitally important that lastminute.com continually deepens the inventory sourced from high-quality suppliers in the travel, entertainment and gift industries across the entire spectrum of goods and services. lastminute.com has relationships with over 9300 suppliers, including international scheduled airlines, hotels, package tour operators, theatres, sports and entertainment promoters, restaurants, speciality service providers, gift suppliers and car hire, both in the UK and internationally. To name a few, their suppliers include Lufthansa, Air France, Alitalia, British Midland, United Airlines, Virgin Atlantic Airways, Starwood Hotels and Resorts Worldwide, the Savoy Group, Sol Melia, Kempinski Hotels, English National Ballet, the Royal Albert Hall and Conran Restaurants.

By leveraging existing technology and capabilities lastminute.com has developed a framework for rapid expansion. The company believes that alternative distribution platforms such as interactive digital television, mobile telephone and personal digital assistants are ideally suited to offer last-minute deals. To date lastminute.com has focused on companies in the interactive television, mobile telephone and personal digital assistant markets. Accordingly, it has entered into agreements with companies such as Cable and Wireless Communications, Telewest, BT Cellnet, Orange, AvantGo and Psion to offer its content using these new channels. The recent launch of a transactional voice-recognition portal is a European first.

At the end of September 2001 lastminute.com announced strong fourth-quarter results, completing an encouraging full year. lastminute.com remains on track to reach operating profit in the UK and France in around two quarters' time:

▶

Case Study 10.3 *continued*

- Total transaction value grows by 3.6 times year on year to £124.2 million (2000: £34.2 million) and by 60 per cent quarter on quarter to £46.9 million.
- Gross profit up 5.2 times year on year to £17.2 million.
- Gross margin increases by 4.1 percentage points year on year to 13.9 per cent.
- Loss (before goodwill amortization) down 20.5 per cent quarter on quarter to £7.4 million.
- Operating cash outflow reduced to £6.8 million for quarter 4 2001, a reduction of 59.4 per cent over quarter 4 2000.
- Customer conversion rate up from 5.5 to 13.9 per cent year on year.
- On track to break even at an operational level in the UK and France in approximately six months' time.

For more information, see **www.lastminute.com**

Questions

- Explore the developments in the share price of lastminute.com, and explain the main reasons behind its fluctuation.
- Discuss how does lastminute.com co-opetes with expedia.com, and compare and contrast their offerings.
- Examine travelocity.com, expedia.com, ebookers.com and travelstore.com, and:
  - identify how they differentiate their offerings;
  - explain their added-value services;
  - identify their unique selling points.
- Discuss and illustrate the differences between the business models of traditional vs electronic travel agencies.

To the degree that new suppliers based in cyberspace are able to add value to the total tourism product, they will correspondingly increase their market share and change the structure of current tourism channels. The electronic travel agent located in an inexpensive location somewhere in the world will prevail. Intelligent agents will identify the best available products for the needs of each individual customer and hence add value to each phase of the transaction. Following the success of on-line travel agencies, such as Expedia, which enables individuals to build their itineraries and purchase their tourism products, new ideas and concepts are currently tested in order to identify products that will serve both tourism demand and supply. One of these ideas is the Electronic Travel Action, which uses the Internet in order to undertake a real-time auction for products that would otherwise remain unsold. This development allows the distribution of perishable items at a price the market is willing to bear, revolutionizes the yield management concepts by maximizing revenue for suppliers, and provides a low-cost advertising medium for principals (Tjostheim and Eide, 1998). Pilot action promotions by Braathens Airlines in Norway and other organizations worldwide have clearly demonstrated that the market develops rapidly and these new distribution channels offer valuable services for both consumers and principals. Unless traditional agencies understand and use the new tools to revolutionize their distribution channels they will be significantly disadvantaged, as consumers are capable of taking up opportunities themselves.

Figure 10.3 The future of travel agencies

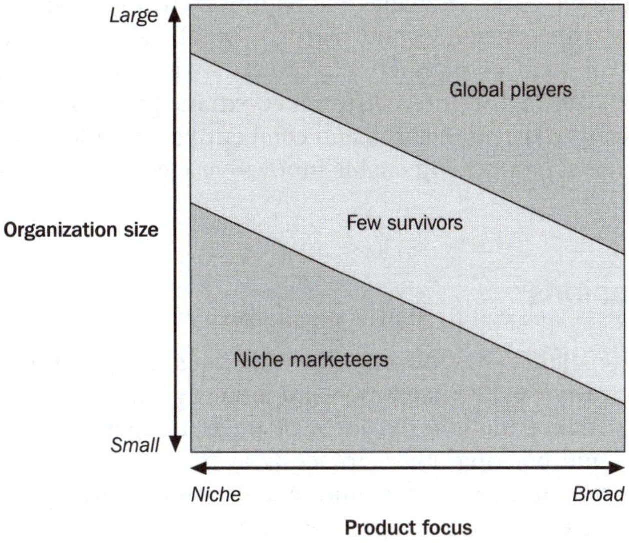

Source: After Paul Richer in WTO (1999)

Successful travel agencies of the future will need to transform themselves from being booking offices to being travel managers and advisers, as well as adding value to the travel experience. Richer suggests that the size and focus of operation will be critical (WTO, 1999) as illustrated in Figure 10.3, and two strategic directions can therefore be followed.

Smaller agencies will need to develop a clearly focused, specialized product, often relevant to their local communities. These agencies will need to offer differentiation value, by designing high-quality personalized travel arrangements for which consumers will be willing to pay a premium. Innovative methods offering differentiated tourism products will be needed for niche markets. Taking full advantage of technology will be essential in order to identify specific products that satisfy the tourism demand, while ICTs will be invaluable for market segmentation, consumer profiling, partnership marketing and adding value to tourism products.

Large players with a global portfolio of activities will be able to take advantage of their global brand power and network. Operating a large volume of transactions will enable them to offer cost value by delivering less expensive products than their competitors. This will be achieved through economies of scale, standardization, high-volume operations and special deals with partners. These agencies will need to capitalize on technology in order to identify special/last-minute deals, as well as to formulate partnerships with suppliers that have ample capacity to offer on a discount basis. They will also distribute packages of mass tour operators, which will be characterized by standardization, low prices and fairly low quality.

These two strategies will probably dominate the travel industry in the future. ICTs will be the nucleus for both type of organizations, as in the former case technology will have to increase efficiency and reduce costs while in the latter it will increase value by identifying, bundling and supplying the extra elements of the desired product. Both strategies will require agencies to use ICTs in order to communicate with consumers and partners, build their on-line and off-line brand and deliver tourism products efficiently. In addition integrating their entire operation within the Internet/intranet/extranet framework will be critical for their effectiveness, profitability and competitiveness. Adding value to the process and the travel product will enable innovative agencies to enhance their position.

10.7 Conclusions

The ICT revolution has introduced a wide range of opportunities and challenges for travel agencies. Perhaps more importantly, the Internet revolution is gradually changing the core business of travel agencies from being information providers and booking offices to acting as travel advisers. Travel agencies need therefore to employ ICTs dynamically and re-engineer their processes and functions in order to add value in the distribution channel. This will safeguard their position in the future.

Chapter questions

1 What is the role of travel agencies in the tourism industry, and what is the value they add to the tourism product?

2 Why do different types of travel agencies have different ICT needs and requirements?

3 Explain the travel agency legacy systems and the implications for their interactivity with other members of the industry.

4 What are the critical internal and external functions supported by ICTs?

5 Can the Internet disintermediate travel agencies?

6 How can travel agencies take advantage of the emerging ICTs?

7 What are the on-line opportunities for travel agencies of the future?

8 What is re-intermediation, and how can travel agencies achieve it?

9 Can travel agencies survive if they do not use the Internet?

10 Can exclusively on-line travel agencies, such as Expedia and lastminute.com, survive in the future?

Further reading

Alford, P. and Kärcher, K. (2001) The Endeavour Extranet: Building and Managing an B2B eCommunity in the British and Irish Travel Industry, http://www.genesys.net/karcherenter_0101.pdf (accessed 12/2001).

Beaver, A. (1993) *Mind Your Own Travel Business: A Manual of Retail Travel Practice*, Beaver Travel Publishers, England.

Bennett, M. (1993) Information technology and travel agency: a customer service perspective, *Tourism Management*, **14**(4), 259–266.

Edwards, G., Dawes, C. and Kärcher, K. (1998) The Imminus Travel and Tourism Intranet, ENTER Conference, Istanbul, Turkey, January 1998, http://www.genesys.net/karcherenter_0198.pdf (accessed 12/2001).

Holloway, C. (1989) *The Business of Tourism*, 3rd edn, Pitman, Plymouth.

Inkpen, G. (1998) *Information Technology for Travel and Tourism*, 2nd edn, Addison Wesley Longman, London.

Minghetti, V. and Mangilli, V. (1998) InTRAsystem: an advanced Internet-based information system for managing business travel, *Information Technology and Tourism*, **1**(1), 33–44.

O'Brien, P. (1999) Intelligent assistants for retail travel agents, *Information Technology and Tourism*, **2**(3/4), 213–228.

Renshaw, M. (1992) *The Travel Agent, Centre for Travel and Tourism*, Business Education Publishers, Sunderland.

Smith, C. and Jenner, P. (1994) Travel agents in Europe, *Travel and Tourism Analyst*, no. 3, 56–71.

Van Rekom, J., Teunissen, W. and Go, F. (1999) Improving the position of business travel agencies: coping with the information challenge, *Information Technology and Tourism*, **2**(1), 15–30.

Wardell, D. (1998) The impact of electronic distribution on travel agents, *Travel and Tourism Analyst*, no. 2, 41–55.

Websites

Travel agencies

Travel Agency Directory: **www.travelgate.co.uk**
Paul Richer's articles in TTG: **www.genesys.net/framepublica.htm**
Thomas Cook: **www.thomascook.co.uk**
Lunn Poly: **www.lunnpoly.com**
MyTravel: **www.mytravelco.com**
Colletts Travel: **www.collettstravel.co.uk**

Electronic travel agencies

EBookers: **www.ebookers.com**
Expedia: **www.expedia.com**
lastminute.com: **www.lastminute.com**
QXL: **www.qxl.com**
priceline.com: **www.priceline.com**
Travelocity: **www.travelocity.com**
American Express: **www.americanexpress.com/travel**
Travel Web: **www.travelweb.com**

Travel associations

ABTA: **www.abta.com**

Travel agency systems

www.tti.org
www.genesys-consulting.com/ttg/index.htm
www.imminus.com/yourbusiness/travelendeavour.html

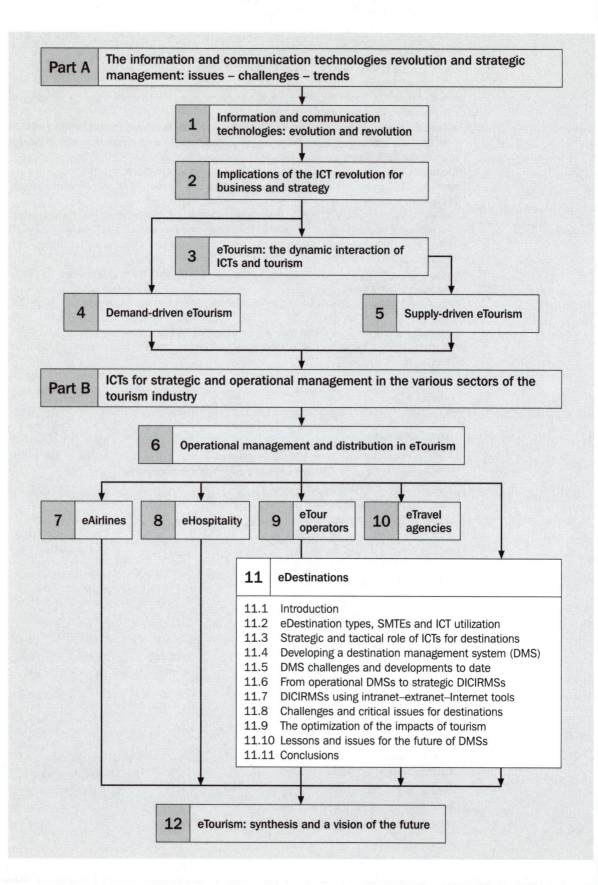

Part A — The information and communication technologies revolution and strategic management: issues – challenges – trends

1 — Information and communication technologies: evolution and revolution

2 — Implications of the ICT revolution for business and strategy

3 — eTourism: the dynamic interaction of ICTs and tourism

4 — Demand-driven eTourism

5 — Supply-driven eTourism

Part B — ICTs for strategic and operational management in the various sectors of the tourism industry

6 — Operational management and distribution in eTourism

7 — eAirlines

8 — eHospitality

9 — eTour operators

10 — eTravel agencies

11 — eDestinations

11.1   Introduction
11.2   eDestination types, SMTEs and ICT utilization
11.3   Strategic and tactical role of ICTs for destinations
11.4   Developing a destination management system (DMS)
11.5   DMS challenges and developments to date
11.6   From operational DMSs to strategic DICIRMSs
11.7   DICIRMSs using intranet–extranet–Internet tools
11.8   Challenges and critical issues for destinations
11.9   The optimization of the impacts of tourism
11.10 Lessons and issues for the future of DMSs
11.11 Conclusions

12 — eTourism: synthesis and a vision of the future

11

eDestinations

Chapter objectives

The purpose of this chapter is to explore the strategic implications of ICTs for destinations. The chapter illustrates how destinations become umbrella brands for all local suppliers and attractions and explains that ICTs and destination management systems can provide strategic tools for planning, managing and marketing destinations. Thus, the learning objectives may be defined as:

- Understand the sources of competitiveness and explore how technology can influence destinations and local enterprises
- Elaborate how ICTs can help destinations develop their brand
- Demonstrate that destination management systems can constitute a network interconnecting all tourism, hospitality and travel companies locally
- Explain that destination management systems can assist both local organizations and regions to achieve and maintain competitive advantage
- Discuss the particular requirements of small and medium-sized enterprises
- Explore how ICTs can integrate the entire industry and economy locally through the development of ICT info-structure

11.1 Introduction

Destinations are recognized as the *raison d'être* for tourism. They satisfy the need for travelling, and it is the attractions at the destination that generate the motivation to visit. Destinations are increasingly recognized as an amalgam of products, facilities and services that comprise the 'total tourism product' or the 'travel experience'. Paris as a destination, for example, brings together a number of tangible elements and attractions (e.g. local attractions, museums, theatres and parks), a number of intangible aspects (e.g. ambience, culture, art) as well as facilities/services for tourists and also locals (e.g. hotels, restaurants and catering, coaches, taxis, metro and other transportation facilities). All these aspects together develop the destination image and product. Traditionally, planning, management, marketing and coordination of destinations are being undertaken by either the public sector (at national, regional or local level) or by partnerships between stakeholders of the local tourism industry (Cooper et al., 1998; Mill and Morrison, 1998).

Destinations increasingly attract tourists from distant or long-haul markets. Thus, the need to disseminate information globally will continue to increase as destination-naive travellers require more information. Domestic markets also expand rapidly. They are usually characterized by short get-away breaks, with trip decisions made on impulse, based on previous experience. However, both markets require timely and accurate information that will reflect the individual needs of travellers. Demand patterns also change as the contemporary, sophisticated and wired travellers seek new experiences, often based on information. Tourists request a wide variety of information on areas, facilities, attractions and activities at destinations both before departure and upon arrival.

It is therefore a combination of both technological enablers and demand drivers that have propelled the realization of destination management systems (DMSs). ICTs have hitherto not been regarded as a critical instrument for the development and management of destinations. However, destination management organizations are gradually realizing the potential opportunities emerging through ICTs and use technology in order to improve their function and performance as well as for communicating their marketing message globally. It gradually becomes evident that destinations that provide timely, appropriate and accurate information to consumers and the travel trade have better chances of being selected. The ability of destinations to satisfy the information and reservation needs of buyers efficiently, by providing appropriate and accurate information on-line, will be critical for their future attractiveness. Hence, ICTs and DMSs in particular can support destinations in strengthening their competitiveness.

11.2 eDestination types, SMTEs and ICT utilization

Although the principles of ICT use at destinations remain largely the same, different types of destinations may require different ICTs. Understanding the type of destination can support marketers in developing appropriate ICT solutions by identifying the right level of information and reservation requirements for the

Figure 11.1 Types of destination – main target markets and activities undertaken

Type of destination	Customers	Activities
Urban	Business–MICE	Meetings–incentives–conference–exhibitions Education–religion–health
	Leisure	Sightseeing–shopping–shows–short breaks
Seaside	Business–MICE	Meetings–incentives–conference–exhibitions
	Leisure	Sea–sun–sand–sex–sports
Alpine	Business–MICE	Meetings–incentives–conference–exhibitions
	Leisure	Ski–mountain sports–health
Rural	Business–MICE	Meetings–incentives–conference–exhibitions
	Leisure	Relaxation–agriculture–learning activities–sports
Authentic third world	Business–MICE	Exploring business opportunities–incentives
	Leisure	Adventure–authentic–charities–special interest
Unique–exotic–exclusive	Business–MICE	Meetings–incentives–retreats
	Leisure	Special occasion–honeymoon–anniversary

Source: Based on Buhalis (2000b)

main market segments attracted. Developing a destination typology is a difficult task, as different visitors use destinations for different purposes. Nevertheless most destinations can be classified in several categories that represent their principal attractiveness, as illustrated in Figure 11.1.

Understanding and appreciating the type of destination, principal target markets and distribution mechanisms for a region are critical in order to analyse, design and implement appropriate systems. SMTEs dominate the tourism provision and contribute a considerable proportion of benefits. However, as discussed in Chapter 8, unless SMTEs find mechanisms to establish their on-line presence and to communicate effectively with their clientèle they will suffer competitive disadvantages. In addition to individual efforts, SMTEs should also establish collaborative ventures at the destination level, which would assist small firms to pool resources and share development and operation costs. Partnerships between private and public sectors as well as close collaboration are critical for the success of such schemes (Buhalis and Cooper, 1998; Buhalis, 1998). Networks of shared costs/resources/information can assist small hotels to alleviate some of the constraints of being small and to assist them to obtain more benefits from scale economies. This cooperation needs support by public tourism organizations as well as associations of local tourist enterprises. Cooperative participation of SMTEs on the Internet and electronic marketplace through the development of DMSs is therefore suggested as a strategic direction.

11.3 Strategic and tactical role of ICTs for destinations

DMSs provide new tools for destination marketing and promotion, as they use ICTs to disseminate information and to support a reservation function for products and facilities at specific destinations. There are many definitions of a DMS, but in essence a DMS is a collection of computerized information inter-actively accessible about a destination. DMSs typically include information on attractions and facilities and often incorporate the ability to undertake some reser-vations. DMSs are usually managed by destination management organizations (DMOs), which may be private or public organizations, or a combination of both. There is an increasing literature on DMSs, although there is still limited agree-ment on the role and functionality of a DMS (Archdale et al., 1992; Vlitos-Rowe, 1992; Sheldon, 1993, 1997; Pollock, 1998a, 1998b, 1999; Archdale, 1994; Buhalis, 1993, 1994, 1995, 1997; Cano and Prentice, 1998; O'Connor and Rafferty, 1997; Frew and O'Connor, 1998, 1999; Wöber, 1998; WTO, 1999, 2001).

Hitherto the majority of DMS developments have been led by *public tourist organizations*. **National tourism organizations** as well as regional and local bodies are traditionally involved in the information provision and marketing for desti-nations. They undertake mass media advertising, provide advisory services for consumers and the travel trade, run **Tourist Information Centres** (TICS), produce and distribute brochures, leaflets and guides both at destinations and at the places of origin of the tourists, and have the strategic responsibility of the entire destination. DMSs facilitate this function by administering a wide range of requests and by providing information to an ever-increasing tourism supply, in an efficient and appropriate way. Thus, ICTs provide a way to improve the acces-sibility of, as well as the quantity and quality of, information on the destination's facilities while presenting travellers with options to minimize their search costs (Sheldon, 1993). Moreover, destinations take advantage of database marketing techniques, in order to identify and target profitable market niches, by tailoring market-driven products for particular customers.

DMSs emerge as a major promotion, distribution and operational tool for both destinations and SMTEs. They can assist developing a flexible, tailor-made, specialized and integrated tourism product. By enabling users to search and select individual tourism products, DMSs can support travellers to create their person-alized destination experience. At the organizational level, DMSs provide the essen-tial info-structure for DMO to coordinate their activity and to provide sufficient information and direction to their overseas offices to promote the destination. As illustrated in Figure 11.2, DMOs and DMSs emerge as interfaces between destina-tion tourism enterprises (including principals, attractions, transportation and intermediaries) and the external world (including tour operators, travel agencies and ultimately consumers).

In several cases, DMSs have been used for integrating the entire supply at the destination. Their contribution to strategic management and marketing is demonstrated by their ability to integrate all stakeholders at destinations and also to reach a global market at a fairly affordable cost. DMSs usually include a product database, a customer database and a mechanism to connect the two. The more advanced systems tend to include a number of the additional services and features, as illustrated in Figure 11.3.

A number of DMSs gradually emerge for all destinations around the world, offering on-line information and in some cases facilitating reservations. Increas-ingly, DMOs provide innovative information that allow people to plan their itin-

Figure 11.2 Tourism distribution mechanisms and the role of DMOs and DMSs

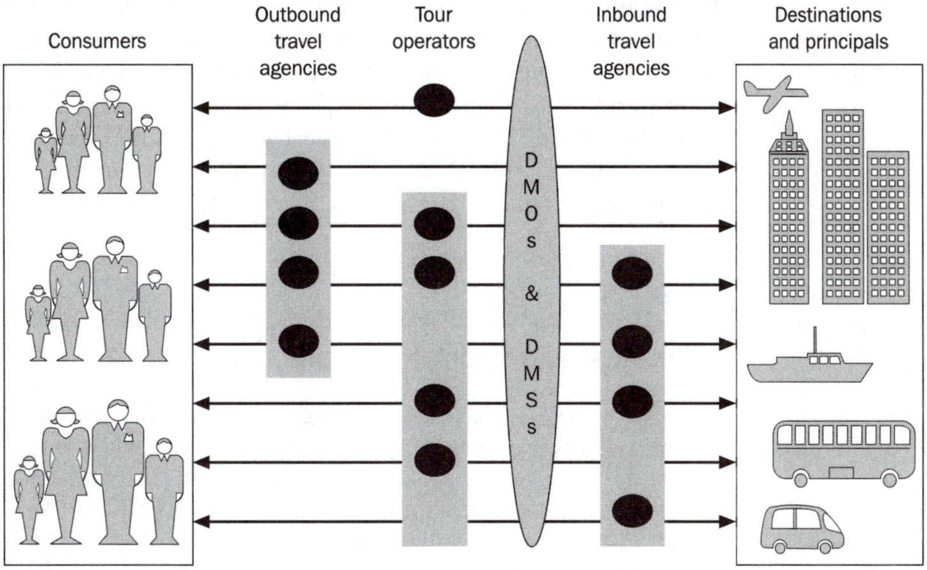

erary and develop their individualized package on-line or purchase commercial packages from tour operators. eCommerce also emerges, with a number of DMSs moving to fully functional websites that can support the entire range of customer purchasing requirements. Tiscover in Austria and Gulliver in Ireland have been leading these developments and gradually other destinations including Holland

Figure 11.3 Services and features for DMS advanced systems

- Information search by category, geography, keyword
- Itinerary planning for customer
- Reservations
- Customer/contact database management
- Customer relationship management functions
- Market research and analysis
- Image library and PR material for press
- Publishing to electronic and traditional channels
- Event planning and management
- Marketing optimization and yield management
- Data editing and management
- Financial management
- Management information systems and performance evaluation
- Economic impact analysis
- Access to third-party sources, such as weather, transport timetables and travel planning, theatre and event ticket reservations

Source: Based on WTO (2001)

and Jersey follow their example. Singapore recently changed its no-reservation policy and incorporated reservations in collaboration with the Hoteliers Association (**www.newasia-singapore.com**). In addition, many destinations assist travellers to develop their itinerary on-line. australia.com, as demonstrated in Case Study 11.1, offers a number of pre-set itineraries for its main tourist regions, while Singapore offers a comprehensive tour planner based on the dates of the tour and the key interests of the holiday maker. Often micro-sites are developed for specific events or for special interest tourism. Australia managed all the

Case Study 11.1

The Australian portal australia.com

The ATC launched its first consumer website in 1996. This site contained 11 000 pages of motivational and destinational content, listings of products, factual information, competitions, feedback and a search for Australia specialist travel agents. Then in 1998 a gateway site sitting above the global site was implemented for North America, followed soon after by several other regions. The gateways brought content from the global site to a higher level, together with links back into the global site. This enabled the regions to present content that was of more relevance to their customers at an earlier point in their browsing. As part of the gateway process, translations were also implemented for gateway content complementing sections of the global site. In 1999 a third layer was placed above the gateways, the 'splash page', to capture user information and route the user to the relevant gateway. Extensive consumer research was conducted to determine how potential travellers access on-line travel sites, their information needs and expectations. The Internet has revolutionized the travel industry by providing a new way for consumers to 'experience' a destination, plan their itineraries and purchase travel products.

The ATC's consumer website, australia.com, is targeted at the international travel market to provide instant access to motivational information that can influence consumers to choose Australia as their holiday destination. The site is the primary call to action in all of the ATC's consumer and trade marketing programmes and is backed by A$28 million in consumer advertising (2001/02). In 2000/01, the site delivered 38 million pages of information to an estimated 5 million unique users. The number of users grows at a rate of more than 50 per cent annually and by 2002/03, 12 million unique users are expected to visit the site. This increase points to the ever-growing importance of on-line technologies and confirms the ATC's strategic move towards web-based marketing. In December 2000 the ATC began a process of redevelopment of australia.com, which will result in the site becoming a vertical portal providing users with a relevant, captivating and informative on-line experience, targeted at users' cultural background, language preference, travel styles, behaviours, interests and needs. The site, launched in January 2002, will be a dynamic platform upon which the ATC will deliver and distribute interactive, branded and targeted multilingual content to drive conversion of actual travel to Australia by potential travellers.

For more information, see **www.australia.com**

Questions

- Discuss the advantages and disadvantages of destination management systems offering on-line bookings.
- Explore how the brand of a destination, like Australia, can be enhanced through its on-line presence.

information about the 2000 Olympic Games on-line, taking the opportunity to involve prospective tourists with the Australian brand and product.

11.4 Developing a destination management system (DMS)

Once DMOs have realized the opportunities arising from the Internet and set to explore these advantages they often find a number of challenges. WTO (1999) suggests 'that there is every reason why destination marketing organizations should be participating on the web and no excuse not to do so. Whilst some DMOs spend millions of dollars in implementing sophisticated integrated systems, it is perfectly possible to develop a website that may require an initial investment of just thousands of dollars'. It is therefore gradually being recognized that each and every destination in the world will somehow develop its Internet presence and will undertake some eMarketing. This may vary from sophisticated and fully integrated systems to stand-alone websites. There are currently a number of DMSs available in the marketplace, including software and solutions offered by Tiscover, WorldNet, Integra and Infocentre. Destination organizations therefore need to decide whether they wish to purchase software off the shelf and develop their own content or whether they would prefer to build their own website from scratch. A number of steps therefore need to be followed to design the system specifications and to undertake a comprehensive cost and benefit analysis between the alternative options. The process of developing a website for a destination can be described in the following steps:

1. Develop strategic overview, brand, look and feel of the destination offering.
2. Prepare an eTourism destination strategy.
3. Secure specialist support from ICT, marketing and DMS experts.
4. Advise and consult with all key stakeholders including principals, transportation companies, tour operators and local travel organizations.
5. Determine functional specifications and the business model of the site.
6. Establish technical specifications, procurement and update programme.
7. Request tenders and decide the partners working on the project.
8. Select system suppliers and/or software developers.
9. Organize the data collection and input to content management tools.
10. Build, pilot and test the DMSs and the website.
11. Host and maintain the DMS and the various sites.
12. Project manage its implementation.
13. Register the site with search engines and maintain good ranking.
14. Provide analysis of users and their usage of the site.
15. Develop feedback mechanisms and establish a process of continuous improvement.
16. Establish long-term strategy and account for technological upgrades.
17. Monitor, evaluate and review process regularly (WTO, 1999, 2001).

Figure 11.4 provides a summary of a step-by-step guide to the process of developing and implementing an Internet presence for a destination.

Figure 11.4 WTO's guide to designing a destination website

Specify the website functionality and the business requirements

- Domain name should be obvious and easy to find and remember, while priority listing in all major Internet search engines should be safeguarded
- Sites should allow different stakeholders to access different elements easily and efficiently
- The design of the page needs to be attractive and simple as well as clear and easy to navigate, avoiding complex designs
- Sufficient customization should be allowed for particular market segments; a 'my-page' function can allow users to build their own profile and preferences
- Speed of download is critical; the server specifications and design are critical in this aspect
- Content needs to be current, accurate, relevant, properly classified and cross-referenced; it should also be expandable to greater detail, with more maps, images and links for users that need to research something further
- Full searchability on the site and also on the sites of other trusted partners will allow the user to find all required information
- The site needs to facilitate bookings on-line, either directly on the site or through trusted partners' sites; partnerships with existing organizations that perform this function as a core business may be more cost-efficient than developing a booking engine
- Links to other sites that meet the quality criteria of the destination should be offered and reciprocal agreements with a wide range of other sites, portals and service providers should be developed
- An efficient mechanism for handling bookings and enquiries, as well as an invitation to users to provide feedback and to 'participate' in the design of the site should be extended

Develop a business model and consult with stakeholders

- Determine the size of destination and number of individual attractions, products and facilities to be included
- Invite wide consultation with all members of the tourism industry and ensure support from all levels of decision-making. Understanding the business models of partners is critical in developing a viable and useful website and service for all involved
- Determine the levels of financial support available for the project and the time-scale of the financial support
- Examine the distribution mechanisms at the destination and explore the structure of the channels
- Decide on the frequency of updating information, the availability and cost of content and the potential partners in this process
- Explore partnership opportunities with organizations that share the same values and can assist in developing the various elements of the site
- Estimate and forecast value of transactions and decide on the cost and benefit of each transaction
- Establish a financial model with consultation and determine commission levels, fees structures and initial costs, ensuring that the operation of the website is financially viable and at the same time makes commercial sense to partners
- Develop a long-term cost and benefits analysis, taking into consideration that technological developments will require a complete upgrade of all hardware and software every 2–3 years

Prepare a structure and design the technical factors and aspects

- Structure needs to support multi-entry points to reflect the motivations of the prospective users and to facilitate early arrivals to satisfactory results with a minimum of effort
- Undertake market research to identify and evaluate existing DMSs
- Decide whether you would like to build your own system, or purchase or lease one of the existing systems
- Decide whether to host your own web server or buy the service from the Internet
- Explore the software and hardware strategy for building the page and bring together technical developers with the content providers and users groups. Ensuring flexibility and interoperability and predicting communications and transactions standards in the future is critical at this stage
- Develop a balance between creative and multimedia material and availability of software on users' computers, download times, and complexity in navigation
- Content and editorial teams need to develop material in a way that can tell a story

Figure 11.4 continued

- Develop micro-sites, directly accessible, for special interest groups or for particular functions such as bookings, legislation and visa formalities, weather, currency
- Designing the website needs to take place in certain phases and at each stage 'naive' users should pilot-use the website and provide feedback
- Decide how many languages the site is going to appear in, according to the destination marketing strategy and make arrangements for translations
- Decide on whether you would like to appoint an agency to assist with the website development steps outlined above

Origination of destination product, editorial and graphics material

- Gradually digitize all product resources, transparencies, prints, maps, video and slides
- Content needs coordination to support the brand, products and all aspects
- All material needs to be stored in all formats supporting the different required uses
- Text needs editing to reflect the terminology of the target markets – not the destination
- Map-driven websites assist users to locate all aspects of content, products and facilities
- Ensure currency of editorial and content material and develop mechanisms for updates

Evaluation of pilot site, implementation, monitoring and evaluation

- Once the software is developed it needs to be tested and all problems need to be identified
- All data need to be validated for accuracy and currency
- Editing the website in every language needs to be undertaken
- The site needs to be tested by independent users and feedback, complaints and suggestions taken into consideration
- The performance of the site needs to be monitored constantly and reactive mechanisms should be developed
- Performance indicators, such as robustness, down-time, search engines positioning, number of users per page, visits and bookings, should be identified and measured frequently
- Feedback and input by users need to be taken into consideration and to be used for site upgrades

Promoting the website

- Once the site is approved and up and running it should be registered with all possible search engines and its ranking position should be maintained
- It is critical that both off-line and on-line marketing assists the launch and visibility of the site
- Incorporating the URL in all aspects of the brand is critical
- Build a customer database and capture personalized information
- Use competitions, auctions and chat rooms to develop a community and regularly communicate marketing messages
- Give customers reasons to come back to the site or to recommend the site to others, for example through postcards or updates on their areas/attractions they visited

Source: After WTO (1999, 2001)

11.5 DMS challenges and developments to date

Despite the fact that studies on destination-oriented systems have been traced back to as early as 1968, it was not until the late 1980s that the proliferation of DMSs emerged (Archdale et al., 1992). This delay is explained by a number of factors:

- lack of adequate and affordable technology at an earlier stage and in the pre-Internet era;
- lack of standardization of the industry and the early systems;

- lack of IT expertise among tourism professionals;
- concentration of marketing efforts in the local markets;
- relatively less intensive competition;
- domination of small and independent tourism enterprises around the world;
- conflicting interests of different players in the tourism industry.

Since the early 1990s and the availability of the Internet, when many destination-related systems emerged, only a handful of success cases can be reported. There are plenty of difficulties in implementing and operating DMSs and only a very small number of DMSs have survived their development and pilot stages to become operational and offer the promised benefits. Research on DMSs has attributed the limited developed to a number of barriers, demonstrated in Figure 11.5 (Buhalis, 1995; Pringle, 1994; Wayne, 1992).

Figure 11.5 Barriers to the successful development of DMSs

- Lack of strategic orientation
- Inability to strengthen competitiveness of the local industry
- Technology leading rather than following marketing strategies
- Less integrated approach than appropriate
- Inability to provide total services for tourism demand and supply
- Limited geographical basis, which makes the system non-feasible
- Premature innovation in a traditionally reserved industry
- Lack of standardization and compatibility
- Withdrawal of public sector interest and funding
- Product rather than demand orientation

In addition, a high failure rate has been observed, as several DMSs failed to attract the support and commitment required from both the private and public sectors. DMSs have also failed to develop viable products that could be utilized from either the independent or institutional tourism demand. The majority of public tourism organizations' projects have exclusively supported the information-only side, excluding the most important part of the transaction, the sale/reservation. Two systems offer an exception to the rule: Gulliver, the Irish DMS, and the Austrian Tiscover. Both systems have adopted their technological basis and their ownership status and remain two of the few operational and successful systems in the world (O'Connor and Rafferty, 1997; Frew and O'Connor, 1998, 1999; Proll et al., 1998).

11.6 From operational DMSs to strategic DICIRMSs

The DMS concept can be taken a step forward to formulate a more comprehensive and substantial system, which can revolutionize all aspects of destination management as well as integrate all tourism actors at the local level. Destination integrated computerized information reservation management systems (DICIRMSs) address the entire range of needs and services required by both tourism enterprises and consumers for specific destinations. In its conception a DICIRMS is an advanced DMS, digitizing the entire tourism industry and integrating all aspects of its value chain. DICIRMSs provide the info-structure for communications and business processes between all stakeholders, including consumers, principals, distributors and DMOs. Although a variety of the elements proposed for these systems already exists in some DMSs, there is currently no operational DMS offering such a comprehensive and integrated service to its users. The main differences between DMSs and DICIRMSs are described in the following points, which also demonstrate the strategic character of DICIRMSs in comparison with the primarily operational DMSs (Buhalis, 1993, 1994, 1995, 1997):

- At the *destination* level, DICIRMSs need to incorporate and coordinate the entire range and population of tourism providers. The complete tourism inventory of destinations needs to be available in order to facilitate customer choice as well as to support comprehensive destination management. This is particularly difficult for SMTEs, which may not have the equipment, the resources or the inclination to connect. However, a destination-wide initiative is critical for bringing together all stakeholders at the destination level. Ideally each SMTE should have a computerized system on its premises, which would support access to a DMS in order to diffuse information on availability, rates and reservation details, as well as to acquire a wide variety of services for both tourists and entrepreneurs. Ultimately, full interaction between SMTEs front and back offices with a DMS would maximize the efficiency of transactions and would empower the destination to operate as a system of wealth creation. SMTEs that cannot afford to install a computer system or lack capable personnel would initially be able to communicate via conventional media, such as telephone, fax or telex, through a dedicated operator and should be given incentives to acquire a computerized system. Access to banking systems is of equal importance in order to facilitate payments by credit cards.
- A DICIRMS should be *multi-integrated*, supporting **destination integration**; it should therefore use the entire range of available ICTs to coordinate all local providers and stakeholders in order to integrate the local economy diagonally. This will assist the maximization of multiplier effects and would support destinations to optimize benefits from their involvement in tourism. The organization involved in the management of DICIRMSs needs to be based on public–private sector partnerships (PPPs). They should be independent agencies, supporting management and marketing at both the micro- and macro-levels. DMOs need to undertake strategic management and marketing for both destinations and SMTEs as an entity. Therefore a partnership between the public and private sectors in the management of the DMOs would be ideal for the management of DICIRMSs. DICIRMSs need to be part of the public tourism organization support to the industry and its function for destination marketing and information dissemination. The public sector should also provide financial support as part of their infrastructure/info-structure development and marketing budgets.

The public sector should also be responsible for certifying the accuracy, quality and neutrality of information, as well as to protect consumers and SMTEs. Local chambers of commerce, associations of hoteliers and travel agencies, as well as other stakeholders should also be involved in order to ensure wider participation and high involvement of local suppliers. Research centres, universities and other knowledge developers can contribute to the systems. Ultimately, DICIRMSs should introduce diagonal integration at the destination by bringing together all actors and by creating synergies through collaboration.

■ DICIRMSs need to operate on a wide area network at the destination and to be accessible through the Internet as well as through mobile devices. *Computerization* and networking of the entire population of enterprises at destinations are therefore essential for establishing the destination management info-structure. Technological convergence and the need for interoperability increasingly require these systems to be able to operate on a wide range of technological platforms, including mobile devices, and therefore systems need to be developed to conform with latest standards and flexibility. The consistent reduction of ICT costs makes basic equipment affordable even to tiny organizations.

■ *information provision* is an integral part of DICIRMSs as they should disseminate information about everything related to a destination. They need to represent the entire destination itinerary providing comprehensive lists and contacts with any type of service providers at the destination level. Information should be accurate, timely and unbiased, while being classified in a 6A framework – that is, amenities–accessibility–attractions–activities–ancillary services–available packages, as illustrated in Figures 11.6 and 11.7. In addition, site and event attractions, available facilities and amenities as well as the transportation/accessibility options to and within the destination should be listed. Both individual products, such as accommodation establishments, restaurants and other catering business, transportation, entertainment as well as 'packages' created by principals, travel agencies, tour operators and other companies should be displayed. Failure to demonstrate all available options would jeopardize the completeness of DICIRMSs and the confidence that these systems can provide the 'best available deal'. The accuracy of information will also be crucial for the credibility of DICIRMSs. As a result, regular inspections

Figure 11.6 The 6A framework for the analysis of tourism destinations

■ Attractions (natural, man-made, artificial, purpose-built, heritage, special events)

■ Accessibility (entire transportation system comprising routes, terminals and vehicles)

■ Amenities (accommodation and catering facilities, retailing, other tourist services)

■ Available packages (pre-arranged packages by intermediaries and principals)

■ Activities (all activities available at the destination and what consumers will do during their visit)

■ Ancillary services (services used by tourists such as banks, telecommunications, post, newsagents, hospitals etc.)

Figure 11.7 Contents of a destination integrated computer information reservation management system

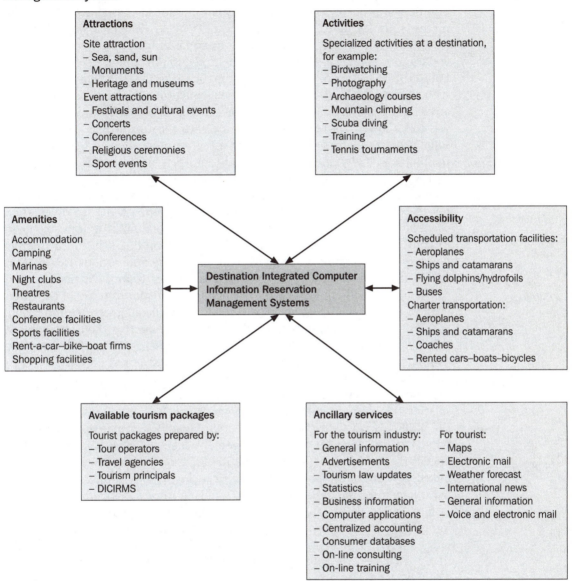

Source: Adapted from Buhalis (1993, p. 376)

by the management body as well as the local authorities, in combination with heavy penalties for deliberate misguidance, will improve the quality of information. A wide range of ancillary services should also be distributed through DICIRMS networks for both consumers and the industry.

■ *reservations and purchasing* of the vast majority – if not all – of local tourism products are critical in the ability of DICIRMSs to provide a comprehensive service. The ultimate aim of tourists who contact a tourism information centre is to gain information in order to eventually make a booking. Therefore, destinations that make it easy for prospective travellers to book all aspects of their trip on-line will probably increase their visitation rates. It is vital that all tourism products display up-to-date availability and prices, while provision of instant confirmation and ease of payment are essential as with all other eCommerce applications. Many DMOs that have attempted to implement reservations have found this to be one of the most problematic issues that they have had to deal with. Some DMOs discovered that their constitution prevented them from any commercial activities, and thus accepting reservations and eCommerce was not allowed. Others faced problems with local principals who felt that some other properties were accepting a higher proportion of bookings than themselves. Finally, intermediaries and tour operators in particular often feel that a DICIRMS offering on-line reservations threatens and competes with their packages. In several cases these tour operators have pressurized principals not to collaborate with DICIRMSs and also threatened DMOs to divert their clientèle to other regions. In Ireland tour operators took the tourism board to court over its decision to allow reservations on-line. The intra-channel power of tour operators on peripheral, insular and remote regions as well as on SMTEs needs to be addressed through creating alternative distribution and communication channels. DICIRMSs therefore can address some of the intermediary power and dependency issues. DMOs have no alternative but to ensure that they offer all facilities available to assist prospective travellers book at their convenience. Several destinations, including Jersey, Holland, Ireland and Austria, have fully functional reservation sites and already appreciate clear benefits. The Holland Tourism Board recently announced a change of strategy that focuses on 'assisting buyers buy, rather than helping sellers sell', encapsulating the essence of eCommerce in tourism.

■ DICIRMSs also facilitate the strategic and operational *management* at destinations. Offering tools for macro-management enables DMOs to integrate their operations and to create an info-structure for coordinating the entire tourism industry at the destination. DICIRMSs can assist both supply and demand management at the destination level, by using information, trends and forecasting, and by developing pro-active and re-active management scenarios. This information, in combination with management processes for tourism enterprises and visitor management techniques, can assist destinations to optimize their benefits. At the micro-level, DICIRMSs can provide managerial tools for principals and can support them in performing a number of their business functions. eHRM can assist recruitment locally, and eLegislation may update them with legislation issues and regulations. In addition, DICIRMSs can develop ASP services offering application hosting and distributing software such as PMS, reservations, accounting, payroll, project management etc. Pooling resources together will allow smaller principals in particular to take advantage of the emerging tools at an affordable cost (Paraskevas and Buhalis, 2002). DICIRMSs therefore can facilitate both operational and strategic decision-making processes both for destinations and enterprises.

■ Perhaps more importantly, DICIRMSs emerge as a *system of wealth creation* and as a destination-wide value chain, which can improve the competitiveness and sustainable development of both destinations and SMTEs, while enhancing consumers' experience (Pollock, 1998a). Consequently, DICIRMSs can support long-term prosperity of host populations, by improving economic impacts and capitalizing on multi-integration at the destination level. In essence, the DICIRMS concept represents the evolution of DMSs. It emerges as a more comprehensive and complete system for integrated tourism destination management. In addition to the information provision and reservation functions that most DMSs tend to offer, DICIRMSs institute a strategic information system and concentrate on strategic functions, coordinate tourism suppliers at destination level in order to enhance the total tourism satisfaction, analyse competitor destinations and complaints, forecast tourism demand and perform yield management, disseminate marketing intelligence, collect and analyse tourism statistics, build local partnerships and encourage the integration of local economies, and provide the entire range of software required for the management of independent enterprises. DICIRMSs bridge the gap between demand and supply by enabling direct selling while cooperating with all existing distribution partners. A variety of customer services can also be provided as DICIRMSs will enable tourists to access several ancillary services and also facilitate their communication with their home base.

Thus, DICIRMSs can be defined as an integrated destination management strategic tool. They should aim at assisting the enhancement of the long-term profitability and competitiveness of the local private sector by reinforcing its marketing processes and intra-channel negotiation power. They should also aim at enhancing the management of tourism impacts at the destination level by intensifying integrated and sustainable economic development. DICIRMSs should also aim at improving interpretation and interaction of socio-cultural rituals and enhancement of environmental concern for destination regions. Not only do DICIRMSs support the provision of seamless tourism product; they also assist DMOs to perform strategic management by utilizing a vast range of information, a destination-wide neural system and a global electronic exchange facilitated through the Internet, extranets and intranets.

11.7 DICIRMSs using intranet–extranet–Internet tools

Until the arrival of the Internet, information about the destination could only be distributed through tourism information centres as well as dedicated terminals in airline branches, offices of national and regional tourism boards etc. The information systems used then were mainly built to support local, regional and national tourism office employees interacting with the public, mainly through the phone or in person. The arrival of the Internet revolutionized the distribution of the information and assisted destinations to communicate directly with people all over the world. The evolution of the Internet enabled these internal systems to develop to wide area networks and comprehensive intranets cost-effectively. This integrated the entire business processes of DMOs and is the basis of great efficiency in their organizations.

11.7.1 Internal systems and intranets

Intranets are used for coordinating the operations of DMOs and for sharing all information, documents, images and videos globally. Developing knowledge management systems supports employees to follow developments in a number of markets simultaneously and to share expertise and experiences across the offices they operate. Finland's tourism board has pioneered intranet developments, as illustrated in Case Study 11.2. Wöber (1998) illustrates that marketing information access and use can improve the efficiency of the tourism organisations.

Case Study 11.2

The Finnish Tourist Board info-structure

The Finnish Tourist Board (FTB) has pioneered the use of the Internet for developing a network for managing tourism in Finland. ICT is used as an integral part of the tourism board's operations and as a tool for cross-industry coordination. The system includes:

- MIS, the Finnish Tourist Board's market information system, which offers a data management and distribution system. Launched in 1992 and updated in 1997, this is the internal system for FTB and is distributed to all its offices internationally. The system allows FTB staff to manage and organize sales and marketing campaigns, to coordinate their marketing and branding activities, as well as to distribute documents and administrate the tourist board globally. Access is also given to other professionals.
- RELIS, the Research, Library and Information Service, which provides the backbone to the national travel research and product documentation. The service connects the travel industry to research and education organizations.
- PROMIS, the national database of Finnish travel products and services, which provides a wide range of up-to-date information on travel products, services and contact information. External PROMIS partners provide and update data and include regional and city tourism organizations and other tourism professionals. Most of the information and images are copyright free and can be used for brochures and other promotional campaigns. The professional marketing information service offers a tourism database covering the whole of Finland.

Most of these databases are accessible via the Internet. In summer 2000, services for the tourist industry were improved considerably by opening an Internet connection to the PROMIS information system, which the Finnish Tourist Board has developed together with the industry. The number of cooperation partners in the PROMIS information system exceeded 130 by the end of that year. The amount of information in the PROMIS system consequently rose by over 40 per cent from spring to autumn, to more than 5000 tourist products. Over 20 new information producers joined the system. Cooperation partners can now add and update information on-line. The Internet service was expanded, with eight new languages being added to the site. At the end of the year the site presented tailored pages on Finland as a tourist destination, in 13 languages. Product information in the PROMIS system was used increasingly in brochures, with the information also available on the Internet. Christmas pages were also produced, along with extranet pages for participants in the Savotta Travel Market and a site for arranging sales events complete with registration procedures. During the year the structure and content of traditional marketing tools were developed intensely. Development focused especially on electronic marketing tools (web and WAP). A massive renewal of the Finnish Tourist Board's website began towards the end of 2000. The entire site, containing about 2500 pages, was to be renewed by summer 2001.

Source: Based on WTO (1999, 2001) and Finnish Tourist Board (**www.mek.fi**)

Questions

- Discuss the main functions of a destination management organization that can be integrated on-line.
- Who are the key players that need to have access to a destination management organization extranet, and why?
- Discuss the costs and benefits for the development of a comprehensive and integrated destination management system.

11.7.2 Interconnecting partner systems and extranets

Extranets can support DMOs to develop links with all their trusted partners and to establish close collaboration. A number of activities can be supported through extranets. Reservations to all local facilities require an extranet connection, as on one hand DMSs will need to have access to on-line inventory and on the other suppliers will need to be able to update their offerings, pricing, special offers and descriptions on a regular basis. Often bookings are outsourced to a specialized company and extranets are used to manage the booking process seamlessly. For example, accommodation bookings on the **www.holland.com** website are facilitated by Bookings Inc (**www.bookings.org**).

Relations with the press can be enhanced as DMOs can communicate, distribute and archive press releases, images, statements, key meetings, reports, events and other useful material on-line. Being able to support the needs of journalists effectively and provide sufficient and consistent material can help to gain considerable coverage in the media.

However it is the development and coordination of the local value chain that extranets can facilitate better than any other technique. Bringing together the entire industry locally and distributing market intelligence are critical for enhancing collective competitiveness. Coordinating all stakeholders, including the entire range of government departments that have an influence on tourism, is also beneficial so that they can coordinate action, legislation and planning processes. An extranet can help DMOs to produce reports, studies, statistics and other widely available material. Registered partners can have access to this material and use it according to agreed restrictions. Market information can assist professionals with their marketing and planning activities. Research institutions, knowledge producers and consultants can also provide useful material for the local industry. Extranets can also be used for training the local industry, and gradually links with local universities and training organizations can assist the local industry to study on-line, perhaps pursuing distance-learning degree courses. In addition, tourism business services, including marketing, financial management and accounting, taxation, human resources and legal advice can be instrumental in supporting the industry improving its operational and strategic management. The British Tourism Authority's trade website (**www.tourismtrade.org.uk**) is a good example of a DMO extranet.

11.7.3 Connecting with all stakeholders through the Internet

The Internet has revolutionized the ability of DMOs to communicate efficiently with all their stakeholders on a global basis; this is particularly beneficial for remote and insular regions. As a result of Internet developments, DMOs are now able to play a much more critical role in the promotion, management and marketing of their destinations. As a result, for the first time ever they can get close enough to their end-consumers and other partners to develop a mutually beneficial relationship. DMOs increasingly use the Internet therefore to communicate with their customers before and during their visit. They are able to develop specialized markets and to support special interest groups on a global basis. For example, the British Tourism Authority focuses on the sports market by developing a dedicated part of the website (**www.visitbritain.com/sport/**).

Several DMSs are now on-line and there are considerable benefits evident. WTO (1999) suggests that the major advantages offered by the Internet for destinations include:

- it increases business for the destination and the local suppliers;
- it generates revenue for the DMO through reservations and value-added services;
- it improves communications and relationships with both individual travellers and targeted groups;
- it reduces costs associated with communications as well as printing, mailing and distributing brochures;
- it creates good public relationships for the destination, the DMO and other local organizations.

From the strategic perspective, DMOs for the first time ever have the opportunity to reduce the power of intermediaries over destinations and principals. By being able to provide information directly to the consumers and by developing bridges between principals and the end-users, they effectively institute a certain level of disintermediation. Innovative DMOs therefore have the tools and are able to re-address the intra-channel power issue and to renegotiate their position in the marketplace. Coordination of all principals and stakeholders at the destination level becomes much more efficient through the new tools and effective interaction allows DMOs to coordinate and integrate the entire destination offering and brand. Developing and maintaining value chains at the destination, by facilitating flexible product formulation and adaptation, also enable DMOs to address an endless range of target markets. Offering a 'multi-entry' strategy provides the opportunity for consumers to initiate their search by the variables that represent their priority. As illustrated in Figure 11.8, a consumer may enter a web page seeking information on a particular activity, life-style, property, service, package holiday, budget or even age and stage in life-cycle. The Internet has therefore revolutionized destination marketing, management and planning, by allowing DMOs to develop and maintain dynamic and interactive relationships with the entire range of stakeholders, including consumers, principals and intermediaries.

11.8 Challenges and critical issues for destinations

There are several *challenges* in the process though. Firstly, developing and maintaining credibility is a major challenge, as often DMOs do not have comprehensive and consistent data, image banks and information on facilities and attractions. Ensuring the currency and accuracy of information is significant not only for ensuring users' satisfaction, but also for avoiding legal action against the organization. Perhaps the most difficult task is to change the mind frame of a number of actors in the industry. Intermediaries tend to see DMSs as competitive to their products, and as a result they develop an antagonistic relationship. Principals are often willing to cooperate only if there is concrete evidence that the DMS can offer bookings and immediate financial gains, while they avoid investing in establishing links or developing the system.

Choosing an *on-line domain name* and *brand* is also a major challenge as the Internet becomes populated with similar domain names frequently trying to attract visitors from official sites to other commercial ones. The on-line domain name should reflect the brand and attributes of the destination and at the same time be easily memorable and accessible. DMSs should aim to register the **nameofdestination.com** name, reflecting the consumer tendency to add the.com element to the key brand name. This has worked well for the australia.com, jersey.com and holland.com websites. One of the major challenges many destinations have is *cyber-squatting*. Once they try to register their name they discover that it is registered by a private organization, using it as either a tourism- or non-tourism-related website for profit or for non-profit activities, or simply occupying the space and expecting to sell the domain. For example, Paris and Seychelles discovered that the **www.paris.com** and **www.seychelles.com** domains are occupied by an organization requesting a considerable amount of money for releasing the names. **Britain.com** is registered by the London Tourism Board, diverting viewers to the **londontown.com** website, while **www.visitbritain.com** is the official British Tourism Authority website but **www.visit-britain.com** belongs to a private operator. Other city/region name web pages have little to do with tourism. For example, **boston.com** belongs to the Boston Globe newspaper while **athens.com** is occupied by a pastry and bakery company. A number of alternatives are therefore registered, including **www.newasia-singapore.com** for Singapore and **www.tourspain.es** for Spain. Perhaps the most interesting legal case on destination cyber-squatting is under way as Barcelona council managed to gain **barcelona.com** back from its owners who have consequently appealed in the American courts (see Case Study 11.3).

Figure 11.8 Multi-entry search variables for destination management systems

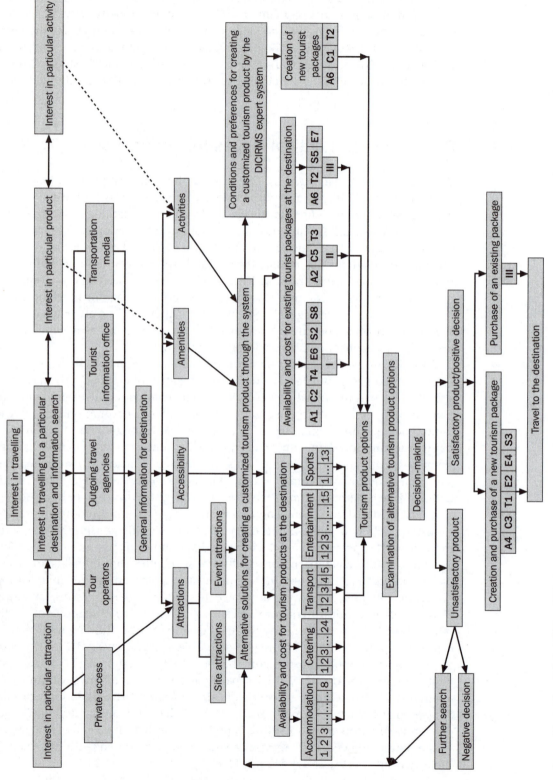

Source: Adapted from Buhalis (1993, p. 376)

The World Wide Web on the Internet emerged as the pervasive and robust platform for the distribution of multimedia-based DICIRMSs globally. The entire range of *distribution* mechanisms should be utilized for DICIRMSs and interoperability and interconnecting with all systems should be ensured. This should include mobile and interactive digital television platforms, which will be critical for tourism distribution in the future. Access should also be available through any telecommunications media utilized by consumers and the travel trade, such as computer communication, videotex, fax, telex and telephone.

Case Study 11.3

Cyber-squatting – the barcelona.com legal battle

Barcelona.com was originally registered in early 1996 by Concepcio Riera of Barcelona and her husband, Joan Nogueras Cobo, and was developed as a website that serves as a source of news and tourism information related to Barcelona. In May 2000, the city filed a claim for the address with the Internet Corporation for Assigned Names and Numbers (ICANN) Uniform Domain Name Dispute Resolution Policy (UDRP). In order for a complainant to succeed in a domain-nabbing attempt under the UDRP, the rules say the current holder must have no legitimate claim to the address and that they must have registered the address – or are using it – in 'bad faith'. The first decision of the court ruled the domain was currently being used in a way that met at least one of the UDRP's 'bad faith' definitions, including to 'attract, for commercial gain, Internet users by creating a likelihood of confusion with complainant's mark as to the source, sponsorship, affiliation or endorsement of your website or location or product or service on your website or location'.

In March 2002, the US District Court for the Eastern District of Virginia upheld a ruling requiring barcelona.com to return its domain name to Barcelona City Council. In addition to ruling that the domain violated Barcelona's trademark, the court also found that barcelona.com's owners had asked Barcelona City Council to pay for the domain name's return and had 'grossly exaggerated the value of the barcelona.com business prospects'. This was the first court case to assert that the Anti-cybersquatting Consumer Protection Act could be applied to foreign trademark violations. The owners of the domain name are appealing the decision but the travel portal and city guide changed its name to easybarcelona.com after the ruling. Meanwhile traffic to barcelona.com is diverted to the municipality web page **www.bcn.es**.

In spring 2001, the Australian city of Brisbane lost bids for the domains brisbane.com and brisbanecity.com. Similar cases that also were decided in favour of the original domain-name holders included disputes over stmoritz.com, portofhelsinki.com and portofhamina.com.

Source: Based on **http://arbiter.wipo.int/domains/decisions/html/2000/d2000-0505.html** Also on **www.easybarcelona.com/courtruling.pdf**

Questions

■ Identify 20–30 major cities around the world, and explore who owns the URLs that bare their names.

■ Who should be responsible for branding a destination on-line?

■ How can destinations maintain their brand integrity on-line and off-line?

Figure 11.9 Distribution of a destination integrated computer information management system

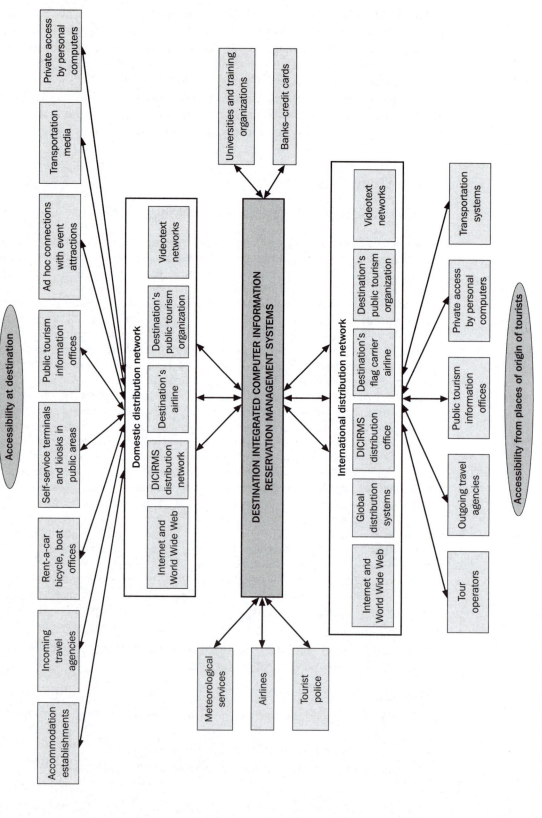

Source: Adapted from Buhalis (1994, p. 268; 1993, p. 377)

DICIRMSs should be accessible to all prospective visitors, business partners and travel intermediaries on all technological platforms, as demonstrated in Figure 11.9. At the destination area, local and wide area networks can facilitate interconnectivity among all tourism suppliers. Intelligent self-service kiosks with interactive multimedia capabilities can also assist visitors who arrive at destinations to identify and purchase suitable tourism products. At the tourists' place of origin, ICIRMSs will mainly be distributed through the Internet, mobile devices and IDTV. In addition, links to CRSs, global distribution systems and videotext networks can support the distribution network of the system. When customers book directly, they can possibly benefit by a fraction of intermediaries' commission, as a special discount. Reservations should be guaranteed against adequate deposit and a cancellation policy should clarify the obligations of both tourists and suppliers.

The low cost involved in distributing information through the web, in combination with its pace of development and usage by consumers, demonstrates that this media will be pivotal in developing and distributing DICIRMSs. The global acceptance of both the interface and programming language in the Internet, in combination with its open, interconnected operational environment, also provides a certain degree of homogeneity and compatibility between DICIRMSs representing different regions, enabling users to browse through similar types of information for alternative destinations. This, in fact, is one of the prerequisites expressed by the travel trade in order to utilize DICIRMSs.

11.9 The optimization of the impacts of tourism

DICIRMS can also play a critical role in the optimization of the impact of tourism. As far as economic benefits are concerned, DICIRMSs are instrumental in promoting diagonal integration at the destination level. Eventually most destinations will develop and use a destination system of some sort. Increasingly, therefore, it becomes evident that DICIRMSs will be unable to provide long-term competitive advantages for destinations on their own. Constant innovation should lead their development and operation and being one step ahead of competition will be critical. Instead DICIRMSs would be instrumental in assisting destinations and SMTEs to avoid competitive disadvantages by rival regions that utilize similar systems. Being able to think strategically and take advantage of the opportunities emerging through the technological revolution is a prerequisite for achieving the described strategic benefits for both destinations and SMTEs. Education and training on strategic marketing and information technology in combination with development of vision for destinations will effectively determine the degree of benefits a destination will achieve.

The competition nature in the tourism industry changes dramatically towards increasing profit margins, rather than tourism volumes. One of the main implications is, therefore, that instead of destinations and SMTEs competing with each other for the same market, the focus should shift towards identifying and co-operating with more lucrative tourism distribution channels that can provide higher profit margins. DICIRMSs should assist destinations and SMTEs to bridge their distance with consumers enhancing their intra-channel power and their ability to negotiate with intermediaries. Thus, DICIRMSs should not only compete to attract consumers from substitute destinations, but also attract them from more traditional tourism distribution channels that currently minimize SMTEs' profit margins. DICIRMSs can play a pivotal role in the rationalization of the industry and the empowerment of principals in their intra-channel negotiations with intermediaries. This approach facilitates a certain degree of disintermediation and provides alternative and/or complementary destination-based tourism distribution channels, reducing intra-channel conflicts and enabling the re-engineering of the power allocation. As a result, there is great potential for enhancing the competitiveness of destinations and SMTEs, provided that a commitment to the appropriate implementation and development of a DICIRMS is undertaken by all parties involved.

Additionally, DICIRMSs can have a major contribution towards the improvement of the socio-cultural and environmental impacts at the destination level. They can assist the setting and monitoring of **carrying capacity** limits. DICIRMSs also allow consumers to develop realistic expectations about both destinations and SMTEs. This not only increases their satisfaction, but also enhances their consciousness and respect for the socio-cultural and environmental resources of destinations. DICIRMSs can also play a part in the training of host populations at destinations, enabling them to improve their professional competence and achieve a better understanding of visitors' needs; the overall result should be an improvement in the relations between tourists and host populations. Finally, DICIRMSs should demonstrate the environmental fragility of destinations, and urge both locals and visitors to take action in order to support its sustainability. Thus, the utilization of ICTs, and DICIRMSs in particular, can play an instrumental role in destinations' ability to improve their economic, socio-cultural and environmental impacts and to sustain their resources. Specifically, remote, peripheral and insular destinations as well as small and medium-sized tourism enterprises will increasingly depend on ICTs and DICIRMSs for the optimization of their impacts in the future (Buhalis, 1997).

11.10 Lessons and issues for the future of DMSs

Despite the many, and often dissimilar, needs and wants of the various stakeholders, there are also many homogeneous requirements. Stakeholders demand reliable and accurate systems that provide user-friendly interfaces for communications with consumers, suppliers and the travel trade. Functional, effective, efficient and profitable DICIRMSs would be of a great benefit to all stakeholders. It is clear that coordination and cooperation are essential. Incompatibilities and divergences that emerge from the different stakeholders' criteria can only be overcome if communication is established, and if the common aim of making DICIRMSs successful drives the deployment of these systems. The public sector has been leading the development of DMSs and it should adopt DICIRMSs as part of its overall responsibility for the coordination, planning, management and marketing of destinations. However, DMOs have traditionally been slow in

recognizing that their active involvement may be the key in fostering cooperation among the different stakeholders. Despite their role as planners, coordina-
tors, regulators and promoters of destinations, DICIRMSs have done little to
assume the role of 'active ICT leaders' in guiding and stimulating change that
purposely benefits all stakeholders at the destination region; only a few excep-
tions can be observed globally, namely Tyrol, Ireland, Australia and Singapore.
DMOs need to be catalysts for the development of tourism at any destination,
and therefore, determine the conditions of tourism operations and encourage
collaboration of all local suppliers through DICIRMSs.

The success criteria for DICIRMSs, as shown in Figure 11.10, clearly raise a
question of feasibility. A close collaboration between public and private sectors

Figure 11.10 Success criteria for DMS stakeholders

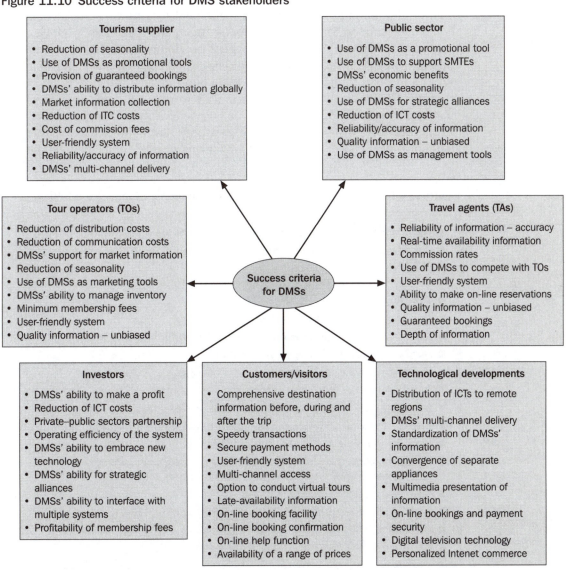

Tourism supplier
- Reduction of seasonality
- Use of DMSs as promotional tools
- Provision of guaranteed bookings
- DMSs' ability to distribute information globally
- Market information collection
- Reduction of ITC costs
- Cost of commission fees
- User-friendly system
- Reliability/accuracy of information
- DMSs' multi-channel delivery

Public sector
- Use of DMSs as a promotional tool
- Use of DMSs to support SMTEs
- DMSs' economic benefits
- Reduction of seasonality
- Use of DMSs for strategic alliances
- Reduction of ICT costs
- Reliability/accuracy of information
- Quality information – unbiased
- Use of DMSs as management tools

Tour operators (TOs)
- Reduction of distribution costs
- Reduction of communication costs
- DMSs' support for market information
- Reduction of seasonality
- Use of DMSs as marketing tools
- DMSs' ability to manage inventory
- Minimum membership fees
- User-friendly system
- Quality information – unbiased

Success criteria for DMSs

Travel agents (TAs)
- Reliability of information – accuracy
- Real-time availability information
- Commission rates
- Use of DMSs to compete with TOs
- User-friendly system
- Ability to make on-line reservations
- Quality information – unbiased
- Guaranteed bookings
- Depth of information

Investors
- DMSs' ability to make a profit
- Reduction of ICT costs
- Private–public sectors partnership
- Operating efficiency of the system
- DMSs' ability to embrace new technology
- DMSs' ability for strategic alliances
- DMSs' ability to interface with multiple systems
- Profitability of membership fees

Customers/visitors
- Comprehensive destination information before, during and after the trip
- Speedy transactions
- Secure payment methods
- User-friendly system
- Multi-channel access
- Option to conduct virtual tours
- Late-availability information
- On-line booking facility
- On-line booking confirmation
- On-line help function
- Availability of a range of prices

Technological developments
- Distribution of ICTs to remote regions
- DMSs' multi-channel delivery
- Standardization of DMSs' information
- Convergence of separate appliances
- Multimedia presentation of information
- On-line bookings and payment security
- Digital television technology
- Personalized Intenet commerce

Source: Buhalis and Spada (2000)

at the destinations, and communication as well as coordination between the different levels of tourist offices throughout the country, would be instrumental in the success of DICIRMSs. Significantly, the intervention of the public sector's agencies in the development of these systems is necessary for the mitigation of conflicts and for enabling the systems to achieve their full potential. Hence, greater emphasis should be placed on the importance of private–public sector partnerships for the successful development and implementation of DICIRMSs (Buhalis and Spada, 2000). The systems that will succeed in the future will probably need to demonstrate a number of characteristics, as illustrated in Figure 11.11.

In addition, using extranets and intranets through DICIRMSs can facilitate the development of innovative and user-friendly platforms for efficient and timely exchange of ideas and information between suppliers. An informed understanding of these attributes will support the penetration of DICIRMSs for the benefit of entire destinations, particularly for peripheral locations. A crucial objective should be to support SMTEs and encourage their participation and involvement, which in turn ensures the wider economic development of the destination. In addition, DICIRMSs should be used for education, business support and advice and as a mechanism of close collaboration and diagonal integration. More importantly, DICIRMSs should act as a neural network at the destination level that enables the industry to act and coordinate its actions proactively and reactively.

It is becoming increasingly evident that only destinations that can demonstrate long-term vision, commitment and strong strategic objectives will be able

Figure 11.11 Characteristics of successful destination systems of the future

- Vision, commitment and strategic understanding at the top
- Complete and comprehensive representation of the entire range of tourism enterprises and facilities
- Accurate information, tourism product pricing and unbiased inventory display
- Guaranteed acceptance of confirmed bookings
- Strong political and industrial support
- Secure and adequate financial bases, based on a realistic business model
- Interconnectivity and interoperability of systems
- Multi-channel strategies capitalizing on all technologies
- Strong links with all distribution partners and mechanisms
- Technology must always follow business models, not lead them
- Wide number of added-value services, based on personalized information
- Micro-sites for niche markets and specialized groups
- Convenient payment methods for consumers, guaranteed commission payment for all intermediaries involved in a booking and prompt suppliers settlement
- Easy, clear and accessible interfaces
- A degree of standardization of DMSs and DICIRMSs
- Marketing of DICIRMSs to both consumers and travel trade on-line and off-line
- SMTEs should be involved at an early stage and gain ownership

to take advantage of the emerging DICIRMS opportunities. They need to capitalize on expertise and knowledge generated globally and make brave steps towards the development and implementation of these systems. Tiscover in Tyrol, Austria is the world leader, as demonstrated in Case Study 11.4.

Case Study 11.4

Tiscover: development and growth

Following the success of Tiscover in Tyrol and Austria, the system has gradually established a family of destination tourism portals operated in partnership with a number of central European DMOs. The Tiscover partner sites include the country portals www.tiscover.com, www.tiscover.de, www.tiscover.ch, and www.tiscover.at. In addition to these Tiscover country portals, where all partners cooperate, each destination can also present itself independently, using identical technology but appearing with a completely different look and feel (for example, www.austria-tourism.com versus www.tiscover.at; and www.tirol.at versus www.tiscover.at/tirol). Hence, Tiscover is creating a community-based approach to tourism marketing that encourages healthy competition within a framework of cooperation. This 'co-opetition' allows destination marketing organizations to establish and position themselves without the hefty costs associated with building a technical system and an on-line user base and brand from scratch. This is an example of co-opetition at its best, as system and on-line marketing and distribution costs and risks are shared, but the unique identities of the destinations are preserved.

The Tiscover portals allow consumers to research destinations the way they choose. The portals feature in-depth tourist information for each destination and country, currently providing content on over 3200 tourist regions, towns and cities. They offer at-a-glance guides to top tourist attractions and cultural events, coupled with real-time on-line bookings and reservations for thousands of accommodation providers. On-line bookability is now a crucial part of tourism websites and is fully functional with Tiscover. The portals also feature weather reports and feeds from webcams positioned in popular tourist areas. The live destination portals in Austria, Germany and Switzerland are popular, with over 30 m visitors in 2000. The country portals were estimated to attract 55 m on-line visits and 200 m page views during 2001. The sites generated over €196 m in turnover for Tiscover's partners during 2000.

Taking advantage of the common platform has a number of advantages. The costs of building this kind of solution independently, with content as comprehensive as this, would be staggering, as many tourist boards have already found. Several tourist boards have invested a huge amount into making the Internet work for them. Most of this has been spent on establishing domains and on systems that often have not lived up to expectations. The Internet domain names that tourist bodies have purchased are usually not the best ones, because those are already owned by commercial parties. The systems they have bought may do a good job of managing their internal content but often fail to maximize the opportunities for eMarketing and eDistribution for consumers.

Because of the increasing number of channels of distribution both on-line and off-line, the cost of setting up an adequate system as well as the advertisement and marketing costs of building brand awareness gradually increase. The only cost-efficient way to benefit from this kind of technology is by harnessing a coopetition model. The DMO partners in Tiscover have the advantages of all the technical systems, including a stable

Case Study 11.4 *continued*

on-line database and a secure booking facility, on a full ASP (application service provision) basis, meaning all they need to get started is a PC with a modem.

The market for on-line bookings is growing dramatically. According to research from the European Travel Monitor 1999–2000, although Austria accounts for only 6 per cent of all European travel, the country accounts for over 13 per cent of on-line travel and tourism bookings, thanks to the fully functional Tiscover model. In the present economic climate, tourist boards have to work harder than ever to attract visitors both domestically and from abroad. A community approach will allow them to learn from each other's experience, to share costs and to market their destinations more effectively.

Source: Contributed by Dr Karsten Kärcher, Tiscover AG, Austria

Questions

■ Identify the success factors for destination management systems.

■ Explore whether a destination management system should represent a destination at a local, regional, national or multinational level.

11.11 Conclusions

ICTs and DICIRMSs in particular emerge as essential tools for both tourism demand and supply, as they establish a flexible and profitable communication bridge and a strategic management tool. They effectively provide the info-structure at the destination level and can network the entire range of principals and operators on a neural network. DICIRMSs are expected to have a brighter future, provided that the industry learns several lessons from the embryonic DMSs' development experiences. Destinations that embrace advanced ICTs and DICIRMSs in particular will be able to improve their strategic positioning, improve their competitiveness and optimize their benefits from tourism.

The success of eDestinations will be determined by their ability to develop interactive computerized systems, such as DICIRMSs, in order to coordinate their offering, interact with consumers, support SMTEs, integrate their entire provision and develop their brand on-line and off-line. It is inevitable that only a few DICIRMSs will be able to develop all the functions outlined and become a strategic tool for destination operational and strategic management. Vision and innovation will be critical for the competitive destination of the future.

Chapter questions

1 Why are destinations regarded as the *raison d'être* for tourism?

2 Who is responsible for coordinating the destination brand?

3 What are the relationships between tourism destination planning and marketing, and how can ICTs facilitate these processes?

4 What are the tourism demand factors that propel DMS developments?

5 What are the advantages and disadvantages of building rather than purchasing a DMS?

6 What are the internal functions of DMOs that can be supported by ICTs?

7 What is the difference between DMSs and DICIRMSs?

8 Should DMSs facilitate reservations, or should that be left to the private sector?

9 What strategic competitive advantages can be facilitated through DICIRMSs?

10 What are the key services that DMSs can offer to tour operators?

11 How can DMSs support the on-line and off-line branding of destinations?

12 How can DMSs work closely with on-line and off-line travel agencies?

13 How can DICIRMSs improve economic tourism impacts at the destination?

14 How can DICIRMSs improve socio-cultural tourism impacts at the destination?

Further reading

Buhalis, D. (1997) Information technologies as a strategic tool for economic, cultural and environmental benefits enhancement of tourism at destination regions, *Progress in Tourism and Hospitality Research*, **3**(1), 71–93.

Buhalis, D. (2000) Marketing the competitive destination of the future, *Tourism Management: Special Issue – the Competitive Destination*, **21**(1), 97–116.

Buhalis, D. and Spada, A. (2000) Destination management systems: criteria for success, *Information Technology and Tourism*, **3**(1), 41–58.

Frew, A. and O'Connor, P. (1998) A comparative examination of the implementation of destination marketing system strategies: Scotland and Ireland, in Buhalis, D., Tjoa, A.M. and Jafari, J. (eds), *Information and Communications Technologies in Tourism, ENTER 1998 Proceedings*, Springer-Verlag, Vienna, pp. 258–268.

Frew, A. and O'Connor, P. (1999) Destination marketing system strategies: refining and extending an assessment framework, in Buhalis, D. and Scherlter, W. (eds), *Information and Communications Technologies in Tourism, ENTER 1999 Proceedings*, Springer-Verlag, Vienna, pp. 398–407.

O'Connor, P. and Rafferty J. (1997) Gulliver – distributing Irish tourism electronically, *Electronic Markets*, **7**(2), 40–45

Pollock, A. (1998) Creating intelligent destinations for wired customers, in Buhalis, D., Tjoa, A.M. and Jafari, J. (eds), *Information and communications technologies in tourism, ENTER 1998 Proceedings*, Springer-Verlag, Vienna, pp. 235–248.

Sheldon, P. (1993) Destination information systems, *Annals of Tourism Research*, **20**(4), 633–649.

Wöber, K. (1998) Improving the efficiency of marketing information access and use by tourism organisations, *Information Technology and Tourism*, **1**(1), 45–59.

WTO (2001) *eBusiness for Tourism: Practical Guidelines for Destinations and Businesses*, World Tourism Organization, Madrid.

Websites

International organizations

www.world-tourism.org
www.etc-europe-travel.org
www1.oecd.org/dsti/sti/transpor/tourism
europa.eu.int/comm/enterprise/services/tourism/index_en.htm

Directories

Tourism offices: www.towd.com
Countries: www.countries.com
Cities: www.cities.com
Destinations directory: www.tourism-office.org
Antor: www.antor.com
Visit Europe: www.visiteurope.com

Destinations

Andorra: www.turisme.ad
Arizona: www.arizonaguide.com
Australia: www.australia.com
Australian Tourism Organization: www.ats.com; www.australia.com
Austria: www.tiscover.com
Barcelona: www.barcelona.com and www.easybarcelona.com
Belgium: www.visitbelgium.com
Britain: www.bta.org.uk
Caribbean: www.caribtourism.com
Cayman Islands: www.caymanislands.com
Croatia: www.htz.hr
Cyprus: www.cyprustourism.org
Denmark: www.dt.dk
Estonia: www.tourism.ee
Finland: www.mek.fi
Florida: www.flausa.com
Germany: www.germany-tourism.de
Gibraltar: www.gibraltar.gi/tourism
Great Britain: www.visitbritain.com
Greece: www.gnto.gr
Greenland: www.greenland-guide.dk/gt/default.htm
Guernsey: tourism.guernsey.net
Hungary: www.hungarytourism.hu
Iceland: www.icetourist.is
Ireland: www.ireland.travel.ie
Isle of Man: www.gov.im/tourism
Italy: www.enit.it
Japan: www.jnto.go.jp
Jersey: www.jersey.com
Latvia: www.latviatravel.com

Liechtenstein: www.searchlink.li/tourist/index.asp
Lithuania: www.tourism.lt
Louisiana: www.louisianatravel.com
Luxembourg: www.luxembourg.co.uk
Malta: www.tourism.org.mt
Netherlands: www.holland.com
New Mexico: www.newmexico.org
New Zealand: www.purenz.com
Northern Ireland: www.ni-tourism.com
Norway: www.tourist.no
Poland: www.poland.pl
Portugal: www.portugal.org
Romania: www.turism.ro
Russia: www.russia-travel.com
Scotland: www.visitscotland.com; www.Scotland.net
Singapore: www.newasia-singapore.com
Slovakia: www.sacr.sk
Slovenia: www.tourist-board.si
South Africa: www.satour.org
South Pacific Tourism Organisations: www.tcsp.com
Spain: www.espagne.infotourisme.com; www.tourspain.es
Sweden: www.gosweden.org
Texas: www.traveltex.com
Thailand: www.amazingthailand.th
Tunisia: www.tourismtunisia.com

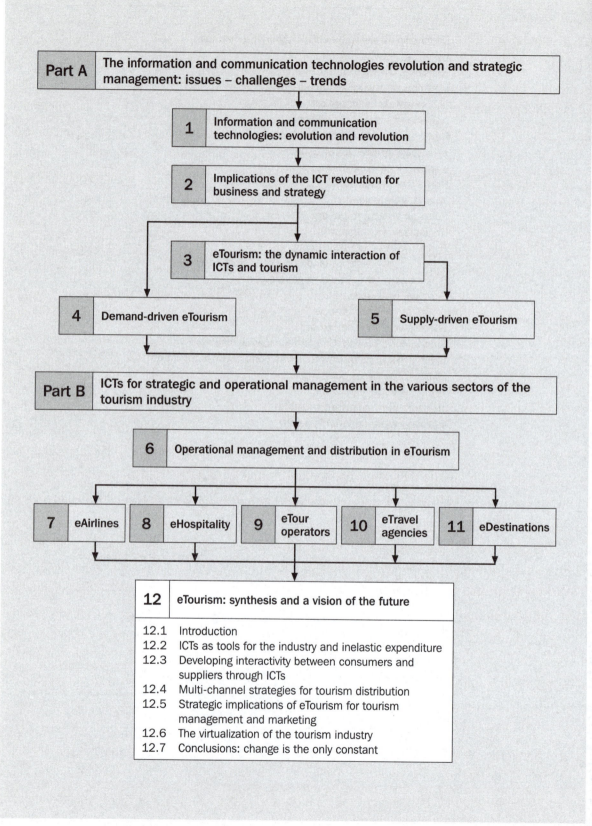

12

eTourism: synthesis and a vision of the future

Chapter objectives

The purpose of this chapter is to synthesize the arguments explored in previous chapters and to provide some indications for the future of eTourism. The chapter identifies several themes such as interactivity with consumers and the emerging ePlatforms and examines how they will influence the tourism industry of the future. Implications are drawn for a wide range of tourism stakeholders. The chapter argues that the tourism organization of the future will need to improve its virtuality in order to improve its competitiveness. Thus, the learning objectives may be defined as:

- Understand that ICTs are critical sources of competitiveness and that they will become more significant for the tourism organization of the future
- Elaborate how ICTs can support tourism organizations, destinations and intermediaries to strengthen their brand on-line and off-line
- Discuss the particular requirements of small and medium-sized enterprises and what they need to do to strengthen their position in the future
- Understand that tourism organizations will need to be proactive and reactive with regard to the utilization of ICTs for serving consumers
- Demonstrate that tourism organizations need to develop their virtuality in order to gain significant benefits
- Explain that innovative operators will be able to take advantage of the emerging opportunities
- Appreciate that change is the only constant in tourism and that eTourism will exacerbate this

12.1 Introduction

We have established that information is the life-blood of the travel industry, and that ICTs are becoming the information, communication and operation back-bone of tourism. ICTs are driving the emerging globalization of tourism demand and supply. They provide effective tools both to consumers for identifying and purchasing suitable products and to suppliers for developing, managing and distributing their offerings on a global scale. ICTs therefore become an imperative partner and they increasingly determine the interface between consumers and suppliers as well as the ability of the industry to develop, manage and market suitable tourism products globally. Hence, effective use of ICTs is pivotal for the competitiveness and prosperity of the industry and all stakeholders (Buhalis, 1998; O'Connor, 1999b; Vlitos-Rowe, 1995; Sheldon, 1997).

eTourism is the umbrella term that describes all ICT management tools and techniques used by the industry to empower its planning, development, management and marketing functions. The term brings together back- and front-office applications as well as interfaces with consumers and between partners. However, by analysing the emerging trends it is quite evident that in the last few years, and particularly since the commercial introduction of the Internet in 1995, ICTs have revolutionized tourism. They have enabled the industry to progress its offering and delivery mechanisms more than the previous three decades all together. This chapter synthesizes the ICT progress of the tourism industry in the last few years and develops a framework for future developments.

12.2 ICTs as tools for the industry and inelastic expenditure

The tourism industry is rapidly entering the eTourism era globally. The Internet and gradually mobile devices and interactive digital television (IDTV) are gaining significant importance. They increasingly contribute a significant portion of bookings for travel organizations and already several organizations distribute all their products electronically. Having gone through a long period of consumers being 'lookers' but not 'bookers', many tourism organizations have learned the lesson, improved their on-line provision and gained the confidence of the public. Although many businesses treat ICTs as a separate division and department, it is increasingly becoming evident that the 'e' element is embedded in all processes. ICTs already facilitate all travel transactions, as they provide significant tools and offer the info-structure for the business processes to take place. These days, if ICT systems cease to function for a few minutes, most airlines and larger hotel properties become paralysed, since most of their functions are dependent on these systems. Therefore, ICT investment gradually becomes inelastic and nobody will be able to escape the ICT impacts on strategic and operational management. Technology will be incorporated in all functions, processes and partnerships and unless managers design their systems properly they will have difficulty achieving their business plans.

However, ICTs are currently far from faultless and reliable tools. They often fail to fulfil the functions and services promised in their specifications. Technological deficiencies are often coupled with organizational inefficiencies and incompetencies, resulting in less than satisfactory performance. Although technology is frequently blamed, it is actually management and marketing shortcomings that generate many of these problems and prevent consumers and organizations from maximizing the prospective benefits. Frequently, this can be attributed to the inability of top management to appreciate the capabilities of ICTs and the unparalleled opportunities emerging for the tourism industry. As a result, the use of ICTs in tourism is often less satisfactory and less cost-effective than anticipated. This frequently leads to early disappointment, which in turn often leads to further inappropriate decisions being made. Therefore, for the tourism organization of the future, ICT vision and expertise will be required to act as a guide through the constant transformation in the marketplace.

The industry not only needs to improve its interactivity with consumers, but also to readdress product issues and all elements of the marketing mix. This will enable the value offered to customers to be maximized, creating value in terms of both money and time. The emerging ICTs and the re-engineering of business processes in tourism generated a paradigm shift, altering the structure of the entire industry and developing a whole range of opportunities and threats for all stakeholders. Careful ICT management will be crucial for tourism organizations to safeguard their interests. Starting too early may mean that huge amounts of money will need to be invested into innovative technologies that are far ahead of their time and have a limited penetration to consumers. Leaving it too late may also damage the prospects of an organization as it will be much more difficult to acquire significant market share. Hence, ICT developments represent a revolution for the tourism industry that could be compared to the introduction of the jet engine.

12.3 Developing interactivity between consumers and suppliers through ICTs

eTourism offers new tools and mechanisms for direct communication with consumers and empowers the interactivity to unprecedented levels. Consumers, for the first time ever, can access information on everything, on a 24-hours/365-days-a-year basis, from the convenience of their armchair. More importantly, they can access an amazing wealth of supplementary resources, which are often provided by non-commercial entities, building their knowledge and expertise on a wide range of issues. Transparency, empowered through web-based interactivity as well as the introduction of the euro in Europe, enables consumers to compare prices and to rationalize their choices.

The development of new ICTs creates the 'new' tourist. Experienced and sophisticated travellers become knowledgeable and seek exceptional value for money and time, as well as participation in special-interest activities. Thus, the relative importance of package tours, which are often based on low quality/low prices, is expected to decline in favour of independently organized tourism. A relatively new movement towards environmental preservation and appreciation of local cultures, history and societies is also evident in tourism and gains great support from travellers. Consumers are less tolerant of environmentally degraded regions and mass-tourism resorts. Increasingly, customers require real experiences that involve rich cultural, artistic, environmental and social resources. ICTs already enable environmentally sensitive information to be publicly accessible, restricting the over-marketing of regions and supporting only genuinely suitable places. Frequently, holiday makers develop amateur web pages and share their experiences in a region with other people, supported by photographs and video footage.

The WTO (1988) argues that 'the key to success lies in the quick identification of consumer needs and in reaching potential clients with comprehensive, personalised and up-to-date information'. Every tourist is different, carrying a unique blend of experiences, motivations and desires. To an extent, the new sophisticated traveller has emerged as a result of previous experience and new ICT tools. Tourists from the major generating regions of the world have become frequent travellers, are linguistically and technologically skilled and can function in multicultural and demanding environments overseas. Hence, customer satisfaction increasingly depends on the accuracy and comprehensiveness of specific information on destinations' accessibility, facilities, attractions and activities. Travellers require not only value for money but also value for time for the entire range of their dealings with tourism organisations. This includes the research, purchasing, consumption and feedback processes of the traveller's circle. These trends reflect people's shortage of time as well as the high-quality requirements already evident in Western societies. Increasingly, ICTs assist travellers to access reliable and accurate information as well as to undertake reservations in a fraction of the time, cost and inconvenience required by conventional methods. ICTs are therefore instrumental in improving the service quality and in contributing to higher guest/traveller satisfaction. A wide range of ICT developments that empower consumers and support their satisfaction were indicated in Chapter 4.

Tourists tend to participate in the experience by being active and by spending their time on their special interests. Leisure time will increasingly be used for 'edutainment', i.e. the exploration of personal interests for both personal and professional development. Flexibility, in both consumer choice and service delivery processes, becomes a key element. The use of ICTs in the industry is driven by both the development of the size and complexity of tourism demand, as well as by the rapid expansion and sophistication of new tourism products that address mini-market segments. Increasingly, new, experienced, sophisticated, demanding travellers seek information about more exotic destinations and authentic experiences, as well as require to interact with suppliers to satisfy their specific needs and wishes. The contemporary/connected consumer is far less willing to wait or put up with delays, to the point where patience is a disappearing virtue.

The gradual development of ambient technologies and the 3G mobile devices will provide the 'Internet on the move' and will empower consumers further by providing location- and time-dependent information, offers and services. Not only will travellers be able to search the entire inventory of a destination or a town for availability and prices but they will also be targeted by organizations that add special value or offer reduced prices. This can allow consumers to browse for information when they need it, cut down the search time and make them more responsive to elements of the environment they visit as well as to their personal needs as required at each stage.

12.4 Multi-channel strategies for tourism distribution

As demonstrated in previous chapters, a number of electronic platforms have emerged to facilitate the distribution of tourism and travel products. This has altered the tourism intermediation function. Traditionally, the travel distribution role has been performed by outbound travel agencies, tour operators and inbound travel agents or handling agencies (Buhalis and Laws, 2001). They were supported by a number of *traditional electronic intermediaries* (or eTourism intermediaries) such as computer reservation systems (CRSs), global distribution systems (GDSs) and tour operators' videotext systems (leisure travel networks) that enabled them to communicate with principals and to facilitate the reservation function. In addition, tour operators used teletext to display late deals and special offers directly to consumers' TV. These eTourism intermediaries gradually developed links between themselves and often they merged or created close partnerships. GDSs, for example, progressively consolidated their position to four major systems, namely SABRE, Amadeus, Galileo and Worldspan, while videotext systems developed connections with CRSs and GDSs to allow travel agencies to access more principals (Kärcher, 1996; French, 1998).

However, the development of the Internet as well as the gradual development of mobile devices and interactive digital television facilitate the development of a whole range of new eTourism intermediaries. Effectively everybody who has access to consumers through a portal, a vertical portal (vortal), an electronic newspaper or mobile service tries to sell tourism. On the one hand they recognize the suitability of the tourism products for eCommerce and on the other they desperately try to create revenue streams for their services. This has blurred the differences between technological platforms and eTourism intermediation further. As a result, tourism organizations need to develop multi-channel strategies to be able to address the needs of the marketplace. This effectively means that they need to assess the entire range of eTourism intermediaries, including Internet, mobile, digital television and calling centre channels, on top of the high street presence. Traditional eTourism intermediaries, such as GDSs, CRSs, videotext and teletext, should also be examined, to evaluate their potential in the long and short term. These media will still be critical, at least during the transition period, when legacy systems will prevent players from upgrading their systems. Evaluating all channels will allow tourism players to develop a strategy that will support them to capitalize on all available media for communicating effectively and profitably with their consumers. It is also important to realize that different channels and platforms will be used by different market segments and also at different stages of the travel experience. The competitiveness of tourism organizations of the future therefore will depend on their ability to manage effectively multi-channel strategies and to support commerce through all potential channels and eCommerce opportunities, namely:

- iCommerce: Internet-empowered commerce
- tCommerce: interactive digital television commerce
- mCommerce: mobile devices commerce
- cCommerce: calling centre-empowered commerce
- wCommerce: walk-in commerce in traditional shops

12.4.1 eTourism intermediaries: the revolution of intermediation

Leiper's (1995) tourism system can be used to explain the transformation of the ICT supported distribution channels, as illustrated in Figure 12.1. This demonstrates that the tourism system is composed of the place of consumers' origin and the destination, with a number of tourism firms offering their services. In the transit region there are transportation companies and traditional inter-mediaries and the system has been supported by GDSs, teletext and viewdata for most of the 1990s. However, the Internet and eCommerce developments in the late 1990s and the adoption of tourism as one of the prime B2B (business-to-business) and B2C (business-to-consumers) applications have changed the situation rapidly (Buhalis, 1998; O'Connor, 1999b; Smith and Jenner, 1998). On one hand, the development of the Internet as a universal and interactive means of communication, and on the other, the parallel change in consumer behaviour and attitudes, have radically changed the traditional way tourism and travel products have been distributed (Werthner and Klein, 1999; O'Connor and Frew, 2000).

The Internet is used widely as a means to deliver up-to-date content. As a result, it created the conditions for the emergence of a wide range of new eTourism

Figure 12.1 Old eTourism Intermediaries

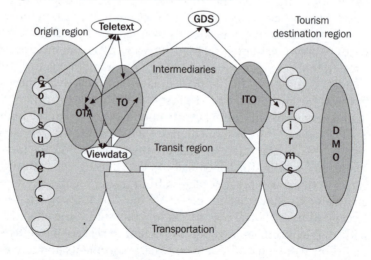

Source: After Buhalis and Licata, 2002

players. The proliferation of eTourism intermediaries followed a period of euphoria, when a great member of players hoped that they would generate a high volume of profit by targeting the tourism industry and by selling tourism products on-line. As demonstrated in previous chapters, tourism suppliers (particularly airlines, car-rental firms and hotels chains) took advantage of the new opportunities and developed eCommerce applications by allowing users to access directly their reservation systems. This included single-supplier provisions, such as British Airways (**www.britishairways.com**), Marriott Hotels (**www.marriott.com**) and Avis (**www.avis.com**). Moreover, several destinations developed destination management systems (DMSs) to distribute their smaller properties and to present the destination as a holistic entity (e.g. **www.tiscover.com**, **www.holland.com**). The major GDSs, following a period of inertia, gradually entered the on-line market by developing interfaces for consumers (e.g. **www.travelocity.com**, owned by Sabre, and **www.trip.com**, owned by Galileo), although they are still less proactive than newer players (O'Connor, 1999b; Buhalis, 1998, 2000a; Richer and O'Neill-Dunne, 1999).

A number of new eTourism intermediaries have also emerged to take advantage of the Internet capabilities. Most of these are new entrants, often owned or powered by existing but non-tourism organizations. Web-based travel agencies were established (e.g. **www.expedia.com**, **www.ebookers.com**, **www.travelocity.com**), while off-line agencies developed their on-line provision (e.g. **www.thomascook. com**, **www.lunnpoly.com**). Internet portals (e.g. **Yahoo**, **Altavista**, **Excite**) and vertical portals (vortals) (e.g. **www.ski.com**, **www.golfonline.com**, **www.tennis. com**) also created on-line travel distribution channels, often by sourcing their travel content from external on-line agents and suppliers. Media companies such as newspapers (**travel.telegraph.co.uk**) and television networks (**www.cnn.com/ travel**) gradually integrated their off-line content with their on-line provision and were expanded to include eCommerce capabilities on their sites. On-line last-minute agencies also emerged to enable distressed inventory to be distributed efficiently (e.g. **www.lastminute.com**). priceline.com reversed the pricing method and allowed passengers to search for suppliers that would be prepared to serve them for the amount of money that consumers specified. Finally, a number of sites (e.g. **www.qxl.com**, **www.ebay.com**) specialized in the sale of distressed stock through auctions. Following these developments several multi-supplier web pages emerged to support airlines to reduce the influence of on-line travel agencies such as expedia.com (e.g. **www.opodo.com**, **www.orbitz.com**). The proliferation of eTourism intermediaries confused consumers and the industry since many marketing managers rushed to ensure that their products were represented in all distribution channels and realized the difficulty and cost of doing so. Standardization of processes and operating systems represent a major barrier for multichannel strategies, as demonstrated in Chapter 9.

In addition to these new, Internet-based eTourism intermediaries, there is a gradual emergence of further organizations using mobile devices (mobile phones, palm tops etc., as well as vehicle-fitted devices) and interactive digital television to distribute tourism. More traditional calling centres have also emerged to support consumers who would prefer to speak to agencies for trouble-shooting or for completing a transaction. A framework identifying a number of new eTourism intermediaries, based on the three emerging ePlatforms (Internet, mobile devices

Figure 12.2 New eTourism intermediation and intermediaries

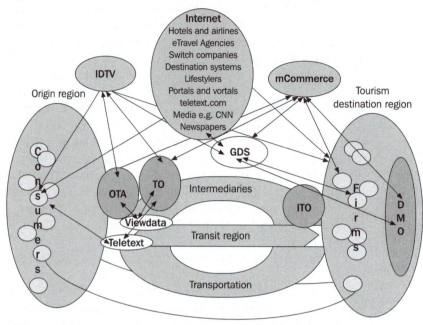

Source: After Buhalis and Licata, 2002

and IDTV) is demonstrated in Figure 12.2. Figure 12.3 also demonstrates examples of traditional and new eTourism intermediaries (Buhalis and Licata, 2002).

12.4.2 eTourism intermediaries: using multi-channel strategies

Advanced communication technologies, the gradual commercialization of IDTV and the growing availability of tourism products and services on mobile networks (mCommerce) will intensify competition further. Therefore, traditional eTourism intermediaries, such as GDSs, videotext and teletext, as well as principals and destinations, should re-assess the way they conduct business to ensure that they remain competitive and benefit from the emergent opportunities. Using innovative interfaces and advanced business models, they can redesign their strategies and distribute their products to wider audiences, enhancing their position. This will be increasingly critical in a market that focuses on direct marketing and cost/commission cuttings (Jarvela et al., 1999). However, ICT developments are expected to create major problems for organizations that fail to adopt and modernize, as new eTourism intermediaries will be competing to maximize their market share by adding value and benefits for both business and leisure end-users.

The advantages and disadvantages of the emerging ePlatforms, namely the Internet, mCommerce and interactive digital TV, will determine their abilities to develop their market share and facilitate transactions (Buhalis and Licata, 2002).

Internet opportunities

The Internet provides access to a great number of people and offers the opportunity to develop closer relationships with customers. Enabling consumers to

Figure 12.3 Traditional eTourism intermediaries vs new eTourism intermediaries

Traditional eTourism intermediaries	New eTourism intermediaries	
GDSs: – Sabre – Amadeus – Galileo – Worldspan	Principals: – Airlines	www.flybmi.com www.airfrance.com www.opodo.com www.orbitz.com
Viewdata	– Hotels	www.marriott.com www.oscar.gr
Teletext	Destinations	www.tiscover.at www.holland.com
	Switch companies	www.utell.com
	Travel agencies	www.lunnpoly.com www.expedia.com www.travelocity.com
	Last-minute bookings	www.lastminute.com
	Portals	www.yahoo.com www.lycos.com
	Vortals	www.tennis.com www.igolf.com
	Newspapers	travel.telegraph.co.uk
	News media	cnn.com
	Auction sites	www.qxl.com www.ebay.com

communicate with organizations on a 24-hours, 365-days-a-year basis, it supports organizations in implementing customer relationship management programmes and enhances the opportunities for a better understanding of customer needs. This interaction generates a whole range of new requirements for organizations, as they need to be accessible and available constantly. Hence, calling centres and interactive teams have been developed by a wide range of organizations to support their Internet distribution. Although this is expensive to develop and maintain, many tourism organizations have reduced their distribution and overhead costs. This is because they can afford to pay less commission (or no commission in some airlines' case) to intermediaries and at the same time reduce their labour cost, as consumers do the manual work of data entry, instead of employees of the company. The Internet has therefore been identified as a clear beneficial distribution platform for many innovative tourism organizations.

The volatile customer base is a major opportunity, as organizations can expand their offering to new segments and geographical regions. The Internet can also help principals to identify and target customers more accurately and effectively. A wide range of segmentation questions is often asked in the profiling of consumers during the Internet registration process. As a result, specific market segments are frequently diverted to specialized parts of the Internet provision.

Moreover, tour operators and leisure travel networks can benefit from the globalization of the selling process, as they increasingly need to mass-customize their products. Transcending geographical borders allows them to penetrate foreign markets and to embrace a much wider consumer pool, towards expanding their market share. The use of multimedia is less important currently, as the bandwidth restrictions do not allow the potential for multimedia content diffusion to be fully realized by industry. However, great potential exists for the utilization of multimedia to convey graphic information and animation about tourism products. This can include videos, maps, interactive presentations etc. Once the technical problems are resolved, innovative tourism organizations would be able to take advantage of the enormous opportunities emerging through multimedia. Broad bandwidth and the asymmetric digital subscriber line (ADSL) technology will be critical for allowing the transmission of digital information at high bandwidths on existing phone lines, for supporting Internet users at home.

However, the lack of human contact during the interaction and the lack of face-to-face up-sell/cross-sell opportunities provide some new challenges for tourism organizations. Since on-line users do not have physical contact with the actual seller, it is more difficult for the seller to instigate further sales, or to lead customers to purchase more expensive or additional products. However, as demonstrated in Chapter 9, evidence from Scandinavian countries demonstrates that the Internet is more successful in cross-selling. If designed properly, consumers can be encouraged to add extra elements out of their own initiative and to enquire about issues on-line, without being embarrassed about asking questions of a human agent. As the interaction between the consumer and the tourism organizations is demand-driven, it may actually address the needs, personality, pace and phobias of the consumer in a better way. Instead of meeting an often-inexperienced travel consultant in a high street shop, after having struggled to park and then waited in the queue for their turn, a number of travel companies already offer specialized support through their calling centres and enable consumers to ask specific questions of a product/property/destination specialist. Traditional intermediaries, such as Thomas Cook, can enhance their provision for their customers who would prefer to go on-line, while maintaining their traditional markets. Security issues are still perceived as significant, but increasingly consumers who use on-line services appreciate the benefits and realize eCommerce is more secure than many other forms of purchasing. Hence, the Internet and the on-line support may actually improve the service and experience for the consumer.

Interactive digital television (IDTV) distribution opportunities

IDTV is a wide-reaching, populist channel and it is expected that a number of commercial tourism applications will be fully functional. Although the technical capability for distributing tourism through the IDTV is already available, there have been limited commercial applications hitherto. IDTV is expected to have a major impact on tourism distribution. As most households already possess a TV set, it is widely used and people have an affiliation with it. It requires no technical understanding, and hence imposes no knowledge-based barrier. IDTV requires a set-top box, which in most cases can be obtained free with the subscription to a digital broadcaster's services. Thus, IDTV will be accessible to a greater portion of the population than the Internet and it will allow a greater penetration into the home market as well as to a greater age spectrum. Viewers frequently trust their favourite TV channels for accessing information, news and political debate. Television is turned on habitually in households and often provides entertainment, information and debate.

A new wave of digital television technology will be emerging in the very near future, with significant implications for the tourism industry as a result. Consumers are expected to use IDTV widely at the inspiration stage of their holiday planning. Being able to watch programmes on destinations, travel themes and activities and facilities is expected to inspire consumers to identify suitable travel activities; then search facilities will enable them to download multimedia information, video-on-demand and other information to support their search functions. IDTV will probably inspire greater confidence in the on-line buyer, as transactions could be perceived to be safer than they would be on the Internet as IDTV will operate on 'closed' networks. IDTV is expected to change the travel distribution channel dramatically, as it will support easier access to consumers and allow the provision of multimedia information on demand and also integrate a wide range of technologies. IDTV-based tourism distribution benefits from several factors, including:

- rich communication medium, offering multimedia presentations, video-on-demand and more realistic footage of destinations and tourism facilities;
- enables a more relaxed atmosphere than when using the Internet;
- interactive and allows video-on-demand, with full motion pictures and sound;
- presents content to the family/group rather than simply to the individual, therefore it will be targeted more to the home than the business market;
- does not need to be switched on through a procedure;
- easy to use and people are already using it habitually.

However IDTV is still developing technologically and, as such, it may not yet be fully functional and ready to be used in the home market on a large scale. Although IDTV usage is currently limited and can reach only a limited customer base, its customer base will expand rapidly in the future. It is therefore only a matter of time until the technology will be developed to a degree that will enable the full capitalization of the potential. Technological convergence and the expansion of commercial services on IDTV will empower organizations to take advantage of the full potential. IDTV will become more advanced, incorporating an increasing number of eCommerce features that will render it superior to the Internet in terms of product information provision and ease of purchase.

Tour operators and high-street travel agents feel that high costs may prove to be a barrier for companies wishing to participate in IDTV marketing and distribution ventures. High entry cost barriers may favour exclusively larger brands, posing a serious obstacle to smaller companies, especially those operating exclusively on-line. However, with a likely cross-over between the Internet and IDTV, this situation may change in the near future.

The degree of customer interaction with IDTV is also still unknown. Despite the greater possibility for multimedia presentations, television has been a 'lean backwards'-type media. Customers can sit back and watch what happens on the screen, but not necessarily interact and customize in the same way they would on the Internet. So far there has been limited capability for active interaction in analogue channels, mainly through teletext, and that has been used extensively for tourism. Special and last-minute offers are distributed through this channel and travel updates are accessed regularly. It will be the convergence between different technologies that will change the perception of TV from an entertainment unit to an interactive service station, offering entertainment, information and interaction with the external world. The introduction of IDTV eMail, for example, will gradually force viewers to change their attitude towards TV. By the year 2005 IDTV is expected to play a significant role in leisure travel distribution and it should be considered as a major enabler and ePlatform for global travel distribution. Within a few years, the Internet and IDTV ePlatforms will be complementary and mutually reinforcing, running in parallel in the future, empowering cross-promotion and cross-navigation. This will inevitably develop the larger eTourism provision. However the two ePlatforms may potentially aim at different:

- markets and segments: higher socio-economic classes vs lower income;
- different times: morning/noon/evening/night;
- geographical locations: countries/regions;
- uses: business trips vs leisure products and family holiday;
- locations of use: office/home/on the road.

Convergence will support tourism organizations to produce seamless experiences for users and it will enable each platform to perform best on its established strengths. The Internet is expected to be a clear leader in the search, inventory development and transaction front. IDTV is expected to empower the multimedia element, which will allow consumers to download and watch real video footage from tourism destinations, products and services. Hence, IDTV will play a major role in the 'inspire' stage, when consumers seek inspiration before they start searching for their tourism products and experiences and also at the 'detailed search' stage, when particular facilities, attractions and activities will be accessed.

Mobile and mCommerce distribution opportunities

Mobile devices and mCommerce will be critical for the eTourism of the future. Mobile devices are gradually emerging as a major distribution ePlatform for tourism. WAP technologies provided the first opportunity to develop data communication with mobile phones. However, WAP technologies offered limited capabilities and failed to live up to expectations. This can be attributed to marketing 'over-hype', which promised 'Internet-on-the-go', developing unrealistic expectations that were not consistent with the prevailing technology and business models. As a result, there is currently a genuine mistrust among consumers regarding mobile commerce and information.

However, the opportunity for providing location-dependent information and reservation is critical for tourism and for the constantly moving consumer. The third-generation (3G) mobile devices are expected to arrive by 2005 and they will provide great opportunities for travel distribution through this platform; they and future-generation mobile services will combine high-speed mobile access with Internet protocol (IP)-based services and will support users in transmitting voice, data and even moving images by improving the data-transmission speed. 3G can also provide services like Internet connection, transmission of large-scale data and moving contents photographed by digital cameras and videos, and software downloading. This will support a whole new way of communicating, accessing information, conducting business, learning and being entertained while on the move, providing great opportunities for tourism organizations. With access to any service anywhere, anytime, from one terminal, the old boundaries between communication, information, media and entertainment will gradually disappear, offering convergence between technologies and tourism services.

Eventually, mobile devices will develop their technical capabilities to allow users to undertake a number of tasks simultaneously. This can include making video calls to the office, surfing the Internet, accessing tourism information, or playing interactive games with friends at home, regardless of user location. 3G technologies will be able to deliver a wide range of market-focused applications through advanced, lightweight and easy-to-use terminals with intuitive interfaces. Tourism organizations therefore have the opportunity to develop innovative value chains and user benefits, driving genuine market demand to their services. This will be particularly important for travellers requiring services at their present location. Mobile operators will be able to present a range of vendors and operators, at close proximity, offering choice, competition and affordability.

The way 3G is introduced in a particular market depends entirely on the business plans of the mobile operators, and the licence requirements imposed by the regulatory authorities. Japan's NTT DoCoMo launched the world's first commercialized third-generation ('FOMA') mobile communication service, on October 2001. In Europe and the USA a number of regulatory and economic issues need to be resolved, on top of the technical ones. The auction process of 3G mobile network licences has forced operators to compete ferociously to get one of the valuable bandwidth slots. Managing user expectations for mobile services, as well as economic models and profitability issues, are critical aspects of this development, especially since most European operators have invested heavily in gaining 3G licences.

It is clear that mCommerce will follow the Internet ePlatform, as a number of Internet-based operators will offer services through different platforms. Tourism providers already use WAP and SMS for distributing information, for allowing consumers to check flight arrivals and departures, and for checking in. Examples mentioned include airlines (e.g. Finnair: **www.finnair.fi/wap/index.wml**), destinations (e.g. Tyrol: **wap.Tiscover.at**), electronic travel agencies (e.g. Expedia to Go: **www.expedia.co.uk**) and hotels (e.g. Amari: **wap.amari.com**). Tourism organizations are expected to expand their Internet provision to support mobile devices once the technology is in place. Mobile devices may be more useful to frequent business travellers and to people that habitually purchase familiar tourism products, rather than to novices who need to search and identify the most suitable product before purchasing. mCommerce can also support last-minute sales as well as reservations and changes near to departure or arrival time.

Many telecommunication companies have started developing on-line travel services, in partnership with electronic travel agencies and other suppliers. For example, Genie has already developed partnerships with expedia.com, British

Airways and lastminute.com to enable WAP-based tourism distribution. The challenge really lies in developing content and information that can be streamed through many different platforms. Perhaps the business model used for mCommerce will need to be different from that of the Internet, as consumers are willing to pay for getting connected to WAP portals. Therefore tourism organizations may be able to charge telecommunication companies fees for content and therefore share their income from the connection time.

In addition, Bluetooth technology will enable the silent communication between personal devices and equipment used by the industry. For example, a customer arriving in a hotel or an airport will eventually be able to check-in *en route*, confirm arrival to the airport/hotel through a Bluetooth device, receive navigation directions and instructions and go straight to the correct flight gate or room. Similarly, checking-out procedures can be simplified considerably by Bluetooth technologies that will request the bill, authorize it and communicate credit-card details before departure. This change is predicted to revolutionize the tourism industry further as it will need to be both proactive in designing appropriate products and reactive in having the info-structure in place to communicate with consumers, respond to their requirements at each stage and maximize their profitability. For the consumer, looking after them before, during and after their purchasing will be the only way to add value and differentiate the product, offering competitive advantage.

Once mCommerce is fully operational it is expected to institute a major change in the way tourism products are purchased, as it will support location-dependent distribution. mCommerce will also allow consumers to purchase products on the go and it will help them identify available products and services locally. As a result, consumers may be reluctant to search in advance and may rely more heavily on services offered at the destination. Similarly mCommerce will allow organizations to target consumers provide special promotions, offers and services. However, technical difficulties experienced by 3G developers as well as unproven business models may delay the commercialization of these services.

12.4.3 eTourism convergence and platforms

The Internet, IDTV and mobile communication devices are clearly identified as the three most significant ePlatforms for the future. They enable consumers to obtain more information, in more detail, in a more independent manner, matching their increased knowledge about destinations and products as well as their sophistication. Technological convergence will enable tourism organizations to use the same content and information to distribute through all three platforms for different markets, users, times, locations and occasions. All electronic distribution channels will ultimately be running on enhanced, open and complementary technologies. The initial business travel bias of the Internet platform will eventually be followed by the leisure traveller, as more consumers trust on-line providers to arrange their inventory and as more organizations develop their offering on-line. The introduction of IDTV is also likely to have a strong impact on the home/leisure market.

The technical capabilities of the competitive tourism organizations are improving rapidly. More advanced and reliable technologies and database packages reduce the need for human operator intervention and allow greater precision in the quality of data. Therefore, the updating and maintenance of databases gradually become easier. This has been achieved through the automation of product information updating processes and the use of 'intelligent' web forms, where user-entered data can be inserted automatically in databases. In addition, the employment of ICT experts gradually reduces technical problems and helps organizations to concentrate on their business. Hence the Internet offers more opportunities for differentiation, for market, products and services development, and for taking advantage of records through data-warehousing and data-mining for dynamic marketing.

The use of new distribution channels and the launch of value-added services and features across all ePlatforms and distribution channels clearly affect the competitiveness of all tourism intermediaries. The commercial introduction and subsequent potential take-off of tourism services based on IDTV and mobile technology will enable new eTourism intermediaries to achieve a further penetration into both home and business markets. The eminent convergence of the Internet, IDTV and mobile telephony will provide a further competitive advantage for new eTourism intermediaries as they will be adopting a multi-platform approach to serve different users at different times and situations. New eTourism intermediaries (e.g. on-line travel agents, portals) in the electronic distribution market challenge traditional eTourism intermediaries (e.g. GDSs and viewdata) as they gradually penetrate the marketplace, gain direct access to consumers and increase their market share. The timely delivery of relevant, content-rich information is one of the main differentiating factors in the on-line market. New eTourism intermediaries are expected to take advantage of the ePlatforms capabilities and increase their presence in the marketplace. Traditional eTourism intermediaries will either have to modernize to the new realities, by developing their on-line presence and adopting a multi-channel strategy, or face significant losses in their market share and value.

Only competitive, flexible and dynamic eTourism intermediaries will use both old and new ePlatforms to survive and expand in the future. Mergers, alliances, partnerships and re-developments will all be used regularly to enable partners to remain competitive. Inevitably there will be several winners who will use all available ePlatforms to deliver products in the most suitable way for their market segments. However, a large proportion of players will fail to modernize fast enough to develop suitable business models and market propositions. These players will probably suffer catastrophic consequences. The only winners in the future will be consumers and those principals and intermediaries who adopt a dynamic, flexible and innovative strategic and tactical management.

12.5 Strategic implications of eTourism for tourism management and marketing

ICTs provide the tools to re-engineer and rationalize the tourism industry. However, the reliability and functionality of the tools as well as their cost need to be improved, while their use should be advanced. This will enable the development of all the direct links required and the establishment of close partnerships between all stakeholders in the industry, as illustrated in Figure 12.4. The forecasted developments will effectively be able to bring a whole range of new benefits for the consumer as well as for innovative and forward-looking tourism suppliers. These developments are expected to have major implications for tourism management and marketing of tourism enterprises. The technological developments need to be backed and stimulated by innovative and robust management and marketing of tourism organizations if they are to fulfil their entire potential (Fesenmaier et al., 1999).

12.5.1 Strategic implications of eTourism for the consumer of the future

Consumer benefits include more information/knowledge about products, services and destinations. This allows consumers to have a higher involvement in planning their travel and in building their own itineraries. As a result, niche markets can grow rapidly by enabling tourism organizations to offer consumers themed, specialized and personalized experiences. More information and competition also allow consumers to shop around and often to reduce the price they have to pay for tourism products. On-line bargaining allows suppliers to sell their distressed capacity and maximize their yield, while offering competitive pricing for the leisure/flexible traveller. A greater level of transparency is also evident, enabling consumers to search the best available product for each occasion. Although the English language dominates both the Internet and international tourism, new tools emerge to assist non-English speakers, such as automatic translation or regional sites on the local language.

Security of transactions and quality assurance of both services and information are critical for consumer satisfaction. Although prospective travellers are still concerned about giving their credit-card details on the Internet, advanced encryption techniques pioneered by credit-card companies are gradually making the Internet safer and increasing consumer confidence. It needs to be emphasized that transaction security over the Internet is also a perceptual issue. In most cases, consumers trust unknown waiters or shop assistants to disappear with their credit card while settling their accounts or happily give their credit-card details to strangers over the phone or fax in order to purchase products and services. However, they are often reluctant to provide credit-card details in a much more secure, encrypted electronic transaction, which is often fully automated. It is reported that electronic intermediaries, such as Expedia and Travelocity, have not experienced any security problems despite selling several million tickets on-line. The objective danger for on-line fraud will gradually be reduced, as encryption systems and credit-card companies improve on-line transaction security. As consumers start purchasing goods on the Internet and realize that there are no major risks, their security concerns will decrease rapidly.

It is widely reported that consumers will be the main winners of technological developments, as they will have more choice, more interactivity and more personalized products to choose from. Never before have consumers had as much power as they have today and never before could consumers influence their tourism product more than in the 21st century.

Figure 12.4 eTourism: stakeholder ICT requirements for the future

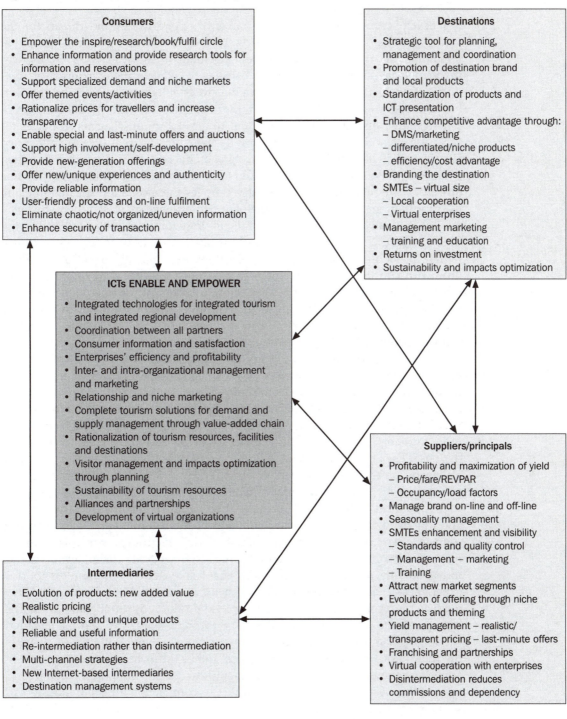

Consumers

- Empower the inspire/research/book/fulfil circle
- Enhance information and provide research tools for information and reservations
- Support specialized demand and niche markets
- Offer themed events/activities
- Rationalize prices for travellers and increase transparency
- Enable special and last-minute offers and auctions
- Support high involvement/self-development
- Provide new-generation offerings
- Offer new/unique experiences and authenticity
- Provide reliable information
- User-friendly process and on-line fulfilment
- Eliminate chaotic/not organized/uneven information
- Enhance security of transaction

Destinations

- Strategic tool for planning, management and coordination
- Promotion of destination brand and local products
- Standardization of products and ICT presentation
- Enhance competitive advantage through:
  - DMS/marketing
  - differentiated/niche products
  - efficiency/cost advantage
- Branding the destination
- SMTEs – virtual size
  - Local cooperation
  - Virtual enterprises
- Management marketing
  - training and education
- Returns on investment
- Sustainability and impacts optimization

ICTs ENABLE AND EMPOWER

- Integrated technologies for integrated tourism and integrated regional development
- Coordination between all partners
- Consumer information and satisfaction
- Enterprises' efficiency and profitability
- Inter- and intra-organizational management and marketing
- Relationship and niche marketing
- Complete tourism solutions for demand and supply management through value-added chain
- Rationalization of tourism resources, facilities and destinations
- Visitor management and impacts optimization through planning
- Sustainability of tourism resources
- Alliances and partnerships
- Development of virtual organizations

Suppliers/principals

- Profitability and maximization of yield
  - Price/fare/REVPAR
  - Occupancy/load factors
- Manage brand on-line and off-line
- Seasonality management
- SMTEs enhancement and visibility
  - Standards and quality control
  - Management – marketing
  - Training
- Attract new market segments
- Evolution of offering through niche products and theming
- Yield management – realistic/transparent pricing – last-minute offers
- Franchising and partnerships
- Virtual cooperation with enterprises
- Disintermediation reduces commissions and dependency

Intermediaries

- Evolution of products: new added value
- Realistic pricing
- Niche markets and unique products
- Reliable and useful information
- Re-intermediation rather than disintermediation
- Multi-channel strategies
- New Internet-based intermediaries
- Destination management systems

12.5.2 Implications of eTourism for principals and SMTEs

ICT developments introduce a wide range of opportunities and threats for the various players in the tourism industry. Airlines have been pioneering the use of technology for their marketing and management since the early 1970s. Increasingly they take advantage of ICTs in order to achieve better control of their distribution costs and processes, as well as to establish innovative and interactive partnerships with consumers and intermediaries. This has propelled them to redesign their distribution channels and to develop multi-channel strategies for accessing their clientèle. In addition, ICTs have propelled airlines to collaborate closely, initially through code-sharing agreements and gradually to full stretched alliances. Similarly car rental, trains and ferry companies are heading in the same direction, although the airline industry is by far the most sophisticated in using ICTs for their marketing and management. Hotels have increased their efficiency and are gradually taking advantage of technology for promoting and distributing their products. International corporations also use ICTs in order to coordinate remote properties and to expand their operations globally. Developing direct links with consumers enables hotels to maximize their yield by offering special prices and negotiated corporate rates on the Internet. At the micro-level, tourism suppliers/principals can maximize their long-term profitability, through close interaction with their clientèle, yield management and networking as well as through developing value-added chains and enhancing virtual close cooperations.

A wide range of opportunities and challenges also emerges for smaller and medium-sized tourism enterprises (SMTEs). Traditionally, the vast majority of tourism suppliers are small and family-run. Hence they face enormous difficulties in marketing their products globally and compete with their larger counterparts. SMTEs frequently perceive ICTs as a problem and challenge. Although they have more available tools, they still lack the expertise and knowledge to maximize their use. They feel that ICTs take away some of their independence, as they have to depend on technology experts for their systems. SMTEs need to take advantage of the emerging ICTs in order to reduce their marginalization from the mainstream tourism industry and to make their products available to institutional and independent buyers. The development of the Internet empowers even tiny tourism organizations to be represented in the electronic marketplace and to network with consumers and partners alike. ICTs facilitate the amalgamation of independently produced products and enable the delivery of seamless tourism experiences. They may also be able to achieve competitive advantages if they manage to develop and position their niche products as unique and authentic. Enhancing the professionalism of SMTEs, through marketing and management training, can support smaller companies to cooperate and compete by developing their knowledge as well as virtual size. Hence, innovative entrepreneurs who appreciate the power of the new media and design and support a suitable presence in the electronic marketplace are able to compete on an equal footing with some of their larger competitors.

Innovative suppliers are also empowered by achieving a greater degree of internal efficiency and effectiveness and by optimizing their operations. They can also develop links with their trusted partners and stakeholders in order to coordinate collaboration and interaction towards developing and delivering seamless products. Cooperation at the local level can enable them to increase their presence in the international markets and also to reduce the handicaps caused by lack of expertise, resources and capital. In this sense, the tourism value chain is enhanced to a wealth-creation system for all participants. Opening a window to the entire world through the Internet enables organizations to communicate with their clientèle and to interact dynamically, enhancing the exposure of the enterprise.

However, tourism suppliers have a number of difficult ICT decisions to face. The pace of ICT developments illustrates that unless an organization innovates in a dynamic way and keeps up to date with both technological and industrial developments it can be left out in the cold. Investing wisely in the right technological solution, at the right time, is critical for a tourism enterprise. But perhaps more crucial is to appreciate the impact of ICT developments on the industry structure. This will enable organizations to identify the best strategic action that they should take (Porter, 2001). Predicting the impact of ICT on players and formulating the right alliances, distributing through the right channels and targeting the right customers will increasingly be at the centre of tourism organization strategies. ICTs can determine and facilitate a number of these strategic decisions and, vice versa, a number of these strategic decisions can be fulfilled only if the right technologies are in place. Technology is therefore at the heart of strategy considerations for tourism organizations and at the same time the tourism industry generates great ICT requirements for fulfilling its strategy.

Increasingly, the quality of service and the ability to differentiate tourism products depend on the level of ICT usage. Enterprises take advantage of the emerging ICT tools and become capable of interacting closely with their consumers. They also become capable of adapting to tourism demand requirements by constantly updating their products. Using ICTs, the industry can create seamless experiences through developing ad hoc partnerships with local suppliers. Identifying niche markets through ICTs as well as packaging and distributing customized products also enable tourism organizations to differentiate their offering and provide suitable products for niche markets at premium prices. Failure to take advantage of the emerging technology may equally lead to competitive disadvantages, when organizations fail to adapt to change and to provide facilities and services offered by competitors. Only organizations that offer instantaneous, flexible and customized tourism products will be able to succeed in the global marketplace. Hence, suppliers need to be both proactive and reactive in order to optimize their potential. ICTs have changed the best operational practices in the industry and only innovative operators will be able to take advantage of the emerging tools in the future. ICTs are therefore instrumental in enabling tourism organizations to achieve competitive advantages.

12.5.3 Implications of eTourism for travel intermediaries

The Internet has also changed travel intermediation dramatically. There is a clear trend for *disintermediation*, i.e. the drive to eliminate travel intermediaries from the value chain. Hitherto, travel agencies and tour operators have been the main travel intermediaries. Travel agencies have also been the major brokers/retails of tourism services and the interface of the industry with consumers. For leisure tourism, tour operators have amalgamated tourism products and packaged them, acting as a wholesaler. Traditional travel intermediation is, to a certain degree, endangered, as some of its conventional functions, such as information provision and communication with wholesalers and principals, become available directly to consumers through the Internet. Suppliers/principals are empowered to communicate directly with their clientèle and also to offer some of the savings made on the distribution channel (commission and labour cost) as a discount to the customer. easyJet and Ryanair, for example, discounted tickets purchased on the Internet by £5. The recent commission capping by airlines around the world also reinforces this and demonstrates clearly that unless intermediaries add value to the tourism product they will gradually lose their market share as more consumers will be purchasing tourism products directly from suppliers.

To the degree that the Internet empowers consumers to develop and purchase their own itineraries, travel agencies (retailers) are more threatened. This is due partly to the fact that hitherto the majority of travel agencies have limited their role to that of booking agencies, jeopardizing the quality of information they provide and the value that they add to travel arrangements. This is a result of the low levels of professionalism, training and knowledge observed in holiday shops or travel agencies selling mainly packaged holidays. Travel agencies that fail to offer substantial value to the customer will gradually be eliminated from the distribution chain.

Traditional travel agencies, therefore, need to reassess the situation and decide which market segment they would like to concentrate on. Adequate equipment, training and service are critical in order to maintain their competitiveness in the long term. Travel agencies need to transform from being booking offices to being travel managers and advisers, as well as to add value to the travelling experience. Two strategic directions can therefore be followed: travel agencies can offer differentiation value, by designing high-quality personalized travel arrangements, which consumers value highly and are willing to pay a premium for. Alternatively, they can offer cost value, by delivering less expensive products than competitors, through standardization, high volume and consolidators. These two strategies will probably dominate the travel industry in the future years. In addition, intermediaries can develop their Internet interfaces and enhance their presence in the electronic market. This is evident for few companies, such as Thomas Cook or TUI, who constantly re-engineer their interfaces to enhance efficiency, maintain their clientèle and enlarge their target markets internationally. Travel intermediaries need to enhance their core competencies and concentrate on their travel adviser's role, i.e. to provide expertise and save time for consumers. Innovative agencies can offer value through providing expert advice, by enabling consumers to understand better their own requirements and by directing them to the most appropriate products in the marketplace. This is a very skilled service to perform, as it requires human/psychology skills and a deep knowledge of the great variety of the tourism products globally.

Larger travel agencies, such as multiples and vertically integrated organizations, need to move to multi-channel strategies that include click (book on-line), walk (travel agencies) and talk (call centres) to maximize their market penetration and customer service. Re-designing retail shops is also critical for walk-in prospective travellers. Customer-friendly desks, which enable consumers to see the travel clerk's screen, as well as offer a relaxed and holiday atmosphere, are also important. Providing direct access to specialized agencies, with experience in particular destinations or products, is critical, and this is where the Internet and calling centres can be of great assistance. Integrating calling centres with the Internet allows consumers to call experts without having to explain the transaction they have been trying to undertake on-line from scratch. To improve the efficiency of transactions, agents should be able to retrieve the parameters already determined on-line, on the same screen with the consumer, and to guide them on-line. Recruiting eMail addresses on-line and off-line can also provide a very useful marketing tool for providing appropriate products and ancillary services.

Staff are extremely valuable and will need to be looked after in order to maximize productivity. Paying high incentives and ensuring job satisfaction are critical for developing professionalism, reducing turnover and providing significant financial saving on recruitment and training costs. Looking after staff through recruitment and training is also important. Unless travel agencies enhance their service to becoming travel counsellors they will be severely threatened and they will lose significant market share as more travellers become confident in making their own arrangements on-line.

Most tour operators have taken advantage of ICTs in order to increase their efficiency and manage their inventory better. They also use ICTs extensively for distributing their package holidays through retail in the current distribution channel. However, hitherto they have been extremely reluctant to re-engineer their business processes and to use ICTs for communicating directly with consumers in order to strengthen their position. This may be attributed to the vertical integration experienced in Europe and the reluctance of tour operators to disturb their travel agency operations or to upset their travel agency partners who are responsible for the promotion of their packages. Only a few operators, such as Kuoni and TUI, have developed credible websites that facilitate B2C trading.

The Scandinavian experience clearly demonstrates that all tour operators need to develop more sophisticated interfaces with consumers, if they wish to maximize their market share. Players who fail to do so will jeopardize their future competitiveness. Tour operators can enhance their customer relationship management on-line, as customers are happier to give personal information on the Internet. Also developing partnerships with established brands that enjoy a high penetration to specific market segments, such as Ministry of Sound for the 18–30 age segment or Barbour for the affluent middle-aged nature lover, can also be very beneficial. Research has consistently demonstrated that there is very small loyalty to tour operators. The Internet provides an opportunity for tour operators to understand and satisfy consumers better, as well as to employ customer relationship management to improve loyalty. The Scandinavian example also demonstrates that once consumers book on-line, they are reluctant to book over the phone or through travel agencies again. This demonstrates that it is critical to capitalize on the on-line opportunity and lock consumers in at an early stage. In addition, incremental sales on insurance, foreign currency, car rentals etc. are greater on-line, partly because these are unprompted and customer-driven. Not only can tour operators increase the value offered, and therefore gain loyalty, but they can also increase their direct revenue and save on commission.

Tour operators should also perhaps use ICTs in order to build individual packages by helping clients to 'mix and match' products. The provision of electronic brochures is expected not only to improve tour operators' flexibility, by enabling them to amend the information provided without massive costs, but also to reduce their promotional and distribution costs. Kuoni is one of the main examples in this area, as it allows customers to differentiate their packages by adding items, prolonging stays or personalizing some of the package elements. Tour operators can also utilize ICTs in order to increase the value added to the tourism package by differentiating elements of the tourism experience. Smaller and independent operators will probably benefit more from ICT developments, as larger ones are expected to continue their cost-advantage strategy, which helps them deliver low-cost packages.

There is also a trend for *reintermediation*, as traditional intermediaries reinvent their role to safeguard their position in the future and new intermediaries emerge to facilitate the intermediation process. They use sophisticated ICTs to both enhance the value of the tourism product and reduce the cost for their clientèle, by maximizing their efficiency and minimizing their distribution costs. Successful intermediaries of the future will be concentrating on the human element, providing customized advice and assistance. These trends are already evident in the business travel sector, where the majority of agencies offer their counselling service for a fee, rather than commissions on bookings. In leisure, tourism travel agencies can also enhance their competitiveness by offering cost reductions through vertical integration and buying in bulk from tour operators and suppliers.

As illustrated in previous paragraphs, a number of new intermediaries emerge to take advantage of the ICT tools and the tourism market. These new eTourism intermediaries have often had no previous involvement in tourism but take advantage of advanced technologies or established relationships with consumers. Their aggressive strategies have in many cases changed the industry structure, impacting dramatically on the competitiveness of their rivals. Perhaps the best known example is Expedia, which was launched and is still partly owned by Microsoft. Its meteoric growth has damaged companies with years of experience in the field, such as American Express and Rosenbluth Travel. A number of other entities have emerged and acquired a significant market share, taking advantage of the relationships with consumers (e.g. newspapers or night clubs).

Different market segments will use dissimilar distribution channels for selecting and purchasing their tourism products. For example, older people and people who travel infrequently will probably continue purchasing tourism products from traditional travel agencies. However, younger travellers as well as business and frequent travellers increasingly use on-line providers to arrange their itineraries and eventually purchase their tickets. The growth of eCommerce in tourism depends on the security of Internet transactions, the reliability and quality of information available on the Internet, and the convenience of the entire process. It is therefore critical for each travel intermediary to undertake a thorough analysis of their strengths and weaknesses and to develop their offerings, taking advantage of the emerging ICT opportunities and avoiding the threats for disintermediation evident in the marketplace.

Appreciating the starting point and the main motivations for travel will enable tourism marketers to support the four key stages of holiday bookings, namely: dream, research, book, fulfil. All stages are marginally served currently, as high-street travel agencies are often perceived as brochure warehouses and offer little value to holiday planning or inspiration. TV footage of holiday destinations or specific activities (such as golf, skiing or painting) support the dream element but have a limited role in the booking and fulfilment stages. Travel portals will allow consumers to develop individualized digital brochures and will support the research and fulfil functions through the Internet, IDTV or mobile devices. A number of service providers on the Internet, digital television or mobile networks will enable the booking function. Eventually all these elements will be coordinated seamlessly, revolutionizing travel distribution.

12.5.4 Implications of eTourism for destinations and the public sector

Destinations emerge as umbrella brands that will incorporate all local suppliers in the region. The public sector has traditionally played an instrumental role in planning, coordinating and marketing the destination and is expected to take advantage of the emerging ICT tools and enhance the competitiveness of destinations as a whole. Destinations can be major beneficiaries of ICT developments by developing destination management systems to coordinate their entire industry. ICTs introduce a great opportunity for closer cooperation at the local level and bridge the gap between suppliers and consumers. Consequently, destinations are empowered to communicate directly with their prospective tourists. DMSs are expected to be instrumental in achieving a certain degree of disintermediation, by encouraging consumers to book directly with local principals.

For the first time ever they can use ICT strategic tools for their management, planning and marketing as well as for bringing together all local enterprises. ICTs can assist destination management organizations (DMOs) to re-engineer the planning, management and marketing of destinations by operating a decision support mechanism, which will focus on existing issues, legislation and markets. They can also use complex forecasting mechanisms to assess future scenarios and demonstrate the best alternative decision for all stakeholders. ICTs should provide the essential 'info-structure' for the networking of all local enterprises and enhance regional development. This can be achieved only by using ICTs to integrate regional economies in order to support the maximization of economic multipliers as well as the optimization of tourism impacts. Sustainability and re-development of resources will also need to be monitored and reinforced through ICT applications. Destination marketing also needs to focus on SMTEs and to ensure that they are represented in the electronic marketplace and enhance their competitiveness (Buhalis, 1993, 1994).

Advanced Destination Integrated Computerized Information Reservation Management Systems (DICIRMSs) can address the entire range of needs and services required by both tourism enterprises and consumers for specific destinations (Buhalis, 1995, 1997). DICIRMSs can revolutionize all aspects of destination management as well as integrate all tourism actors at the local level. Although a variety of the elements proposed for these systems already exists in some DMSs, there is currently no operational DMS that provides such a comprehensive and integrated service to its users and plays a strategic role in the coordination and promotion of its destination. As far as economic benefits are concerned, DICIRMSs are instrumental in promoting diagonal integration at the destination level, while they play a pivotal role in the disintermediation of the industry and the empowerment of principals in their intra-channel negotiations with intermediaries. Increasingly, however, it becomes evident that DICIRMSs will be unable to provide long-term competitive advantages for destinations, as most destinations will eventually develop and use these systems. Instead DICIRMSs will be instrumental in assisting destinations and SMTEs to avoid competitive disadvantages by rival regions that utilize similar systems. In addition, DICIRMSs would enable destinations and SMTEs to bridge their distance with consumers, enhancing their intra-channel power and their ability to negotiate with intermediaries. Being able to innovate constantly and to take advantage of the opportunities emerging through the technological revolution are critical for achieving the described strategic benefits for both destinations and SMTEs. Education and training on strategic marketing and ICTs, in combination with development of vision for destinations, will effectively determine the degree of benefits a destination would be able to achieve. DICIRMSs emerge as a strategic tool of wealth creation as well as a complementary distribution channel. These systems can help DMOs re-establish equity in the allocation of power and profit margins between tourism distribution channel members. They can also help host populations to optimize the impacts of tourism locally.

DICIRMSs are expected to allow DMOs and SMTEs to readdress the structure of the distribution channel, to gain intra-channel distribution power and to improve their returns on investments. To a certain extent, these developments can assist dynamic DMOs to control their destiny, to reduce pressure by multinational intermediaries and other organizations to accept a cost-orientation strategy, to differentiate their products and to attract niche markets. DICIRMSs empower the tourism product coordination locally as well as reinforce the DMOs' role and power within the tourism distribution channel. As a result, both locals and visitors can benefit in the long term, while the sustainability of local resources can be augmented.

12.6 The virtualization of the tourism industry

Tourism operates within a business environment undergoing a great transformation of business practices from the industrial era to the new information era. The importance of power sources is transformed from material resources to information processing, redefining the competitiveness of all enterprises in the global marketplace. As demonstrated in Chapter 2, Davidow and Malone (1992) suggest that virtual corporations that offer virtual products and services produced instantaneously in response to customer demand will be competent corporations of the

21st century. Technology facilitates informational networks to link up and bring together their core competence to create a *best-of-everything* organization. This new corporate model requires challenging interaction structures as it effectively redefines the traditional boundaries of the organizations It is based on *co-destiny*, meaning that each partner is dependent on *trusted* employees, partners and consumers. The key reason and competence of the virtual enterprise is speed. Opportunities do not last long in the global marketplace. Companies that wait to develop what they need for themselves will simply be left behind. In contrast, companies that can access world-class competencies can exploit fast-changing opportunities by sharing costs, skills and access to global markets.

Examining the functions and operation of the tourism industry illustrates that in reality tourism organizations have always shared quite a number of the characteristics of virtual corporations, due to the nature of the industry. As they depend constantly on suppliers and partners for the formulation and delivery of tourism products, they frequently formulate ad hoc partnerships with other independent enterprises. This is evident in traditional distribution channels of leisure tourism. Tour operators contract hoteliers and local handling agencies at destinations to organize and deliver tourism products on their behalf. They also use travel agencies and other retailers to promote, demonstrate and distribute their packages to consumers. Hoteliers also formulate partnerships with local suppliers for raw materials and equipment. Most of the SMTEs also contract experts such as accountants, ICT experts and lawyers for their specific services, on either a regular or an ad hoc basis. Thus, they outsource non-core functions of their business, as it is not economical to maintain the services of expensive professionals permanently. Tourism enterprises are also forced to take advantage of some of the characteristics of virtual corporations, as they need to adapt their product constantly to satisfy tourism demand, use information extensively, develop partnerships, and outsource a significant amount of functions in order to achieve economies of scope.

The emergence of virtual corporations and the re-engineering anticipated in the way the tourism industry organizes itself will have much more profound implications for the organizations of the future. The ICT revolution provided the tools for efficient networking and collaboration with partners throughout the value-added chain. In addition, the increasing concentration of tourism supply has resulted in the globalization of the industry. As a consequence, it has reinforced the need for the development of virtual corporations, which will develop partnerships and deliver suitable products to consumers efficiently on an international scale. Tourism organizations need to develop their virtuality further by taking advantage of the new ICT tools and the global marketspace. ICTs make it possible to communicate seamlessly with all service providers and to individualize tourism offerings at an affordable cost. Virtual corporations that develop partnerships with other principals and deliver integrated packages that satisfy the entire range of needs for market segments will achieve competitive advantage and increase their market share. These corporations do not necessarily need to be located near the consumer. Instead the ICT networks and tools as well as partnerships with other enterprises enable corporations to develop a virtual proximity to consumers and their needs (Schertler et al., 1995; Williams, 1993).

ICTs re-engineer the production, marketing, operational and distribution functions of tourism enterprises. This supports the development of networks of tourism provision between strategic partners. In addition, ICTs allow the successful outsourcing of non-core functions to specialists, and thus support economies of scope. New innovative practices are introduced to instigate close relationships with both consumers and principals, increasing the total efficiency and effectiveness of the tourism industry. Understandably, larger organizations take greater advantage of the emergent technologies earlier than smaller ones, and ICTs facilitate their further expansion. Paradoxically, however, small enterprises can enjoy more benefits in developing and managing their virtuality, as they have always had a closer proximity to consumers and a need to develop partnerships for the delivery of their products.

The introduction of these facilities empowers networking throughout the industry and also improves the interactivity between tourism production and distribution partners, supporting a closer cooperation towards the provision of seamless products. ICTs increasingly transform distribution to an electronic marketplace, where access to information and ubiquity are achieved, while interactivity between principals and consumers provides major opportunities (Morath, 2000). The Internet also promotes the mass-customization of tourism products as it helps the industry to target niche markets of significant size in different geographical locations. Hence, the Internet propels the re-engineering of the entire process of producing and delivering tourism products, as well as boosting interactivity between partners that can design specialized products and promotion in order to maximize the value-added provided to individual consumers. Ultimately, ICT tools reinvent the packaging of tourism to a much more individual-focused activity, offering great opportunities for principals and intermediaries and enhancing the total quality of the final product (fitness to purpose).

Despite the aforementioned benefits, to date eTourism virtuality has remained primitive. This jeopardizes the opportunities for tourism corporations to develop credible interfaces with other members of the value chain and thus prevents them from developing their virtuality. A number of organizations have failed to appreciate the benefits of *co-opetition* and *co-destiny*, when organizations collaborate with players that they would normally regard as competitors. A wide range of issues must therefore be resolved before the tourism industry can take full advantage of ICT and maximize its virtuality. The 'I' framework, as illustrated in Figure 12.5, demonstrates that intelligent tourism will require all tourism stakeholders to develop their ability to innovate and to use information strategically in order to develop close partnerships with other members of the value chain to serve the individual consumer.

Eventually ICTs will create the info-structure for industry collaboration at the macro- and micro-levels, as well as an electronic cyber-market for consumers. This will gradually support the virtuality of the industry and boost its ability to use all its Internet, intranet and extranet tools in order to produce virtual products and develop interactive and seamless services. Inevitably only innovative tourism suppliers will be able to survive in the future. The time-scale of the transformation is determined by a number of parameters and will differ for each market segment and location. Nevertheless tourism providers who fail to take advantage of the industry transformation will lose significant market share.

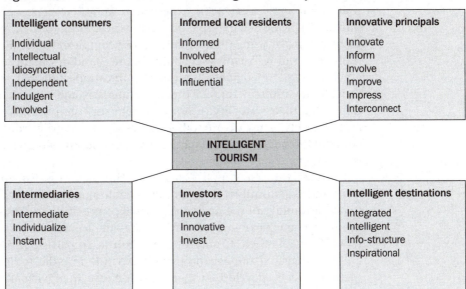

Figure 12.5 The 'I' framework – increasing the virtuality of eTourism

12.7 Conclusions: change is the only constant

The analysis in this book clearly demonstrates that tourism marketing constantly evolves, taking advantage of the emerging ICT tools. ICTs empower tourism marketing and management as they provide cost-effective tools for organizations and destinations to target appropriate market segments and to develop strategic tools. They also support the interactivity between tourism enterprises and consumers, and as a result they re-engineer the entire process of developing, managing and marketing tourism products and destinations.

ICTs can introduce great benefits in the efficiency, differentiation, cost reduction and response time of tourism organizations. Consequently, ICTs stimulate radical changes in the operation, distribution and structure of the tourism industry. The proliferation of technology throughout the tourism distribution channels essentially means that both consumers and professionals use the newly available tools in order to retrieve information, identify suitable products and perform reservations. Thus, the visibility of tourism principals in the marketplace will be a function of the technologies and networks utilized to interact with their individual and institutional customers. This will, therefore, determine their ability to distribute their product efficiently and to communicate interactively with their clientèle. Should tourism principals neglect the significance of ICTs in their distribution function, they will effectively jeopardize their competitiveness and become marginalized. Hence, tourism enterprises need to understand, incorporate and utilize ICTs, in order to be able to serve their target markets, improve their efficiency, maximize profitability, enhance services and maintain long-term prosperity for both themselves and destinations. ICTs have a great influence on the strategic management of contemporary organizations, as a paradigm shift is experienced, transforming the 'best' business practices.

Several key trends drive the utilization of ICTs in tourism. Consumers will be much more sophisticated and experienced, and therefore they will be much more difficult to please. Changing requirements according to their mood and environment will make segmentation much more complex. The availability of new and more powerful ICTs empowers both suppliers and destinations to enhance their efficiency and re-engineer their communication strategies. Increasingly, ICTs provide the info-structure for the entire industry and support all stakeholders in improving their virtuality. Innovative tourism enterprises use ICTs strategically and tactically. They divert staff resources and expertise from mechanistic processes to interacting and servicing consumers, adding a higher added value in the transactions.

However, the emerging ICTs also pose threats for tourism enterprises, destinations and organizations that maintain traditional operational practices and fail to take advantage of the new tools. Global competition expands rapidly and only innovative and flexible organizations are able to develop products and services that will enable them to survive in the future. In particular, SMTEs will need to enhance their ICT understanding and expertise in order to design and promote niche products, develop partnerships, increase their virtual size and compete with large and powerful competitors and partners in the distribution channel. Travel intermediaries and in particular travel agencies and tour operators are already threatened by disintermediation, as principals develop direct relationships with consumers and aim to bypass them. Intermediaries will increasingly need to re-engineer their operations to focus on value-added services, rather than the mechanistic procedures of product searches and reservations. This will empower intermediaries, such as travel agencies and tour operators, to survive in the future and to maintain or develop their market share.

The booking process is gradually being rationalized; this helps both consumers and the industry to save considerable time in identifying, blending, reserving and purchasing tourism products, facilitating a closer match between tourism demand and supply. Prospective tourists can browse the Internet and identify a rich variety of offers in order to make travel choices suited to their personal requirements. The focus is thus shifted towards individual travel and dynamic packages, targeting mini-segments. Using ICTs empowers organizations to offer personalized services, as they can research and recognize the needs of individual customers. Inclusive tourism is also facilitated as people can use technology to minimize the time spent on identifying the availability and price of suitable packages. Hence, the intermediation of the tourism industry becomes more complex on a daily basis and ICTs increasingly dominate the tourism distribution channel. A number of new players are attracted, aiming at acquiring part of the market through a whole range of product propositions and value-added elements. They range from traditional agencies and operators and electronic intermediaries to vertical and lifestyle portals that extend their service to travel. In most cases they need to collaborate with one of the leading global distribution systems in order to access the complex algorithms determining the best airline routes and fares. In addition, they often negotiate corporate rates and special offers with particular suppliers. Keeping up to date with all distribution developments and deals, while protecting brand properties, supporting regular and loyal customers and at the same time remaining profitable, is a taxing task. Each enterprise will need not only to deal effectively and profitably with the entire range of distribution channels, but also to develop its own interfaces to communicate directly with their clientèle. Managing the entire range of new eTourism intermediaries and adopting a multi-channel strategy are therefore two of the most complex tasks for any tourism manager.

However, it should be recognized that ICTs are not a panacea; they require restructuring of several management practices in order to ensure that organizations can achieve their strategic objectives. ICTs can contribute to both sides of the balance sheet and both opportunities and threats emerge as a result. Therefore, a thorough and realistic audit of ICT capabilities and requirements as well as a cost-and-benefit analysis are required by all tourism organizations. This will help them to appreciate their position and to design the most appropriate action in order to enhance their competitiveness. Certain prerequisites are applicable for achieving success. Long-term planning and strategy as well as top management commitment will be needed to ensure that ICTs are dealt with as part of the strategic planning and management of tourism enterprises. Planning should not be rigid and inflexible, but rather innovative and dynamic, allowing organizations to be proactive and reactive to consumer requirements and industry developments. A rational management and marketing strategy is needed to ensure that competent ICTs tools are used, although it needs to be recognized that first movers often face greater risks if the marketplace is not ready for a new technological development or if that technology is not fully developed yet.

Investment in capable human resources should be a priority as intellect becomes one of the most significant assets for tourism organizations. Intellect will need to concentrate on the marketing area to ensure a great appreciation of consumer needs, as well as on the technological side, where an up-to-date understanding of the new tools and their potential is needed to challenge old and outdated practices. Training throughout the business hierarchy will need to ensure not only that all employees are competent users of the emerging ICTs, but also that they can develop a commitment in using innovative and dynamic methods for communicating and interacting.

The need for cooperation emerges through the need to improve service and provides seamless travel experiences, as well as through the new realities imposed by contemporary economic developments, such as deregulation and globalization. ICTs provide unprecedented opportunities for horizontal, vertical and diagonal integration, which assist the industry in improving its provision to consumers as well as strengthening its effectiveness. Developing the virtuality of tourism organizations, through ICT-powered partnership and cooperation, requires a certain degree of standardization and interconnectivity between systems and processes. Interconnectivity, compatibility and standardization of the information technology used in tourism will enable inter- and intra-organizational cooperation, avoid 'technology islands', and facilitate access for consumers. The degree of standardization achieved in interfaces and processes will determine the compatibility and interactivity among technologies, partners and users. Consequently, standardized communication protocols and platforms are required to reinforce interactive tourism product design, presentation and delivery, intermediation, payment systems and telecommunication infrastructure.

ICTs generate a paradigm shift in the tourism industry, which transforms the best business practices and redefines the role and the competitiveness of all tourism enterprises and destinations. A wide range of business processes re-engineering is being experienced in the tourism industry, where most players are redesigning their inter- and intra-organizational processes, based on the newly available ICT tools, to facilitate interaction and interconnectivity. Adaptation and innovation will enable the tourism industry to develop its organizational competitiveness. Amending the strategic direction of each sector and of the industry as a whole will empower the tourism industry to address the opportunities and avoid the threats arising from the ICT revolution. A thorough re-engineering of all business processes needs to ensure that tourism organizations do not simply automate but also redesign all interfaces and interactions with stakeholders. Marketing, rather than forcing product-driven technologies, should drive this process. Vision and commitment by corporate management at both the micro- and macro-levels will be critical for the successful adaptation of the industry.

Although there is a fair degree of uncertainty in tourism ICT development, it is evident that change wil be the only constant. Tourism organizations that need to compete will need to compute. Unless the current tourism industry improves its competitiveness by utilizing the revolutionary technology, there is a danger that exogenous players will enter the marketplace, jeopardizing the position of existing players. Only creative and innovative suppliers will be able to survive the competition and to develop their virtuality in order to serve all their stakeholders. Winners will include players who will be able to identify consumer needs and requirements and develop their info-structure in order to bring together all partners required to maximize the added value and optimize customer satisfaction. The unpredictable nature of consumer requirements, the speed of change of all parameters on the external environment, the transparency of offering and the proliferation of tourism suppliers on a global scale make this process very challenging. Therefore continuous innovation in the tourism industry needs to ensure that a wide range of prerequisites such as rational organization, training, and quality-assurance methodologies are in place in order to enable destinations and suppliers to capitalize on new ICT capailities. The emerging ICT tools therefore require constant innovation, investment in human resources and the development of strategic vision and commitment. *Intellect* and *innovation* will drive the ICT utilization in tourism, and they will determine the competitiveness of tourism enterprises and destinations.

Chapter questions

1 How can tourism organizations benefit from constant interactivity with consumers?

2 What are the main challenges emerging from this interactivity?

3 Why do tourism organizations require multi-channel strategies?

4 Which channels will dominate the market in the future?

5 How can destinations integrate all local actors through ICTs?

6 Why have calling centres gained significance since the development of eCommerce?

7 Which of the new eTourism intermediaries will survive, and why?

8 What will be the main opportunities and challenges of interactive digital television for tourism?

9 Explain why future generations of mobile technology are expected to revolutionize the tourism industry once again.

10 What is eTourism convergence, and what are the critical implications for the tourism organization of the future?

11 How can consumers participate more in designing their customized tourism products?

12 Can SMTEs survive in the future, and what are the conditions for strengthening their competitiveness?

13 Explore the concept of co-destiny with regards to ICTs in the tourism industry.

14 Why is co-opetition critical in the business?

15 How can destination management organizations enhance their info-structure?

16 What will be the major drivers of competitiveness in the future, and how will ICTs support them?

Further reading

Buhalis, D. and Licata, C. (2002) The eTourism intermediaries, *Tourism Management*, **23**(3), 207–20.
Buhalis, D. (1998) Strategic use of information technologies in the tourism industry, *Tourism Management*, **19**(3), 409–423.
Buhalis, D., and Schertler, W. (1999) *Information and Communication Technologies in Tourism, Conference Proceedings ENTER 1999*, Springer-Verlag, Vienna.
Buhalis, D., Tjoa, A.M. and Jafari, J. (1998) *Information and Communication Technologies in Tourism: IT and the dynamic tourism market place*, Springer-Verlag, Vienna.
Fesenmaier, D., Leppers, A. and O'Leary, J. (1999) Developing a knowledge based tourism marketing information system, *Information Technology and Tourism*, 2(1), 31–45.
Fesenmaier, D. Klein and S. Buhalis, D. (eds) (2000) *Information and Communication Technologies in Tourism, Conference Proceedings ENTER 2000*, Springer-Verlag, Vienna.
O'Connor, P. (1999b) *Electronic Information Distribution Technology in Tourism and Hospitality*, CAB, Oxford.
Sheldon, P.J. (1997) *Tourism Information Technology*, CAB, Oxford.
Sheldon, P. Wöber, K. and Fesenmaier, D. (eds) (2001) *Information and Communication Technologies in Tourism, Conference Proceedings ENTER 2002*, Springer-Verlag, Vienna.
Werthner, H. and Klein, S. (1999) *Information Technology and Tourism – A Challenging Relationship*, Springer-Verlag, New York.
Wöber, K., Frew, A. and Hitz, M. (eds) (2002) *Information and Communication Technologies in Tourism, Conference Proceedings ENTER 2002*, Springer-Verlag, Vienna.

Websites

IFITT: **www.ifitt.org**
Travelmole: **www.travelmole.com**
Eyefortravel: **www.eyefortravel.com**
Travel Industry Association: **www.tia.org**

Glossary

Added value The contribution of the organization, measured as the difference between the market value of the output and the cost of the inputs to the organization.

Advertising Paid and non-personal dissemination of information, ideas, goods or services by an identifiable advertiser in order to influence buyers to buy.

Allotment Contract allocation of space (hotel rooms or transport seats) to a tour operator on a pay-as-much-as-you-sell basis.

Amadeus One of two main European global distribution systems (GDSs) developed by Air France, Iberia, Lufthansa and SAS.

Application service provider (ASP) Company that provides and hosts application software on remote servers on a wide area network, allowing firms to outsource some of their IT functions.

Artificial intelligence (AI) The science and engineering of making intelligent software and hardware that can solve problems and achieve goals as humans.

Authentication Process of verification of transaction participants before payments are authorized, access is allowed or documents are delivered. Critical for on-line transactions and eCommerce.

Average room rate The average daily rate paid by guest in hotels.

B2B (business-to-business) eCommerce between businesses through the Internet.

B2C (business-to-consumer) eCommerce between commercial organizations and consumers.

B2G (business-to-government) eCommerce and electronic communication between commercial organizations and governments.

Bandwidth The capacity of the telecommunications channel or the volume of data that can be transmitted over the Internet in a fixed period of time. Refers to the speed of interaction across a network.

Banner An on-line, graphic advertisement on a web page used to direct viewers to the advertiser's web page.

Bluetooth A short-range wireless technology enabling links between mobile computers, mobile phones, portable handheld devices, and connectivity to the Internet.

Brand The identity of goods or services as demonstrated by a name, term, sign, symbol, design, or a combination of these, aiming to differentiate goods or services in the minds of buyers.

Business process An interrelated number of activities that create an output that provides value for internal or external customers.

Business process re-engineering (BPR) The radical rethinking and redesign of business processes, which employs the capabilities of new information and communication technologies to improve the performance or organizations.

Business travel/tourism Travelling for business purposes and particularly for attending meetings, incentives, conferences and exhibitions (MICE).

Carrying capacity The maximum capacity of a destination or facility that allows tourism activity without detrimental effects to the environment or deterioration of the visitor experience.

Centralized computing Central computer-controlled processing for multiple users.

Channel conflict Disagreement among distribution channel members over processes, goals, roles and rewards.

Charter Privately hired aircraft, ship, train or bus for a group of tourists.

Chat group Real-time on-line forum for discussing issues of public and personal interest.

Click and brick Using eCommerce whilst maintaining retail stores and off-line distribution channels.

Code sharing Practice of sharing the same airline identification code by two or more airlines to demonstrate seamless service between carriers and to achieve higher ranking on global distribution systems.

Collaboration Process integration involving strong coordination and interdependence between processes and partners.

Commission Payment of a percentage of the value of the transaction by a supplier to an intermediary as a reward for contribution to the distribution of the service. Override commission signifies a higher-than-normal commission as an incentive for directional sale. Commission capping signifies a maximum amount that suppliers are prepared to pay distributors.

Competitive advantage Significant advantage over competitors gained by perceptual appreciation of product value by consumers. It is normally achieved through lower prices or by providing differentiated and unique products that justify higher prices.

Competitive analysis The process of identifying key competitors, objectives, strategies, strengths, weaknesses, opportunities and threats as well as the analysis of the expected results for alternative prospective strategic actions.

Competitive intelligence Information about the competitors and their actions informing the strategic analysis of an organization.

Competitive strategies Offensive or defensive strategies that aim to provide strategic competitive advantage and to increase the competitiveness of an organization.

Computer A programmable device that can execute previously stored instructions (software).

Computer program (or software) Set of instructions in a programming language that specifies the order and actions performed by the computer.

Computer reservation system (CRS) Used for inventory management by airlines, hotels and other facilities. CRSs can allow direct access through terminals for intermediaries to check availability, make reservations and print tickets.

Computer system A system consisting of computers and other computer-controlled devices that process data by executing programs.

Connectivity Ability to transmit data between interconnected devices.

Consumer User of goods and services (although may not be the customer/buyer).

Consumer buying behaviour The process of purchasing a product and the buying behaviour of the final consumer.

Convergence Trend of integrating computing and communication technologies into single devices.

Cookie Small text file that a web browser stores in a folder on a web user's PC to facilitate repeat usage of a website.

Cooperation Establishing links between individuals and organizations to share knowledge or resources towards achieving common goals in the market place.

Cooperative marketing Joint promotional activities between two or more parties.

Cooperative strategy Strategic alliance or joint venture strategy between two or more parties.

Co-opetition Strategic alliance or joint venture strategy with competitor(s) in an industry.

Corporate strategy A longer-term plan of major objectives, purposes or goals and policies and actions for achieving strategic objectives.

Cost and benefit analysis (CBA) Systematic evaluation of the costs and benefits of a project. It also attempts to quantify the broader socio-environmental costs and benefits to be derived from particular strategic initiatives.

Cryptography Process of encrypting and decrypting messages in order to increase security.

Culture The set of basic values, perceptions, wants and behaviours learned by a society member through the socialization process.

Customer loyalty The degree that a customer remains loyal to a specific facility, destination, intermediary or brand.

Customer relationship management (CRM) Software that facilitates interaction with customers by planning, controlling and scheduling promotional activities before, during and after the travelling experience.

Database Structured collection of computer-stored and controlled data that relate to a specific business, situation or problem.

Data mining Data-analysis tools that allow the establishment of consumer behaviour patterns in large transaction databases.

Data warehouse Hardware and software that use transaction data for analysing patterns rather than transaction processing.

Decision-support system (DSS) Interactive information system supporting decision-makers in semi-structured and unstructured situations through the provision of information, forecasting and simulation models, as well as data-manipulation tools.

Demand for tourism Number of tourists visiting a facility or destination. Actual demand refers to those who participate in tourism. Potential demand refers to those consumers who may participate in the future. Suppressed demand refers to those that would like to participate but cannot due to illness, time limitations or financial reasons.

Demographic segmentation Segmentation based on demographic variables such as age, sex, family size, family life cycle, income, occupation, education, religion, race and nationality.

Destination A well-defined geographical area that attracts visitors. Destinations can be seen as amalgams of tourism products offering an integrated experience to consumers.

Destination integration The coordination of all stakeholders at the destination for the optimization of tourism impact at the micro- and macro-levels.

Destination management organization (DMO) Partnership organization between the private and public sectors responsible for the promotion and coordination of tourism in a region.

Differentiation Strategy emphasizing the unique benefits or attributes of a product or service.

Digitalization Process of incorporating information technology in all business processes and practices of an organization.

Digital signature Digital record that validates a transaction by serving the purpose of a virtual signature.

Digital subscriber line (DSL) Digital technology for achieving high-speed data communications using copper telephone lines.

Direct marketing Marketing and commerce activities between sellers and buyers, without any involvement from intermediaries.

Disintermediation Removal of intermediaries from the distribution channel and facilitation of direct interaction between sellers and buyers.

Distance learning Computer-enabled learning, away from the knowledge provider.

Distributed computing System that allows individuals to do their own work on personal computers and use a telecommunications network to link to other devices.

Distribution channel (marketing channel) Set of interdependent organizations involved in the process of making a product or service available for use or consumption by the consumer or industrial user.

Domain name The name used to reference a computer on the Internet.

Dumb terminal Input/output device linking users with the central computer where all processes take place.

eBusiness The use of digital tools for business functions and processes.

Economies of scale Cost savings per unit due to high volume of production.

Economies of scope Cost savings per unit due to separate producers sharing facilities.

Edutainment Combining of education and entertainment during holidays.

Electronic auctions Auctions conducted on the Internet.

Electronic cash (eCash) Small amounts of money stored in an electronic form, usually on a smart card, mobile phone or digital wallets.

Electronic commerce (eCommerce) Internet-facilitated commerce, using electronic means for promoting, selling, distributing and servicing products.

Electronic data interchange (EDI) Electronic transmission of standard business data and documents, such as purchase orders and invoices, between organizations.

Electronic funds transfer (EFT) Electronic transfer of money from one account to others, mainly used between organizations.

Electronic market Virtual marketplace where buyers and sellers negotiate, submit bids, agree on orders and transact electronically.

Encryption Process of making messages indecipherable except by those who have an authorized decryption key.

Enterprise resource planning (ERP) Inter-organizational information system that provides a common, integrated electronic infrastructure for all business processes within an organization.

Executive information system (EIS) Interactive system providing managers access to information for monitoring operating results and general business conditions.

Expert systems A computer system or program that uses artificial intelligence techniques to solve problems that ordinarily require a knowledgeable human. Expert systems perform knowledge engineering, by extracting a set of rules and data from experts through extensive questioning.

Extranet Private network that is accessible only by trusted business partners using secured connections over the Internet.

Fare tracker Intelligent agent that monitors the prices of airline tickets and notifies consumers on special fares.

Feasibility study Systematic assessment of the prospects for a new venture, which normally consists of cost and benefit analysis, market trends and financial projections.

File transfer protocol (FTP) Standard protocol used on the Internet for moving files across the Internet.

Firewall System (hardware and software) that protects networks from unauthorized intruders.

Flag carrier National and often government-operated airline.

Focus strategy Competitive strategy that addresses the specific needs of a specific market segment.

Frequent-user programme Promotional programme aiming to increase customer loyalty through a number of benefits.

Galileo One of two main European global distribution systems.

Generic strategies Three generic strategies of cost leadership, differentiation and focus for achieving the objectives of an organization.

Geographical information systems Information system based on spatial or geographical coordinates.

Global marketing Multi-national marketing that integrates or standardizes marketing actions across different countries.

Global organization Organization that operates in many countries around the world.

Global System for Mobile Communication (GSM) One of several technical standards for transmitting cellular phone calls.

Growth–share matrix Portfolio-planning method that evaluates a company's strategic business units (SBUs) in terms of their market growth rate and relative market share. SBUs are classified as stars, cash cows, question marks or dogs.

Hard disk Device that stores and retrieves data using magnetized regions on a rotating disk.

Hardware Physical devices and connections in a computer system.

Hit Request for data from a web page or file.

Hospitality industry The entire range of organizations offering hospitality and catering services.

Host computer Computer on a network that is a repository for services available to other computers on the network.

Hotel An establishment providing accommodation, food and drink.

HTML (hypertext markup language) Standard that defines the structure and layout of a web document by using a variety of tags and attributes.

HTTP (hypertext transfer protocol) Protocol used for coding and displaying pages on the World Wide Web.

Inclusive tour A package of transport, accommodation and possibly other travel services sold as one product for an inclusive price.

Incoming tour operator Agency or organization providing handling services for tourists at destinations.

Industry and competitive analysis Monitoring, evaluating and disseminating information from external and internal environments.

Information and communication technologies (ICTs) The hardware, software and netware used by information systems.

Information superhighway The entire range of networks facilitating access to unlimited information and supporting electronic transactions.

Information systems (IS) Systems that use information technology to capture, transmit, store, retrieve, manipulate or display information.

Info-structure All kinds of ICTs that provide the infrastructure for organizations to operate.

Infrastructure All forms of construction required by an inhabited area that support and make economic development possible.

Innovation The generation and exploitation of new ideas that may be commercially exploitable.

Intangibility Services cannot be seen, tasted, felt, heard or smelled before they are bought.

Integrated service digital network (ISDN) Set of standards to handle voice and computer data on existing copper telephone networks.

Integration The close coordination of business practices processes and firms.

Intelligent agents Long-lived, semi-autonomous, proactive and adaptive software systems to which one can delegate tasks.

Intermediary Third party between sellers and buyers, such as retailing or distributors, that helps organizations to promote, sell and distribute their goods to final buyers. Intermediaries include middlemen, physical distribution firms, marketing-service agencies and financial intermediaries. In tourism, there is a plethora of intermediaries, including travel agencies, tour operators, handling agencies and conference organizers.

Internet Self-regulated global network of computers interconnecting independent hosts around the globe.

Internet service provider (ISP) Firm that provides access to the Internet.

Internet tools The whole constellation of resources that can be accessed using Gopher, FTP, HTTP, telnet, USENET, WAIS and some other tools.

Interoperability The ability of heterogeneous hardware and software components to work together seamlessly, conveniently and inexpensively.

Intranet Internal communication (LAN or WAN) network, using Internet-type interfaces accessible only by authorized employees and protected by the company's firewall.

Knowledge A combination of instincts, ideas, rules and procedures that guide actions and decisions.

Knowledge management A system aiming to promote the retention and sharing of knowledge within an organization.

Legacy system Outdated information resources currently available in an organization. They usually include existing mainframes, personal computers, serial terminals, networks, databases, operating systems, application programs and all other forms of hardware and software that a company may own.

Legacy thinking Outdated business processes that fail to take advantage of the emerging ICT capabilities.

Load factor The percentage relationship of transport capacity sold to capacity operated.

Local area network (LAN) Network connecting personal computers and other equipment within a local area to help people share equipment, data and software.

Mainframe computer Computer used to control large databases, perform high-volume transaction processing and generate reports from large databases.

Management The process of utilizing material and human resources to accomplish designated objectives, involving the activities of planning, organizing, directing, coordinating and controlling.

Management information system (MIS) Information system that provides information for managing an organization.

Market A network of dealings between the actual and potential sellers and buyers of a product.

Market development Strategy for an organization to develop activities in a new market.

Market penetration Strategy aiming to increase sales of current products to current market segments.

Market positioning Setting a clear, distinctive and desirable place for a product relative to competitors in the minds of target customers.

Market research Examination of consumer patterns, products and marketing methods.

Market share The ratio of sales of a firm's product to total sales of that type of production in a particular market.

Marketing Process that determines needs and wants of target markets and a mechanism of creating and exchanging products and value with others.

Marketing intelligence Information about developments in the marketplace that assists managers to perform strategic and tactical marketing.

Marketing management The analysis and control of market information and the planning, development and implementation of action that leads to creation and development of offerings that satisfy market demands and generate organizational benefits.

Marketing mix Set of controllable tactical marketing tools, including produce, price, place, promotion, process, people and politics that firms use to target specific market segments.

Marketing research The function that examines consumer and purchasing patterns in order to identify marketing opportunities and to examine the suitability of existing products and offerings.

Mass tourism Large-number participation in tourism activities, often in seaside resorts.

Media Non-personal communications channels including print media (newspapers, magazines, direct mail), broadcast media (radio, television), display media (billboards, signs, posters) and electronic media (Internet, SMS, eMails).

Mission statement Defines the purposes of an organization and demonstrates the values and expectations of the stakeholders.

Mobile commerce (mCommerce) Mobile and wireless technology-enabled eCommerce.

Modem (modulator/demodulator) Device for encoding and decoding computer-generated digital data in order to be transmitted over analogue telephone lines.

Multimedia Use of multiple types of data such as text, pictures and sounds, within the same application.

National Tourism Organization (NTO) Governmental body responsible for the development, promotion and coordination of tourism at a country level.

Network Series of interconnected devices plus communication channels linked together.

Network computing Computing in which some of the computing is done on each user's computer, but the processing is controlled centrally.

Neural network Information system that recognizes objects or patterns based on examples that have been used to train it.

Occupancy The percentage relationship of accommodation capacity used to determine available capacity in hotels.

Oligopolio A market in which there are few sellers.

Oligopsonio A market in which there are few buyers.

One-to-one marketing Relationship marketing in which suppliers treat each customer as an individual.

Operating system Complex program that controls the operation of computers and networks.

Outsourcing Purchasing process-critical products or services from outside, rather than producing them inside the organization.

Package Combination of two or more travel elements (e.g. airline ticket and accommodation) sold as a single product for an inclusive price.

Perishability Services cannot be stored for later sale or use and therefore need to be sold in time.

Personal computer (PC) Single-user and self-sufficient desktop or portable computer.

Personal digital assistant (PDA) Handheld device containing personal information which increasingly includes cell phone and Internet capabilities.

PEST (political, economic, social and technological) analysis Examines the external environment looking at those four factors.

Platform The basic type of computer, operating system and network that an information system uses.

Point-of-sale (POS) The location at which a sale takes place.

Point-of-sale (POS) system Integrated information system that facilitates sales, records orders and generates customer bills.

Portfolio matrix analysis Technique that analyses the range of products possessed by an organization (its portfolio) against relative market share and market growth.

Price The amount of money charged for a produce or service.

Product The physical objects, services, people, places, organizations and ideas that are offered to a market for attention, acquisition, use or consumption at a price.

Product development The development of a concept into a physical product or service that can be promoted in the marketplace.

Product differentiation strategy Strategy that ensures that products are perceived as unique propositions in the marketplace.

Program Set of instructions in a programming language that specifies the data processing to be performed by a computer.

Programming Development of computer code during the development phase of an information system project.

Promotion Communication and persuasion techniques aiming at convincing customers to purchase a product.

Promotion mix Combination of advertising, personal selling, sales promotion and public relations aiming at achieving marketing objectives.

Proprietary standards Technical standards that are owned by a corporation and licensed to others.

Protocol Set of rules determining how computers communicate with one another over a network.

Pull Information system that depends on the user requesting information.

Push Information system that provides information to the user automatically.

Re-intermediation Redefining and re-employing traditional intermediaries in a transaction as well as establishing new electronic intermediaries in place of disintermediated traditional intermediaries.

Relationship marketing The process of creating, maintaining and enhancing strong, value-laden relationships with customers and other stakeholders.

Resort representative (rep) Tour operator's employee based in a resort, facilitating local handling at the destination.

Scalability Ability to significantly increase or decrease capacity according to levels of demand without major disruption or excessive costs.

Scheduled Regular transportation service operated according to a published timetable.

Search engine Program that trawls the Internet to identify web pages that seem to be related to groups of words or phrases supplied by the user.

Seasonality Consistent pattern of demand movements repeated yearly.

Segmentation The process of dividing a market into distinct groups of buyers with different needs, characteristics or behaviours and identifying specific market segments for targeted marketing campaigns.

Server Specialized computer linked to other computers on a network in order to perform specific types of tasks requested through those computers.

Smart card Plastic card containing programmable information.

Software Programs that control the processing performed by a computer system.

Stakeholders The entire range of actors who have an interest in the organization and, therefore, may wish to influence aspects of its mission, objectives and strategies.

Strategic business-planning grid Portfolio planning method that evaluates a company's strategic business units using indexes of industry attractiveness and the company's strength in the industry.

Strategic business unit (SBU) Unit of a company with an identifiable management, mission and objectives that can be planned independently from other divisions of a company.

Strategic information systems Systems designed to support the strategic management decision processes and implementation.

Strategic planning Formal planning system for the development and implementation of the strategies related to the mission and objectives of the organization. Determines a set of managerial decisions that determine the long-term strategy of an organization.

Strategy The processes determining the major objectives and goals of an organization as well as the methods for achieving them.

Suppliers Firms and individuals that provide the resources needed by the company and its competitors to produce goods and services.

Supply chain The process and movement of goods between supplier and organizations.

Supply chain management (SCM) Management of all the activities along the supply chain, from suppliers to internal logistics within a company, to distribution to customers. This includes ordering, monitoring, billing, and so on.

Sustainable competitive advantage Long-term competitive advantage through constant innovation.

SWOT (strengths, weaknesses, opportunities, threats) analysis Examines the strengths and weaknesses present internally in the organization, coupled with the opportunities and threats that the organization faces externally.

Target market Market segment that shares common needs or characteristics and that an organization decides to target for promoting its products.

TCP/IP (transmission control protocol/Internet protocol) Set of standards for sharing data between different computers running incompatible operating systems.

Terminal Computer equipment normally consisting of a keyboard and visual display unit (VDU) screen linked to the computer.

Third generation (3G) Mobile communications technology that can handle data quickly and efficiently alongside voice calls and will underpin mCommerce activities.

Tour operator Intermediary that buys individual travel services from its suppliers and sells as a package.

Tourism industry Describes both private firms and establishments providing facilities and services for tourists as well as the public-sector authorities planning and managing tourism in a region.

Tourism suppliers or principals All actors that design, develop, operate and deliver a tourism service, including hotels, transportation companies, entertainment organizations etc.

Tourist board National, regional or local organization aiming to develop, promote and coordinate tourism in a region.

Tourist information centre (TIC) Office offering information about visitor attractions, facilities and services, and undertaking accommodation reservations.

Travel agent Intermediary selling travel services on behalf of principals.

Uniform resource locator (URL) The address scheme used to locate documents on the Internet.

Unique selling proposition (USP) The benefit an organization promotes as an incentive to purchase the product.

User-friendly Describes technological solutions with easy-to-use interfaces.

Value chain Methodology that identifies the set processes used in an organization for adding value linking with the main functions of an organization.

Variability Services vary greatly, according to the service provider and the time, place and conditions at which they are offered.

Videotext (or viewdata) Dumb terminals used by travel agencies for accessing databases hosted by tourism suppliers for search availability and making reservations.

Virtual organization Organization in which major processes are outsourced to partners.

Virtual reality A simulation of reality that engages the participant's senses and intellect through a simulated environment.

Web page A hypertext document accessible directly via the World Wide Web.

Wholesaling All activities involved in selling goods and services to those buying for resale or business use.

Wide area network (WAN) Telecommunications network that spans a wide geographical area such as a state or country.

Wireless application protocol (WAP) Standard technology framework allowing mobile phone users to access information on the Internet.

World Wide Web The universe of hypertext servers that allow text, graphics, sound files etc. to be mixed together.

XML (extensible markup language) Allows users to create their own customized tags, enabling the definition, transmission, validation and interpretation of data between applications and organizations.

Yield management The process of trying to maximize revenue by selling the same product (such as a seat on a flight) to different customers at different prices depending on the demand and supply.

Bibliography

ABTECH (1993) The use of technology by UK travel agencies, ABTECH technology report, ABTECH, London.

Adam, R. (1990) A licence to steal? The growth and development of airline information systems, *Journal of Information Science*, **16**(1), 77–91.

Adamson, M. and Toole, D. (1995) Multimedia in the home: the battle for the living room, Financial Times report, Telecoms and Media Publishing, London.

Airtours (1999) *Annual Report and Accounts*, Airtours, London.

Anckar, B. and Walden, P. (2001) Introducing web technology in a small peripheral hospitality organisation, *International Journal of Contemporary Hospitality Management*, **13**(5), 241–250.

Ansoff, I. (1965) *Corporate Strategy*, McGraw-Hill, New York.

Archdale, G. (1993) Computer reservation systems and public tourist offices, *Tourism Management*, **14**(1), 3–14.

Archdale, G. (1994) Non European initiatives and systems, in Schertler, W., Schmid, B., Tjoa, A. and Werthner, H. (eds), *Information and Communications Technologies in Tourism*, Conference proceedings ENTER'94, Innsbruck 12–14 January, Springer-Verlag, Vienna, pp. 56–63.

Archdale, G., Stanton, R. and Jones, G. (1992) *Destination Databases: Issues and Priorities*, Pacific Asia Travel Association, San Fransisco.

Augier, M., Shariq, S. and Vendelø, M. (2001) Understanding context: its emergence, transformation and role in tacit knowledge sharing, *Journal of Knowledge Management*, **5**(2), 125–137.

Bakos, Y. (1991) A strategic analysis of electronic marketplaces, *MIS Quarterly*, **15**(3), 295–310.

Barnatt, C. (1995) Office space, cyberspace and virtual organisation, *Journal of General Management*, **20**(4), 78–91.

Barsoum, K. (1999) eCommerce is the great enabler, *Management Today*, March, **5**.

Beaumont, J. and Sparks, L. (1990) Information technology is a source of competitive advantage, *International Journal of Information Resource Management*, **1**(1), 28–36.

Beaver, A. (1992) Hotel CRS – an overview, *Tourism Management*, **13**(1), 15–21.

Beaver, A. (1993) *Mind Your Own Travel Business: A Manual of Retail Travel Practice*, Beaver Travel Publishers, England.

Beekman, G. (2001) *Computer Confluence: Exploring Tomorrow's Technology*, 4th edn, Prentice Hall, Uppper Saddle River New Jersey.

Beldona, S., Beck J. and Qu, H. (2001) Implementing enterprise resource planning in a hotel: towards theory building, *International Journal of Hospitality Information Technology*, **2**(1), 9–22.

Bennett, M. (1993) Information technology and travel agency: a customer service perspective, *Tourism Management*, **14**(4), 259–266.

Bennett, M. and Radburn, M. (1991) Information technology in tourism: the impact on the industry and supply of holidays, in Sinclair, T. and Stabler, M. (eds), *The Tourism Industry: An International Analysis*, CAB International, Oxford, pp. 45–67.

Blois, K. (1987) IT and marketing strategies in service firms, *Service Industry Journal*, **7**(1), 14–23.

Boberg, K. and Collison, F. (1985) Computer reservation systems and airline competition, *Tourism Management*, **6**(3), 174–183.

Bollinger, A. and Smith, R. (2001) Managing organizational knowledge as a strategic asset, *Journal of Knowledge Management*, **5**(1), 8–18.

Bradley, S., Hausman, J. and Nolan, R. (eds) (1993) *Globalisation, Technology and Competition: The Fusion of Computers and Telecommunications in the 1990s*, Harvard Business School Press, Boston, Massachusetts.

Braham, B. (1988) *Computer Systems in the Hotel and Catering Industry*, Cassell, London.

Bubley, D. and Bennett, P. (1994) Information superhighways: the new information age, Financial Times report, London.

Buhalis, D. (1993) Regional integrated computer information reservation management systems as a strategic tool for the small and medium tourism enterprises, *Tourism Management*, **14**(5), 366–378.

Buhalis, D. (1994) Information and telecommunications technologies as a strategic tool for small and medium tourism enterprises in the contemporary business environment, in Seaton, A. et al. (eds), *Tourism – the State of the Art: the Strathclyde Symposium*, John Wiley, Chichester, pp. 254–275.

Buhalis, D. (1995) The impact of information telecommunication technologies on tourism distribution channels: implications for the small and medium-sized tourism enterprises' strategic management and marketing, PhD thesis, University of Surrey.

Buhalis, D. (1997) Information technologies as a strategic tool for economic, cultural and environmental benefits enhancement of tourism at destination regions, *Progress in Tourism and Hospitality Research*, **3**(1), 71–93.

Buhalis, D. (1998) Strategic use of information technologies in the tourism industry, *Tourism Management*, **19**(3), 409–423.

Buhalis, D. (1999) Information technology for small and medium-sized tourism enterprises: adaptation and benefits, *Information Technology and Tourism*, **2**(2), 79–95.

Buhalis, D. (2000a) Information technology in tourism: the state of the art, *Tourism Recreation Research*, **25**(1), 41–58.

Buhalis, D. (2000b) Marketing the competitive destination of the future, *Tourism Management*, **21**(1), 97–116.

Buhalis, D. (2000c) Information technology and tourism, in Gartner, W. and Lime, D.W. (eds), *Trends in Outdoor Recreation, Leisure and Tourism*, CAB International, Oxford, pp. 47–63.

Buhalis, D. (2001) The tourism phenomenon – the new tourist and consumer, in Wahab, S. and Cooper, C. (eds), *Tourism in the Age of Globalisation*, Routledge, London.

Buhalis, D. and Cooper, C. (1998) Competition or co-operation: small and medium sized tourism enterprises at the destination, in Laws, E., Faulkner, B. and Moscardo, G. (eds), *Embracing and Managing Change in Tourism*, Routledge, London, pp. 324–346.

Buhalis, D. and Keeling, S. (1999) Distributing B&B accommodation in York, UK: advantages and developments emerging through the Internet, in Buhalis, D. and

Scherlter, W. (eds), *Information and Communications Technologies in Tourism*, ENTER 1999 Proceedings, Springer-Verlag, Vienna.

Buhalis, D. and Laws, E. (2001) *Tourism Distribution Channels*, Continuum, London.

Buhalis, D. and Licata, C. (2002) The eTourism intermediaries, *Tourism Management*, **23**(3), 207–220.

Buhalis, D. and Main, H. (1998) Information technology in small and medium hospitality enterprises: strategic analysis and critical factors, *International Journal of Contemporary Hospitality Management*, **10**(5), 198–202.

Buhalis, D. and Schertler, W. (eds) (1999) *Information and Communication Technologies in Tourism*, Springer-Verlag, Vienna.

Buhalis, D. and Spada, A. (2000) Destination management systems: criteria for success, *Information Technology and Tourism*, **3**(1), 41–58.

Buhalis, D., Tjoa, A.M. and Jafari, J. (eds) (1998) *Information and Communication Technologies in Tourism*, Springer-Velag, Vienna.

Burt, S. and Dawson, J. (1991) The impact of new technology and new payment systems on commercial distribution in the European Community, Series studies: commerce and distribution, European Community, DG XXIII, report XXIII/518/91, Brussels.

Byrne, J., Brandt, R. and Port, O. (1993) The virtual corporations, *Business Week*, **8**(2), 36–40.

Bywater, M. (2001) Travel distribution: who owns whom in the European travel distribution industry, in Buhalis, D. and Laws, E. (2001) *Tourism Distribution Channels*, Continuum, London.

Cano, V. and Prentice, R. (1998) Opportunities for endearment to place through electronic visiting: WWW homepages and the tourism promotion of Scotland, *Tourism Management*, **19**(1), 67–73.

Chaffey, D., Mayer, R., Johnston, K. and Ellis-Chadwick, F. (2000) *Internet Marketing*, Prentice Hall, Upper Saddle River New Jersey.

Chervenak, L. (1991) CRS: The past–the present–the future, *Lodging*, June, 25–43.

Chervenak, L. (1993) Hotel technology at the start of the millennium, *Hospitality Research Journal*, **17**(1), 113–120.

Clemons, E.K. and McFarlan, F.W. (1986) Telecom: hook up or lose out, *Harvard Business Review*, **64**(4), 91–97.

Collins, G. and Malik, T. (1999) *Hospitality Information Technology*, Kendall/Hunt, Iowa.

Connolly, D., Olsen, M. and Allegro, S. (2000) The hospitality industry and the digital economy: summary of the IH&RA Think Tank, Lausanne, Switzerland.

Cook, S. (2001) Travel planners: how they use the web today, presentation at ENTER2001 Conference, Montreal.

Cooper, C. and Buhalis, D. (1992) Strategic management and marketing of small and medium-sized tourism enterprises in the Greek Aegean islands, in Teare, R., Adams, D. and Messenger, S. (eds), *Managing Projects in Hospitality Organisations*, Cassell, London, pp. 101–125.

Cooper, C. and Buhalis, D. (1998) The future of tourism, in Cooper, C.R. et al. (eds), *Tourism: Principles and Practices*, Addison Wesley Longman, London.

Cooper, C., Fletcher, J., Gilbert, D., Shepherd, R. and Wanhill, S. (eds) (1998) *Tourism: Principles and Practices*, Addison Wesley Longman, London.

Copeland, D. (1991) So you want to build the next SABRE System, *Business Quarterly*, **55**(33), 56–60.

Copeland, D. and McKenney, J. (1988) Airline reservation systems: lessons from history, *MIS Quarterly*, **12**, 535–370.

Curtis, J. (1999) WAP! Three letters that will blow the net wide apart, *Revolution*, 10 November, 24–30.

Davenport, T. (1993) *Process Innovation: Reengineering Work through Information Technology*, Harvard Business School Press, Boston, Massachusetts.

David, F. (1997) *Strategic Management*, 6th edn, Prentice Hall, Upper Saddle River New Jersey.

Davidow, W. and Malone, M. (1992) *The Virtual Corporation: Structuring and Revitalizing the Corporation for the 21st Century*, Harper Business, New York.

Davidson, R. (2001) *Business Travel*, 2nd edn, Addison Wesley Longman, London.

Davis, T. and Darling, B. (1996) ABC in a virtual corporation, *Management Accounting*, **78**(10), October, 18–26.

Day, G. (1986) *Analysis for Strategic Marketing Decisions*, West Publishing, Eagan Minnesota.

Dempsey, M. (2000) When convergence turns into digital collision, *The Financial Times*, Information Technology survey, 19 January, p. IV.

Deng, S. and Ryan, C. (1992) CRS: tool or determinant of management practice in Canadian travel agents?, *Journal of Travel and Tourism Marketing*, **1**(1), 19–38.

Dennis, P. (1998) Marriott International on the Internet: a success story, presentation at the ENTER'98 Conference, Istanbul.

Dertouzos, M. (1997) *What Will Be: How the New World of Information Will Change Our Lives*, Piatkus Books, London.

Earl, M. (ed.) (1988) *Information Management: the Strategic Dimension*, Clarendon Press, Oxford.

EC (1990) Council Directive of 13 June 1990 on package travel, package holidays and package tours, (90/314/EEC), *Official Journal of the European Communities*, No. L 158/59, 23 June, 59–64.

EC (1993) Growth, competitiveness, employment: the challenges and ways forward into the 21st century, White Paper, Bulletin of the European Communities, Supplement 6/93, Luxembourg.

EC (1994) Integrated programme in favour of SMEs and the craft sector, Commission of the European Communities, COM (94) 207, final, Brussels.

Edwards, A. and Graham, A. (1997) *International Tourism Forecasts to 2010*, Travel and Tourism Intelligence, London.

Edwards, G., Dawes, C. and Kärcher, K. (1998) The Imminus travel and tourism intranet, in Buhalis, D. et al. (eds), *Information and Communication Technologies in Tourism*, ENTER 1998 Proceedings, Springer-Verlag, Vienna, pp. 190–201.

Emmer, R., Tauck, C., Wilkinson, S. and Moore, R. (1993) Marketing hotels using global distribution systems, *The Cornell Hotel Restaurant Administration Quarterly*, **34**(6), 80–89.

Evans, D. (2000) Third world war, *Business and Technology*, January, 22–24.

Feeny, D. (1988) Creating and sustaining competitive advantage with IT, in Earl, M. (ed.), *Information Management: The Strategic Dimension*, Clarendon Press, Oxford, pp. 98–117.

Feldman, J. (1987) CRS in the USA: determining future levels of airline competition, *Travel and Tourism Analyst*, **3**, 3–14.

Ference, G. (2001) Improving organisational performance using survey-driven databases, *The Cornell Hotel and Restaurant Administration Quarterly*, April, 12–27.

Fesenmaier, D., Leppers, A. and O'Leary, J. (1999) Developing a knowledge based tourism marketing information system, *Information Technology and Tourism*, **2**(1), 31–45.

Fesenmaier, D., Vogt, C. and Mackay, K. (1992) Researching consumer information: exploring the role of pre-trip information search in travel decisions, Proceedings of Travel and Tourism Research Association: tourism partnership and strategies: merging vision with new realities, 23rd Annual Conference, 14–17 June, Minneapolis, pp. 32–36.

Fesenmaier, D., Klein, S. and Buhalis, D. (eds) (2000) *Information and Communication Technologies in Tourism*, Springer-Verlag, Vienna.

Finlay, P. (2000) *Strategic Management: an Introduction to Business and Corporate Strategy*, Financial Times–Prentice Hall, London.

Freedman, D. (1991) The myth of strategic IS, *CIO*, **4**(10), 42–48.

Freeman, C. and Perez, C. (1988) Structural crisis of adjustment: business cycles and investment behaviour, in Dosi, G., Freeman, C., Nelson, R., Silverbery, G. and Soete, L. (eds), *Technical Change and Economic Theory*, Francis Printer, London.

French, T. (1998) The future of global distribution systems, *Travel and Tourism Analyst*, **3**, 1–17.

Frew, A. and Horan, R. (1999) eCommerce in the UK hotel sector: a first look, *International Journal of Hospitality Information Technology*, **1**(1), 77–87.

Frew, A. and O'Connor, P. (1998) A comparative examination of the implementation of destination marketing system strategies: Scotland and Ireland, in Buhalis, D. et al. (eds), *Information and Communication Technologies in Tourism*, ENTER 1998 Proceedings, Springer-Verlag, Vienna, pp. 258–268.

Frew, A. and O'Connor, P. (1999) Destination marketing system strategies: refining and extending an assessment framework, in Buhalis, D. and Scherlter, W. (eds), *Information and Communications Technologies in Tourism*, ENTER 1999 Proceedings, Springer-Verlag, Vienna, pp. 398–407.

Gamble, P. (1990) Culture shock, computers and the art of making decisions, *International Journal of Contemporary Hospitality Management*, **2**(1), 4–9.

Gamble, P. (1994a) Strategic issues for the management of information services from the tourism to the hospitality industry – lessons for the future, in Cooper, C. and Lockwood, A. (eds), *Progress in Tourism, Recreation and Hospitality Management*, vol. 5, John Wiley, Chichester, pp. 273–288.

Gamble, P. (1994b) Applications of information technology, in Witt, S. and Moutinho, L. (eds), *Tourism Marketing and Management Handbook*, 2nd edn, Prentice Hall, London, pp. 202–206.

Gates, W. (1999) *Business@the speed of thought*, BCA, New York.

Gee, C. (1981) *Resort Development and Management*, Educational Institute of the American Hotel and Motel Association, Michigan.

Gee, C., Makens, J. and Choy, D. (1989) *The Travel Industry*, 2nd edn, Van Nostrand Reinhold, New York.

Go, F. (1992) The role of computerised reservation systems in the hospitality industry, *Tourism Management*, **13**(1), 22–26.

Go, F. and Welch, P. (1991) Competitive strategies for the international hotel industry, *The Economist* Intelligence Unit, special report no. 1180, London.

Goeldner, C., Ritchie, B. and McIntosh, R. (2000) *Tourism: Principles, Practices, Philosophies*, 8th edn, John Wiley, New York.

Grönroos, C. (1990) Relationship approach to marketing in service contexts: the marketing and organisational behaviour interface, *Journal of Business Research*, **20**, 3–11.

Groth, J.C. (1993) Critical factors in exploiting technologies, *Management Decision*, **31**(3), 34–48.

Gupta, U. (1996) *Management Information Systems: A Managerial Perspective*, Thomson Learning–Course Technology, Boston.

Gupta, U. (2000) *Information Systems: Success in the 21st Century*, Prentice Hall, Upper Saddle River New Jersey.

Haeckel, S. and Nolan, R. (1993) Managing by wire, *Harvard Business Review*, **71**(5), 122–132.

Hale, R. and Whitlam, P. (1997) *Towards the Virtual Organisation*, McGraw-Hill International, London.

Hall, M. (2000) *Tourism Planning: Policies, Processes and Relationships*, Addison Wesley Longman, London.

Halsall, F. (1996) *Data Communications, Computer Networks and Open Systems*, Addison Wesley Longman, London.

Hammer, M. (1990) Reengineering work: don't automate, obliterate, *Harvard Business Review*, May–June, 89–103.

Hammer, M. and Champy, J. (1993) *Reengineering the Corporation: A Manifesto for Business Revolution*, Nicholas Brealey, London.

Handy, C. (1995) Trust and the virtual organisation, *Harvard Business Review*, May–June, 40–50.

Hanlon, P. (1999) *Global Airlines Competition in a Transnational Industry*, 2nd edn, Butterworth-Heinemann, Oxford.

Hax, A. and Majluf, N. (1991) *The Strategy Concept and Process: A Pragmatic Approach*, Prentice Hall, Upper Saddle River New Jersey.

Hensdill, C. (1998) Hotels technology survey, *Hotels*, February, 24–42.

Hickey, G. (1993) Strategic IS/IT planning, in Peppard, J. (ed.), *IT Strategy for Business*, Pitman, London, pp. 75–99.

Hickey, J. (1988) Hotel reservation systems and source of business, *Travel and Tourism Analyst*, **2**, 23–36.

Hitchins, F. (1991) The influence of technology on UK travel agents, *Travel and Tourism Analyst*, **3**, 88–105.

Hoffman, J. (1995) Tourism and end consumer networks: the message in the living room, presentation at the ENTER'95 conference: Information and Communication in Tourism, Innsbruck, 18–20 January.

Hollister, N. (1995) The mobile office: towards the virtual corporation, Financial Times Management Reports, London.

Holloway, C. (1989) *The Business of Tourism*, 3rd edn, Pitman, Plymouth.

Holst, A. (2001) Tour operator Internet sales, Tourism Distribution Conference, Access Conferences, June, Nice, France.

Hopper, L. (1990) Ratting SABRE – new ways to compete on information, *Harvard Business Review*, **68**(3), 118–125.

Horner, S. and Swarbrooke, J. (1996) *Marketing Tourism, Hospitality and Leisure in Europe*, Thomson Business Press, London.

Ingold, A., McMahon-Beattie, U. and Yeoman, I. (2000) *Yield Management*, 2nd edn, Continuum, London.

Inkpen, G. (1998) *Information Technology for Travel and Tourism*, 2nd edn, Addison Wesley Longman, London.

International Hotel Association (1992) Yield management – revenue control, Hotel Automation Advisory Group Report at the IHA Congress, Bangkok, 11–15 October, International Hotel Association, Paris.

Jackson, C. (1989) Building a competitive advantage through information technology, *Long Range Planning*, **22**(4), 29–39.

Jarvela, P., Loikkanen, J., Tinnila, M. and Tuunainen, V. (1999) Business models for electornic commerce in the travel services, *Information Technology and Tourism*, **2**(3/4), 185–196.

Jewell, G., Williamson, B. and Kärcher, K. (1999) The Airtours Cruise intranet: streamlining the distribution of information knowledge and money, in Buhalis, D. and Schertler, W. (eds), *Information and Communication Technologies in Tourism*, ENTER 1999 Proceedings, Springer-Verlag, Vienna, pp. 337–346.

Johnson, G. and Scholes, K. (1999) *Exploring Corporate Strategy*, 5th edn, Prentice Hall, London.

Jones, N. (1999) European online commerce and travel: serving the directed shopper, Jupiter Communications presentation at the conference Changing Distribution Channels in the Travel Industry, 8–9 December, London.

Jones, P. (ed.) (1996) *Introduction to Hospitality Operations*, Cassell, London.

Jones P. and Lockwood, A. (1989) *The Management of Hotel Operations*, Cassell, London.

Jones P. and Pizam, A. (1993) *International Hospitality Management – Organisational and Operational Issues*, Pitman, London.

Jupiter (1999) *Online Consumer survey*, Jupiter Communications, London.

Kalakota, R. and Whinston, A. (1996) *Frontiers of Electronic Commerce*, Addison Wesley Longman, London.

Kärcher, K. (1996) The four global distribution systems in the travel and tourism industry, *Electronic Markets*, **6**(2), 20–24.

Kärcher, K. (1997) *Reinventing the Package Holiday Business: New Information and Telecommunications Technologies*, DeutscherUniversitätsVerlag, Gabler, Germany.

King, W., Hufnagel, E. and Grover, V. (1988) Using information technology for competitive advantages, in Earl, M. (ed.), *Information Management: the Strategic Dimension*, Clarendon Press, Oxford, pp. 75–86.

Klein, S., Schmid, B., Tjoa, A.M. and Werthner, H. (1996) *Information and Communication Technologies in Tourism*, Springer-Verlag, Vienna.

Knowles, T. and Garland, M. (1994) The strategic importance of CRSs in the airline industry, *Travel and Tourism Analyst*, **4**, 4–16.

Konig, J. and Strauss, C. (2000) Rostering integrated services and crew efficiency, *Information Technology and Tourism*, **3**(1), 27–39.

Kotler, P. (1998) *Marketing Management: Analysis, Planning and Control*, 8th edn, Prentice Hall International Editions, New Jersey.

Kotler, P., Bowen, J. and Makens, J. (1996) *Marketing for Hospitality and Tourism*, Prentice Hall, Upper Saddle River New Jersey.

Ladkin, A. (2000) *The Meetings, Incentives, Conferences and Exhibitions Industry*, Travel and Tourism Intelligence, London.

Ladkin, A. and Spiller, J. (2000) *The Meetings, Incentives, Conferences and Exhibitions Industry: An International Research Report*, Travel and Tourism Intelligence, London.

Lattin, T. (1990) Hotel technology: key to survival, in Quest M. (ed.), *Horwath Book of Tourism*, Macmillan, London, pp. 219–223.

Laudon, K. and Laudon, J. (2002) *Management Information Systems: Managing the Digital Firm*, 7th edn, Prentice Hall, Upper Saddle River New Jersey.

Leidner, D. (1999) Information technology and organisational culture: understanding information culture: integrating knowledge management systems into organisations, in Galliers, R., Leidner, D. and Baker, B. (eds), *Strategic Information Management: Challenges and Strategies in Managing Information Systems*, Butterworth-Heinemann, Oxford, pp. 523–550.

Leiper, N. (1995) *Tourism Management*, RMIT Press, Melbourne.

Levine, M. (1987) Airline competition in deregulated markets: theory, firm strategy and public policy, *Yale Journal of Regulation*, **14**, 393–394.

Lieberman, W. (1993) Debunking the myths of yield management, *Cornell Hotel Restaurant Administration Quarterly*, **34**(1), 34–41.

Lindsay, P. (1992) New hospitality products supply and demand: session introduction, *Tourism Management*, **13**(1), 11–14.

Loebbecke, C. and Jelassi, T. (1997) Concepts and technologies for virtual organising: the Gerling journey, *European Management Journal*, **15**(2), 138–146.

Lorenz, A. (1999) Mobile mania, *The Sunday Times*, Business Focus, **3**, p. 5.

Lynch, R. (1997) *Corporate Strategy*, Financial Times–Pitman Publishing, London.

Marcussen C. (1999a) *Internet Distribution of European Travel and Tourism Services*, Research Centre of Bornholm, Denmark.

Marcussen C. (1999b) The effects of Internet distribution of travel and tourism services on the marketing mix: no-frills, fair fares and fare wars in the air, *Information Technology and Tourism*, **2**(3/4), 197–212.

Marcussen, C. (2000) Tour operators in Scandinavia and Finland on the Net: a European perspective, *Anatolia*, **11**(1), 6–21.

Marsan, J. (2001) Hotels technology survey, *Hotels*, February, 78–94.

Martin, W., Brown, C., DeHayes, D., Hoffer, J. and Perkins, W. (1999) *Managing Information Technology: What Managers Need to Know*, Prentice Hall, Upper Saddle River New Jersey.

McFarlan, W. (1984) Information technology changes the way you compete, *Harvard Business Review*, **62**(3), 98–103.

McGee, J. and Thomas, H. (1988) Technology and strategic management: a research review, in Earl, M. (ed.), *Information Management: the Strategic Dimension*, Clarendon Press, Oxford, pp. 7–53.

McGuffie, J. (1994) CRS development in the hotel sector, *Travel and Tourism Analyst*, **2**, 53–68.

McKenna, R. (1993) *Relationship Marketing: Successful Strategies for the Age of the Consumer*, Addison Wesley, Reading.

Metakides, G. (1994) Opening address, paper presented at the European Information Technology Conference'94, Brussels, 6–8 June.

Middleton, V. (1988) *Marketing in Travel and Tourism*, Heinemann, London.

Middleton, V. (1994) *Marketing in Travel and Tourism*, 2nd edn, Butterworth-Heinemann, London.

Middleton, V. and Clark, J. (2001) *Marketing in Travel and Tourism*, 3rd edn, Butterworth-Heinemann, Oxford.

Mietus, J. (1989) European Community regulation of airline computer reservation systems, *Law and Policy in International Business*, **21**(1), 93–118.

Mill, P. and Morrison, A. (1998) *The Tourism System*, 3rd edn, Kendall Hunt Publishing Company, Dubuque, Iowa.

Minghetti, V. and Mangilli, V. (1998) InTRAsystem: an advanced Internet-based information system for managing business travel, *Information Technology and Tourism*, **1**(1), 33–44.

Mintzberg, H., Ahlstrand, B. and Lamplel, J. (1998) *Strategy Safari*, Prentice Hall, London.

Mintzberg, H., Quinn, J.B. and Ghoshal, S. (eds) (1998) *The Strategy Process*, revised European edn, Prentice Hall, London.

Moon, D. (1994) Deployment of computer networks in leisure packaged tour marketing in the USA, *Journal of Vacation Marketing*, **1**(1), 43–60.

Morath, P. (2000) *Success @ e-business*, McGraw-Hill, London.

Morrison, A. (1994) Marketing strategic alliances: the small hotel firm, *International Journal of Contemporary Hospitality Management*, **6**(3), 25–30.

Morrison, A., Taylor, S., Morrison, A. and Morrison, A. (1999a) Marketing small hotels on the world wide web, *The Hospitality Review*, **1**(3), 22–29.

Morrison, A., Taylor, S., Morrison, A. and Morrison, A. (1999b) Marketing small hotels on the world wide web, *Information Technology and Tourism*, **2**(2), 97–113.

Murphy, L., Forrest, E., Worthing, C. and Brymer, R. (1996) Hotel management and marketing on the internet, *Cornell Hotel and Restaurant Administration Quarterly*, **37**(3), 70–82.

Negroponte, N. (1995) *Being Digital Paperback*, Coronet Books, Hodder and Stoughton, London.

Obeng, E. and Crainer, S. (1994) *Making Reengineering Happen*, Financial Times–Pitman Publishing, London.

O'Brien, D. (2000) Smile – you are on the web, *The Sunday Times*, Culture Section, 9 January, p. 51.

O'Brien, J. (1996) *Management Information Systems: Managing Information Technology in the Networked Enterprise*, Irwin, Chicago.

O'Brien, P. (1999) Intelligent assistants for retail travel agents, *Information Technology and Tourism*, **2**(3/4), 213–228.

O'Connor, P. (1995) *Using Computers in Hospitality*, Cassell, London.

O'Connor, P. (1999a) *Using Computers in Hospitality*, 2nd edn, Cassell, London.

O'Connor, P. (1999b) *Electronic Information Distribution Technology in Tourism and Hospitality*, CAB, Oxford.

O'Connor, P. and Frew, A. (2000) Evaluating electronic channels of distribution in the hotel sector: a Delphi study, *Information Technology and Tourism*, **3**(3/4), 177–193.

O'Connor, P. and Horan, P. (1999) An analysis of web reservations facilities in the top 50 international hotel chains, *International Journal of Hospitality Information Technology*, **1**(1), 77–87.

O'Connor, P. and Rafferty J. (1997) Gulliver – distributing Irish tourism electronically, *Electronic Markets*, **7**(2), 40–45.

Oliva, R. (2001) Rise and fall: as the initial hype of Internet offerings comes to a plateau, hotels find true ways to use the Web to their advantage, *Hotels*, **35**(6), 12–14.

Orkin, E. (1988) Boosting your bottom line with yield management, *Cornell Hotel and Restaurant Administration Quarterly*, **28**(4), February, 52–56.

O'Toole, K. (2001) IT trends survey 2001, *Airline Business*, August.

Oz, E. (2000) *Management Information Systems*, 2nd edn, Thomson Learning–Course Technology, Boston.

Paraskevas, A. and Buhalis, D. (2002) Web-enabled ICT outsourcing for small hotels: opportunities and challenges, *Cornell Hotel and Restaurant Administration Quarterly*, **43**(2), 27–39.

Parsons, G. (1983) Information technology: a new competitive advantage, *Sloan Management Review*, **24**(1), 3–14.

Peacock, M. (1995) *Information Technology in the Hospitality Industry: Managing People, Change*, Cassell, London.

Peppard, J. (ed.) (1993) *IT Strategy for Business*, Pitman, London.

Perry, J. and Schneider, G. (2001) *New Perspectives on eCommerce*, Thomson Learning–Course Technology, Boston.

Piercy, N. (1983) Retailer information powers: the channel marketing information system, *Marketing Intelligence and Planning*, **1**(1), 40–55.

Pollock, A. (1998a) Creating intelligent destinations for wired customers, in Buhalis, D. et al. (eds), *Information and Communication Technologies in Tourism*, ENTER'98 Conference Proceedings, Springer-Verlag, Vienna, pp. 235–247.

Pollock, A. (1998b) New technologies as help for integrated quality management, in European Tourism Forum Conference Proceedings, Vienna, Austria 1–3 July, pp. 78–87.

Pollock, A. (1999) Marketing destinations in a digital world, *Insights*, May, A149–158.

Poon, A. (1988) Flexible specialisation and small size – the case of Caribbean tourism, SPRU, DRC discussion paper, no. 57.

Poon, A. (1989) Competitive strategies for new tourism, in Cooper, C. (ed.), *Progress in Tourism Recreation and Hospitality Management*, vol. 1, Belhaven Press, London, pp. 91–102.

Poon, A. (1990) Flexible specialisation at small size: the case of Caribbean tourism, *World Development*, **18**(1), 109–123.

Poon, A. (1993) *Tourism, Technology and Competitive Strategies*, CAB International, Oxford.

Poria, Y. and Taylor, A. (2001) I am not afraid to pay when I am on the Net: minimising social risk for lesbian and gay consumers when using the Internet, *Journal of Travel and Tourism Management*, **11**(2/3), pp. 127–142.

Porter, M. (1980) *Competitive Strategy: Techniques for Analysing Industries and Competitors*, Free Press, New York.

Porter, M. (1985a) *Competitive Advantage*, Free Press, New York.

Porter, M. (1985b) Technology and competitive advantage, *The Journal of Business Strategy*, Winter, 60–70.

Porter, M. (1989) Building competitive advantage by extending information systems, *Computerworld*, 9 October, **23**(41), 19.

Porter, M. (2001) Strategy and the Internet, *Harvard Business Review*, **103D**, March, 63–78.

Porter, M. and Millar, V. (1985) How information gives you competitive advantage, *Harvard Business Review*, July–August, **63**(4), 149–160.

Pringle, S. (1994) Destined to fail? An investigation of the Hi-Line Destination Marketing System, in Seaton, A., Wood, R., Dieke, P. and Jenkins, C. (eds), *Tourism – The State of the Art: The Strathclyde Symposium*, John Wiley, Chichester, pp. 500–509.

Prochak, M. (1997) Virtual enterprise goes boldly into the transformed universe, *Business and Technology*, July, 10.

Proll, B., Retschitzegger, W., Wagner, R. and Ebner, A. (1998) Beyond traditional tourism information systems: the Web-based approach TIScover, *Information Technology and Tourism*, **1**(1), 15–31.

Puhretmair, F., Lang, P., Tjoa, A.M. and Wagner, R. (2001) The XML-KL approach: XML-based integration of tourism and GIS data for HTML and WAP clients, in Sheldon, P., Wober, K. and Fesenmaier, D. (eds), *Information and Communication Technologies in Tourism*, Springer-Verlag, Vienna, pp. 73–82.

Rach, L. (1997) The connected consumer: implications for hospitality sales and marketing, *Hospitality Sales & Marketing Association International*, **13**(3), 23–26.

Rambler, M. and McGrew, G. (2000) The case for ASPs: opportunities and challenges with the ASP model, *Lodging Magazine*, December, **http://www.cyntercorp.com/ sections/news_articles/articles/200012ASP.asp**

Rayport, J. and Sviokla, J. (1994) Managing in the marketspace, *Harvard Business Review*, **72**(6), 141–150.

Renshaw, M. (1992) *The Travel Agent, Centre for Travel and Tourism*, Business Education Publishers Ltd, Sunderland.

Reynolds, G. (1992) *Information Systems for Managers*, West Publishing, Eagan USA.

Richards, G. (1995) Retailing travel products: bridging the information gap, *Progress in Tourism and Hospitality Research*, **1**(1), 17–29.

Richer, P. (2000) The death of the brochure, *Travel Trade Gazette*, 4 December, 24.

Richer, P. and O'Neill-Dunne, T. (1999) *Distribution Technology in the Travel Industry Strategies for Marketing Success*, Financial Times Retail & Consumer, London.

Robledo, M. (1999) DBM as a source of competitive advantage for the hotel industry, in Buhalis, D. and Schertler, W. (eds), *Information and Communication Technologies in Tourism*, Springer-Verlag, Vienna, pp. 36–45.

Robson, W. (1997) *Strategic Management and Information Systems: an Integrated Approach*, 2nd edn, Pitman, London.

Rowe, M. (1989) Yield management, *Lodging Hospitality*, **45**(2), February, 65–66.

Runge, D. and Earl, M. (1988) Getting competitive advantages from telecommunications, in Earl, M. (ed.), *Information Management: the Strategic Dimension*, Clarendon Press, Oxford, pp. 125–145.

Russell, S. and Norvig, P. (1995) *Artificial Intelligence*, Prentice Hall, Upper Saddle River New Jersey.

Schertler, W., Schmid, B., Tjoa, A.M. and Werthner, H. (eds) (1994) *Information and Communication Technologies in Tourism*, Springer-Verlag, Vienna.

Schertler, W., Maier, M. and Rohte, S. (1995) The end user acceptance of new information and communication technologies in tourism, in Schertler, W. et al. (eds), *Information and Communication Technologies in Tourism*, Conference proceedings ENTER'95, Springer-Verlag, Vienna, pp. 46–52.

Schertler, W., Schmid, B., Tjoa, A.M. and Werthner, H. (eds) (1995) *Information and Communication Technologies in Tourism*, Springer-Verlag, Vienna.

Schmid, B. (1994) Electronic markets in tourism, in Schertler, W. et al. (eds), *Information and Communication Technologies in Tourism*, Conference proceedings ENTER'94, Innsbruck 12–14 January, Springer-Verlag, Vienna, pp. 1–8.

Shaw, G. and Williams, A.M. (1990) Tourism economic development and the role of entrepreneurial activity, in Cooper, C. (ed.), *Progress in Tourism Recreation and Hospitality Management*, vol. 2, Belhaven Press, London, pp. 67–81.

Sheldon, P. (1993) Destination information systems, *Annals of Tourism Research*, **20**(4), 633–649.

Sheldon, P. (1994) Information technology and computer systems, in Witt, S. and Moutinho, L. (eds), *Tourism Marketing and Management Handbook*, Prentice Hall, London, pp. 126–130.

Sheldon, P. (1997) *Information Technologies for Tourism*, CAB, Oxford.

Sheldon, P., Wöber, K. and Fesenmaier, D. (eds) (2001) *Information and Communication Technologies in Tourism*, Springer-Verlag, Vienna.

Simmons, L. (2000) Last call for offline sales?, *Revolution*, 4 May, 32–35.

SITA (2001) Wireless applications for airports, **http://www.sita.net/objects/download/ reference/wirelessairport.pdf**

Sloane, J. (1990) Latest developments in aviation CRSs, *Travel and Tourism Analyst*, **4**, 5–15.

Smith, C. and Jenner, P. (1994) Travel agents in Europe, *Travel and Tourism Analyst*, **3**, 56–71.

Smith, C. and Jenner, P. (1998) Tourism and the Internet, *Travel and Tourism Analyst*, **1**, 62–81.

Snepenger, D., Meged, K., Snelling, M. and Worrall, K. (1990) Information search strategies by destination naive tourists, *Journal of Travel Research*, **29**(1), 185–208.

Stipanuk, D. (1993) Tourism and technology: interactions and implications, *Tourism Management*, **14**(4), 267–278.

Strassmann, P. (1990) *The Business Value of Computers: an Executive Guide*, The Information Economics Press, Connecticut.

Strauss, J. and Frost, R. (1999) *Marketing on the Internet: Principles of On-line Marketing*, Prentice Hall, Upper Saddle River New Jersey.

Sun (1998) *Electronic Commerce Essentials: Trading in the Electronic Age*, Santa Clara, California.

Symonds, M. (1999) The net imperative: business and the Internet, *The Economist*, 26 June, 8–44.

Swarbrooke, J. and Horner, S. (2001) *Business Travel and Tourism*, Butterworth-Heinemann, Oxford.

Szabo, K., Stucki, P., Blatter, M., Simeon, P., Ruff, M., Horezku, C. and Pauli, K. (1994) Development of a CD-ROM based multimedia application in an open system environment, in Schertler, W. et al. (eds), *Information and Communication Technologies in Tourism*, Conference Proceedings ENTER'94, Innsbruck 12–14 January, Springer-Verlag, Vienna, 108–115.

Tapscott, D. (1996) *The Digital Economy: Promise and Peril in the Age of Networked Intelligence*, McGraw-Hill, New York.

Tapscott, D. and Caston, A. (1993) *Paradigm Shift: the New Promise of Information Technology*, McGraw-Hill, New York.

Tapscott, D., Ticoll, D. and Lowy, A. (2000) *Digital Capital: Harnessing the Power of Business Webs*, Harvard Business School Press, Boston.

Teare R. and Olsen M. (1992) *International Hospitality Management – Corporate Strategy in Practice*, Pitman, London.

The pH Group (1993) Micro economic analysis of the tourism sector, a study by the pH Group for the DGXXIII, European Community, Brussels.

Thomas, M. (1998) Innovation and technology strategy: competitive new technology firms and industries, in Giaoutzi, M., Nijkamp, P. and Storey, D. (eds), *Small and Medium Size Enterprises and Regional Development*, Routledge, London, pp. 44–70.

TIA (1997) *Travel and Interactive Technology: A Five Year Outlook*, Travel Industry Association of America, Washington DC.

TIA (2001a) *eTravel Consumers: How They Plan and Buy Leisure Travel Online*, Travel Industry Association of America, Washington DC.

TIA (2001b) *Travelers' Use of the Internet*, 2001 edn, Travel Industry Association of America, Washington DC.

Tidd, J., Bessant, J. and Pavitt, K. (1997) *Managing Innovation: Integrating Technological, Market and Organisational Change*, John Wiley, Chichester.

Tjoa, A.M. (ed.) (1997) *Information and Communication Technologies in Tourism*, Springer-Verlag, Vienna.

Tjostheim, I. and Eide, J.O. (1998) A case of an on-line auction for the World Wide Web, in Buhalis, D. et al. (eds), *Information and Communication Technologies in Tourism*, ENTER 1998 Proceedings, Springer-Verlag, Vienna, pp. 149–161.

Truitt, L., Teye, V. and Farris, M. (1991) The role of computer reservation systems: international implications for the tourism industry, *Tourism Management*, **12**(1), 21–36.

Turban, E. and Aronson, J. (2001) *Decision Support Systems and Intelligent Systems*, 6th edn, Prentice Hall, Upper Saddle River New Jersey.

Turban, E., Lee, J., King, D. and Chang, H. (2002) *Electronic Commerce: A Managerial Perspective*, Prentice Hall, Upper Saddle River New Jersey.

Van Hoof, H., Ruys, H. and Combrink, T. (1999) Global hoteliers and the Internet: use and perceptions, *International Journal of Hospitality Information Technology*, **1**(1), 45–63.

Van Rekom, J., Teunissen, W. and Go, F. (1999) Improving the position of business travel agencies: coping with the information challenge, *Information Technology and Tourism*, **2**(1), 15–30.

Vaughan, R. (1995) Travel retailing has passed its sell by date, *Travel Trade Gazette*, 11 January, **2143**, 66.

Vlitos-Rowe, I. (1992) Destination databases and management systems, *Travel and Tourism Analyst*, **5**, 84–108.

Vlitos-Rowe, I. (1995) *The Impact of Technology on the Travel Industry*, Financial Times Management Reports, London.

Wanhill, S. (1998) Intermediaries, in Cooper, C., Fletcher, J., Gilbert, D., Shepherd, R. and Wanhill, S. (eds), *Tourism: Principles and Practice*, 2nd edn, Longman Publishing, London, pp. 423–446.

Ward, J., Griffiths, P. and Whitmore, P. (1990) *Strategic Planning for Information Systems*, John Wiley, Chichester.

Wardell, D. (1987a) Airline reservation systems in the USA: CRS agency dealerships and the gold handcuff, *Travel and Tourism Analyst*, **1**, January, 45–56.

Wardell, D. (1987b) Hotel technology and reservation systems: challenges facing the lodging industry, *Travel and Tourism Analyst*, **2**, June, 33–47.

Wardell, D. (1998) The impact of electronic distribution on travel agents, *Travel and Tourism Analyst*, **2**, 41–55.

Wayne, N. (1992) Hi-Line, in Yee, J. (ed.), *Proceedings of the PATA Destination Database Conference*, Singapore, 9–10 December, PATA Intelligence Centre, San Francisco, pp. 70–74.

Werthner, H. and Klein, S. (1999) *Information Technology and Tourism – A Challenging Relationship*, Springer, New York.

Wheatcroft, S. and Lipman, G. (1990) European liberalisation and world air transport: towards a transnational industry, Economist Intelligence Unit, special report, no. 2015, London.

Whiteley, D. (2000) *eCommerce: Strategy, Technologies and Applications*, McGraw-Hill, London.

Wijnhoven, A. and Wassenaar, D. (1990) Impact of information technology on organisations: the state of the art, *International Journal of Information Management*, **10**(1), 35–53.

Williams, P. (1993) Information technology and tourism: a dependent factor for future survival, in Ritchie, B. et al. (eds), *World Travel and Tourism Review: Indicators, Trends and Issues*, vol. 3, CAB International, Oxford, pp. 200–205.

Winston, P.H. (1992) *Artificial Intelligence*, 3rd edn, Addison Wesley Longman, Massachusetts.

Wiseman, C. (1985) *Strategy and Computers: Information Systems as Competitive Weapons*, Dow Jones-Irwin, Homewood, Illinois.

Wöber, K.W. (1998) Improving the efficiency of marketing information access and use by tourist organisations, *Information Technology and Tourism*, 1(1), 45–59.

Wöber, K., Frew, A. and Hitz, M. (eds) (2002) *Information and Communication Technologies in Tourism*, Springer-Verlag, Vienna.

WTO (1975) *Distribution Channels*, World Tourism Organisation, Madrid.

WTO (1988) *Guidelines for the Transfer of New Technologies in the Field of Tourism*, World Tourism Organisation, Madrid.

WTO (1995) *Global Distribution Systems in the Tourism Industry*, World Tourism Organisation, Madrid.

WTO (1999) *Marketing Tourism Destinations Online*, World Tourism Organisation, Madrid.

WTO (2000) *World Tourism Organisation's Tourism 2020 Vision*, World Tourism Organisation, Madrid.

WTO (2001) *eBusiness for Tourism: Practical Guidelines for Destinations and Businesses*, World Tourism Organisation, Madrid.

Zipf, A. and Malaka, R. (2001) Developing location based services for tourism: the service providers' view, in Sheldon, P., Wober, K. and Fesenmaier, D. (eds), *Information and Communication Technologies in Tourism*, Springer-Verlag, Vienna, pp. 83–92.

Index

Accounting, 12–13, 36, 77, 87, 101, 164,
 185, 188
Acquisitions, 49
Added value, 12, 49–50, 52, 55, 65, 112,
 149–51, 155, 179, 232, 257, 336
Advertising, 39, 153–4
 Fee, 79
 Online, 122, 144
 Off-line, 144
Airlines, 37, 48, 51, 91, 139, 144, 148,
 194–213, 328
 Alliances, 138–9, 196, 199, 209–11, 213
 Baggage handling, 203–4, 206
 Capacity management, 150
 Cargo, 203
 Charter, 198
 Complaints, 103
 Crew, 199–202
 CRS, 194–7, 202
 General Sales Agencies (GSA), 204
 No-frills, 112, 131, 167, 198
 Online sales, 121
 Operational management, 198–203
 Partners management, 203
 portal, 209–10, 213
 Procurement, 204
 Reservations, 103, 121–5, 159, 194
 Scheduled, 198
 Station control, 202
 United, 103
Airport, 194–213
 Baggage handling, 203–4, 206
 Infrastructure, 203
 Management, 202–3, 328
Alliances, 45, 49, 51, 53, 64, 68, 163–5,
 196, 329
 Airlines, 138–9, 196, 199, 209–11, 213
Allotment, 242–3
Amadeus, 195–7, 211, 319
Application Service Providers (ASP), 211
 Airlines, 211
 Destination, 292
 Hotel, 235

Applications
 Business, 10
 Information technology, 88
 Simulation, 24
 Tourism, 87
Artificial Intelligence, 7, 14, 24
Asymmetric Digital Subscriber Lines
 (ADSL), 17, 92, 320
Authentication, 186
Average room rate, 223

Back office, 139
Bandwidth, 21, 84, 320
Benchmarking, 56
Bluetooth, 22, 324
 In hotels, 235, 324
Booking, 87–9
 Process, 93
 System, 93, 267
Brand, 43, 156, 167–9, 200, 268
 Building, 163
 Destination, 297
 Enlargement, 163
 Integrity, 211
 Loyalty, 157
Broadband, 21, 84, 320
Brochure, 168, 252
Bulletin Boards, 33
Business
 Functions, 12, 31, 138–9, 178, 184, 230
 Management, 12, 77
 Model, 23, 43, 61, 167, 318
 Processes, 10, 61, 99
 Strategy, 10, 11, 68, 211
 Travel, 11, 111, 166
Business process reengineering (BPR) 41,
 60–1, 70, 78, 99, 139, 150, 154, 162,
 335–40
Business to Business (B2B), 39–40, 42, 111,
 316
Business to Consumers (B2C), 39, 42, 316
Business to Government (B2G), 39, 42
Buyer, 57

Call centres, 153
Capacity, 126
  Distressed, 139
  Excess, 126
Car rental, 123
  Reservations, 122, 159
Carrying capacity, 301–2
Change, 40, 337–40
Channel, 25
  Conflict, 182, 293, 334
  Control, 182
  Leadership, 182, 334
  Multi-channel, 175, 315–25, 328, 338
  Negotiation, 153, 293
Charter airlines, 198
Chat rooms, 20, 33
Clicks and mortal, 272
Code sharing, 213
Co-destiny, 66, 336
Commission, 39, 167, 319, 331–2
  Capping, 208, 330
Communication, 16, 34, 67
  Cost, 31, 290
  Gaps, 3
Community, 33–5
Competition, 12, 30, 41, 51, 54–6
  Analysis, 48
Competitive
  Advantage through ICT, 150–63, 328–9
  Advantage, 6, 12, 14, 31, 43, 49, 52, 54,
    56–7, 59, 104, 150–63, 328
  Analysis, 45, 100
  Disadvantage, 14, 58, 105, 161–3
  Drivers, 95–6
  Edge, 55
  Intelligence, 154
  Position, 50, 57
  Strategy, 12, 43, 49
  Sustainable advantage, 160–1
Competitiveness, 6, 15, 31, 44, 48–51,
    57–8, 67, 78–9, 99, 149, 312, 340
  Destination, 340
  Enterprises, 340
  Organizational, 3, 25
Complaint
  Web sites, 127, 314
Computer, 7
  Design, 20
  Programme, 34
  System, 2
Computer Reservation System (CRS), 19,
    83, 93–6, 102, 179, 187, 194–6,
    315–17

Airline, 194–7, 202
Hotel, 223, 225–6
In travel agencies, 263–4
Connectivity, 115–25
Consumer, 6, 42, 55, 64, 68, 79–80, 102, 326
  Barriers, 125–6
  Behaviour, 55, 158, 314
  Catalysts, 125–6
  ICT needs, 94, 327
  Needs, 55, 130
  Patterns, 3
Content, 70, 316
Control, 10, 45, 186
  Operations, 55
  Performance, 55, 139
Convergence, 22, 41, 234, 290, 322, 324–5
  Technological, 96–7
Cooperation, 17, 336
  Marketing, 281
Corporate Strategy, 43
Cost
  Advantage, 151–5
  Communication, 3, 16, 95
  Cutting, 61
  Distribution, 52
  Drivers, 96
  Effective, 79, 149, 156, 339
  Focus, 50
  Labour, 164
  Leadership, 49–50, 52–4
  Operational, 3, 31
  Reservation, 95
  Stream, 58
Cost/benefit analysis, 152
Culture, 68
Customer Relationship Management
    (CRM), 19, 78, 150–1, 169–70
  Airline, 211
  Travel agencies, 265
Customer, 31, 66
  Care, 235
  Demand, 67, 110–34
  Loyalty, 41, 56
  Requirements, 54
  Satisfaction, 132–4, 314, 326, 340
Cyber-squatting, 168, 299

Data
  Mining, 24, 325
  Modelling, 24
  Processing era, 77
  Processing, 11, 60
  Warehouse, 54, 325

Database, 12, 138
  Hotel, 19
  Relational, 24
Decision, 13
  Making, 9, 16, 55, 68
  Support systems, 13–14, 203
Demand, 45, 48, 110–34
  Forecasting, 145–50
  Leisure, 110, 320
  Management, 149–50
Destination Integrated Computer
    Information Reservation Management
    System (DICIRMS), 299–93, 333–4
  Impacts optimisation, 301–2
Destination, 76, 82, 94, 96–9, 122, 146,
    280–306, 314, 327
  Collaboration, 234
  Facilities, 280–306, 314
  ICT, needs, 94, 327
  Information, 122–3, 128, 280
  Integration, 96–9, 289
  Internet presence, 125, 327
  Management organization (DMO), 95,
    138, 146, 282, 292, 295–7, 333–4
  Management systems (DMS), 95, 102,
    147, 179, 223, 280–95
  Management, 292, 333–4
  Marketing, 285, 333–4
  Naïve tourist, 131
  Portals, 38, 315
  Promotion, 295, 333–4
  Stakeholders, 295–7, 302–4
  Strategic planning, 146–7, 280, 293,
    333–4
  Types, 280–1
  Unspoilt, 115
  Web sites, 125, 314
  Web-site, 286–7
Differentiation, 40, 49–50, 325, 332
  Advantage, 43, 54, 71, 155–9, 232
  Branding, 146
  Marketing, 52
  Product, 52, 57, 332
Digital
  Devices, 22, 322–4
  Television, 9, 20, 23, 116, 315–16,
    320–5
Digitization, 76
Discussion forums, 3
Disintermediation, 39, 166, 174, 178,
    329–33
  For tour operators, 254–6, 329–33
  For travel agencies, 270–2, 329–33

Distribution
  Airlines, 209
  Channel, 23, 31, 56–7, 112, 174–9,
    178–82, 195, 276, 317, 334, 338
  Cost, 52
  Hotel, 36, 232–4
  Mechanism, 31, 54, 194–6, 281, 299
  Strategies, 163, 165
Diversification, 47
Domain name, 79, 153, 297
Dumb terminals, 484

Economies of scale, 55, 128
Economies of scope, 34, 55
Education, 3, 6, 163
Edu-tainment, 128
Efficiency, 56, 68
Electronic
  Auctions, 23, 208
  Business, 38
  Commerce, 12, 17, 23, 39–40, 42, 70,
    77, 83, 118–19, 122, 142, 148, 154,
    209, 227, 254, 268, 284, 292, 317,
    332
  Communication, 70
  Funds transfer, 87, 126
  Interaction, 81, 336
  Mail, 3, 15–16, 20, 102, 208
  Market, 25, 38, 139, 281
  Platforms, 25, 53, 56, 99, 317–18,
    325
  Ticket, 208
  Tools, 7, 182–9, 312–13, 329
Electronic Data Exchange (EDI), 17, 90
End-user, 23–4, 139
Enterprise resource planning, 59
Entertainment, 3, 20, 23, 322
  In room, 236
Entrepreneurs, 30, 141, 144
Environment, 43, 51, 68
  External, 10, 13–14, 41, 43–5, 49, 51, 53,
    56, 68–9, 76, 149–51
  Preservation, 314
eTourism, 75–171
  Definition, 76–7
Europe, 112
European Commission, 30, 140, 143,
    247–50
Events, 149
  Attractions, 158, 290
Executive information systems, 14, 51
Expedia, 58, 78, 139, 148, 159, 162, 317
Expert systems, 14, 24

Extranet, 17, 69–70, 99–100, 102, 138, 186–9
  Airlines, 203–6
  Destination, 295–6, 304, 333–4
  Functions, 101, 138
  Hotels, 225–7
  Tour operators, 246–50, 329–33
  Travel agencies, 267

Family
  Run, 140, 148
  Hotel, 142, 231–4
Fax, 89
Feedback, 45, 49
File Transfer Protocol (FTP), 15, 102
Financial
  Functions, 178
  Management, 36, 59, 77, 185, 188
  Problems, 58
Firewall, 17, 186
Flag carrier, 198
Flexible, 78, 131, 314
  Organizations, 65
  Specialization, 67, 130
  Tourism, 128–9
Focus strategy, 49, 53, 157
Food and beverage, 145
  Department, 145
Forecasting, 13, 333
Frequent
  Flyer club, 56, 139, 170, 195, 209, 212
  Travellers, 122–3, 128, 272
Front office, 139
Fulfilment, 39

Galileo, 195, 211, 226, 319
Geographical
  Constraints, 64
  Expansion, 78
  Information Systems, 24
  Market, 50
Germany, 111, 113
Global
  Competition, 164
  Economy, 30
  Expansion, 328
  Market share, 39, 52, 162, 313
  Market, 69
  Marketplace, 12, 35, 41, 52, 63, 104, 138–9, 328, 335
  Practice, 64
Global Distribution System (GDS), 93–5, 102, 164, 179, 187, 315–17

Airlines, 194–6, 203
Hotels, 225–6
Travel agencies, 263–4
Global System for Mobile
  Communications (GSM), 21, 322
Globalization, 3, 12, 55, 81, 95, 170, 209, 312
Glocalization, 34
Government, 30, 42, 68, 94–5
  Drivers, 96
Groupware, 7, 8
Growth, 55
  Share matrix, 47
Guest History, 56, 139, 224–5

Hardware, 6–8, 17, 22, 76, 79, 83
Hi touch-hi tech, 237
Hospitality, 76
  Enterprise, 87, 89
  Industry, 82, 97
Hotel, 36, 41, 123, 144, 153, 220–37
  Chains, 6, 91, 139
  Corisande, 31–2
  Employees, 186
  Housekeeping, 36
  Investment, 145
  Marketing, 36, 142, 220
  Proactive management, 150
  Reservations, 121–5, 131, 142, 159, 222, 233
  Resort, 41
  Small, 31–2, 112, 141–2, 148
  Specialized, 156
  Technologies, 7, 19
  Type, 220–1
  Web site, 142
Human, 33
  Resources, 30, 36, 48, 57, 59, 67
  Resources management(HRM), 77, 161, 183, 185, 188, 230
Humanware, 6, 7
HyperText Mark-up Language (HTML), 15

i-mode, 120
Impacts optimization, 147, 301–2
Inclusive package, 112, 128, 131, 290
Incoming travel agency, 180
Independent
  Enterprises, 102
  Tourist, 128
Individual
  Holidays, 112
  Tourism products, 158
  Travellers, 92, 160

Industrial revolution, 2, 31
Industry structure, 329
Information
  Acquisition, 7
  Application, 7
  Dissemination, 7, 280
  Distribution, 16
  Management, 10, 24, 31, 77
  Processing, 7
  Quality, 24, 31
  Retrieval, 7, 20
  Search, 121–6, 130
  Society, 31
  Speed, 31
  Storage, 7, 9
  Superhighway, 20, 92
  Systems, 77, 174
  Technology, 2
Information Communication Technologies
    (ICT), 1–26
  Life cycle, 153
  Requirements, 174
  SMTEs, 141, 231–4, 328–9, 333–4
Information system, 9, 10
Infospace, 81, 104–5
Infostructure, 3, 10, 40, 67, 70–1, 105,
    147, 209–10, 312, 333, 338–40
Infrastructure, 10, 138, 165, 196, 339
  Digital, 39
Innovation, 6, 10, 41, 53, 55–6, 67, 162, 340
  Constant, 157, 340
Innovative
  Distribution strategies, 179
  Management, 162, 326, 338
  Organization, 63, 80, 155, 174, 320, 328,
    338
  Planning, 59
  Process, 58
  Technologies, 10
Intangible
  Aspects, 280
  Services, 76
Integrated
  Destinations, 96–9, 289, 333–4
  Systems, 13
Integrated Service Digital Network (ISDN),
    17, 92
Integration
  Destination, 289, 333–4
  Diagonal, 128
  Horizontal, 163
  Technological, 25, 96
  Vertical, 148, 164, 181

Intellect, 7, 30, 163, 340
Intelligent
  Agents, 7, 14, 33, 158, 269
  Applications, 22–4
  Electronic assistant, 21
  Networking, 61
Interactive, 67, 320, 336
  Marketing, 16
  Management, 16
Interactivity, 16, 41, 71, 79, 105, 144, 336
Interfaces, 9, 17, 22–3, 312, 320
Intermediary, 39, 77, 79, 82, 95, 139, 148,
    315–25, 327, 329–33
  Electronic, 139, 168, 315–25
  ICT needs, 94, 327
  Tour operator, 242–58, 329–33
  Traditional, 126, 315
  Travel agency, 262–74, 329–33
Internal analysis, 45
Internet, 2–3, 15–16, 69–70, 99–104, 138,
    174, 183
  Airlines, 194, 206–8
  Consumer choice, 110, 326, 327
  Designer, 17
  Destinations, 296–7, 327, 333–4
  In hotels, 227–31
  In tour operators, 250–1, 329–33
  In travel agencies, 267–70, 329–33
  Protocol, 15
  Service provider, 125–6
  Users, 115–25, 139
Interoperability, 22–5, 225, 247–50, 290
Inter-organizational, 12, 31, 138, 164
  Functions, 101, 138
  Network, 91
Intranet, 17, 69–70, 99–101, 138, 174,
    183–6
  Airlines, 199–203
  Destinations, 294–5, 304
  Functions, 101, 138
  Technology, 101
  Tour operators, 244–6, 329–33
  Travel agencies, 265–7, 329–33
Intra-organizational, 12, 31, 38, 138,
    339
  Network, 91
  Functions, 101, 138, 178
Inventory
  Control, 86, 101, 184
  Management, 93

Kiosks, 9, 23, 84
  Airline, 212

Knowledge, 24, 34, 186
  Base, 14, 17
  Economy, 30–1
  Management, 24, 138, 186

Lastminute.com, 79, 145
Learning, 66
  Resource, 30
Legacy system, 79, 112
  Airline, 211
  Tour operator, 256, 329–33
Leisure, 3
  Facilities, 144–5
  Industry, 82
  Time, 3, 314
  Travel, 111, 122–3, 320
Lifecycle, 68
Lifestyle, 68, 115, 158
Load factor, 201
Local
  Economy, 97–8
  Society, 98
Local Area Networks (LAN), 12, 91, 212
Location dependent information, 159
Long-haul travel, 115
Loyalty, 55–6
  Customer, 183
  Schemes, 56, 139

Macro
  Economic, 30, 98, 340
  Environment, 17
Mainframes 2, 11, 15, 83–4
Management Information systems, 11, 13, 86
  Era, 60
Management, 10, 69, 77
  Control, 6, 13
  Of tourism, 138
  Process, 51, 63
Market, 67
  Attractiveness, 45, 57
  Development, 47
  Domestic, 280
  Drivers, 96
  Penetration, 47
  Research, 55, 155
  Segment, 34, 50, 54–6, 71, 112, 121–2, 129–30, 157, 315, 319, 332
  Share, 43, 105, 162
Marketing, 48, 59, 68–9, 77, 133, 152
  Functions, 24, 178, 230
  Intelligence, 154

Mix, 68, 145, 159, 168
  One-to-one (1-2-1), 56, 68, 158, 170, 209
  Process, 63
  Research, 53, 68, 155
  Through ICT, 152
Mass
  Customization, 320, 329
  Destination, 152
  Market, 20
  Production, 49, 65, 97, 128, 152
  Tourism, 152, 314
Media, 23, 86, 122
Mergers, 49, 181
Micro
  Economic, 31
  Level, 340
Mission, 43, 45, 48, 185
Mobile
  Commerce, 120–1, 322–4
  Communication, 89, 322–4
  Computing, 23
  Devices, 9, 21, 80, 317, 322–4
  Multimedia, 120–1
  Networks, 21
  Operators, 160
  Personal digital Assistant, 212
  Phones, 7, 9, 21–2, 212
  Telephone, 89
Modem, 17
Multi-channel Strategy, 175, 315–25, 328, 331, 334, 338
  Airlines, 212, 328
  Hotels, 234, 328
  Tour operators, 329–33
  Travel agencies, 329–33
Multimedia, 9, 15, 86, 320–1
  Interfaces, 17, 24
  Mobile phones, 21
  Presentations, 24
Multiplier effects, 98

Netware, 7, 8
Network, 7, 16–17, 23, 92
  Architectures, 23
  Computer, 6, 34, 91
  Enterprise, 61, 63
  Era, 60–1, 139
  Intelligence, 30
  Interconnected, 150
  Neural, 149–50
Neural
  Networks, 149–50
  Organizations, 150

New tourism, 128, 313
Niche
  Marketing, 155
  Markets, 34, 251
North America
  Travel patterns, 112

Occupancy, 41, 94, 185
Old tourism, 128
One to one (1-2-1) Marketing, 56, 68, 158, 170, 209
Online
  Bookings, 124–5, 154, 162, 228, 267
  Demand, 115
  Motivation for purchasing, 120
  Population, 115–25
  Purchases, 118–19, 131, 320
  Search, 126, 130
  Travel planning, 124–7
Ontology, 249
Operating system, 13
Operational
  Management, 150, 194
  Matrix, 47
  Practices, 78
  Systems, 13
Opportunity, 44, 48, 148
  Business, 52, 325
  Cost, 51
  Market, 65
  SMTEs, 141, 231, 328–9, 333–4
Organizational Change, 63, 337–40
Origin, 82
Outsourcing, 53, 64–5, 151, 163, 209, 336

Package, 112, 131
  Destination, 290
  Tour operator, 131, 160, 181, 242–57
Paradigm shift, 30, 60–3, 70, 337, 340
Partners, 55, 65, 69, 71, 79, 164, 281
  External, 63
  Local, 329
Performance, 12, 46, 48
  Indicators, 49
  Monitor, 139
Peripheral Regions, 33, 115
Personal
  Brochures, 92
  Computer, 2, 9, 12, 84
  Information, 91–2
  Relationship, 56, 67

Personal Digital Assistant (PDA), 21–2, 212
Personalization, 33, 56, 130
  In hotels, 224
  Tour operator package, 257
PEST Analysis, 46
Planning, 162
  Destination, 280
Platform, 33, 53, 290, 325
  ICT, 56, 317–18
Point of sales, 87
Portals, 79, 315
  Airline, 209–10, 213
Portfolio
  Analysis, 45–9
  Management, 163, 165
Price
  Comparison, 111
  Methods, 317
  Tactics, 52
Principals, 94, 328–9
  Airlines, 194–213, 328
  IT needs, 94
Procurement, 48, 77, 185, 188
  Airlines, 199, 204, 209
  Hotels, 228–30
Product
  Development, 47
  Differentiation, 43, 50–4, 155, 332
Productivity, 3, 6, 13
profit
  For profit organizations, 144–6
  Margin, 57, 154
  Not-for-profit organizations, 146–7
  Operational, 145
Profitability, 51, 57, 187, 328
  Targets, 146
Promotion, 41, 322
  Airlines, 209
  Campaigns, 79, 164
Property Management System (PMS), 7, 19, 101, 222–5
  Fidelio/Opera, 19, 59, 225
Proprietary
  Electronic tools, 99
  Standards, 247–9
  System, 21
Public
  Sector, 6, 178
  Tourism organization, 281–2
Pull factors, 141–5
Push factors, 141–5

Quality, 53, 56
  Control, 56
  Of access, 140

Refocus, 59
Regional development, 30
Reinforcing, 60
Reintermediation, 39, 178, 329–33
  Of travel agencies, 270–2, 329–33
  For tour operators, 254–6, 329–33
Relationship marketing, 24, 69, 209
Reservations, 84, 103, 121, 159, 314
  Airline, 103, 121–5, 159, 194, 314
  Destination, 291, 314, 333–4
  Hotel, 220, 233
Reskilling, 59
Resort representatives, 112
Resources, 6, 52, 55, 329
  ICT, 11
  Internet, 20
  Utilization, 52
Restaurant, 35
Retooling, 59

Sabre, 194, 226, 319
Search
  Engine, 15, 123
  For tourism, products, 111
  Internet, 130
Seasonality, 95, 158, 187
Security, 126, 326
  Airline, 211
Segmentation, 110–25, 130–2, 157, 319, 322
Self service
  Check in, 212
  Terminals, 85
Server, 15–16
Small
  Hotel, 141, 231–4
  Medium Tourism Enterprise (SMTEs), 102, 140–4, 187, 231, 281–2, 292, 328–9, 333–4
  Organization, 30, 66–7
Smart card, 24
Social
  Class, 153
  Impacts, 301–2
  Interaction, 128
Society, 9
Software, 6–8, 22, 76, 85
  In tourism, 83–7
  Standard, 86

Special
  Information, 156
  Interests, 128, 149, 156
Speed, 41, 80
Stakeholders, 6–7, 17, 25, 43–4, 55, 64, 67–9, 71, 77–9, 99, 102–4, 141–5, 326, 328
  Airline, 206
  Destination, 147, 286, 333–4
  Destination, 295, 302–4
  Interests, 44
Standardization, 56
  Process, 317
Stock exchange, 58, 145
Strategic
  Alliance, 45, 49, 51, 53, 64, 68, 163–5, 196, 329
  Analysis, 44
  Business unit (SBU), 45–6, 93, 144–5, 195
  Decisions, 163–5
  Focus, 157
  Function, 139, 200
  Initiatives, 55
  Management, 43–4, 51–2, 61, 69, 100, 147–70, 313, 339
  Objectives, 13–14, 144–7
  Options, 45
  Planning, 144–7, 162, 339
  Process, 49
  Resources, 52, 329
  Tools, 52, 306, 312–3, 329, 337
  Vision, 61
Strategic Information Systems, 12, 14, 101
  Era, 60–1
Strategy, 3, 31, 43–4, 49, 185
  Implementation, 49, 51
  Generic, 49, 52
Suppliers, 6, 52, 57, 64, 69
  ICT needs, 94, 327–9
Supply, 45, 48, 138–71
  Chain, 188
  Driven ICT, 138–71
Sustainable competitive advantage, 160–1, 328–9
Switch companies, 225–6
SWOT analysis, 45, 48
Synergies, 57, 59
System(s) architecture, 86

Tactical
  Function, 139
  Management, 148
  Planning, 200

Target market, 68, 156
TCP/IP, 15
Technology 2, 41
  Evolution, 22, 175
  Management, 30–41, 313
  Revolution, 24, 81, 132–4
  Tools, 6, 134, 165, 182–9, 312–13, 329, 337
Tele-
  Banking, 33
  Entertainment, 33, 322
  Learning, 33
  Medicine, 33–4
  Working, 33–4
Telecommunications, 7, 42
  In tourism, 89–93
Telephone, 6, 7
Teletext, 90
Television, 20, 317, 320–4
  Cable, 20
  Digital, 23, 116, 301, 315–16, 320–5
  Networks, 317
  Satellite, 20
Telex, 89
Terminal, 7
Third-generation(3G), 21–2, 161, 314, 322–4
Threats, 44, 47
  SMTEs, 141
Tickets, 111, 167
  Air, 194, 211
  Electronic, 208
  Systems, 265
Time, 50, 52, 80
  Advantage, 139, 159
Tools
  Management, 46
  Strategic, 52, 306, 337
  Technological, 6, 134, 164–5, 312–13, 329, 337
Tour operator, 37, 41, 97, 160, 181, 183, 242–58, 329–33
  Brochure, 252
  Disintermediation, 254–6, 329–33
  Function, 242–3
  Functions, 242–3
  Inventory control, 101
  Package, 131
  Reservations, 243
  Specialized, 252
  Types, 242–3
  Videotext, 243–4, 246, 315

Tourism board, 146
  Local, 280
  National, 146–7, 280
  Regional, 280
Tourism, 2, 76, 81
  Consumers, 3, 102, 130, 327
  Demand, 76, 110–34
  Future, 329–33
  Growth, 81
  Industry integration, 98, 289
  Industry, 76, 81, 95–9
  Multipliers, 98
  Suppliers, 3, 327–9
  Supply, 76
  System, 80–3, 99, 112, 174–5
Tourist, 94
  Experienced, 132
  Information centre, 280–4
  Motivation, 110
  Product, 93
  Visitor attractions, 290, 314
Training, 17, 57–8, 66, 162–3
Transaction, 39, 55, 77
  Airlines, 199
  Mechanisms, 102
  Support systems, 13
Transport, 82, 316
Travel agent, 11, 65, 82, 112, 123, 159, 180, 262–76
  Disintermediation, 270–2, 329–33
  Function, 262
  Reservation systems, 263–4
  Sales, 268
  Types, 262–3
Traveller
  Frequent, 110, 170, 212
  Satisfaction, 129–34, 314, 340
  Sophisticated, 110, 128, 160, 314
Travelocity, 58, 78
Trends, 45, 71, 150

Uniform Resource Locator (URL), 15
United Airlines, 103, 123
Un-metered access, 126
User, 23
  Interfaces, 7, 86, 24, 161, 312
  Friendly, 6, 12, 304

Value, 43, 138
  Added, 49–50, 52, 55, 65, 112, 149–51, 155, 179, 232, 257, 336
  Chain, 35–8, 43, 49, 71, 80, 165, 329
  Company financial value, 145

Videotex or Viewdata, 89–90, 93, 243–4, 246, 263–4, 315
Virtual
  Corporation, 63–7, 81, 139, 334
  Organization, 63, 334–7
  Products, 63
  Reality, 92
  Size, 67, 328, 338
  Tourism industry, 334–7
Vortal, 315

Web
  Airline, 194
  Complaints, 127, 314
  Site design, 144
  Site, 70, 80, 123–5, 314

Wholesaler, 180
Wide Area Networks (WAN), 12, 91
Wireless
  Applications, 21
  Solutions, 212
Wireless Application Protocol (WAP), 21, 120, 154, 323–4
World Tourism Organisation, 113–14
World Wide Web (WWW), 15, 30, 102, 139

XML, 21, 247–50

Yield management, 139, 145, 158, 167, 184, 328
  Airline, 199
  Hotels, 223